Craft Sources

THE ULTIMATE CATALOG FOR CRAFTSPEOPLE

Paul Colin and Deborah Lippman

M. EVANS AND COMPANY, INC.  NEW YORK 10017, NEW YORK

M. Evans and Company titles are distributed in
the United States by the J. B. Lippincott Company,
East Washington Square, Philadelphia, Pa. 19105;
and in Canada by McClelland & Stewart Ltd.,
25 Hollinger Road, Toronto M4B 3G2, Ontario

Library of Congress Cataloging in Publication Data
Colin, Paul, 1946-
    Craft sources, the ultimate catalog for craftspeople.
    Includes index.
    1. Handicraft—United States—Directories.
2. Handicraft—Bibliography.   I. Lippman, Deborah,
joint author.   II. Title.
TT12.C64   745.5′07   75-12543
ISBN 0-87131-183-6
ISBN 0-87131-184-4 pbk.

Contents

Foreword

TIME magazine termed one of the more significant aspects of the American culture boom of the 1960's the "craft explosion." The name stuck, and ten years later it is still used to describe the ever-mushrooming American Crafts scene. *TIME* attributed the new crafts consciousness to an increase in leisure time, coupled with a desire on the part of a growing number of people to return to the traditional values of independence, and self-sufficiency. Whatever the reason, handicrafts are growing more popular every day, and the public's interest has not gone unnoticed by publishers, who produce hundreds of books, magazines, and articles in every craft field. It is no wonder that the average craftsperson looking for information is often confused or bewildered by the multitude of available texts and publications. This book, we hope, will provide craftspeople with a shortcut for locating useful source material.

Craft Sources, The Ultimate Catalog for Craftspeople, is a guide to the available books, magazines, organizations, suppliers, and schools; for professionals, amateurs, and educators in the crafts field. It is intended as a general handbook; we make no claims to comprehensiveness. In compiling the information contained in the book, we endeavored to present material that was readily available or especially conspicuous in the public eye. However, the task of providing access to the art and science of most of the handicrafts practiced in America today, proved to be a Sisyphean one. We found ourselves chasing our own tail in trying to keep up with the new books, publications and organizations. Therefore, out of necessity we had to limit our material to what was available at the time immediately before writing (spring 1974), and sources which we considered classics in their field and therefore indispensible to any research guide. We also included interviews with craftspeople to provide invaluable first-hand information and, we hope, some insight into their personal involvement with crafts.

This book could not have been written without the generous help of scores of craftspeople who provided direction for our research and therefore made much good out of our ignorance. We would like to especially thank Gary Williams for writing such a complete and detailed section on wood crafts. We also wish to thank Susan Dresner and Barbara Linden for their illuminating articles on crafts and education. Bruce McClelland deserves our heartfelt gratitude for spending countless hours transforming the washed out latent images from poorly exposed photo negatives into clear, readable prints.

We are also grateful to the following for permission to reprint material included in *Craft Sources:*

Charles Counts for his poem "Fragments."

Dover Publications, Inc. for a quotation from *The Pueblo Potter* by Ruth L. Bunzel, 1973.

Drake Publishers, Inc. for "How to Repair a Flopping Plow," from *Drake's Modern Blacksmithing and Horseshoeing* by J. C. Holstrom, 1971.

Watson Guptill Publications, New York, for a quotation from *Modern Leather Design* by Donald Willcox, 1969.

William Morrow and Company for a quotation from *Potworks* by Billie Luisi, 1973.

Throughout, we have used bold face type to indicate direct quotations from previously published materials. We believe that all necessary permissions for these have been secured. If we have inadvertently made any errors we will be glad to correct them in future editions.

We wish to thank Pamela Veley for valuable assistance in turning a chaotic and often puzzling manuscript into a book; and of course thanks to Herbert Katz without whose advice and inspiration this book could have never been published.

Basketry

BASKETS AS TEXTILE ART, by Ed Rossbach. Van Nostrand Reinhold, New York, 1973. 199 pages. illustrations, photographs, bibliography, index. $14.95.

Basketmaking has remained virtually unchanged for thousands of years. This quality of stability in a century characterized by rapid change imbues baskets with a sense of the mysterious and strange, a timelessness that the author celebrates in words and photographs.

Mr. Rossbach discusses a wide variety of baskets, pausing to consider those commonly used today as well as those housed inside museums. He illustrates the various forms of baskets and examines the special qualities of each one. Yet the emphasis is not on structural analysis or on the practical how-to side of basketry, nor is the interpretation historical or anthropological but, rather, personal. This book was to have been a collection of photographs accompanied by brief descriptions, but soon developed into a vehicle for the author's own ideas about basketry and an opportunity for him to express his own insights into the basketry process and its relation to other art procedures. Those who share Mr. Rossbach's love of basketry will be grateful for this opportunity to join him in this tribute to one of man's most ancient and enduring crafts.

> When young and old in circle around the firebrands close,
> When the girls are weaving baskets and the lads are shaping bows
>
> —Macaulay

PALMETTO BRAIDING AND WEAVING. by Viva J. Cooke and Julia M. Sampley. E. A. Seemann Publishing Company, Miami, Florida, 1972. 127 pages. 81 black-and-white photographs and drawings. $5.95.

The classic work on palms and weaves, republished after twenty-five years. Full of detailed, comprehensive, and clearly stated information. The authors begin simply with the selection and preparation of materials, and continue to introduce more sophisticated techniques and processes as the book progresses. They provide instruction for the making of a number of projects such as hats, mats, baskets, and decorative items.

EARTH BASKETRY. by Osma Gallinger Tod. Crown Publishers, New York, 1972. 169 pages. illustrations, photographs, index. $2.98.

The beginning weaver will find little use for this handbook. In all but a few instances, the diagrams are unclear. The instructions, though conveniently placed opposite the appropriate diagrams, are not set off typographically, ex-

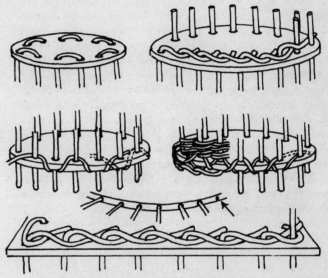

WOODEN BASES WITH HOLES BORED FOR SPOKES.

cept in the case of a page-long series of instructions where the typeface is reduced in size. Such a format makes it virtually impossible to read and work at the same time.

More experienced weavers might be interested in the section on basket bird nests, which comes complete with a chart of dimensions according to species. Another pleasant feature is the section on novelty baskets, giving clear directions for five ways to use corn husks. The book also contains a list of natural basketry materials found in the United States.

INDIAN BASKETRY. by George Wharton James. Dover Publications, New York, 1972. 271 pages. illustrations, photographs, index. paperback edition $3.50.

A pioneering study first published in 1901 as an attempt to promote understanding and appreciation for the fast-fading art of Indian basketry. The author traces the development and underlying principles of Indian basketmaking and design in the major tribes of the Southwest and the Pacific coast area. Much of the information was garnered through interviews with Indian craftsmen and the book contains extensive discussions of the place of the basket in Indian life, legend, and ceremony.

The author describes various native weaving materials and dyes, and presents information about weaving and stitching techniques in enough detail to enable a skilled weaver to reproduce many of the authentic and often extinct forms and motifs. He also offers some brief hints to the collector on buying baskets from the Indians, hints that are outdated today but are sociologically interesting. An appendix contains an illustrated reprint of Roland B. Dixon's "Basketry Designs of the Maidu Indians of California," which was published in the April-June 1900 issue of *American Anthropologist*.

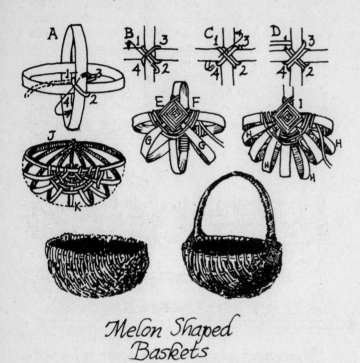

Melon Shaped Baskets

heart. A basket made from willow is extremely strong and long lasting. It retains its color well and is very light in weight. It also costs quite a bit less than a similar one made of cane.

Ms. Maynard suggests that beginners practice the basic weaves and borders on a homemade "practice board" constructed from a piece of pegboard measuring about 10 by 14 inches. Insert in the board a number of pegs 3 inches long cut from #15 cane to form an oblong or a square. A beginner can use the board to master each weave thoroughly before using it on the basket; the work on the board will also help clarify the diagrams, as the illustrations in the book look more like the work on the board than on the actual basket.

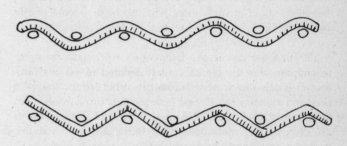

The difference between cane and willow randing

The two Navajo gods of war were born of two women; one was fathered by the sun, the other by a waterfall. When the children were born, they were placed in identical baby baskets. The footrests and the back battens of the baskets were made of sunbeams, the hoods of rainbows, the side strings of sheet lightning, and the lacing strings of zigzag lightning. One child was covered with a black cloud and the other with the female rain.

Source: INDIAN BASKETRY, by George Wharton James.

The line illustrations of the baskets, which serve primarily to give information about size and shape, are unattractive but serviceable, and the instructional diagrams, despite the spaghettilike appearance of many of the weavers, are clear and easy to follow as are the written instructions that accompany them.

If the step-by-step directions and advice are followed, the no-longer-beginning weaver should be ready to design and execute an original basket by the time chapter seven, the design section, has been reached. Even after the reader attains proficiency, this book will still retain its usefulness, for the author's suggestions for new work patterns are stimulating, and her hints and tips offer some very practical, and often overlooked, advice.

MODERN BASKETRY FROM THE START. by Barbara Maynard. Charles Scribner's Sons, New York, 1973. 172 pages. illustrations, 128 black-and-white photographs. $10.00.

Because basketry is difficult to learn without actually seeing the moves being made in person, the author recommends in her introduction that novice weavers try to get some practical instruction in addition to reading the book. This is sound advice, but if any book can make those procedures graspable, this is it. The book opens with a description of tools, basic materials, and processes. The description of each tool is accompanied by a drawing of the tool and a diagram illustrating the process in which it is most frequently used. In addition to a discussion of cane and its varieties and uses in basketry, Ms. Maynard emphasizes the benefits of willow weaving, a subject about which very little has been written but which is very dear to her

WEAVING WITH CANE AND REED: MODERN BASKETRY. by Grete Kroncke. Van Nostrand Reinhold, New York, 1967. 96 pages. black-and-white photographs, diagrams. $4.95.

Geared to the beginner, this book is a good place for would-be basket weavers to start. The author offers a brief discussion of materials as well as some practical suggestions: use plastic clothespins to hold reeds in place until they are ready to be glued, and afterward until the glue dries; even naturally colored reeds must be well rinsed before dyeing since manufacturers frequently use chlorine or acid in the cleaning process; never soak a reed for too long since soaking can cause permanent discoloration and a tendency to fray.

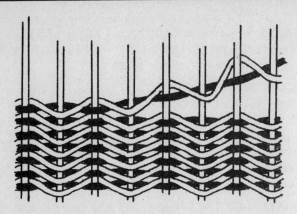

Pattern weaving with two different colors. The dark reed lies flat, while the white reed forms a loose zigzag over the stakes to create the angular pattern

The first section of the book deals with basic basketry techniques, and the second half is devoted to various projects, beginning with very simple yet attractive baskets with premade wooden bases, and progressing to all woven baskets, lampshades, and sewing boxes. Several of the projects are designed for combinations of dyed reeds, and a simple procedure for home dyeing with fabric dyes is offered.

The instructions and diagrams are quite clear and easy to follow, and the projects are numerous and varied.

Zebra pattern

NEW WAYS WITH RAFFIA. by Grete Kroncke. Van Nostrand Reinhold, New York, 1970. 96 pages. 124 illustrations and diagrams, index. $4.95.

Raffia, a connective tissue in plants, is made up of long, narrow cells that form a fiber. Raffia can be obtained from a variety of plants and trees. Yarn made from flax for textile use consists of raffia, though today when we refer to raffia we usually mean the fibers from the leaves of the raffia plant.

In recent years a new synthetic raffia (Swistraw or Raffne) has appeared on the market. It looks like natural raffia and has many of the same good qualities, plus several

admirable traits not found in natural raffia that make it especially suited for knitting and crocheting, though not as suited for wrapping around cord or reed.

This book contains projects utilizing both natural and synthetic raffia to create many lovely and diverse articles. Directions are given for crocheting, embroidering, and knitting with Swistraw, as well as for weaving projects using natural raffia. Neither the written instructions nor the diagrams for most of the projects seem especially clear and in the projects that utilize another craft technique, such as knitting, a knowledge of that technique is assumed. However, anyone who is interested in raffia as a medium, or anyone with a bit of experience in handling it, will probably find that they can puzzle out the instructions with just a bit of perseverance.

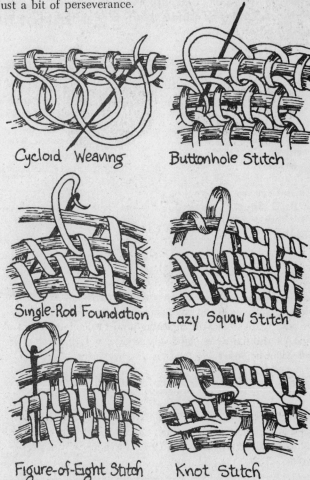

INDIAN BASKET WEAVING. by the Navajo School of Indian Basketry. Dover Publications, New York, 1971. 103 pages. paperback edition $1.75.

It is too bad that the useful information contained in this volume is marred by a generally condescending and unpleasant attitude toward the Indian craftsmen. Nevertheless, the book explains in detail exactly how to make a variety of Navajo baskets. Each chapter details the materials needed and techniques employed, including suggestions for possibilities of color and design as well as information on dyes, polishes, and stains.

The following books will probably mystify beginners but will provide experienced basket makers with a rich source of inspirational material. The government publications are ethnologically interesting, but be forewarned: they were written long ago and reflect early twentieth-century conceptions of Indian life and status. They were also written by anthropologists and not basket makers, and therefore contain some technical inaccuracies.

POMO BASKETRY. by Elsie Allen. Naturegraph Publishers, Healdsburg, California, 1972. illustrations, photographs. paperback edition $2.00.

PIMA INDIAN BASKETRY. by H. Thomas Cain. Heard Museum, Phoenix, Arizona, 1962. 40 pages. illustrations, photographs (some color), bibliography. paperback edition $1.50.

BASKETRY. by F. J. Christopher. Dover Publications, New York, 1952. 180 pages. illustrations, photographs. paperback edition $1.25.

INDIAN BASKET WEAVING. by the Navajo School of Indian Basketry. Dover Publications, New York, 1971. illustrations, photographs. $1.75.

PUEBLO CRAFTS. by Ruth Underhill. U. S. Department of the Interior, 1944. (Publications Service, Haskell Indian Junior College, Lawrence, Kansas). 147 pages. illustrations, photographs. $.80.

BASKETRY OF THE SAN CARLOS APACHE INDIANS. by Helen H. Roberts. The Rio Grande Press, Glorieta, New Mexico, 1972. 218 pages. photographs.

Suppliers

Ace Rattan Products, Inc.
60-19 54th Place
Maspeth, N.Y. 11378
brochure

Alnap Company, Inc.
66 Reade Street
New York, N.Y. 10007
catalog. (reed.)

Artis
9123 East Las Tunas
Temple City, Cal. 91780
catalogs $1.50 to $2.50
(Swistraw)

Bamboo and Rattan Works, Inc.
901 Jefferson Street
Hoboken, N.J. 07030
brochure.

Dick Blick Company
P.O. Box 1267
Galesburg, Ill. 61401
catalog.

Craft Service
337-341 University Avenue
Rochester, N.Y. 14607

Handcraft Wools
Box 378
Streetsville, Ontario, Canada
catalogs.

The Handcrafters
1 West Brown Street
Waupun, Wis. 53963
brochure $.50.

Indian Summer
1703 East 55 Street
Chicago, Ill. 60615
catalog. (rush.)

Nasco
Fort Atkinson, Wis. 53538
and P.O. Box 3837
Modesto, Cal. 95352

Hazel Pearson Handicrafts
4128 Temple City Boulevard
Rosemead, Cal. 91770
catalog (Swistraw.)

H. H. Perkins
10 South Bradley Road
Woodbridge, Conn. 06525
brochure. (rush.)

Peoria Arts and Crafts Supplies
1207 Main Street
Peoria, Ill. 61607
catalog $.50.

Whitaker Reed Company
90 May Street
Box 172
Worcester, Mass. 01602
catalog

The Workshop
P.O. Box 158
Pittsford, N.Y. 14534
brochure $.25.
(reed, cane, rush.)

Beads

BEAD DESIGN. by Ruth Wasley and Edith Harris. Crown Publishers, New York, 1970. 216 pages. illustrations, photographs (some color), index. $7.95. paperback edition $3.95.

Although the authors present instructions for various items such as jewelry, fruits, and holiday ornaments, the most comprehensive and outstanding feature of this book is the section on beaded flowers. There are over one hundred different varieties of flowers, including some of the more exotic varieties like night-blooming cereus, Anthurium, and sugarplum trees.

The designs are original and beautiful, but the instructions are not clear and the diagrams and text do not correspond on all points.

BEAD EMBROIDERY. by Joan Edwards. Taplinger Publishing, New York, 1966. 200 pages. illustrations, bibliography, index. $9.95. paperback edition $5.95.

Over half of this book is devoted to the history of beadwork around the world. The author covers a lot of ground and offers many examples. (Unfortunately, there are no photographs, and sketches of outstanding historical beadwork do not convey any sense of the original.)

The book then moves on to the principles of design in beading. The author favors a "buildup" technique of repeating geometrical patterns: a process of adding, subtracting, and rearranging groups of beads until a pleasing effect has been achieved. She believes that beads like room to move about in and that careful planning of comparatively few beads is the surest way to successful results.

Even when the author gets down to the actual methods of beading, her approach is still rather general and historical as opposed to step-by-step or procedural. She does present clear instructions for beaded dollhouse furniture, a basic pattern for knitting beads, and two beaded trimming patterns. The real contribution here, though, is not so much how-to as historical and inspirational.

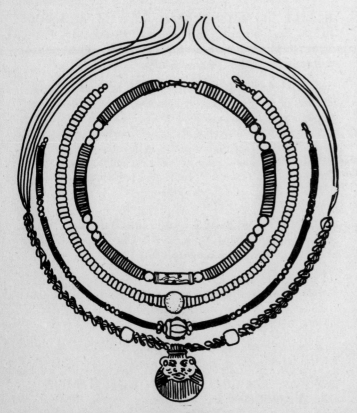

Sketch for necklaces, Susan Sonnenberg

Interview

Susan Sonnenberg has been beading for almost as long as she can remember. As a child, she vacationed with her family in Wisconsin; this was Indian country, and soon young Susan became a favorite of the neighboring tribe. She was presented with her own beading loom and she began to make necklaces and belts in the traditional manner. As she grew older, Susan allowed her beading talent to take second place to her interest in costume design. She attended art school for theatrical costuming, but found that her love of beads kept asserting itself in one way or another. "I was constantly sewing sequins, pearls, and rhinestones onto everything I made." She went out to Los Angeles to help a friend establish a new boutique, supplying her with original jewelry to sell. These pieces, primarily leather and bead designs, were an instant success, and Susan found herself with a new career. A partnership with another friend soon developed, and Juniper Trading Company was born.

Susan now concentrates solely on beaded jewelry. She buys only old or unusual beads, such as Egyptian mummy beads, jade, and turquoise, including things that traditionally might not be regarded as beads (animal figures, whistles, buttons), but that have holes built into their construction. She finds her materials at auctions, in old coin shops, and in worldwide traveling expeditions. She does not work directly from traditional or ancient designs, but due to the nature of her materials she strives for a traditional appearance. Susan concentrates on textural interest, color, and size change, particularly on graduated sizes.

Juniper designs have been enjoying an incredible popularity. They have been featured in *New York* Magazine's "Best Bets" column, in shows at the Fairtree Gallery and Bloomingdale's department store in New York City, and were specially featured in an article in *Women's Wear Daily*.

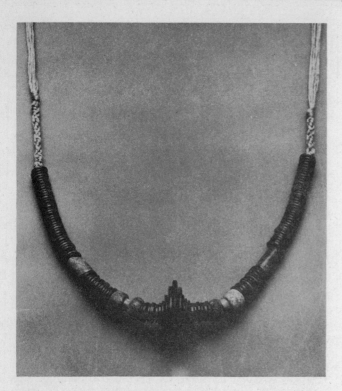

Necklace, Susan Sonnenberg

Necklace, Susan Sonnenberg

SIMPLY BEADS: AN INTRODUCTION TO THE ART OF BEADING FROM NORTH AND CENTRAL AMERICA, AFRICA, AND THE MIDDLE EAST. by Betty J. Weber and Anne Duncan. 1971. distributed by the Western Trimming Corporation, 8575 West Washington Boulevard, Culver City, California 90230. 25 pages. illustrations, photographs (some color). $1.50.

A brief, very pleasant exploration into the beadcraft of other cultures. Color photographs illustrate original artifacts and modern adaptations for which there are clear diagrams and written instructions. Among the projects presented are an Indian flower necklace, a peyote Indian rope choker, a God's-eye amulet, and an African mandala.

THE PEARL AND BEAD BOUTIQUE BOOK. by Virginia Nathanson. Hearthside Press, Great Neck, New York, 1972. 192 pages. illustrations, photographs (some color), index. $8.95.

Clear directions and diagrams for seventy-five projects: crocheted bags, neckties, belts, earrings, bracelets, evening bags, jewelry, flowers, and vegetables. There is quite a bit of overlap in the floral section from the author's previous book; many of the projects are uninspired, and others are just downright funny (the beaded and crocheted toilet tissue cover for example), but the book supplies beginning beaders with a firm enough ground in basic techniques to enable them to go on to create designs other than those presented.

THE ART OF MAKING BEAD FLOWERS AND BOUQUETS. by Virginia Nathanson. Hearthside Press, Great Neck, New York, 1967. 192 pages. illustrations, photos (some color), index. $8.95.

A very good introduction to the craft of beading flowers. The author covers the major techniques thoroughly through simple, step-by-step instructions and diagrams.

Half the book is a compilation of projects, not only for flowers, but also for potted plants, miniature plants, holiday and table decorations, table accessories, and bouquets. There is also a section on caring for beaded bouquets and another on how to design and arrange them.

BOUQUETS FROM BEADS. by Virginia Osterlan. Charles Scribner's Sons, New York, 1971. 222 pages. illustrations, photographs (some color). $12.50.

Excellent instructions for basic beading techniques and an intelligent discussion of flower arranging, both Oriental and Western. Step-by-step instructions for making forty-four flowers, novelties, and Christmas patterns.

RANDOM THOUGHTS ON COLOR AS APPLIED TO THE MEDIUM OF BEADS

1. Using color in a flower arrangement is making a design within a design. All those guiding principles previ-

BABY'S BREATH

Materials

3 inches of white beads for each unit (Units are made the same for both large and small arrangements. For large arrangements, the smaller units are combined. Use five of them mounted on a piece of 16- or 18-gauge wire. For the miniature, use the units singly and mount them on a short piece of 18-gauge wire.

26- or 28-gauge wire (brass, green, or silver)

Twig

String approximately 3 inches of beads; crimp end of wire.

Push six or seven beads to within 5 inches of the crimped end of wire and make a loop of the beads. If you turn the loop rather than the wires, it will be easier for you to get a tight loop. Twist the two wires together for ½ inch.

On the left side of the twisted wires, ½ inch out, make another loop of six or seven beads; twist wires together to where the wires are twisted below the first loop. (Fig. 1)

Directly opposite the second loop and to the right of the first, make a third loop of six or seven beads.

Twist together the two wires at the base of the third loop until you have twisted back to the untwisted wire (A).

At the base of the first unit of three loops, twist more wire together for 1 inch.

Make another loop of six or seven beads, 1 inch to the left of the first unit of three loops.

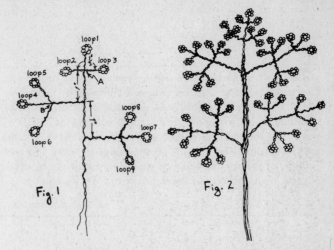

Fig. 1   Fig. 2

Twist the wires at the base of this loop for ½ inch; make another loop of beads to the left ½ inch out, and twist the wires together to B.

Make a third loop of beads directly opposite and to the right of the second loop, ½ inch out. Twist the wires back to B. Twist the two bare wires together for 1 inch.

Make another unit of three seven-bead loops in the same manner on the right side of the first two units, then twist the two wires together.

Cover the two wires with tape and they are ready either to be combined for a large spray and stemmed, or to be used individually and stemmed (Fig. 2).

Source: THE ART OF MAKING BEAD FLOWERS AND BOUQUETS. by Virginia Nathanson.

---

ously described must be applied to color: proportion, balance, line, focus, and repetition. At the same time these color rules must be applied to our medium—beads.

2. A new element enters and that is light reflection. One color bead will reflect on another, intensifying some and toning down others.

3. Certain hues which in an opaque bead would have weight, have lost it because of light and sparkle. A student should become used to the idea of selecting beads by their visual weight, which includes translucence and color.

4. It is always safe to use only opaque beads or only transparent beads. Experience will give you confidence to mix several kinds in one bouquet to achieve an even better translation of impression.

5. All high-intensity colors in one arrangement tend to be wearing. Save this for holidays. All high-intensity colors in one flower brings on the gas station syndrome.

6. If there is any doubt as to which way a color is cast, try it next to the true spectrum color. You can easily see if a red is leaning toward blue or yellow.

7. Blue and violet are at their best in daylight. They "retire" under artificial light.

8. Red should be used sparingly. Unless you find cut red beads with sparkles, it builds up and kills itself. Two or three values of red in the same flower, a bright or dark contrasting center, or a pattern with lots of air seems to save the red flower from suicide.

9. Yellow is very forward and gay but it also builds up. Use some quiet yellows along with the bright ones. Many flowers have brilliant yellow centers in nature. If the identical bright yellow is used, an undesirable spotty look might appear. Try the toned-down yellows.

10. Violet is such a receding color that it needs a bright background such as yellow-green leaves, or it should be used in combination with white flowers. Leftover deep purple beads make beautiful, deep dramatic centers.

11. Look for dark navy-blue beads instead of black. Black, in color language, is the absence of light. Black beads can be very lifeless.

Source: BOUQUETS FROM BEADS. by Virginia Osterlan.

BEADS AND MACRAME: APPLYING KNOTTING TECHNIQUES TO BEADCRAFT. by Grethe La Croix. Sterling Publishing, New York, 1971. 48 pages. illustrations, photographs (some color). $2.95.

A little information on the basic techniques of embroidery, macrame, and beading. Several projects, the more difficult of which (such as a macrame and beaded handbag) do not receive comprehensive treatment from the standpoint of text or diagrams.

The most important thing to remember about beading is that your creations must be unique, inimitable by machines. Use unusual and beautiful materials and don't be afraid of spending a lot of money for a small amount of beads if you're not sure of the degree of your commitment. If you are sure, don't be afraid of spending an even greater amount of money on a larger supply of beads. It is, after all, the beads which are the substance of the design.

—Susan Sonnenberg

Suppliers

American Handicrafts Corporation
110 Mission Street
San Francisco, Cal.
catalog.

Alnap Company, Inc.
66 Reade Street
New York, N.Y. 10007
catalog.

Bead Game
505 North Fairfax Avenue
Los Angeles, Cal. 90036
catalog.
African trading, clay, wood, others.

Bead's Nest
P.O. Box 1257
Cupertino, Cal. 95014
brochure $.15.

Bergen Arts and Crafts
P.O. Box 381
Marblehead, Mass. 01945
catalog.

Bethlehem Imports
1169 Cushman Avenue
San Diego, Cal. 92110
brochure; bead samples $1.00.
African trading, clay, wood, others.

Black Sheep Weaving and Craft Supply
318 South West Second Street
Corvallis, Ore. 97330
catalog $.75.

Dick Blick Company
P.O. Box 1267
Galesburg, Ill. 61401
catalog.

Boin Arts and Crafts
87 Morris Street
Morristown, N.J. 07960
catalog $.50.

California Crafts Supply
Box 3277
Anaheim, Cal. 92802
catalog.

William Condon and Sons Ltd.
P.O. Box 129
Charlottestown, Prince Edward Island
Canada
catalog.

Craft Service
337-341 University Avenue
Rochester, N.Y. 14607
catalog.

Craft Yarns of Rhode Island
603 Mineral Spring Avenue
Pawtucket, R.I. 02862
catalog.

Creative Fibers, Inc.
1028 East Juneau Avenue
Milwaukee, Wis. 53202
catalog $1.00.

Crowe and Coulter
Box 484 ACC
Cherokee, N.C. 28719

East Street
10 Main Street
Chester, Mass.
catalog.

Edgerton's Handcrafts
219 West Town
Norwich Town, Conn. 06360
brochure.

Gager's Handcraft
3516 Beltline Boulevard
St. Louis, Mo. 55416
catalog $1.00.

Glori Bead Shoppe
172 West 4 Street
New York, N.Y.
price list.

Gloria's Glass Garden
Box 1990
Beverly Hills, Cal. 90212
catalog.

Greene Plastics Corporation
Canochet Road
Box 178
Hope Valley, R.I. 02832
catalog.

J. L. Hammett
Hammett Place
Braintree, Mass. 02184

The Handweaver
111 East Napa Street
Sonoma, Cal. 95476
catalog.
clay, wood.

J. C. Larson Company
7330 North Clark Street
Chicago, Ill. 60626
catalog $1.00.

Lemco
P.O. Box 40545
San Francisco, Cal. 94149
catalog.

Lenos Handcrafts
2037 Walnut Street
Philadelphia, Pa. 19103
brochure.

Macrame Studio
3001 Indianola Avenue
Columbus, O.
catalog.

Macrame and Weaving Supply Company
63 East Adams Street
Chicago, Ill. 60603
catalog $.50.

Magnolia Weaving
2635 29 Avenue West
Seattle, Wash. 98199
catalog.
wood and general beads.

Maharani
3209 Hidalgo
Irving, Tex. 75062
brochure; samples $2.50.

Jean Malsada, Inc.
P.O. Box 767
Roswell, Ga. 30075
catalog.

The Mannings
RD #2
East Berlon, Pa. 17316
catalog.

Margola Import Corporation
315 West 36th Street
New York, N.Y. 10018
catalog.

Marian Mumby Ceramic Beads
206 Hanover Drive
Costa Mesa, Cal. 92626
samples $3.65.

Naturalcraft
2199 Bancroft Way
Berkeley, Cal. 94704
catalog $.50.
African trading, general.

Nicole Bead and Craft Company, Inc.
924 Cherry Street
Philadelphia, Pa. 19107
brochure.

Northeast Bead Trading Company
12 Depot Street
Kennebunk, Me. 04043

Owl and Olive Weavers
4232 Old Leeds Lane
Birmingham, Ala. 35213

Hazel Pearson Handicrafts
4128 Temple City Boulevard
Rosemead, Cal. 91770
catalog.

Reeves Knotique
2510 Rambling Court
Riverside, Cal. 92504
catalog $.75.

S & S Arts and Crafts
Colchester, Conn. 06415
catalog.

Sheru Enterprises, Inc.
49 West 38 Street
New York, N.Y. 10018
brochure.

3 Gables Homecrafts
1825 Charleston Beach
Bremerton, Wash. 98310
brochure $.20.
clay, general.

Walbead
38 West 37 Street
New York, N.Y. 10018
catalog.

Warp, Woof, and Potpourri
514 North Lake Avenue
Pasadena, Cal. 91101
catalog.
African trading beads, clay, wood, general.

Yellow Springs Strings
P.O. Box 107
68 Goes Station
Yellow Springs, O. 45387
catalog.
African trading beads, clay, wood.

Yone, Inc.
487 Union Street
San Francisco, Col. 94113
brochure.

York Novelty Import
10 West 37 Street
New York, N.Y. 10018

Candles

CREATIVE CANDLEMAKING. by Thelma R. Newman. Crown Publishers, New York, 1972. 212 pages. illustrations, photographs (some color), suppliers list, bibliography, index. $7.95. paperback edition $3.95.

The definitive book on making candles by molding. Thelma Newman presents an incredible amount of information on the process, history, and materials of candlemaking. She tells how to make molds from household materials such as cardboard tubes, cartons, corrugated forms, glassware, old bottles, plaster, and metal. She gives complete information on making silicone rubber (RTV) molds, sand-casting molds, and balloon molds (for making hollow candles).

How candles were hand painted in the 18th and 19th centuries

Full instructions are given for inserting wicks, measuring wax, and pouring, cooling, and removing candles from molds.

The section on candle decoration contains a discussion on how to press, roll, shape, cut, color, glue, pull, melt, carve, and paint wax to achieve interesting forms, as well as how to use decoupage, encaustic painting, gold and silver leaf, embedments, and layered pouring.

CANDLE ART, A GALLERY OF CANDLE DESIGNS AND HOW TO MAKE THEM. by Ray Shaw. William Morrow and Company, New York, 1973. 160 pages. photographs (some color), suppliers list, index. $8.95.

Most of the designs presented here are created by the pouring method and are produced by simple decorative techniques. Somehow, the term *design* seems a misnomer when applied to just about all of the candles presented in this book. *Ideas* would probably be a more accurate way to describe the results of applying decorative techniques to essentially the same form throughout.

The instructions, however, are clear and well illustrated, and the hints on general candle construction are excellent. In fact, these are probably more useful than the whole gallery of designs.

THE CANDLE MAKER'S PRIMER. by K. Lomneth Chisholm. E. P. Dutton, New York, 1973. 130 pages. illustrations, photographs (some color), index. $7.95.

This book has an especially good section on dipped candles. The author says that when dipped candles are properly made they burn with a brighter, clearer, more even light than poured candles.

During the colonial period, dipped candles were "feathered" by plunging them into very hot water and then shaking them dry. This changed the pore structure of the outer wax and made them burn more evenly. Today, adjustments in the wax formula take care of this problem.

Wax formulas for dipped candles differ from those of poured candles. Ms. Chisholm suggests a formula of 60 percent paraffin to 40 percent stearic acid for dipping.

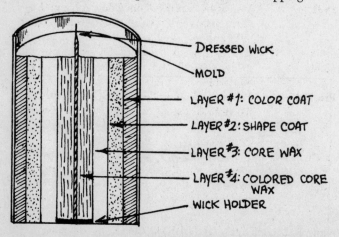

Pour mold full of wax and empty it when layer has formed. When layer becomes opaque and dull, pour next layer.

Bayberry Candles

One and a half quarts of bayberries stripped from bushes in September will make an 8-inch taper. Cover berries with water and boil them for five minutes. Work with small batches. After boiling, set the berries in a cool place until the wax rises to the top of the pot. Skim off the wax. Set this batch aside and repeat the operation until you have completed boiling all your berries.

Remelt the wax and let the impurities settle to the bottom. Strain this batch. Store the wax in tightly sealed cans until you are ready to make candles. The fragrance is fugitive and easily lost.

Dip or mold your candles and then store them in tightly sealed containers to maintain their fragrance.

INTRODUCING CANDLEMAKING. by Paul Collins. Taplinger Publishing Company, New York, 1972. 96 pages. illustrations, photographs, suppliers list. $6.95.

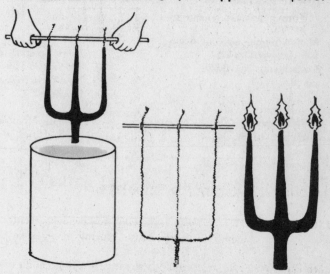

A simple introduction to some basic candlemaking techniques. The author presents candle projects that utilize simple equipment in step-by-step format. The instructions for the molding projects are simple but flawed by an oversight on the part of the author. He says that after the wax has set in the mold it will separate from the sides due to shrinkage. This is not the case at all times. He neglects to mention release agents for this purpose. Moreover, he excludes commercial candle molds which are quite easy to use and inexpensive.

CANDLE CRAFTING, FROM AN ART TO SCIENCE. by William Nussle. A. S. Barnes, Cranbury, New Jersey, 1971. 202 pages. illustrations, photographs, suppliers list, index. $8.95.

This is a fantastic all-around book on candle production. Technical information on wax, wicks, additives, melting points, and so on should be an invaluable aid to craftsmen involved in candlemaking as a business. The author also supplies interesting information on commercial candle and mold production.

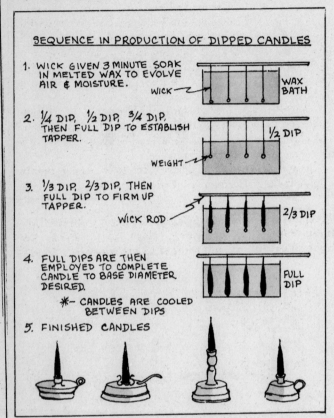

SEQUENCE IN PRODUCTION OF DIPPED CANDLES

1. WICK GIVEN 3 MINUTE SOAK IN MELTED WAX TO EVOLVE AIR & MOISTURE. — WICK — WAX BATH
2. 1/4 DIP, 1/2 DIP, 3/4 DIP, THEN FULL DIP TO ESTABLISH TAPPER. — WEIGHT — 1/2 DIP
3. 1/3 DIP, 2/3 DIP, THEN FULL DIP TO FIRM UP TAPPER. — WICK ROD — 2/3 DIP
4. FULL DIPS ARE THEN EMPLOYED TO COMPLETE CANDLE TO BASE DIAMETER DESIRED. — FULL DIP
   ✳ — CANDLES ARE COOLED BETWEEN DIPS
5. FINISHED CANDLES

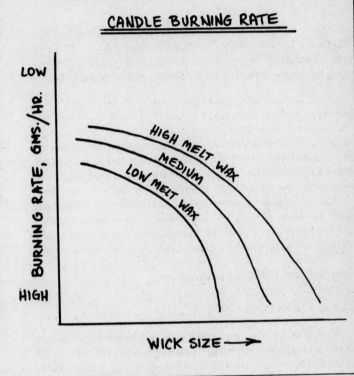

CANDLE BURNING RATE

BURNING RATE, GMS./HR. (LOW ... HIGH)

HIGH MELT WAX / MEDIUM / LOW MELT WAX

WICK SIZE ⟶

Table of Candle Events

13th century	The guild of traveling candlemakers went from house to house making candles in Paris.
15th century	The wood mold method of making candles (before the candles were dipped) was introduced by Sieur Brex of Paris.
18th century	Spermaceti, a crystalline substance from the head of the sperm whale, was used in candlemaking. One candlepower is based on the light given by one pure spermaceti candle weighing one-sixth of a pound, burning at a rate of 120 grams per hour.
1800–1855	Candle-molding machines were developed. These are the prototypes of today's molding machines.
1811	Michel Chevreul discovered fat-splitting separation of natural fats into fatty acids and glycerin. This eventually led to the use of stearin as a low candle dilutent and constituent.
1825	Cambaceres introduced the plaited wick of twisted cotton or linen yarn. The plaited wick bends over and allows ashes to drop and be consumed, thus eliminating the old problem of carbon accumulation.
1825	Michel Chevreul and Gay Lussac took out a patent to manufacture stearic acid.
1830	Paraffin: Reisebach's use of hydrocarbons of the marsh grass series.
1831	De Milly improved on Chevreul and Lussac's method by substituting sodium salt with calcium hydroxide. Candles made by this method are called "Milly" candles.
1834	Morgan developed the continuous wicking machine.
Pre 1847	Palmer invented a wick that had 1/10th of its strands coated with nitrate of bismuth that caused the burned end of the wick to curl over.
1850	James Young of Scotland introduced paraffin for the manufacture of candles (paraffin came from the petroleum seeps of Derbyshire).

Source: CREATIVE CANDLEMAKING. by Thelma Newman.

CANDLES AND CANDLECRAFTING. by Stanley Leinwoll. Charles Scribner's Sons, New York, 1973. 139 pages. illustrations, photographs (some color), suppliers list, index. $8.95.

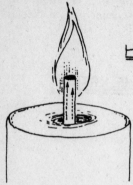

HOW A CANDLE BURNS

LIQUID WAX IS DRAWN UP THE WICK BY CAPILLARY ACTION. THERE HEAT FROM THE FLAME VAPORIZES THE WAX. THE VAPOR IGNITES AND FEEDS THE FLAME.

This book describes the necessary equipment and materials for candlemaking, and then takes up three methods of candle production: dipping, rolling, and molding. The author doesn't go into any of these methods in great detail.

Some of the ideas presented about candle decoration are quite unique, but these are usually commercial candles presented by the author for illustrative purposes and probably would present difficulties for the beginner in execution.

International Guild of Candle Artisans
16 Morningside Drive, S.E.
Grand Rapids, Mich. 49506

Group of people concerned with candlemaking, amateur and professional. Bestows Candle Artisan of the Year award. Publishes *Candlelighter*, monthly, and *Round Robin Digest*, annually.

1. Wick should point a bit off center.

2. Is wick too small?

3. Is wick too large?

4. White ash too much Borax.

5. Black ash, too little Borax.

Candle problems

Candlemaking Suppliers

The following is a list of mail-order sources for candlemaking supplies and decorations. Note that you should always write ahead before ordering to inquire about specific merchandise and prices. Many firms also have price lists and/or catalogs.

Artis, Inc.
P.O. Box 68
Temple City, Cal. 91780

Barker Enterprises
15106 10th Avenue, South West
Burien, Seattle, Wash. 98166

Bersted's Hobby Craft, Inc.
Box 40
Monmouth, Ill. 61462

Cake Decorators and Craft Supplies
Blacklick, O. 43004

The Candle Barn
20 Sterling Road
Watchung, N.J. 07060

The Candle Shop
111 Christopher Street
New York, N.Y. 10011

Candlemaker's Supply
630 North College
Indianapolis, Ind. 96205

Candlewic Company
2101 Black Horse Drive
Warrington, Pa. 18976

Early American Candle Galleries
Box 100
Trexlertown, Pa. 18087

Florida Supply House
P.O. Box 847
Bradenton, Fla. 33507

General Supplies Company, Inc.
P.O. Box 338
Fallbrook, Cal. 92028

General Wax and Candle Company
Box 9398
North Hollywood, Cal. 91609

The Glow Candle Company
Box 10102
Kansas City, Mo. 64111

Hawthorne House, Inc.
103 North Robinson Street
Bloomington, Ill. 61701

Lee Wards
Elgin, Ill. 60120

Lumi-lite Candle Company
P.O. Box 2, Main Street
Norwich, O. 43767

Marjorie's Craft Studio
2620-B West Chester Park
Broomall, Pa. 19009

Natcol Crafts, Inc.
P.O. Box 299
Redlands, Cal. 92373

Novelcrafts Manufacturing Company,
Inc.
P.O. Box T
Rogue River, Ore. 97537

Hazel Pearson Handicrafts
4128 Temple City Boulevard
Rosemead, Cal. 91770

Perterbrook, Inc.
Candle Mill Village
East Arlington, Vt. 05202

Pourette Manufacturing Company
P.O. Box 6818
Roosevelt Way, North East
Seattle, Wash. 98115

Premier Manufacturing Company
P.O. Box 26126
Denver, Colo. 80226

A. I. Root Company
1100-06 East Grand Street
Elizabeth, N.J. 07201

W. Spencer, Inc.
11 Exchange
Portland, Me. 04111

Skil-Craft Corporation
325 West Huron Street
Chicago, Ill. 60610

Walco Products, Inc.
1200 Zerga Avenue
Bronx, N.Y. 10462

Wooley and Company
Box 29
Peoria, Ill. 61601

Yaley Enterprises
358-D Shaw Road
South San Francisco, Cal. 94080

Ceramics

CERAMICS: A POTTER'S HANDBOOK. by Glenn C. Nelson. Holt, Rinehart and Winston, New York, 1971. 348 pages. illustrations, photographs (some color), suppliers list, bibliography. paperback edition, $8.50.

An excellent manual both practically and aesthetically. The author begins with an extended and profusely illustrated discussion of the history of ceramics from early times, leading up to a review of the significant modern works and styles around the world. He then proceeds with a general survey of forming and decorative techniques, a review of kilns, and a more specific and technical investigation of glazes and glaze formulas. There is also a chapter devoted to upholding the morale and enthusiasm of the student about to turn professional. Appendixes offering technical and tabular data conclude this book, a very readable compendia of valuable information.

POTWORKS, A FIRST BOOK OF CLAY. by Billie Luisi. William Morrow and Company, New York, 1973. 154 pages. illustrations, index. $2.45.

This book is designed to help would-be potters with a limited budget but with great enthusiasm. There are an inadequate number of diagrams, and it's hard to visualize many of the techniques without them, but the author has a nice, chatty style and offers some good advice that frequently runs counter to the grain of established tradition. About electric kilns, for example, she has the following to say:

Electric kilns are portable, small-scaled, dependable, and boring, but don't let the last stop you. In recent years new insulating material has been developed that makes it possible to have a light weight, 7–9 cubic feet kiln that fires up to stoneware temperatures, that can be moved, taken apart, added onto, and turned off automatically, if necessary. Such kilns are usually 8 to 10 sided, top-loading, thin-walled (new types of insulation brick are used), and the novice's best friend.

Despite what all the greatest potters say and what all the best authorities write, you can make excellent pots and glaze them beautifully using electric power. It takes only about five times more glaze research to produce interesting, various, and inviting glazes with electricity than it does with a kiln that burns something, i.e., gas, oil, coal, wood. The reason for this extra work is . . . the chemically less active atmosphere that exists in the electric powered firings. Don't be depressed by the obvious bias demonstrated by Rhodes, Leach, Nelson, et al, in favor of natural fuel firing (reducing atmosphere) at high temperatures. Just because industry makes lousy, boring glazes with electric power does not mean that you have to do likewise. Industry manages to make some banal glazes with gas too.

A POTTER'S BOOK. by Bernard Leach. Transatlantic Arts, Levittown, New York, 1948. 294 pages. illustrations, photographs, index. $12.75.

The classic work by the best-known independent studio potter today. From the creative point of view, it is highly recommended and all serious potters should at least be familiar with Mr. Leach's philosophy.

THE COMPLETE BOOK OF CERAMIC ART. by Polly Rothenberg. Crown Publishers, New York, 1972. 276 pages. illustrations, photographs (some color), suppliers list, bibliography, index. $8.95.

This book offers broad, general coverage on materials (other than tools) and techniques. It reads well, but at times it is difficult to follow, especially when the text and instructional photographs are not presented on the same page.

POTTERY WORKSHOP. by Charles Counts. Macmillan, New York, 1973. 198 pages. illustrations, photographs, suppliers list, bibliography. index. $8.95.

An excellent all-purpose handbook for beginners, containing step-by-step photographs for building a potter's wheel, for throwing, for decorating, and for building a kiln. The author provides brief and simple background information on glazes, and supplies several recipes for at home mixing. He also discusses the problems of selling wares, primarily methods of selling on consignment at shows, from workshops, and in shops.

Fragments

COMMON CLAY
    Fragments
We know the past by pieces
    by shards
    broken pieces of pottery found
    beneath the earth's crust
    having once been a part, expressing totality.
Now still a part more and less so
    speaking history to us
    being form in fragment.
What can we name it . . .
    when a way of life still exists
    and itself is a fragment
    being part of the past and
    projecting tenaciously into our time?
Patterns of existence . . . what for?
    this life-way discovered and reported is not a
    hard-fact fragment
    it is a real existence
    flowing
    continuously in today from yesterday
    making tomorrow.
In our totality of today we can see it only
    as a fragment and learn some truth
    in its form. Paradoxically in looking
    we atrophy it making it hard and fast.
But this must be transcended for today was
    yesterday and our living
    will see tomorrow.
Potters are water-carriers of history's truths.

—Charles Counts

National Ceramic Association
P.O. Box 39
Glen Burnie, Md. 21061

Conducts promotional activities, seeks to improve teaching methods, promotes standardization of entries and judging at shows. Sponsors teacher's meetings and business seminars. Publishes *Clay Chatter*, bimonthly, and *Hobby Teacher's Manual.*

AN ILLUSTRATED DICTIONARY OF CERAMICS. by George Savage and Harold Newman. Van Nostrand Reinhold, New York, 1974. 320 pages. illustrations, photographs (some color). $18.95.

More than 3,000 definitions and cross-references, as well as 626 illustrations of ceramic terms, names, and phrases. Also includes a listing of principal European factories and their marks.

POTTERY: THE TECHNIQUE OF THROWING. by John Colbeck. Watson-Guptill Publications, New York, 1971. 144 pages. photographs. $10.00.

Serial photographs and minimum text. The treatment and emphasis on clay preparation is quite good, and the book is helpful (of course, nothing can replace practical experience and a knowledgeable guide as a means of mastering throwing) despite the poor coordination between photographs and text.

SYLLABUS FOR ADVANCED CERAMICS. F. Carlton Ball. Keramos, 1973. 68 pages. illustrations, photographs, index. $3.95.

This manual emphasizes the study of glaze-making and presents a series of tests for the student to carry out which will lead to a greater understanding of glaze materials and how they can be manipulated to achieve desired results. All procedures and outcomes are to be recorded in a notebook. There are recipes for slip glazes and tests for crawling, crackling, lead glazes, stoneware clay bodies, and grogs. Appendixes contain additional recipes for first series cone 10 and cone 5 glazes, as well as study questions.

SYLLABUS FOR BEGINNING POTTERY. F. Carlton Ball. Keramos, 1971. 76 pages. illustrations, photographs, index. $4.00.

Originally intended as a workbook for use in schools, this syllabus is equally appropriate for students not directly involved in a classroom situation. It is meant to serve as a supplement to and not a replacement for other beginning pottery books.

The book opens with the basic rules of studio etiquette and a discussion of the important role the ceramics industry plays in maintaining the quality of life by helping man to satisfy his basic needs for food and shelter: ceramic products aid in the storage, preservation, and preparation of food and also provide brick, tile, glass, and sanitary fixtures. The subject of clay itself is introduced in a brief, nontechnical way, and then followed up by a more precise description of the way the three states of clay—plastic, fluid, and pulverized—are used to form ware and the processes appropriate to each.

A chapter on forms presents methods of analyzing pots and of clarifying individual ideas about design. The author focuses on the cylinder, presenting and discussing twelve types.

The first, he says, is not too bad in shape, but the foot and rim curve in slightly. This was caused by the firing. The more subtle the shape, the more distortion is apparent.

Types 2, 3, 4, and 5 are bad. No care was taken with contours, tops, or edges which curve in. The whole form is so bad that no one element can be considered responsible for the trouble.

The top edge of 6 was flared slightly to counteract shrinkage in the kiln. The rim of 7 was flared even more so and the more exaggerated flare helps to counteract warping of the mouth rim. However, the flare in 7 is really too abrupt for the pot to be a good shape. The flare on 8 is better because it is more subtle. Both 9 and 12 have accentuated rims. These add a touch of detail and help to counteract warping. Such details function as a period at the end of a sentence. The choice of emphasizing or not emphasizing the lip of a pot is up to the potter. Both should be tried and used with care to fit the form and mood of each pot.

Types 2, 3, 4, and 5 could be helped by trimming to resemble 6, 10, or 11, but trimming is laborious and sometimes kills the spirit of the pot by overwork. It is, however, a good exercise for a beginner who needs practice in glazing. A well-trimmed base on 4 would be of no help because of the inward curve of the top. It is too abrupt and there is no reason for it. This type of curve usually makes a pot look thicker and squat. The flared foot on 5 is no good. A slightly flared foot can be an asset, but not here where it is unnecessary. The pot is sturdy without it, and with it would chip easily.

Types 10, 11, and 12 are slight variations of cylindrical form. 10 and 11 are opposite in line; the slight curve, convex or concave, makes a great difference in appearance. The feet on 11 and 12 are unlike the standard foot on 7. They are the natural outgrowth of the direct use of the standard trimming tool and are adaptable, practical, and not offensive.

There is of course a chapter on kilns, one on glazes, and another containing step-by-step procedures for decorative techniques. An appendix contains study questions, and upon completion of the book a student should be able to answer questions like these with ease:

_____ Give five reasons for wedging clay.

_____ Alumina is added to glaze to give what result?

_____ Is a colored clay slip an engobe?

_____ What do you call glazed pottery that has a permeable or porous body?

_____ Name the pyrometric cone temperature series and the cones.

Interview

An interview with Richard Rappaport of the Studio Workshop on East 18th Street, New York City, and Ellen Staller, who teaches at the school and operates *Terra Firma*, a private pottery business with her partner Connie Bates. Connie was out of town at the time of the interview.

Paul   Richard, how did you start this place? Were you a potter?

Richard No, I was trained as an artist. I didn't intend to start a "ceramics" studio. The way it all happened was that I wanted to teach those things that I knew about: drawing, jewelry, painting, water-color, things like that. I bought a small kiln and a wheel—little did I know that six years later we'd have fourteen wheels and one of the biggest ceramics studios in New York. All the other areas have more or less been closed off to a certain degree, except for jewelry. We had a darkroom, weaving, candlemaking, you name it. We had all the arts going at once, and slowly, due to economic factors, we had to remove them. More people seemed to be coming for ceramics, so this is where I wagered to make my money; we couldn't compete with the big schools in a number of things.

Debby What are some of the problems you ran into?

Richard Oh, there are a lot of problems. It depends on the amount of money you want to make and how much effort you're willing to put into it, how much you're committed to what's going on. There are a host of economic problems you have to be aware of when you're going into something like this. You have to have a lot of money behind you: you have to get it started, you have to cover your rent and your materials costs. You have to get the students to come in, too.

Paul   How do you do that?

Richard With a great deal of work! Advertising, keep plugging. For the first three years I failed because I didn't have anybody here. You need a lot of determination, and when things are looking bad just staying with it and saying you have a good place and it's worth it. I know I have a better place than any other place in this city.

Paul   What makes it a better place?

Richard Primarily that it's right for the student. In other words, we're cheaper than anyplace else in the city.

Debby How can you do that? Less greed?

Richard Yes, we're not as greedy, and also, my money flow out is under tight control in terms of teachers, materials. . . . Since I'm here on a day-to-day basis watching the place, I know where all the money is so that I'm able to control it in a very careful way. I also have a very nice arrangement with Ellen and Connie so that I don't have a big flow of money out in salaries. They teach here, but they also maintain their private business in my studio, use my space and materials. It's an even trade. Very few ceramic places are doing that and they have a great deal of trouble. In fact, four or five of them closed down this year. It's too hard. For the amount of work and the amount of profit, it's not really worth it. It's not a game. You know, people go into it thinking it's easy and they're going to be successful, and they have a lot of problems because their prices are high (ours are low), they have rigid schedules (we have no schedules, any time you want you can come in here and find a teacher to work with you and help you).

Paul   How much does it cost a month?

Richard We have different rates set up. In other words, somebody can come for one month, two, three, five hours a week, ten hours, twenty, or all the time. We have a rate of eighty-five dollars for three months, five hours a week. This covers everything: material, kiln time, everything. Most places will make an extra sixty to seventy dollars on you for the cost of the clay and the firing. They're losing those students to places like us; we're swamped; we're operating close to ninety to ninety-five percent capacity.

Debby Did you experiment with other setups before settling on this one?

Richard No. I kept the whole thing more or less to my own personality and my personality is sort of informal.

Ellen You see, Richard stays here all the time. He's here from about nine in the morning until about eleven at night, sometimes later. That's the way he is. He loves this place.

Richard Yeah. I love it but it's also a matter of circumstances. You've got to work hard if you want something to succeed, and I've worked for years seven days a week, fifteen hours a day. It's not the worst thing in the world, but I hope that in another two years I can have a manager running the place so that I can take a break every now and then.

Ellen   Oh, Richard, what would you do? You love being here that much!

Richard   No, I don't. Don't laugh, Ellen, I don't like being here *that* much. The only reason why—no basically, what you have to do is you have to make a lot of money just to survive. To make a profit, to get ahead so that you're not worried about the next month, you have to make a little extra besides. Then you have to make more of a profit so that you can in a few years decide to operate in a way that you feel is right for yourself. Ellen doesn't really understand the full economics of the situation.

Debby   So, would you then say to anybody wanting to open a studio that they'd better be prepared to pension the next ten years of their lives?

Richard   Well, no. You see, it depends on what you want to do.

Ellen   Richard's here to make a profit. Some people just want a studio to work in and use it as a means of covering their expenses. Now that's a totally different thing.

Paul   But Richard, I thought that's how you started.

Richard   Yes, but the picture changed. The economics changed and this thing grew.

Paul   How many students would you say you have now?

Richard   We average one hundred fifty. It shifts around because of the monthly rates and due to seasonal flow. You see, in this business you really have got to love people because you're going to run into so many that you'll have to deal with. You can't antagonize them. You have so much competition right in their own backyards. The reason they come here from far away is because they enjoy this place.

Debby   Richard, you said you weren't a potter. Do you teach?

Richard   Yes. I taught myself pottery when I got the wheel in here. I teach the beginners and I've discovered I have this fantastic gift. I can guarantee that with the exception of maybe one or two people, I can teach them to throw and to throw fairly well in one hour, or, at least well enough so that they have the confidence to want to come back and try it again.

Debby   What's your secret?

Ellen   It's a new skill for beginners. They have absolutely no idea of the control required. It's not just a matter of pressure, it's a matter of pressure at the right points. When Richard teaches a beginner, first he'll throw a pot and let them see how it's done. Then, they'll sit down, start putting their hands on the clay, and Richard will push their hands around step by step so that they get more of a feel for what's going on. Otherwise, they have no idea. They know where to put their hands and that's all.

Debby   What's the hardest part of learning?

Ellen   The hardest thing for beginners is getting it centered. And the rub is that getting it centered is not particularly fun and you just can't do anything until you can get it centered. That's the initial frustration. If you can't get it centered you can't make anything and it's just no fun.

Debby   What's the most important thing for a teacher to do?

Richard   The most important thing for a teacher to do is to make a student relax and feel confident. The thing is, the skill is easy, it's easy to learn.

Terra Firma

Basically, we do two types of work. One kind which is purely commercial and is all very staid and with precise workmanship. People love it and buy it and it's our mainstay. We also do things that are a little more bizarre, and some very large things, and those things are a little weird for some people.

Corn teapot, Ellen Staller

People of late tend to like the new things very much but they're not willing to pay the price. Ceramics has not transcended that price thing yet. People still think of it as a pot and don't want to spend seventy-five dollars on a pot unless it's a jardiniere. People will look at something and say, "What can I use if for?" And I'll say it's a jar, you can use it for anything. And they'll say, "Well, what can I put in it, cookies? I'm not going to spend seventy-five dollars on a cookie jar!" They haven't come to the point where they can have it there just because they like it.

Flower vase, Ellen Staller

A big part of the reason why we do functional objects is that we have to sell them. Initially when we design something we don't think of it in terms of function. We think of how it would look and then put function into it afterward.

My favorite things are those that are functional, but that's sort of a side issue. There's something more to speak of them besides their function. The calla lily, for example, is not extremely functional, but it does work as a jar with pouring spout.

We're very much interested in thrown pieces that become distorted in a certain way and then are complemented by hand-building.

In a lot of our pieces you can see that there's a definite contrast going on between the glaze and the raw clay, gold glaze versus the iron oxide and the color of the clay. Sometimes we make the conflict from the clays themselves. The lily for example. The top is out of porcelain and the bottom is stoneware, so there's that textural contrast.

"We like to have a precise thrown shape, or a delicate thrown shape, and then make the bottom hand-built and very organic. The bottom would be hand-built first and the top would be thrown right on it. It's tricky because you can't let any water get on the bottom and also because you have to recenter a piece that has nothing to do with a center. But if you'd just make the pieces separately and attach them, then it's going to look like that's what you've done, and we want it to look like it comes out of it.

I don't like the glazing very much. It's not secondary, it's very important, and when we glaze it takes a very long time. We paint on designs. We draw them on in pencil and paint three coats of glaze and go through a whole number to get the precision. It's very painstaking so that the conception of the glazing is more fun than the execution. Also, we don't use glaze that much because we're limited by the fact that we only have an electric kiln. With gas kilns you can get a greater range of colors and looks. You can also do salt glazing and raku.

Generally, we use stoneware for reasons of color, texture, and durability. Stoneware is much stronger than terracotta. It's also more plastic to work with.

Our main interest has always been in surface texture and how it relates to the form of a piece.

Everybody thinks it's very strange that Connie and I work so well together. I think that's just an ego thing. People like to think that creation is a totally individual process. To a certain extent that's true, but it remains that way for me and Connie because we both have our individual personalities and we both do different kinds of things. We've found that when our individualities come together, it's really the best. When we work on our own, sometimes things get a little too outlandish.

ELLEN ON MYSTIC POTTERS

Recently, there have been a lot of books that have come out and a lot of people are into, well, sensitivity groups working with clay. There are just two approaches. There's the serious approach and there's the ethereal approach, the mystical approach. Basically, that has nothing to do with ceramics. It's just a game. It's a good way for getting people interested in the subect and it's good for kids, but once you progress beyond a certain stage it's just absurd. Technical things aren't even that important because that's something you pick up as you go along, but the interest, it shouldn't just be, "Oh, wow, the clay's coming from the earth and it's turning into something under my hand," because when you do that you just let it control you. You don't control it at all and you don't produce anything that way.

Shell teapot, Ellen Staller

An electric kiln is probably the best for beginners because you can repeat the same glaze over and over if you've made it the same way. Whereas in a gas kiln, depending upon where you've got it in the kiln, it's going to come out with different colors or different surface texture. Even if you fire a set of teacups and one's on the top of the kiln and one's on the bottom, they're bound to come out looking different.

Some diehards still use a woodburning kiln. You can get certain effects with a woodburning kiln but it's a bit of an anachronism. When you fire a woodburning kiln you have to stoke it every three minutes, and sometimes it will take twenty-four hours to fire. You have to have that kind of craziness.

Most people outside the city use a gas kiln. The city won't zone them and it's very hard to get one here. I don't miss it that much any more.

Building a gas kiln is a very tricky business. It's very hard and a lot of people take years before they finally perfect it, or get it to a point where it's usable. The books make it look easy, but it's really hard because you have to get the updrafts right, all kinds of things like that. Everything has to work right. You can build anything from a book and follow precisely the measurements and it won't work right. Sometimes you'll build it and it will work perfectly the first time, but most people have a lot of trouble, especially if they're firing something like porcelain. Porcelain has to have very even heat and if the heat's uneven it will sag.

ELLEN ON WHEELS

Some people say that kick wheels give you more contact with the clay. There's a basis for this. If you're good, you can control the wheel exactly as you want. There's also that attitude again: it's a spiritual thing that involves your whole body in the throwing process. That to me is ridiculous. I don't care about that. What I care about is what's the best machine to produce what I want to make. I'm concerned with the final product and I want the easiest way of doing it. If I'm doing something large, I'd use an electric wheel because I don't want to pour all my energies into kicking the wheel. But sometimes if I'm making something small I do want to work on a kick wheel, and also sometimes it's just fun if you're in the mood to do it.

Richard, when he teaches beginners, never starts them off on a kick wheel because you just have too many things going at once. If you have to worry about your feet going at the same time as your hands, it's too much to handle. But then again, people very into the spiritual aspect will only put a beginner on a kick wheel because they want to involve them immediately in the whole process. So they get involved in the whole process, but they can't really do anything. They can't really master the skill.

STEP-BY-STEP CERAMICS. by Jolyon Hofsted. Golden Press, 1967. 76 pages. illustrations, photographs (some color), suppliers list, bibliography. $2.50.

A good, inexpensive introduction to ceramics. The author begins with a general discussion of basic principles, workshop layout, and clay preparation. The main body of the book consists of projects arranged categorically according to technique: slabbing, coiling, wheel throwing, press molding, slip casting, and Egyptian pasting. The individual procedures are illustrated by step-by-step photographs, and the finished items are presented in color plates. There is a chapter on glazing which presents information on applying commercially bought glazes; a chapter on kilns and firing processes which contains blueprints for building a kiln; and a short section on raku.

PRACTICAL POTTERY AND CERAMICS. by Kenneth I. Clark. The Viking Press, New York, 1964. 79 pages. illustrations, photographs (some color), bibliography, index. $6.95.

General information about procedures, but no in-depth coverage of any particular technique.

STONEWARE AND PORCELAIN. by Daniel Rhodes. Chilton Book Company, Radnor, Pennsylvania, 1959. illustrations, photographs. paperback edition $3.95.

An important book both technically and philosophically, reflecting the author's feelings about the aesthetic pre-eminence of high-fired ceramics.

Leaf Ashtray

1. Draw a pattern based on illustration, or use a natural oak leaf.
2. Roll clay between slats. Remove slats. Place pattern on clay and roll once over leaf firmly to obtain clear imprint. Cut around leaf with cutting tool. Smooth edges with damp sponge.

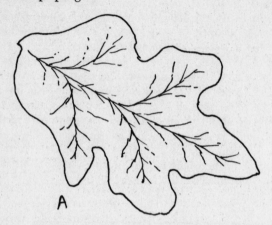

A

3. Make three acorns, each in two parts. Do this by making three balls of clay the size of small grapes. Pull up top stem with fingers.

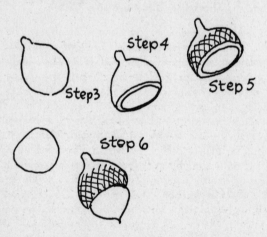

4. Hollow out slightly by pushing in with fingertip.
5. Allowing ball to remain on finger, roll it on a screen to make rough imprint on cap.
6. Form body of acorns by making three balls the size of small peas. Coat one side with slip and set inside cap.
7. Use fingers to shape leaf into a dish. Score one side of the acorns and place on the side to form a cigarette rest.
8. Dry 5–7 days, or for 2 days and 6–8 hours in a warm oven.
9. Paint leaf with green underglaze and acorns with brown underglaze.
10. Fire to 05 cone.
11. Apply three coats of clear glaze.
12. Fire to 06 cone.

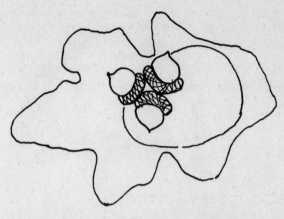

Source: **CREATIVE CERAMICS FOR THE BEGINNER.** by Doris W. Taylor and Anne B. Hart. Van Nostrand Reinhold, New York, 1968. 120 pages. illustrations, photographs, index. $6.95.

THE COMPLETE BOOK OF POTTERY MAKING. by John B. Kenny. Chilton Book Company, Radnor, Pennsylvania, 1968. 242 pages. illustrations, photographs (some color), index. $7.50.

Another excellent handbook for beginners, this book takes the reader on a step-by-step pictorial journey from

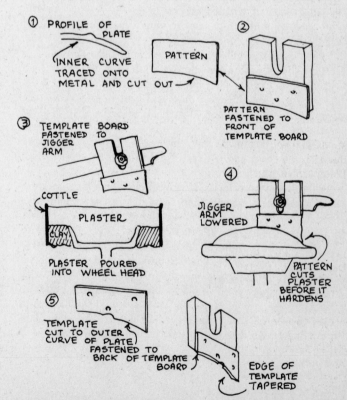

Making a jigger bat and template

simple modeling to throwing, casting, using a turning box, even jiggering—a mechanical method of making tableware in which a lump of clay is placed in a convex plaster bat and turned while a template is held against it. The bat shapes the inside of the plate while the template cuts the outside. Factory equipment for jiggering is heavy and expensive, but the author explains how to build a simple and inexpensive device that can be used with any kick wheel that has some provision for holding a bat in place.

Magazines: Ceramics

Ceramics Monthly
4175 N. High Street
Columbus, O. 43214
Monthly. $6.00 a year for 10 issues.
   Articles directed primarily toward the amateur and hobby potter.

Ceramic Industry
270 St. Paul Street
Denver, Colo. 80206
Monthly. $13.00 a year. $1.00 per single issue.

Ceramic Data Book
Industrial Publications
5 South Wabash Avenue
Chicago, Ill. 60603
   Annual publication containing information on supplies, manufacturers, and equipment. $3.50.

Ceramic Scope
Box 48643
Los Angeles, Cal. 90048
Monthly. $4.00 a year for 10 issues. Subscription includes annual *Ceramic Hobby Industries Buyers Guide*.
   For professionals in ceramic hobby business. Articles on studio organization and management, products, market trends, shows.

Studio Potter
Box 172
Warner, N.H. 03278
Semiannual: $5.00 a year. $2.75 per single issue.
   Features articles, spotlights potters and their works, information of technical, historical, and design nature.

Ceramic A & C
11408 Greenfield Road
Detroit, Mich. 48227
Monthly. $5.00 a year. $.50 per single issue.
   Instructional articles.

Pottery Quarterly
Murray Fieldhous, editor
Northfield Studio, Tring
Hertfordshire, England
Quarterly. $7.00 a year.
   Brief articles, plates, classifieds.

EARLY AMERICAN FOLK POTTERY. by Harold F. Guilland. Chilton Book Company, Radnor, Pennsylvania, 1971. 322 pages. photographs (some color). $12.50.

   The author, who is himself a potter, laments the modern American potter's lack of awareness of the vast design heritage left to him by traditional craftsmen. He concentrates upon a period in American ceramic history rarely touched by historians, 1640 to 1880, the eras of stoneware and earthenware. There are numerous photographs of the well-crafted crocks, pitchers, and storage jars of this period, along with the roach traps, water whistles, and foot warmers.

MORAVIAN POTTERS IN NORTH CAROLINA. by John Bivins. University of North Carolina Press, Chapel Hill, North Carolina, 1973. 300 pages. photographs. $12.95.

   Fifty years after their migration to Bethlehem, Pennsylvania, in 1700, a small group of Moravian brethren acquired land in North Carolina and established a community founded upon a strong religious center.
   John Bivins discusses and reconstructs the life and work of the Old Salem potters in the eighteenth and nineteenth centuries: how they located and transported materials, how they formed, decorated, and fired their pots. He takes special note of the Oriental and English Continental traditions that can be seen in some of the exceptionally beautiful earthenware, salt-fire ware, and stoneware produced during these periods.

TULIP WARE OF THE PENNSYLVANIA-GERMAN POTTERS. by Edwin Atlee Barber. Dover Publications, New York, 1970. 233 pages. photographs. paperback edition $3.00.

   The reissue of the 1903 volume that heralded Barber's discovery of slip decoration in Pennsylvania in the eighteenth and early nineteenth centuries, this is a meticulous historical and technological description.

EARLY POTTERS AND POTTERIES OF NEW YORK STATE. by William C. Ketchum, Jr. Funk and Wagnalls, New York, 1971. 278 pages. illustrations, photographs. $10.00.

   Craftsmen were among the very first settlers of New York. They dug their own clay, ground glazes, and fired kilns. They also moved around a great deal, considering that each relocation meant a new start. They followed the Hudson River northward and the canals westward, often covering remarkable distances.
   The author has gathered facts and figures on individual craftsmen whose existences have been recorded in form throughout New York State. He presents biographical data as well as information on their wares, which were simple household and farm vessels, plates, mugs, and pitchers. At first, the wares were of red clay, which was lead glazed and decorated with white slip or a coggle wheel, and later of the stoneware clay found in the Amboys and Huntington,

Long Island, and which they brushed with cobalt, incised, and salt glazed.

THE PUEBLO POTTER. by Ruth L. Bunzel. Dover Publications, New York, 1973 (originally published in 1929 by Columbia University Press, New York). 134 pages. illustrations, bibliography, index. $3.00.

The creation of beautiful form in clay is subject from the start to two kinds of limitations—those imposed by the nature of the material and by the purpose of the object. From the point of view of art, clay is one of the most versatile of all materials. Endless variation is possible in form, finish, and color. Ornament may be evolved from the plastic nature of the material or applied in colored pigments. Most of the common ceramic techniques have been known and practised in the area studied. Some of them had already been tried and abandoned in prehistoric times.

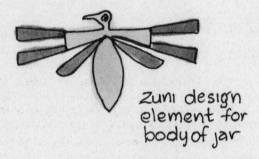

Zuni design element for body of jar

Hopi design for exterior borders of bowls & jars

A second set of limitations, those imposed by utilitarian considerations, seems less obvious. However, the clay vessel of the Southwest is always an article that serves two functions. It is primarily an utensil—in this case a container for food. It is also an object whose form gives pleasure directly to the maker and user. Among the people who provided the basis of this study and indeed, among primitive people in general, it is the utilitarian aspect of objects and activities that holds the center of interest. . . . Despite the preoccupation of our primitive potters with the utilitarian aspects of their product, they are fully aware of its esthetic significance. "Pretty, but not strong," is a comment that is often heard and which evaluates the object in terms of its two functions.

A-D	San Ilde Fonso	G	Hopi
E	Hopi	H	Zuni
F	Zuni	I	Acoma

PIONEER POTTERY. by Michael Cardew. St. Martin's Press, New York, 1971. 327 pages. illustrations, photographs, index. $15.00.

This is not a book for greenhorns, but it is comprehensive and important in its field. The author emphasizes digging and processing clay and glaze materials, and presents technical information and diagrams for sophisticated wood-firing techniques.

PRIMITIVE POTTERY. by Hal Riegger. Van Nostrand Reinhold, New York, 1972. 120 pages. illustrations, photographs (some color), bibliography. $12.95.

A call to the modern potter to rediscover himself and his medium by experiencing through the eyes of primitive man, becoming aware of materials and approaching them in a primitive manner without the tools of modern technology.

Modern studio potters call upon various techniques of forming clay: throwing, casting, and hand-building. The author here is concerned only with the latter. He demands not only a change in procedure, but also in consciousness. Even the potter's conception of time must alter; some pots will take a much longer time to construct than was anticipated and this must be endured. There can be no more propping up of a sagging pot with newspapers or rags; the pot must be built slowly, letting each addition harden a bit before another is added. Yet, the potter using primitive techniques will be working in the sun and must not tarry too long or he will lose all. His awareness of time and its relation to his medium must be constant.

Pot supported on three stones for firing without a kiln

The author discusses not only primitive techniques of shaping and forming pottery, but also of decorating it texturally and with simple glazes, and methods of firing without a kiln, a simple and direct operation that brings the potter into intimate contact with his pots in a way sophisticated firing cannot.

EXPLORING FIRE AND CLAY. by Arne Bjorn. Van Nostrand Reinhold, New York, 1970. 87 pages. illustrations, photographs. $4.50.

Though this is written from an archaeological perspective, the book contains detailed and illustrated information on building and firing woodburning kilns.

The revival of post–World War I English pottery was largely due to the work and teachings of William Staite Murray (1881–1962) and Bernard Leach (1887–   ). These two men had much in common, though they held different opinions about the direction modern ceramics ought to take.

Murray was committed to the production of one-of-a-kind pieces, whereas Leach advocated a cooperative workshop approach aimed at the production of functional pottery at reasonable prices. Leach's workshop approach had a tremendous influence on the work of the 1930s and was a major contribution to the rebirth of this craft.

Murray spent his later years in Africa, but his influence continued in the work of the students he taught at the Royal College of Art (1925–1939), and, more recently, in the work of young studio potters of today. A great many contemporary potters come from an art-school background and, like our society, favor individuality of the artist over tradition. Many of these young potters are even turning from thrown forms to the freer coil and slab techniques to create work that is sculptural rather than functional in nature.

STYLE IN POTTERY. by Arthur Lane. Noyes Press, 1974. 80 pages. illustrations, photographs. $8.95.

Arthur Lane was keeper of the department of ceramics in the Victoria and Albert Museum before his death in 1963. This new edition of his book, originally published in 1948, is updated with extra illustrations and a preface by R. J. Charleston. The purpose is to develop an awareness of the aesthetic qualities that characterize fine ceramics, historical or contemporary. This is accomplished through a study of the means and aims of potters and a survey of pots and potters of the ancient world, Near East, Far East, and preindustrial as well as modern Europe.

NEW DESIGN IN CERAMICS. CRAFT SERIES, VOLUME 7, CERAMICS. by Donald J. Willcox. Van Nostrand Reinhold, New York, 1970. 119 pages. photographs, bibliography. $7.50.

A photographic gallery of contemporary Scandinavian ceramics.

RAKU POTTERY. by Robert Piepenberg. Macmillan, New York, 1972. 159 pages. illustrations, photographs, bibliography, index. $12.95.

Raku is a low-temperature technique of firing porous, low-bisque fired pottery, ordinarily bearing a lead glaze. This technique generally requires the placement of the pottery in a preheated kiln with tongs, and the removal of the still-glowing pot, also with tongs. This form of pottery was most favored by the masters of the Japanese tea ceremony, and because of this it is closely associated with Zen.

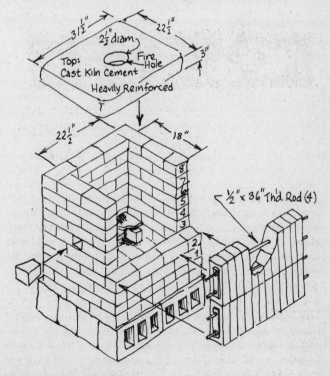

Side loading raku kiln

The author discusses the history of raku and the tea ceremony, not because he feels that contemporary Western potters should model their wares upon traditional forms, but because he believes that the spirit of tea and the spirit are one, and that both underlie the mystery of the metamorphosis of clay.

Almost any type of clay can be used for raku as long as it matures chemically at or above 1600 degrees F., contains enough coarse or refractory material to withstand the thermal shock, responds well to forming, and can successfully survive the firing. Many native clays direct from the ground fill the bill. However, many potters prefer to mix their own clay, and the author offers a number of formulas, including his personal favorite of 75 percent 50-mesh fire clay and 25 percent 45-mesh beach sand. For a more plastic body suitable for working on a wheel, 20 percent Jordan clay is added and the fire clay is reduced to 60 percent and the beach sand to 20 percent.

Raku glazes are like other ceramic glazes except that they mature at temperatures between 1600 and 2000 degrees F. The low temperature maturation allows for a wide range of color and intensity from the various coloring oxides. Lead oxide is the most useful and most used glaze in raku, but it has drawbacks. A raw lead glaze is poisonous and will injure anyone who eats or drinks from lead glazed ware; it may even harm the potter who works with it. Strict precautions must be taken when working with raw lead glazes, and the author takes pains to emphasize and enumerate them.

The book also contains a general discussion of the raku process, forming, applying glaze, making the kiln, firing, and postfiring reduction procedures, which the author considers to be the culmination of the entire raku experience.

RAKU HANDBOOK. by John Dickerson. Van Nostrand Reinhold, New York, 1972. 112 pages. illustrations, photographs, bibliography, suppliers list. $7.95.

This book offers a lot of practical advice, such as what forms lend themselves best to raku, a number of clay recipes, and a description of methods of forming, coupled with a philosophic appreciation of raku as an ancillary of Zen, the means through which the process of self-development can take place. Because he views the craft of raku as so much a part of the aesthetic and philosophical system from which it sprang, the author provides loose guidelines rather than definite instructions in raku procedures. He emphasizes the individual's role as modifier of form and process and creator of new tools to suit his dialogue with the clay. He views the direct ordeal of sudden fire as the ultimate test of both pot and potter—the quality of the pot reflecting the quality of the man. Nothing that is done in raku is without meaning, each step is part of the Zen process of becoming. Thus, in his discussion of decoration, the author advises:

Try to be decisive and commit yourself to a strong mark. If you do not like the mark you have made, do not compromise your principles by trying to "touch it up." The mark you make is after all a clear indication of the quality of your thought and dexterity; by falsifying it you succeed only in deluding yourself. Our aim must be to achieve the perfect mark—the physical achievement of the finest idea.

CERAMIC SCIENCE FOR THE POTTER. by W. G. Lawrence. Chilton Book Company, Radnor, Pennsylvania, 1972. 239 pages. illustrations, photographs, bibliography, index. $10.95.

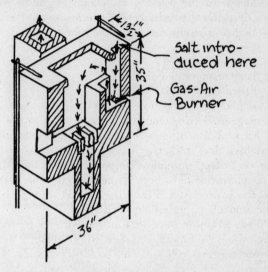

A small downdraft gas-fired kiln for salt glazing experiments

A collection of many facts from numerous scientific investigations designed to help a potter better understand the nature of the materials with which he is working. It is designed for those having no science background and can be understood with only a minimum of effort.

Salt Glazing

Once a kiln is used for salt glazing, its interior becomes loaded with an excess of salt and each subsequent firing augments this situation. This results in the glaze mixture used in any given firing being overshadowed by what has gone before. This may not only produce unexpected results from coloring oxides, but may completely ruin the ware of latter firings. If experimentation with salt glazing is to be at all extensive or effective, it is a good idea to build a small salt-glazing kiln. Be sure to provide thorough ventilation and provisions for the removal of hydrochloric acid vapors.

Source: CERAMIC SCIENCE FOR THE POTTER. by W. G. Lawrence.

CERAMIC FORMULAS: THE COMPLETE COMPENDIUM. by John W. Conrad. Macmillan, New York, 1973. 309 pages. diagrams, bibliography. $8.95.

Designed to be used as a working manual, this book contains more than seven hundred tested formulas for ceramic oxides, stains, glazes, clays, engobes, enamels, and glazes. The formulas are grouped according to type of material and use, and then subdivided by media, use, firing temperature, and technique.

All the materials in the four basic ceramic areas were tested for appropriate characteristics. Clay formulas, for example, were subjected to a uniform procedure that analyzes each formula for the following:

1. Ability of the clay to hold glaze.
2. Fusion of the glaze to the clay.
3. Glaze retention of smooth surface.
4. Degree of transparency of the glaze over the stain and the clay.
5. Clay surface quality.
6. Percentage of clay shrinkage.
7. Plastic quality of the clay.
8. Reduction or oxidation color of clay.
9. Suggested firing temperature.

All formulas have been tested for safety as well as reliability. Many craftsmen have contributed their own favorite or "secret" formulas for publication in this book and other formulas have been garnered from other publications on the basis of the interest they would seem to provide to the student or professional craftsman.

Few ceramists have time or patience to go through all the extensive experiments needed to achieve the various formulas presented here. This book provides a valuable and compact source of information which will enable an individual to develop his own formulas based on the concepts and formulas presented here.

CERAMIC GLAZES, third edition. by Cullen W. Parmelee. revised and enlarged by Cameron G. Harman. Cahners Books, Boston, Massachusetts, 1973. 612 pages. $14.95.

A technical work written as a reference for the ceramics engineer. However, art potters need not be disconcerted by its rather scientific-looking format; it is actually written in a simple and direct manner, and is the most comprehensive study of the subject available.

GLAZES FOR THE CRAFT POTTER. by Harry Fraser. Watson-Guptill Publications, New York, 1973. 160 pages. illustrations, photographs, index. $8.95.

When clayware is fired, the heat decomposes the clay body and liberates gases produced by the burning away of volatiles (primarily carbonaceous materials and steam produced by the liberation of water present in the clay crystal). Most water is driven away at 350 degrees C. (660 degrees F.), but vapor can still be detected at 900 degrees C. (1650 degrees F.), and carbonaceous material usually remains up to 900 to 1100 degrees C. (1650 to 2010 degrees F.) or higher with stoneware or rapid-firing cycles.

If biscuit pottery is refired at a lower temperature than that of its first firing, the amount of decomposition that results from the second firing will be minimal. If, on the other hand, the temperature of the second firing exceeds that of the first, further decomposition will occur and will liberate gases that must, if the pot is glazed, bubble through the glaze layer.

The materials that the potter uses are far from simple. Although the basic starting material consists of clay plus an appropriate amount of water to produce the desired plastic properties, many other ingredients are added to impart desirable characteristics. Feldspars or other glass-forming materials, flint, calcined fireclay grog and other inert materials are added to produce specific effects. The materials used in ceramic bodies are, for the most part, crystalline and remain so during the firing operation. Some glass is, of course, formed in firing which sticks the crystalline materials together and provides the fired strength of the body. The properties exhibited in the final product are determined largely by the amount and types of crystals present and the relative amounts of crystalline and glassy phases present. Body additions, therefore, should be based on a knowledge of the function of each ingredient added and its behavior or reaction to the surroundings which are the other body ingredients. The potter needs to know something about crystals, their structure, morphology and their thermal and physical properties.

The potter is also involved in making glazes which must properly fit the bodies he produces. Glazes with few exceptions are glasses. Glassy materials are entirely different from crystalline materials in that they are amorphous solids, solids which have no repeating structure or orderly atomic arrangement. The potter should know something about the properties and characteristics of glasses, glass formation, viscosity, softening point, thermal expansion and color formation.

Source: CERAMIC SCIENCE FOR THE POTTER. by W. G. Lawrence.

Craft potters usually follow a different firing procedure than do industrial potters due to the difficulties encountered in the application of glazes to articles of low porosity. Unlike the industrial potter (who, desiring to obtain a smooth, impervious glaze surface, glost fires at a lower temperature than he biscuit fires), the craft potter generally biscuit fires up to the point at which most volatiles have been burned away but at which little consolidation has taken place. This results in a pottery that has a high porosity, enabling the glaze to be applied easily by dipping for a firm but even coat.

Once the temperature of the glost fire exceeds that of the biscuit fire, the body begins to decompose further, and gases are released which bubble through the glaze and burst upon reaching the surface to produce pinholes or small craters. Sometimes, as is frequently the case with some stoneware and porcelain glazes, this has an enhancing effect, and other times, it is not to be desired. The author discusses various glazes, clays, glazing, and firing techniques from the point of view of both potter and user so that exactly the right effect can be achieved with the proper know-how. He describes in detail the calculation of glaze composition and formulas. Chapters are devoted to opacifiers, opacification methods, glaze types and methods of producing various effects with glazes, prepared stains, and coloring. The preparation of glazes from the first stages of grinding rock, mixing dry ingredients, to the flocculation and deflocculation by electrolytes is charted. He also examines various defects not deliberately induced by the potter that may appear in the glazed and fired articles. Crawling, for one, can be caused by a number of factors, among which are the presence of oil, grease, or dust on the ware before dipping; the knocking of the unfired glazed surface; overgrinding the glaze; or the presence of soluble salts in the water supply used to sponge the ware or during the turning of the pot on the wheel. This is easily remedied by adding a little vinegar to the water.

CLAY AND GLAZES FOR THE POTTER, revised edition. by Daniel Rhodes. Chilton Book Company, Radnor, Pennsylvania, 1973. 330 pages $12.50.

An extensive, clear treatment of clay, glazes, and calculations.

POTTERY GLAZES. by David Green. Watson-Guptill Publications, New York, 1973. 143 pages. illustrations, photographs (some color), suppliers list, bibliography, index. $9.95.

This is a simple, straightforward presentation of glaze mixing. The author begins by filling in chemical background, and at a slow and kindly pace describes the nature of elements, atoms, atomic weights and compounds, geology, and individual characteristics of minerals, such as silica, lead, and boric oxide, commonly used in glazes. He then proceeds to a step-by-step explanation of glaze calculations, formulas, recipes, methods of glaze application, firing techniques, and correction of faults.

FACTS ABOUT LEAD GLAZES FOR THE ART POTTER AND HOBBYIST and LEAD GLAZES FOR DINNERWARE

Important pamphlets for anyone using lead glazes on functional pottery, these may be obtained from the International Lead Zinc Research Organization, 292 Madison Avenue, New York, N.Y. 10017.

If you buy prepared leaded glazes, purchase them from a company that is a member of the United States Pottery Association's Ceramic Dinnerware Surveillance Program, such as:

The American Clay Company, Indianapolis, Indiana.
The American Beauty Ceramics Corporation, Wiilongly, Ohio.
Ceramichrome, Inc., Cardena, California.
Duncan Ceramic Products, Inc., Fresno, California.
Gare, Inc., Hoverhill, Massachusetts.
Pemperton-Neal Ceramics Supplies, Bellflower, California.
Reward Ceramic Colors Manufacturing, Inc., Glen Brunie, Maryland.

Untitled sculpture 1973, Pat Lay. 5′ x 6′ fired clay, glaze, luster, sand, gravel

There are five factors which must be considered before kiln design can begin.
1. Kind of kiln: updraft, downdraft, salt glaze, etc. Will it be 10, 20, 25, 45, 150 cubic feet or larger?
2. The clay to be fired. The type of clay will determine the type of kiln, size, fuel to be used, etc. A kiln should be designed to enhance pottery and control the effects of the firing according to what the potter wants to achieve.
3. The atmospheric conditions. Oxidation, reduction, and maybe even middle fire must be considered because channel shape, burners, and dampeners can greatly affect the ability of a kiln to oxidize or reduce. This also affects the clay body, glazes, and outcomes.
4. Available fuel. Propane/butane and electric are available just about everywhere and they are clean burning. Natural gas is perfect for city use and wood, coke, coal and oil for use in the country.
5. The location of the kiln. Most areas have codes restricting building and use of kilns.

Source: THE KILN BOOK. by Frederick L. Olsen. Keramos, 1973. 146 pages. illustrations, photographs, index. paperback edition $8.95.

"How To Build an Electric Kiln to Fire Ceramics or Heat Treat Metal at Temperatures of Nearly 2300°," *Popular Mechanics* (February 1968) page 178.

"The fire is the key"

KILNS: DESIGN, CONSTRUCTION, AND OPERATION. by Daniel Rhodes. Chilton Book Company, Radnor, Pennsylvania, 1968. 231 pages. illustrations, photographs, bibliography, index. $9.95.

One of the few books to deal effectively with the art of kiln design for the art potter. The reader is introduced to the

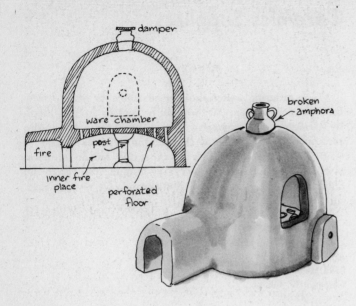

Ancient Greek kiln

subject from a historical vantage point as the author traces the development of kilns from ancient to modern times, including kilns of primitive people and those of the Orient. The remainder of the book is concerned with the practical problems of kiln design, building, and operations. The author presents many original kiln designs illustrated with step-by-step diagrams as well as descriptions of updraft, downdraft, raku, electric, and portable kilns with discus-

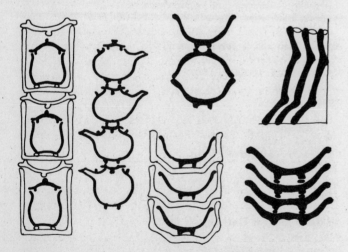

Methods of setting various pottery forms in the kiln

sions of the advantages and limitations of each. He also presents detailed information on how to set the kiln with ware and fire it for a variety of effects.

MAKING AND DECORATING POTTERY TILES. by B. C. Southwell. Watson-Guptill Puiblications, New York, 1972. 128 pages. illustrations, photographs (some color), bibliography, index. $8.95.

Contemporary potters and designers have rediscovered the art of tile-making, an art that is almost as old as ceramics itself.

The most elaborate tiles are those found in Middle Eastern cultures. They are exceedingly rich and are used on an architectural scale not found elsewhere in the world. European tiles, though less elaborate, are no less interesting. Often, they may be read as a social document on their times, describing the dress, customs, and technology of the period. The tremendous diversity of historical tile designs appears, at first, to be an inhibiting factor for anyone wishing to begin producing their own tiles. Frequently, it is the figurative elements in historical tilework that obscure the underlying design values, values that are most important for the creative designer. It is the constructional elements that should be analyzed, not the style or figurative content.

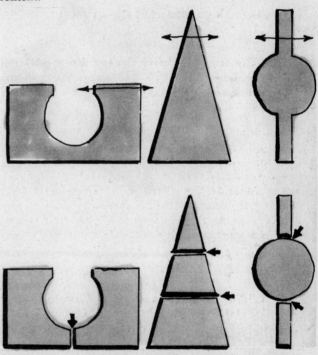

When firing unusual shapes, tiles must be subdivided into sections to prevent warping.

A tile can exist as a single unit; in this case the design values are those related to its surface and physical boundaries. On the other hand, a tile's design may be only part of many other tiles, and notice must first be taken of the total scheme and then the contribution of the individual tile. Most tilework fits one of the following formats: (1) a single tile repeat, following a grid pattern, (2) a repetition of two or more tiles following a grid pattern, (3) a freely composed design without a grid pattern, (4) any single tile existing alone, (5) any combination of the above.

There are no universal rules to solve problems of tile design, only rules that can be discovered and applied in any given situation. B. C. Southwell has found that the most useful method of solving design problems is to view the work from its technical aspects. This will never give a complete answer to design questions, but it will provide a direction in which the imagination can work. The designer is also more free to work in a creative manner if the technical aspects of the job present no threat. The author breaks down and simplifies the basic procedures of tile-making in order to familiarize those new to it. Chapters are devoted to handmade and factory tiles, glaze preparation, and application, with considerable time spent on on-glaze and under-glaze decorations. There is also a very good section on silk-screening including information on building a frame, printing with a paper stencil, and printing with photographic stencils.

Template for cutting handmade tiles

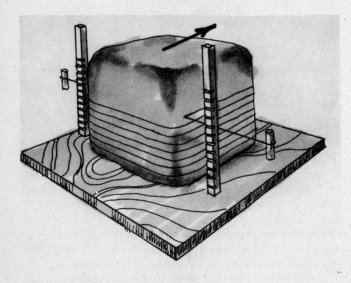

Cutting a block of clay into tiles

Ceramics Suppliers

When ordering materials it is advisable to order a few bulky but cheap items so they can be sent by freight, thereby avoiding the expensive parcel post rate. It is also recommended that you deal with the supplier closest to your area. Kilns and wheels are expensive and do, on occasion, malfunction. The nearer the supplier, the faster the shipment of any new parts or the cheaper the postage rates on any return.

A.R.T. Studio
2725 West Howard
Chicago, Ill. 60645
catalog $1.00.
clay, clay chemicals and components, raku clay, kilns, wheels, cones, modeling tools.

J. T. Abernathy
212 South State Street
Ann Arbor, Mich. 48101
kilns.

AKG Company, Inc.
1442 Christiana Road
Newark, Del. 19711
catalog $.35.
clays, clay chemicals and components, glazes, kilns, cones, wheels.

Allcraft Tools and Supply Company, Inc.
22 West 48 Street
New York, N.Y. 10036
catalog $1.00.
modeling tools.

A. D. Alpine
353 Coral Circle
El Segundo, Cal. 90245
catalog.
bats, kilns and kiln furniture, cones, wheels.

American Art Clay Company
4717 West 16 Street
Indianapolis, Ind. 46222
catalog.
kilns, cones, clay, raku clay, glazes, modeling tools, ceramic tile.

Amherst Potters Supply
44 McClellan Street
Amherst, Mass. 01002
catalog.
clays, clay chemicals and components, kilns, modeling tools, glazes.

Archie Bray Foundation
2915 Country Club Avenue
Helena, Mont. 59601
brochure.
clays, raku clay, clay chemicals and components, cones, modeling tools.

Art Brown
2 West 46 Street
New York, N.Y. 10036
catalog.
clay, modeling tools, wheels.

Art Consultants
100 East 7 Street
New York, N.Y. 10009
catalog.
clay, raku clay, glazes, kilns, kiln furniture, cones, modeling tools.

Ashland Chemical
P.O. Box 2219
Columbus, O. 43216
catalog.
clay chemicals and components.

Babcock and Wilcox Company
161 East 42 Street
New York, N.Y. 10017
catalog.
kiln bricks.

Baynton Electronics Corporation
2709 North Broad Street
Philadelphia, Pa. 19132
catalog.
pyrometric cones.

Judith Baldwin
540 LaGuardia Place
New York, N.Y.
all ceramics supplies.

W. J. Beilman Company
6708 San Haroldo Way
Buena Park, Cal. 90620
catalog.
kilns.

Bergen Arts and Crafts
P.O. Box 381
Marblehead, Mass. 01945
catalog.
clay, glazes, wheels, modeling tools, jigs, kilns, cones.

Dick Blick Company
P.O. Box 1267
Galesburg, Ill. 61401
catalog.
clay, glazes, kilns, kiln furniture, cones, wheels, modeling tools.

Bluebird Manufacturing
100 Gregory Road
Fort Collins, Colo. 80521
catalog.
wheels.

Boin Arts and Crafts
87 Morris Street
Morristown, N.J. 07960
catalog $.50.
clay, kilns and furtniture, cones, wheels, modeling tools.

Bona Venture Supply Company
17 Village Square
Hazelwood, Mo. 63042
catalog $1.00.
ceramic tile, clay, glazes, kilns and furniture, wheels, cones, tools.

Bovin Ceramics
6912 Schaeffer Road
Dearborn, Mich. 48126
general suppliers.

Robert Brent Company
128 Mill Street
Healdsburg, Cal. 95448
brochure.
bats, wheels.

Brodhead-Garrett Company
4560 East 17 Street
Cleveland, O. 44105
glaze materials and equipment.

Burns Brick Company
Macon, Ga. 31200
clay.

Byrne Ceramic Supply Company, Inc.
95 Bartley Road
Flanders, N.J. 07836
catalog.
ceramic tile, glazes, clay, kilns, kiln furniture, wheels, tools.

California Kiln Company
P.O. Box 731
Monrovia, Cal. 91016
catalog.
kilns.

Gilmour Campbell Company
14258 Maiden
Detroit, Mich. 48213
brochure.
decorating and band wheels.

Capital Ceramics
2174 South Main Street
Salt Lake City, Ut. 84115
catalog.
wheels.

Cedar Heights Clay Company
50 Portsmouth Road
Oak Hill, O. 45656
catalog.
clay.

Cerami Corner, Inc.
607 North San Gabriel Avenue
P.O. Box 516
Azusa, Cal. 91702
catalog $1.00.

Ceramic Color and Chemical Company
P.O. Box 297
New Brighton, Pa. 15066
glaze materials.

Ceramic Extrusion
369 Mill Road
East Astoria, N.Y. 14052
catalog.
clay, clay chemicals and components, wheels.

Ceramichrome, Inc.
7155 Fenwick Lane
Westminster, Cal. 92683
brochure.
glazes.

Ceramics, Hawaii, Ltd.
629 Cooke Street
Honolulu, Hawaii 96813
general supplies.

Charl-Stan Company
P.O. Box 348
Chester, Pa. 19016
brochure.
glazes.

Clay Art Center
40 Beech Street
Port Chester, N.Y. 10573
Also 342 Western Avenue
Brighton, Mass.
brochure.
kilns, wheels.

Clay-Stone Company
P.O. Box 2758
Norman, Okla.
brochure.
clay, clay chemicals and components, cones, modeling tools.

Cole Ceramic Laboratories
Gay Street
Sharon, Conn. 06069
catalog.
clay, clay chemicals and components, glazes, kiln furniture, wheels.

The Crafters
Cascade, Wis. 53011
catalog $.50.
glazes, modeling tools, wheels.

The Craftool Company, Inc.
1421 West 240 Street
Harbor City, Cal. 90710
catalog $1.00.
modeling tools, wheels, kiln furniture,
jigs.

Craft Service
337-345 University Avenue
Rochester, N.Y. 14607
catalog.
glazes, kiln furniture, modeling tools.

Creative Industries
8139 Center Street
La Mesa, Cal. 92041
catalog.
wheels.

Creek-Turn Ceramic Supply
Route 38
Hainesport, N.J. 08036
catalog $1.00.
clay, clay chemicals and components,
glazes, cones, wheels.

Cress Manufacturing Company
1718 Floradale Avenue
South El Monte, Cal. 91733
catalog.
kilns.

Cross Creek Ceramics, Inc.
3596 Brownsville Road
Pittsburgh, Pa. 15227
clay, glazes, cones, modeling tools.

Crusader Industries, Inc.
338 West 12 Street
Holland, Mich. 49423
brochure.
kilns, kiln furniture.

W. P. Dawson, Inc.
1147 East Elm Avenue
Fullerton, Cal. 92631
brochure.
kiln and kiln controls.

Denver Fire Clay Company
P.O. Box 5507
Denver, Colo. 80217
catalog.
clay, kilns.

Duncan Ceramic Products, Inc.
5673 East Shields
Fresno, Cal. 93727
catalog $1.00.
glazes, molds.

Earth Treasures
Box 1267, Department PF
Galesburg, Ill. 61401
catalog.
clay, glazes, wheels.

Earthworks, Inc.
2309 West Main Street
Richmond, Va. 23220
catalog.
clay, clay chemicals and components,
raku clay, kilns, wheels, tools.

Eastern Refractories Company, Inc.
P.O. Box 749
Montpelier, Vt. 05602
catalog.
clay.

Endicott Clay Products Company
Fairbury, New Brunswick, Canada
catalog.

Estrin Manufacturing, Ltd.
1767 West 3rd
Vancouver 9, British Columbia
Canada
brochure.
wheels.

Ferro Corporation
4150 East 56 Street
Cleveland, Ohio 44105
glaze chemicals and frits.

George Fetzer—Ceramic Supplies
1205-17th Avenue
Columbus, O. 43211
price list.
clay, glazes, modeling tools, clay components and chemicals.

The Forming Company, Ceramic Supply
2764 North West Thurman Street
Portland, Ore. 97210
catalog.
clay chemicals and components, clay,
glazes, kiln builders, wheels, tools.

Gare Ceramic Supply
165 Rosemont Street
Haverhill, Mass. 01830
glaze material and equipment.

The Robert Gee Pottery
15227 Cascadian Way
Alderwood Manor, Wash. 98036
catalog.
glazes, kiln controls, modeling tools,
bats.

Genco
P.O. Box 7
Minerva, O. 44657
catalog.
clay, clay components and chemicals.

Georgia Art Clay Company
Route 1
Lizella, Ga. 31052
price list.
clay.

A. P. Green Fire Brick Company
Mexico, Mo. 65265

J. L. Hammett Company
Hammett Place
Braintree, Mass. 02184
catalog.
clay, glazes, kilns, wheels, cones, modeling tools.

Hammill and Gillespie, Inc.
225 Broadway
New York, N.Y. 10007
brochure.
clay, clay components and chemicals.

Harris-Linden Ceramics
1772 Genessee Avenue
Columbus, O. 43211
catalog $1.00.
clay, clay chemicals and components,
glazes, kilns, modeling tools.

Harshaw Chemical Company
1945 East 97 Street
Cleveland, O. 44106
glaze chemicals.

C. R. Hill Company
35 West Grand River
Detroit, Mich. 48226
catalog.
general supplies.

House of Ceramics, Inc.
1011 North Hollywood Street.
Memphis, Tenn. 38108
catalog $1.00.
kilns, clays, cones, ceramic tile, glazes,
china paint, modeling tools.

Humisco, Inc.
14 Locust Place
Manhasset, N.Y. 11030
brochure.
wheels.

Hydor Therme Corporation
7155 Airport Highway
Pennsauken, N.J. 08109
catalog.
wholesale pyrometers.

Industrial Minerals
1057 Commercial Street
San Carlos, Cal. 94070
brochure.
clay, clay components and chemicals.

Jay-Bellman
1051 North Edgemont
La Habra, Cal. 90631
kilns.

Johnson Gas Appliance Company
Cedar Rapids, Ia. 52405
catalog.
burners.

Kemper Manufacturing, Inc.
P.O. Box 545
Chino, Cal. 91710
catalog $.50.
wholesale modeling tools.

Kentucky-Tennessee Clay Company
P.O. Box 449
Mayfield, Ky. 42066
catalog.
wholesale clay.

Kilns Supply and Service Corporation
38 Bulkley Avenue
Port Chester, N.Y. 10573
catalog $.60.
clay, glazes, kilns, kiln furniture, modeling tools, wheels, cones.

H. R. Klopfenstein and Sons
Route #2
Crestline, O. 44827
catalog.
wheels.

L and L Manufacturing Company
Box 348
Chester, Pa. 19016
catalog.
glazes, kilns, pyrometers.

Langley Ceramics Studio
413 South 24 Street
Philadelphia, Pa. 19146
clay.

L and R Specialties
120 South Main
Nixa, Mo. 65714
catalog.
clay chemicals and components, wheels, cones, modeling tools.

LA-MO Refractory Supply Company, Inc.
323 Iris Avenue
P.O. Box 10325
New Orleans, La. 70121
catalog.
kiln furniture, fire bricks.

Leslie Ceramic Supply Company
1212 San Pable Avenue
Berkeley, Cal. 94706
catalog.
glazes, clay, china paint, kilns, cones, wheels, tools, brick.

Little Slabroiller
288 South 7 Street
Indiana, Pa. 15701
catalog.
general supplies.

Lockerbie Manufacturing Corporation
7812 Boulder
Highland, Cal. 92346
catalog.
wheels.

Long Island Ceramic Center
1190 Route 109
Lindenhurst, N.Y. 11757
catalog $1.00, free to schools and institutions.

L.T.M. Corporation
855 South Telegraph Road
Monroe, Mich. 48167
wheels.

Macmillan Arts and Crafts, Inc.
9520 Baltimore Avenue
College Park, Md. 20740
catalog.
clays, clay components and chemicals, kilns, ceramic tile, tools, glazes.

Mandl Ceramic Supply
R.R. #1, Box 369-A
Pennington, N.J. 08534
price list; shipping charge for samples.
clay.

Marin Ceramics
55A Tamal Vista Blvd.
Corte Madera, Cal. 94925
catalog.
clay, clay components and chemicals, glazes, kilns, cones, tools.

Marshall Craft
1001 Martin Avenue
Santa Clara, Cal. 95050
catalog.
clay, clay chemicals and components, kilns, cones, burners, modeling tools.

Marubeni America Corporation
200 Park Avenue
New York, N.Y. 10017
catalog.
wholesale.

The Max Corporation
P.O. Box 34068
Washington, D.C. 20034
catalog.
wheels.

Maxon Corporation
P.O. Box 2068
Muncie, Ind. 47302
catalog.
burners.

Mayco
20800 Dearborn Street
Chatsworth, Cal. 91311
catalog.
glazes.

The Edward Orton Jr. Ceramic
    Foundation
1445 Summit Street
P.O. Box 8309
Columbus, O. 43201
brochure.
wholesale pyrometric cones.

Pacifica Crafts
P.O. Box 1407
Ferndale, Wash. 98248
brochure.
bats, wheels.

Paoli Clay Company
Route 1
Belleville, Wis. 53508
catalog.
clay, wheels.

Paragon Industries
Box 10133
Dallas, Tex. 75207
wholesale kilns

Paramount Ceramic, Inc.
220 North State Street
Fairmont, Minn. 56031
catalog $1.00.
clays, raku clay, clay chemicals and components, kilns, glazes, wheels.

Parfex Company
7812 Boulder Avenue
Highland, Cal. 92346
brochure.
wheels.

Oscar Paul Corporation
522 West 182 Street
Gardena, Cal. 90247
catalog.
bats.

Rereny Equipment Company
Department CD
898 Chambers Road
Columbus, O. 43211
catalog.
kilns.

Robert Piepenburg
515 East Windamere
Royal Oak, Mich. 48073
raku tongs.

Pink Stilts
P.O. Box 11337
Columbus, O. 43211
brochure.
modeling tools.

The Pottery Supply House
P.O. Box 192
2070 Speers Road
Oakville, Ont. L6J 5A2, Canada
catalog.
clay, clay chemicals and components, ceramic tile, kilns, wheels, glazes.

The Poverty Bay Pottery and Clay Company
3327 Meridian
North Seattle, Wash.
catalog.
clay, raku clay, clay components and chemicals, kilns, wheels, glazes.

Probst's Watermelon Works Pottery
Box 29
Penland, N.C. 28765
catalog.
clays, raku clay.

Pyrometer Instrument Company, Inc.
234 Industrial Parkway
Northvale, N.J. 07647
catalog.

Quyle Kilns
Murphys, Cal. 95247
catalog.
clay, kilns.

Randall Pottery, Inc.
Box 774
Alfred, N.Y. 14820
brochure.
wheels.

Reduction Production
196 Broadway
Cambridge, Mass. 02139
catalog.
Judge kilns.

Reward Ceramic Color Manufacturers, Inc.
314 Hammonds Ferry Road
Glen Burnie, Md. 21061
glazes.

Richland Ceramics, Inc.
Box 3416
Columbia, S.C. 29203
glazes and general supplies.

Rovin Ceramics
6912 Schaefer Road
Dearborn, Mich. 48126
catalog $.50.
clay, kilns, cones, wheels, modeling tools.

Sacramento Ceramics and Potters Supply
2552-C Albatross Way
Sacramento, Cal. 95815
catalog $1.00.
clay, kilns, glazes, cones, wheels, burners, bats, modeling tools.

Sax Arts and Crafts
207 North Milwaukee Street
Milwaukee, Wis. 53202
catalog $1.00.
clays, ceramic tile, kilns, cones, wheels, modeling tools, cones.

Scargo Stoneware Pottery
Box 304, 30 Potters Way
Dennis, Mass. 02638
brochure.

Seeleys Ceramic Service
9 River Street
Oneonta, N.Y. 13820
catalog.
general ceramic supplies.

Sculpture House
38 East 30 Street
New York, N.Y. 10016
catalog.
glazes, kiln builders, modeling tools, wheels.

Sculpture Service, Inc.
9 East 19 Street
New York, N.Y. 10003
catalog $.50.
clay, modeling tools.

Sheffield Pottery, Inc.
Box 395, Route 7
Sheffield, Mass. 01257
catalog.
clay, glazes, kilns, pyrometric cones.

Shimpo-West
Box 2315
La Puente, Cal. 91746
catalog.
wheels.

Skutt and Sons
2618 South East Steele Street
Portland, Ore. 97202
wheels.

Soldner Pottery Equipment
Box 90
Aspen, Colo. 81611
catalog.
wheels.

Spencer's Pottery, Inc.
5021 South 144 Street
Seattle, Wash. 98168
catalog.
clay, clay components and chemicals, glazes, kilns, wheels, tools.

Standard Ceramic Supply Company
Box 4435
Pittsburgh, Pa. 15201
catalog.
clay and general supplies.

Star Engineering
256 East 4300 South
Ogden, Utah 84403
catalog.
wheels.

Stewart Clay Company
133 Mulberry Street
New York, N.Y. 10013
catalog.
clay, raku clay, kilns, pyrometers, cones, wheels, tools, glazes.

Stewart's of California, Inc.
16055 Heron Avenue
La Mirada, Cal. 90638
catalog.
clays, clay components and chemicals, glazes, wheels, kilns, pyrometers.

Tepping Studio Supply Company
3003 Salem Avenue
Dayton, O. 45406
catalog $1.00.
clays, glazes, kilns, pyrometers, wheels, modeling tools.

Triarco, Inc.
3201 North Kimball Avenue
Chicago, Ill.60618 (outlets in Michigan, Maine, Pennsylvania, and Virginia)
catalog $1.00.
glazes, kilns, wheels, pyrometers, modeling tools, cones.

Trinity Ceramic Supply Company
9016 Diplomacy Row
Dallas, Tex. 25235
catalog.
clay.

Tru-Fyre Ceramic Products Company
5894 Blackwelder Street
Culver City, Cal. 90230
catalog.
glazes.

Unique Kilns Division
HED Industies, Inc.
P.O. Box 176
Pennington, N.J. 08534
catalog.

Van Howe Ceramic Supply Company
11975 East 40
Denver, Colo. 80329
Also 4860 Pan American Freeway North East
Albuquerque, N.M. 87107
catalog $1.00.
clays and clay components, raku clay, kiln furniture and controls, wheels.

S. Paul Ward, Inc.
601 Mission Street
P.O. Box 336
South Pasadena, Cal. 91030
catalog.
clays, clay components and chemicals, kiln furniture, wheels.

Way-Craft
394 Delaware South
Imperial Beach, Cal. 92032
brochure.
clays, clay components and chemicals, kilns, wheels, pyrometers, cones.

Westby Ceramic Supply Manufacturing
408 North East 72 Street
Seattle, Wash. 98115
brochure.
kiln furniture, pyrometers, kilns, kiln controls.

West Coast Kiln Company
635 Vineland Avenue
La Puente, Cal. 91746
brochure.
kiln builders, pyrometers, kiln controls, kilns.

Western Ceramics Supply Company
1601 Howard Street
San Francisco, Cal. 94103
Catalog $1.00, free to schools and institutions if request received on official letterhead.
clays, clay components and chemicals, glazes, wheels, kiln furniture.

Western Stoneware Company
521 West 6th Avenue
P.O. Box 288
Monmouth, Ill. 61462
brochure; samples $.10 a lb. plus postage.

Westwood Ceramics Supply Company
1440 Lomitas Avenue
City of Industry, Cal. 91744
catalog.
clays, clay components and chemicals, wheels, ceramic tiles, kilns.

Wheelcraft, Inc.
2233 140th North East
Bellevue, Wash. 98005
catalog.
wheels.

Jack D. Wolfe Company, Inc.
724 Meeker Avenue
Brooklyn, N.Y. 11222
catalog $1.00.
kilns, wheels, clay, glazes, modeling tools, pyrometers, kiln furniture.

Worden Robinson Art Pottery
715 8th Street, South East
Washington, D.C. 20003
catalog.
clay, wheels, pyrometers.

Yankee Hill Brick Manufacturing Co.
3705 South Coddington Avenue
Lincoln, Neb. 68522
catalog.

Zanesville Stoneware Company
Zanesville, O. 43701
clay.

Ellen Staller has found the best all-around wheels to be Shimpo, regardless of price. They can be obtained from:

Dick Blick Company
Clay Art Center
Earthworks, Inc.
Harris Linden Ceramics
L and R Specialties
Macmillan Arts and Crafts, Inc.
Marin Ceramics
Marubeni America Corporation
The Pottery Supply House
Rovin Ceramics
Sacramento Ceramics and Pottery Supply
Sax Arts and Crafts
Sculpture House
Spencer's Pottery, Inc.
Stewart Clay Company
Stewart's of California, Inc.
Van Howe Ceramic Supply Company
Way-Craft
Westwood Ceramics Supply Company

Country Crafts

THE SEASONS OF AMERICA PAST. by Eric Sloane. Funk and Wagnalls, New York, 1958. 150 pages. illustrations. $7.50.

In rural, preindustrial America the changing of the seasons determined what people did to maintain their existence. Eric Sloane takes the reader through a full year's activities and illustrates with detailed drawings of mills and presses, sleds, pumps and wells, stump-pulling, maple-sugaring, axes, plows, and scythes.

Self-sufficiency, the dropout luxury of the 1960s, may become the necessity of the 1970s, and therefore it's important as well as interesting to find out how things were done by our recent ancestors.

DO, A LITTLE BOOK OF EARLY AMERICAN KNOW-HOW. by Eric Sloane. Walker and Company, New York, 1972. 55 pages. illustrations. $2.95.

Early America was cluttered with a weary lot of "don'ts." People were so strict about not doing this and not doing that. Yet that disciplined life was also enlivened by an amazing number of things to do.

Today, doing things by and for ourselves has become a lost art, and the joy of doing things not just "the old-fashioned way" but plainly the right way is a nearly vanished satisfaction.

Some of this satisfaction can be gained by following Eric Sloane's old delightful dos. For instance:

Do clean woodwork marred by matchstriking, etc., by rubbing it with half a lemon. Fingermarks will also disappear by this method.

Do hang a broom from a nail instead of resting it upon the floor. Letting a broom stand can give it a permanent warp within a few hours.

Foxfire
The Southern Highlands Literary Fund
Rabun Gap, Ga. 30568
Quarterly. $4.00 a year.

Foxfire is a publication concerned with researching, recording, and preserving Appalachian folk art, crafts, and traditions. A typical issue contains articles on quilting, chair-making, soap-making, home remedies, mountain recipes, feather beds, and homemade hominey, plus regional poetry and book reviews. One issue was devoted entirely to log cabin building. These are not superficial "feature" articles, but definitive, detailed treatments of traditional skills and crafts quickly dying out in our culture. *Foxfire* is a real, adult magazine despite the fact that it is published by high school students at the Rabun Gap-Nacoochee School in Rabun Gap and totally lacking in the artificial trappings of the hip, underground urbanities of the coasts.

FOXFIRE BOOK I. Eliot Wigginton, ed. Anchor Press, New York, 1972. 384 pages. illustrations, photographs. paperback edition $3.95.

These are selections from the quarterly by the same name. The book contains information on hog dressing, log cabin building, mountain crafts and food, planting by the signs, snake lore, hunting tales, faith healing, moonshining, and other affairs of plain living.

FOXFIRE 2. Eliot Wigginton, ed. Anchor Press, New York, 1973. 410 pages. illustrations, photographs. paperback edition $3.95.

This volume contains ghost stories, spring wild plant foods, spinning and weaving, midwifing, burial customs, corn shuckin's, wagon-making, and more affairs of plain living.

COLONIAL CRAFTSMEN. by Edwin Tunis. World Publishing Company, New York, 1965. 159 pages. illustrations. $6.95.

FRONTIER LIVING. by Edwin Tunis. World Publishing Company, New York, 1961. 166 pages. illustrated. $6.95.

COLONIAL LIVING. by Edwin Tunis. World Publishing Company, New York, 1957. 156 pages. illustrated. $6.95.

These books are not intended to be read for their practical applications to contemporary life, but rather for the interest that old ways of making things may have.

Take, for instance, the case of the vanished American

hornsmith. At one time, hundreds of common everyday items were made from cow horns. Today, these same articles—combs, glass frames, spoons—are made out of plastic, a cheaper and more easily worked material; and hornsmithing has become a lost art in this country.

Edwin Tunis includes just about every possible aspect of colonial life and craft and broadly describes working methods and equipment.

THE AMERICAN CRAFTSMAN. by Scott Graham Williamson. Finch Press, 1940 (reprinted). 239 pages. illustrations, photographs. $13.00.

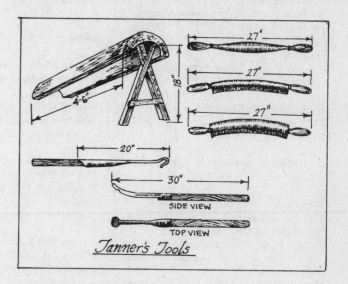

Tanner's Tools

What have now become antiques and collector's items were originally the products of a viable self-sufficient community of craftsmen. Hundreds of these products are illustrated in this book, making it quite useful as a source of inspiration.

THE BOOK OF COUNTRY CRAFTS. by Randolph Wardell Johnston. A. S. Barnes and Company, Cranbury, New Jersey, 1973. 211 pages. illustrations, suppliers list, bibliography, index. $3.98

This is a book aimed at the worker living in country districts who is cut off from ready access to libraries, museums, and the workshops of other craftsmen. The author hopes that it will provide solid, basic information to the lone craftsman and enable him to make a good beginning and steady progress in wood, clay, metals, stones, and color work. Unfortunately, it does not really succeed.

THE GOLDEN AGE OF HOMESPUN. by Jared Van Wagenen, Jr. Hill and Wang, New York, 1963. 280 pages. illustrations, index. paperback edition $2.25.

The New York State Historical Association was the original 1953 publisher of this folk history containing the reminiscences of the eighty-two-year-old author and the old men he knew, men who, like himself, had built their lives around the tilled fields, hillside pastures, and woodlands of east central New York.

The author's "hereditary memory" has kept him in touch with the times when self-sufficiency was the order of the day. He talks of the life, skills, and concerns of the people of the homespun age, and theorizes as to the reasons for both its development and eventual decline.

FROW

CRAFTS OF THE NORTH AMERICAN INDIANS. by Richard C. Schneider. Van Nostrand Reinhold, New York, 1972. 325 pages. illustrations. paperback edition $6.95.

At last, a sensitive, intelligent, and uncompromising approach to Indian crafts. There are no decorative adaptations here; most of the crafts take time, sweat, and patience to accomplish—let alone master. The author is tremendously conscious of the expertise required to execute many seemingly simple tasks and believes that the best way to educate the public in these matters is through their participation. Thus, the reader is shown how to make Indian tools, to work and tan leather, and to try some of the lesser known crafts, such as porcupine quill embroidery. The book makes no claim to comprehensiveness, but what is covered is covered well. The author treats delicately the matter of artifacts carrying religious and spiritual significance (drums, pipes, masks, and so on), because though they are of interest to contemporary craftsmen, he fears their possible degeneration through reproduction without a thorough and sympathetic understanding of their place.

Measurements are presented in generalities; designs and shapes are suggested rather than enforced; there is little precision. Indians followed tribal codes and family preferences, but each craftsman had his own idiosyncracies in sizes, designs, and techniques; the author can only offer what seem to be universal generalizations.

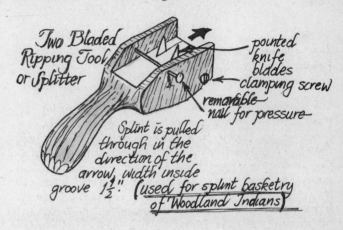

Mr. Schneider asks that those craftsmen who achieve proficiency in North American Indian crafts not add to the already existing market for fraudulent artifacts nor attempt to take away from native craftsmen the small market they have left. Rather, the author hopes they will "gain appreciation and sympathy for the arts and skills of a people. Perhaps in this way we can also generate similar feelings for the Native Americans themselves."

THE COMPLETE HOW-TO BOOK OF INDIAN CRAFT. by Ben Hunt. Collier, 1973. 187 pages. illustrations, photographs, bibliography, index. paperback edition $2.95.

A collection of sixty-eight projects, some using authentic methods, some adapted to modern resources. Contains hand-drawn, handwritten plates by the author.

HOW TO MAKE WHIRLIGIGS AND WHIMMY DIDDLES AND OTHER AMERICAN FOLKCRAFT OBJECTS. by Florence H. Pettit. Thomas Y. Crowell Company, New York, 1972. 349 pages. illustrations, photographs. $6.95.

In addition to whirligigs, the book includes jumping jacks and acrobats that move, patchwork and appliqué quilts, kachina dolls, and much more. It is imaginative, humorous, and encyclopedic in content. Drawings are accurate and beautiful, and many are actual size for tracing. The author also traces the origins of indigenous American folk art from Indians and Eskimos to European colonists.

Early American Life
Robert G. Miner, Publisher
P.O. Box 1831
Harrisburg, Pa.
$6.00 a year.
Official magazine of the Early American Society. Features articles on the arts, crafts, and social history of early America.

Design

TREASURY OF AMERICAN DESIGN, Volumes 1 and 2. Selected by Clarence P. Hornung. Harry N. Abrams, New York, 1972. 876 pages. illustrations (some color). $50.00.

Hundreds of unemployed Depression artists were assigned by the W.P.A. to the task of researching and compiling watercolor records of Early American craftsmanship and folk art. This resulted in the *National Gallery's Index of American Design*, the source from which Clarence Hornung has drawn his selections. The volumes are organized around the nature of the objects considered; for example, cooking utensils, fabrics, toys, and so on. Each object is accompanied by a brief description, although the publication itself is almost exclusively visual (there are 2,150 black-and-white illustrations and 850 in color).

THE UNKNOWN CRAFTSMAN: A JAPANESE INSIGHT INTO BEAUTY. by Soetsu Yanagi, adapted by Bernard Leach. Kodansha International, Ltd., Tokyo and Palo Alto, California, 1972. 230 pages. photographs (some color). $17.50.

An important as well as beautiful book in that it provides a comprehensive view of what almost might be called the original aesthetics of a nation, Japan; and because it nudges American craftsmen into thinking about consolidating the American artistic position in the modern world of nations.

WILLIAM MORRIS AS DESIGNER. by Ray Watkinson. Van Nostrand Reinhold, New York, 1967. illustrations, photographs. $16.50.

Scores of photographic examples of the work of this seminal nineteenth-century designer.

Film

WITH THESE HANDS: THE REBIRTH OF THE AMERICAN CRAFTSMAN. A film produced and distributed by Daniel Wilson Productions, New York. 52 minutes. Color.

Originally shown on ABC-TV, this film explores the lifestyles and work of eight American craftsmen. It is directed toward a large, general audience, and emphasizes the individuality and creativity of each artist-craftsman rather than his use or materials, tools, or techniques. The artists covered are: James Tanner, glassblower and ceramist; Paul

Soldner, potter; Harry Nohr, maker of wooden bowls; J. B. Blunk, sculptor of natural forms from tree stumps and driftwood; Dorian Zachai, weaver; Clayton Bailey, potter; Peter Voulkos, potter and sculptor; and Toshiko Takaezu, potter.

AMERICAN INDIAN DESIGN AND DECORATION. by Le Roy H. Appleton. Dover Publications, New York, 1971. 277 pages. bibliography, index. paperback edition $4.00.

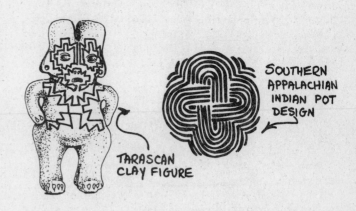

TARASCAN CLAY FIGURE

SOUTHERN APPALACHIAN INDIAN POT DESIGN

THE BOOK OF SIGNS. by Rudolf Koch. Dover Publications, New York, 1930. 104 pages. paperback edition $1.25.

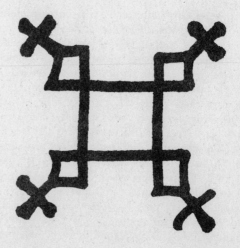

JAPANESE DESIGN MOTIFS. compiled by the Matsuya Piece-Goods Store. Dover Publications, New York, 1973. 216 pages. paperback edition $3.50.

4,260 illustrations of Japanese crests.

JAPANESE STENCIL DESIGNS. by Andrew F. Tuer. Dover Publications, New York, 1967, 139 pages. paperback edition $2.75.

102 stencils.

HANDBOOK OF ORNAMENT. by Franz Sales Meyer. Dover Publications, New York, 1957. 548 pages. paperback edition $3.50.

3,002 illustrations.

ART DECO. by Bevis Hillier. Studio Vista/E. P. Dutton and Company, New York, 1968. 168 pages. illustrations, photographs, index. paperback edition $2.45.

Gold and enamel ring, French, c. 1925

DESIGN MOTIFS OF ANCIENT MEXICO. by Jorge Enciso. Dover Publications, New York, 1947. 192 pages. paperback edition $2.50.

DESIGNS AND DEVICES. by C. P. Hornung. Dover Publications, New York, 1946. 218 pages. 1,836 basic designs. paperback edition $2.00.

SYMBOLS, SIGNS, AND SIGNETS. by Ernst Lehner. Dover Publications, New York, 1950. 224 pages. paperback edition $3.50.

Over 1,350 illustrations.

Talisman to bring success, wealth, and long life

1. *18th century tapestry trademark*

2. *15th century pottery mark*

3. *15th century French stained glass artisan*

4. *18th century French goldsmith hallmark*

5. *16th century Japanese potter*

6. *Mark of early gothic stonemason*

THE ARTS AND CRAFTS MOVEMENT IN AMERICA 1876–1916. Robert Judson Clark, ed. exhibition catalog distributed by Princeton University Press, Princeton, New Jersey, 1973. 190 pages. photographs, bibliography. paperback edition $7.95.

A catalog that focuses on craftsmen and their contributions. It is organized according to geographical distribution.

OBJECTS: U.S.A. by Lee Nordness. The Viking Press, New York, 1970. 395 pages. photographs (some color). $16.95.

This book is a pictorial survey of art objects being created in the United States. The objects encompass diversified materials, varied styles, myriad philosophies, and far-ranging techniques, but each object shares the common feature of having been created by one person alone.

The word *object* is used rather than *handicraft* to allow for purity of connotation. It is an attempt to purge the pejorative connotations that are too frequently associated with the work *handicraft*.

Beyond depicting contemporary objects alone, the book attempts to establish the creator behind each work; he or she is photographed; his contribution noted, and his personal statement if he has chosen to make one, is recorded.

Education

Crafts in the Educational Process

—Susan Dresner

The Problem Is—
What the Problem Is
Defined as Being.

The premise of this article is that our students must be active participants in the learning process, motivated, not by fancy gimmickry, coercion, or formless exploration, but by a structured curriculum reflective of their emotional and cognitive needs. Only then can we say we are educating our children toward becoming responsive, creative, and intellectually confident members of society.

Crafts are usually relegated to a minimal position in the schools. If there is a specialized crafts program, it is usually stuck somewhere in the basement with a part-time instructor and a very limited budget. Otherwise, crafts means hobby-hour in the classroom: for the students, a release from the academic pressure and the monotony of the "more important" subjects, and for the teacher, a free period. In both instances, crafts is considered apart from the standard curriculum. Since the classroom teacher is neither trained in art/crafts instruction nor appreciative of its built-in learning possibilities, the student is left to his own resources, interests, and talents; or (and this is probably the more disastrous), regimented into manufacturing sex and culturally stereotyped items. We are all familiar with these traditional "look-alikes"—for the boys: wooden ships, knives, guns; electric dynamos; metal nameplates; the girls: embroidery; potholders and aprons; jewelry; Indian or historical folklore: miniature canoes and spinning wheels; toms-toms, beadwork; "free-form": papier-maché and clay masks or figurines. We are told the children do not want to do anything different. But are they afforded options with only the customary materials, skills, and models available, and further reinforced by the instructor's narrow perspective of what crafts ought to be. Even with the current entry of the professional craftsperson into the educational mainstream, bringing in multifarious techniques and expressive forms (batiking, macramé, and silkscreening amongst others), there seems to be little hope of moving away from the standard precious ornaments being produced as long

as the role and function of crafts in the schools remain the same. We do not believe the problem lies with the students (it is a fallacy that children lose their creativity once they have left kindergarten) nor with a lack of class time or funds. What must be examined is our approach to curriculum design, and more fundamental, the learning process.

According to Jerome Bruner, learning is a continuous process of deepening understanding of the complex forms of the structure of knowledge. ". . . any subject can be taught effectively in some intellectually honest form to any child at any stage of development." Instead of segmented units of study (in which isolated facts and techniques play the major role), the spiral curriculum is proposed. Fundamental issues, concepts, and values provide a central core from which the curriculum acts as the underpinning material, expanding reinforced knowledge in a spiral fashion. For an example, the concept of causality, essential to the principal disciplines, can be introduced early in the primary grades, and intercalated in the form of increasingly more complex material and applications throughout the academic years.

Implicit in the design of the spiral curriculum is the "core" approach to learning. Integrating concepts and skills with the major academic areas, around one central theme of study, is the most effective way to foster the transferability of knowledge. A dynamic theme like "The Development of the Community" would permit the interrelated study of several subjects: social sciences (geography, history, sociology, anthropology, economics); sciences (biology, physics, topography); mathematics; arts (literature, art, crafts, dance, music). Not only could a concentrated, indepth process of exploration be conducted over a span of time, but the inherent principles and techniques could be transferred on to later learning in a vital and profound way.

The self-contained and subject-oriented class would eventually lose its purpose. Rather, a battery of teachers would develop problem-solving issues from which multiple questions would spontaneously arise (e.g., What does the community need to survive? Why does the community form? What environments are most conducive to the growth of the community? Why does a community decline?). Both the instructors and students would collectively explore these questions, employing a variety of approaches, skills, and resources, toward reaching possible, but nonetheless, tentative solutions. The focus would no longer be on the "right" answer authorized by the teacher; instead, as the issues and concepts become more complex and interwoven, the need to develop and refine intuitive and analytical cognitive skills naturally assumes prime importance. Learning situations are structured by a corps of "specialists" and coordinated by the "core" teacher, taking place within and outside of the school walls. Disciplined study habits are derived from the necessity to "test" appropriate hypotheses. Consequently, both the teachers and students are actively engaged in the learning process.

How does the "core" approach apply to the teaching of crafts? First, crafts must be included as an integral part of the curriculum. The potential learning experiences are enormous: concepts and skills intrinsic to mathematics, the physical and social sciences, and the arts should be built in to all craft lessons. For instance, a project like constructing a model of a primitive river community would necessitate the following concepts/skills: ratio and proportion, scaling, measurements (mathematics); height, width, depth (topography); ecology; grouping patterns (sociology); historical references; space and design. The crafts specialist would work closely with the "core" teacher to develop the spiral curriculum (i.e., concepts, methods, materials, projects), and utilize the resources within the classroom. The connotation crafts has, that of a specialized, supplementary component of the academic program, would be altered. Crafts would assume its deserved place, within the framework of the educational process.

Secondly, the emphasis of most crafts programs has been on explicit skills, formulae, and objectives. Students are expected to know how to use specified tools and materials in the production of a narrow range of craft items. The carryover of experiences and techniques occurs rarely from one grade to the next. We view this approach as inimical to operational learning. What must underlay any craft activity is the development and refinement of both intuitive and analytical thinking (i.e., problem-solving). Students should be given implicit problems to work out so they can exercise their abilities to reflect, evaluate, and generalize. As an example: the problem could be to devise a two-dimensional structure with a three-dimensional projection using only two types of materials and four color tones. The students would first have to visualize the object (understand the problem), be able to conceive a structural analysis of the form, and then, subsequently construct it. This approach demands a great deal from the instructor—a thorough grasp of the structural basis of the subject; knowing the right questions to lead the students to appropriate assumptions; interjecting the necessary techniques and tools at the suitable time. Extensive forethought and preparation—but this is what makes teaching an exciting challenge.

In conclusion, we must scrutinize our own mode of instruction to determine if it effectively fosters the process of creativity. Implicit in the examination are several questions: toward what purposes are we educating? Is the material we are teaching applicable to other areas of study, and furthermore, useful in solving more complex academic problems that might occur later on? Are we providing enough aesthetic and intellectual challenges in order to motivate the students to achieve a sense of excellence? The responses to these queries will hopefully furnish the impetus to design integrative, creative curriculum.

Susan Dresner is a former teacher and
free-lance writer who currently
lives in New York City.

ARTS AND CRAFTS ACTIVITIES DESK BOOK. by Joyce Nobes Laskin. Parker Publishing Company, Englewood Cliffs, New Jersey, 1972. 255 pages. illustrations, photographs, index. $9.95.

In this book are 110 arts and crafts ideas intended as ancillaries to a given study area. Each lesson is condensed into five sections.
A checklist of materials
Motivational techniques
A list of numbered, step-by-step procedures
Follow-up activities and display suggestions
Classroom management hints
The projects are directed more toward the elementary than the secondary school teacher. They are all intended as instructive rather than purely creative or artistic. For example, vitamin art can help the very young child learn to appreciate the value of nutrients. The teacher should pick a single vitamin and discuss its effects with the class. Then,

the whole class should scour magazines and newspapers for representative clippings to be used in a vitamin A collage. They should be encouraged to use materials of varying sizes, and to make letters and write words in addition to using purely visual material.

WITH A FREE HAND. by Adelaide Sproul. Van Nostrand Reinhold, New York, 1968. 144 pages. photographs, bibliography, index. $7.95.

This book covers painting, drawing, graphics, ceramics, and sculpture for children, and describes in detail specific ways of presenting ideas and techniques to children, indicating appropriate ages for introducing various ways of thinking and working.

The author presents various lesson plans and a section of technical notes containing basic procedural information for teachers. It is not necessary to be an accomplished artist to teach art to children, and indeed, most primary school teachers are not art specialists. The only requirement is a sense of personal commitment and involvement, and the one hard-and-fast rule that the author insists upon is that every lesson be thoroughly reviewed before it is taught.

A FESTIVAL OF CRAFT ACTIVITIES FOR ELEMENTARY TEACHERS. by Hilmar O. Leyrer. Parker, 1972. 162 pages. illustrations, index. $8.95.

Over two hundred simple, ready-to-use crafts projects that have already proven themselves successful in the classroom. Projects are organized in chapters according to the craft material employed: leather, paper, wire and metal, and so on.

Jane Ziegler has been making puppets for about two years. Just recently she took a course with Bil Baird that helped her over some of the more troublesome points she had been unable to work out on her own.

Many of the people in the course were teachers—speech therapists. They were using the puppets in their classes. Children would have trouble talking so they would give them a puppet and then the children would use the puppet to project through. There are so many things that you can do with puppetry besides put on a puppet show, things like that, it's just amazing.

THE ROLE OF CRAFTS IN EDUCATION. by R. C. Wilson. U.S. Department of Health, Education, and Welfare Office of Education, Bureau of Research. Final Report Project no. V-013 Contract #OE-6-10-075.

Report of symposium on crafts in education. Four-part organization:
I.   Pre-conference thinking

II.   Substance of talks
III.   Abridged recordings of four seminar groups.
IV.   The author's analysis of the basic issues and problems and the proposals and suggestions that were made.

Among the proposals reached by the various seminars and the symposium as a whole were the following:

That the position of elementary and secondary craft teachers be upgraded with a view towards inducing more competent craftsmen into teaching at a lower level.

That traveling classrooms be established to bring instruction and materials to areas lacking in resources.

That class hours be rescheduled to permit students to have the time necessary for the gestation of concepts and the development of sequential experiences.

That art and crafts courses be long enough to enable students to accomplish something of value.

That visual education is a totally different concept from academic education and has for too long been made to fit into an academic mold to the detriment of both.

That a complete visual education program be integrated into the present educational structures as soon as possible.

That there be an end to the compartmentalizing within the art education field itself; a unifiaction of arts, crafts, and design.

CERAMICS

Chart of Stages of Development indicating what to expect from children who have had an opportunity to explore materials freely and independently.

Kindergarten (4–5)	Rolling and pinching of soft materials (clay and plasticine) into dishes, simple animals, and people.
Grade I (6)	
Grade II (7) Grade III (8)	Still much rolling and pinching, but objects become more representational, pots more useful.
Grade IV (9)	Children begin to make successful coil pots and other complicated shapes in clay.
Grade V (10)	Use of coil and slab methods, built-up and carved pieces, many real and imaginary animals and people.
Grade VI (11)	Further development of the above, plus large coil and slab pieces.
Grade VII (12)	Wheel-throwing can be added now. Hand-built ceramics are often very accomplished. Figure and abstract sculpture.
Grade VIII (13)	Children often becoming very skillful. Many can mix simple glazes and carry out technical chores.

Source: WITH A FREE HAND. by Adelaide Sproul.

EMBROIDERY FOR CHILDREN. by Ann-Mari Kornerup. Van Nostrand Reinhold, New York, 1969. 70 pages. photographs (some color). $6.50.

This is a text directed toward parents and teachers. However, very little is suggested on exactly how to set up an embroidery program for children (in terms of materials and techniques), or evaluations on what various age levels are capable of achieving.

INTRODUCING PATCHWORK. by Alice Timmins. Watson-Guptill Publications, New York, 1968. 96 pages. illustrations, photographs (some color). $7.95.

Patchwork projects can be of great value in elementary education. They can teach a great deal about color and design, cooperation in work, and the importance of accuracy and firm construction. The fitting together of the shapes and the making of templates present mathematical problems to be solved by the child.

The author runs through basic procedures for teachers and offers a few good suggestions for projects. There are no really practical classroom suggestions, and a lot of the layout appears to be wasted space—an annoying quality, especially in a book of this price.

USING FABRICS FOR FUN. by Alice White. Drake Publishers, New York, 1972. 135 pages. illustrations, photographs. $7.95.

Alice White is a senior lecturer at St. Katherine's College of Education in England and the author of a number of books. This one, however, seems to be problematical in that it is difficult to determine whether her audience is the child himself or the parent and teacher. The list of references found at the end of each chapter, and various suggestions that involve a bit of mobility and travel, seem to suggest that this is a book for the teacher, but the somewhat sugary tone, the lack of sophistication in approach, and the lack of concrete classroom tips or suggestions, make this seem doubtful, too.

Teachers of young children can probably derive some good tips and ideas from this book which covers fabric collage, three-dimensional patchwork, tie-dyeing, embroidery and other projects kids are likely to enjoy.

INTRODUCING WEAVING. by Phyl Shillinglaw. Watson-Guptill Publications, New York, 1972. 80 pages. illustrations, photographs. $7.95.

This book is directed toward teachers of young children who wish to introduce weaving as a classroom activity. It contains various suggestions as to possible applications of this craft to other subjects; the use of vegetable dyes, for example, can serve as an introduction to the science of color.

The author outlines the stages in which the children can participate in the weaving process, from the preparation of fibers to the creation of fabrics on different looms. Suggestions are also offered for using dyed fleece in other manners,

such as the creation of decorative panels.

Phyl Shillinglaw's methods obviously met with great success in the classroom—the photographs of student work show that clearly—but the teacher who is totally unfamiliar with either spinning or dyeing may find himself in need of a book which addresses itself more fully to the problems an inexperienced adult encounters in learning this craft.

INTRODUCING BEADS. by Mary Seyd. Watson-Guptill Publications, New York, 1973. 96 pages. illustrations, photographs (some color), suppliers list, bibliography. $7.95.

Beads can be made from anything, and the author demonstrates how to make them from wood, bone, and plastic and gives advice for performing the operations with children. She also makes beads from toothpaste tubes, papier-mâché, gesso, and clay, and devotes a special chapter to their fabrication from shells, pebbles, and seeds.

Beadwork is a wonderful introduction to a variety of subjects other than those ordinarily regarded as craft-related. This book is loaded with historical and cultural information and suggestions on opening up the avenue of approach to a wide variety of topics. It offers entertaining reading, too, as well as a spur to the imaginations of parents and teachers.

ASSEMBLAGE: A NEW DIMENSION IN CREATIVE TEACHING IN ACTION. by Victor D'Amico and Arlette Buchman. The Museum of Modern Art, New York, 1972. 240 pages. distributed by the New York Graphic Society, Ltd. photographs. $10.95.

The author-educator's own experiences with children were the basis for the projects presented here. The text is filled with imaginative insights and sensitive responses to the talents of children. The emphasis is on flexibility and growth rather than on set projects.

Our schools cannot limit the teaching of crafts to only a few processes of the artist/craftsman. The constant development of new materials in every industry suggests an ever widening area in crafts. Surely clay, wood, weaving, needlework, and many others of the "old standards" will maintain their importance, but it is necessary not to become so bound by traditional materials that one excludes the many exciting possibilities of experimentation with new materials and processes. It is, however, very easy to become lost in the jungle of gimmicks and gadgets and to conduct a crafts program without depth or meaning. This usually becomes what is commonly called the "product-centered program." When such a program is in effect, the child rarely has the time or sufficient skill with tools or materials to carry out fully his imaginative ideas. Instead he seeks shortcuts in craftsmanship and hides behind a shield of indifference.

Source: MEANING IN CRAFTS, third edition. by Edward L. Mattil. Prentice Hall, Englewood Cliffs, New Jersey, 1971. 237 pages. photographs, bibliography, index. $8.95.

Teaching Crafts in a Psychiatric Setting

—Barbara Linden

Psychiatric patients spend a great deal of time involved in arts and crafts endeavors. This is documented by the large number of activities and occupational therapists employed by most psychiatric hospitals. The notion of mental patients involved in crafts usually conjures up fantasies of people working out aggressive or hostile feelings by pounding clay or carrying out the passive task of weaving one reed over another to form a not very spectacular basket. These stereotypes, although sometimes reflective of a portion of a larger program, are far from an accurate picture of what a crafts program for psychiatric patients entails.

There are certain basic guidelines for preparing to introduce projects to patients. First, the finished product must be attractive and/or useful. No one, no matter how crazy, wants to become involved in constructing an ugly piece of junk. Second, in many cases the pathology limits the patient's attention span. This necessitates projects which can be completed in a one-hour session, allowing for frequent breaks. Another way of getting around this handicap is to prepare projects which can be completed in steps. When using this method, each step becomes satisfying in itself, which fulfills another often encountered problem—the need for immediate gratification. Third, the teacher must be enthusiastic about the projects. Psychiatric patients often lack affect; that is, they don't show any signs of feeling. Eyes are often emotionless and there are rarely any smiles. There may be complaints of boredom or tiredness. If the therapist seems bored or unenthusiastic, it is certain that there will be little group participation.

In addition to following these basic guidelines, the therapist must be aware of some of the psychiatric facts of life. A patient may seem enthusiastic about starting a project and work the project, such as a simple decoupage, near completion. As the finish approaches, the otherwise careful worker spills shellac over the nearly completed project and it is destroyed. Often, this is sabotage. Many patients have an unconscious investment in low self-esteem; this is pathological. It is crucial for the therapist to recognize when sabotage is likely to occur and to avoid it by working closely with the patient. For this person, the successfully executed, often praised and admired finished product can provide a small step toward a better feeling about him or herself.

There are also the more easily recognized hazards in crafts activities. These include using knives, scissors, sharp metal objects with patients who are self-mutilating or suicidal. There is also the danger of a hostile aggressive patient endangering the therapist or other patients. A more subtle problem arises when certain types of glue or spray paint are used. There is always the chance that a patient will disappear only to return in an altered state of consciousness.

In two and a half years of teaching crafts in a psychiatric setting, I have rarely limited the tools or materials used in my groups, and I have never had any serious mishaps. My method is to acknowledge to the group the dangers of using certain materials, set down strict rules about the use of these materials, and explain the very tedious procedure involved in filling out an accident report. This has proved effective.

Another important psychiatric fact of life of which the therapist must be aware is the effect of psychotropic drugs. It is difficult to teach tasks such as embroidery or precision cutting, which requires a steady hand, to a patient who has thorazine tremors.

From this description of the problems and limitations imposed by the psychiatric setting, it may seem that we have come full circle back to clay and baskets. This is far from the truth. Projects which have proved successful are many and varied. One group of fairly low level patients, many diagnosed as schizophrenics, recently completed a book-binding project. This entailed making a small notebook with folios sewn together and glued into a decorative full-bound cover. In the day hospital where people are hospitalized from nine to five, lamps were constructed which could be taken home as an attractive and useful addition to the patient's room or apartment. The lamps were made by stacking wood disks of various sizes which had holes drilled through the center on a metal rod. The fixture which holds the light bulb was screwed on the top of the rod. The lamp could easily be wired by passing an electrical cord through the rod in the center of the wooden disks. The decorative decisions such as whether to stain and shellac or paint the disks were left to the individual patient's taste. Resist dyeing such as tie-dye and batik has also proved successful and rewarding. Such projects became especially popular after a recent out trip to a local department store where the patients noted that simple tie-dye T-shirts were selling for $15.00 apiece. This was also the case with fabric flowers which were formed on chenille pipe cleaners.

After a session with a music therapist a group of patients became involved in constructing simple musical instruments such as bamboo flutes and maracas. These were then employed in the next music session.

There are many other projects which could be listed, but by now the clay and basket myth has probably been dispelled. Almost any craft project can be used or adapted to a psychiatric setting as long as the needs of the individual patient and general pathological problems are carefully considered.

Barbara Linden teaches crafts at Hillside Hospital on Long Island and is currently completing her graduate requirements in psychiatric social work.

INTRODUCING BATIK. by Evelyn Samuel. Watson-Guptill Publications, New York, 1968. 80 pages. illustrations, photographs (some color), suppliers list, bibliography. $7.95.

This book is an excellent introduction to batik for both children and teachers. Evelyn Samuel presents the usual techniques of batik, but in addition gives a multitude of innovative methods for creating designs on fabric. She suggests dipping various objects into the hot wax and using their intrinsic shape to form decorative patterns. Things like cardboard tubes, nuts and bolts, wedges of wood, and so on are employed. Another technique is to stretch the fabric over different textures (wire mesh, bricks, wood grain) and rub it with a candle or wax crayon. This procedure can be extended to make wax rubbings of larger objects, such as church gravestones or reliefs on buildings. She also suggests that young children just drip the wax onto the fabric in a free form.

Some Javanese and African textiles are dyed using a kind of paste instead of wax, and the author proposes an alternative resist using a mixture of flour and water.

The instructions are lucid and all techniques are illustrated by explicit photos and diagrams. Examples of finished batiks, all of them beautiful and all of them made by children, are presented in color and black-and-white photographs.

INTRODUCING JEWELRY MAKING. by John Crawford. Watson-Guptill Publications, New York, 1969. 111 pages. photographs (some color), suppliers list, bibliography, index. $7.95.

The book is not intended as a handbook on jewelry so much as an introduction to this craft as an adjunct to other arts and crafts activities in schools and colleges.

The greater part of the book deals with the making of simple jewelry from copper, a malleable and inexpensive metal. The author sets forth a complete listing of tools and equipment that will be necessary for completion of each project contained in the book and others that should be on hand for original designs. The first project he suggests is a "facsimile" Celtic brooch or pin, which serves as an excellent way for the students to become acquainted with tools and procedures. He also presents step-by-step instructions for making chains and wire rings. New techniques, such as annealing and hammering, are introduced with complete instructions and illustrations as they are needed. More advanced projects utilize etching techniques, soldering, melting, and enameling.

BEGINNING POTTERY. by Warren Farnworth. Van Nostrand Reinhold, New York, 1973. 128 pages. photographs, suppliers list, bibliography. $5.95.

Designed to help teachers help young children to enjoy their first encounters with clay.

Clay can provide opportunities for exploratory play at the child's own level and a great deal of learning is involved with the fun. Little is gained from the imposition of adult standards of form and technique too early. These usually develop naturally if the teacher provides the kind of situation in which clay can be progressively explored. The author, who is senior lecturer in art and craft at Cartrefle College of Education, has a great deal of practical advice for teachers of young children:

1. Encourage manipulation of clay with hands and fingers.
2. Provide opportunities for using clay in various states: cheese-hard clay for cutting and carving; dry clay for scraping, sawing, chipping and breaking; and even liquid clay for pouring and mixing.
3. Encourage the use of tools—not expensive modeling tools and clay cutters, but odds and ends freely available, like old table knives, pastry cutters, brush handles, and so on.
4. Provide things that can be stuck into clay: seeds, buttons, etc.

The author says that it is wrong to view simple hand modeling as a first step to be passed over as quickly as possible so that the real work of pottery making can begin. The teacher's task is to sustain the child's natural inquisitiveness about clay without engendering in it an element of competitive precocity, where the star pupil is the first to produce an Eiffel Tower model bud vase.

The author provides information on where to obtain clay, digging it with students, preparing it, storing, and handling it, and basic modeling and building techniques in step-by-step fashion. His discussion is thorough, yet general enough to be appropriate for the teacher who is, after all, interested in clay from an educational standpoint rather than that of a would-be craftsman. Most of the author's suggested projects require no special equipment, but he does provide brief information on kiln firing and glazing for those who have access to a kiln, or are willing to build a primitive oven.

Art Education
National Art Education Assoc.
1201 16 Street, North West
Washington, D.C. 20036
Monthly (October to June). $6.00 a year.
Practical and scholarly articles on the problems of teaching art at all levels.

Embroidery

ERICA WILSON'S EMBROIDERY BOOK. by Erica Wilson. Charles Scribner's Sons, New York, 1973. 374 pages. illustrations, photographs (some color), index. $15.00.

Erica Wilson defines embroidery as anything that is done with a needle on any material including canvas, and with her characteristic enthusiasm she sets out to make all the varieties of embroidery accessible and exciting to pro and novice alike.

Any book of so large a scope must have certain deficiencies, and this one is no exception. Finishing information is usually sacrificed to the actual stitching techniques, so that in needlepoint, for example, only a few paragraphs are devoted to blocking the finished work, a process that frequently gives beginners some trouble. However, instructions and diagrams are excellent, clear, and easy to follow, and all the basic stitches are included.

In addition to instructions for crewel and needlepoint, Ms. Wilson's book contains chapters on silk and gold thread embroidery (embroidery on rich fabrics which require special techniques); black work (a form of Spanish embroidery which uses gold thread and black silk on cream linen); whitework (white stitching on a white ground which requires a contrast of texture to achieve its full effect—this is the baccalaureat for embroiderers); stump work (raised work popular in seventeenth- and eighteenth-century England); and a miscellany of monograms; appliqué; and Shisha work (embroidery done in conjunction with mica or mirrors).

Aside from its value as a technical manual, this book makes plain good reading. The photographs are beautiful to look at, and the wealth of historical information is interwoven with fascinating accounts and gossipy anecdotes. One of the author's interesting asides is that the word canvas comes from the Latin *cannabis*, hempen cloth. Erica conjectures (perhaps half whimsically?) that since hemp was used to make rope, sailcloth, and tents throughout history, the tent stitch, the basic stitch in needlepoint, might have received its name as a result of this association.

EMBROIDERY. The Golden Hands Series. Random House, New York, 1973. 128 pages. illustrations, photographs. $4.95.

Eighty completed projects are presented in large, full-color photos; everything from bedspreads to monograms, rugs and pillow covers to wall hangings. At the rear of the book each project is again presented, this time in cookbook fashion listing materials and tools, and a line layout pattern is given. Instructions are clear and concise. A glossary of stitches and general techniques (including finishing methods, tracing and marking, and pillow making) completes the book. Unfortunately, not too much emphasis is placed on original designs or freedom of technique. The beginner who wants handsome, finished products the first few times out will find this a good starting point.

THE CRAFT OF EMBROIDERY. by Alison Liley. Drake Publishers, New York, 1972. 224 pages. $5.95.

A very technical book intended for serious students of embroidery who wish to produce objects of exceptionally high quality. The methods and stitches are illustrated by good, clear line drawings.

The author gives information on exactly what the embroiderer needs to know for guild tests and school tests about embroidery methods and design.

THE COMPLETE GUIDE TO EMBROIDERY STITCHES AND CREWEL. by Jo Bucher. Creative Home Library Books, Des Moines, Iowa, 1971. 353 pages. illustrations, photographs, suppliers list. $8.95.

This book offers 312 stitches explained with lucid and detailed instructions for both right- and left-handed sewing, plus over 1,000 suggestions for their uses on embroidered articles.

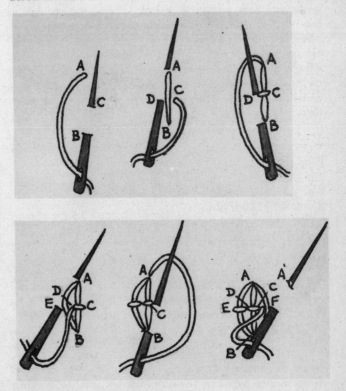

The Renaissance stitch

The author supplies a fine introductory chapter on paraphernalia (a word that originally referred specifically to the materials and tools of embroidery), and a list of stitch uses, cross-referenced stitch names, a stitch index, and a glossary of embroidery terms. Design sources per se are not treated.

PAINTING WITH A NEEDLE. by Nettie Yanoff Brudner. Doubleday and Company, Garden City, New York, 1972. 192 pages. illustrations, photographs, suppliers list, bibliography. $8.95.

An adequate but not outstanding coverage of the basics. Suitable for a beginner.

MACHINE EMBROIDERY: TECHNIQUE AND DESIGN. by Jennifer Gray. Van Nostrand Reinhold, New York, 1973. 232 pages. illustrations, photographs (some color). $12.00.

Advances in sewing machine technology have opened up a whole new range of possibilities to the embroiderer. The author explains the virtues of the embroidery machine and the regular sewing machine with embroidery attachements apart from the time-saving advantages they afford. She provides general instructions on how to use machines to achieve a variety of textures and effects (such as bunching, smocking, and others) in a simply stated text and clear photographs. The main emphasis, however, is on design. This is unfortunate, since her models are somewhat limited in scope and anything that falls outside the styles derivative of contemporary British art is completely neglected. This results in a lack of real information on how and when a sewing machine can be used to take the place of hand embroidery. Traditional stitches and styles are ignored in favor of a kind of frenetic machine design. This is a shame because there is a dearth of good books on machine embroidery for the traditional needleworker, and this one does virtually nothing to remedy the situation.

Embroiderer's Journal
220 Fifth Avenue
New York, N.Y. 10001
Bimonthly. $7.00 a year.
  New ideas in patterns and other needlecraft related articles.

THE STITCHES OF CREATIVE EMBROIDERY. by Jacqueline Enthoven. Van Nostrand Reinhold, New York, 1964. 212 pages. illustrations, photographs. $7.95.

A very complete glossary of embroidery stitches, giving clear and complete step-by-step line drawings and illustrating the finished stitches in photographs. Reproductions of old master paintings show the stitches used in clothing during the Middle Ages and Renaissance.

ECCLESIASTICAL EMBROIDERY. by Beryl Dean. Charles T. Branford Company, Newton Centre, Massachusetts, 1958. 258 pages. illustrations, photographs. $11.00.

This is an unusual and interesting book that is quite comprehensive in its own terms. It contains a complete explanation of traditional materials and tools and how to use them to reproduce old work or create new work. Motifs and symbols receive a thorough historical treatment, and a list of saints and their emblems is generously provided.

A proposal to all Mothers of Great Britain:

1. That no young Virgin whatsoever be allowed to receive the addresses of her first lover but in a suit of her own embroidery—
2. That before every fresh humble servant she be obliged to appear with a new stomacher at the least—
3. That no one be actually married until she hath the child-bed pillows, etc., ready stitched as likewise the mantle for the boy quite finished.

These laws if I mistake not, would effectually restore the decayed art of needlework and make the virgins of Great Britain exceedingly nimble fingered in their business.

—SPECTATOR, 1714

SAMPLERS AND STITCHES. by Mrs. Archibald (Grace) Christie. Hearthside Press, Great Neck, New York, 1972. 155 pages. illustrations, photographs (some color). $6.95.

A facsimile of a 1920 English encyclopedia, this contains instructions for two hundred stitches and their applications.

STITCHERY: FREE EXPRESSION. by Ann Woelders. Van Nostrand Reinhold, New York, 1973. illustrations, photographs. $7.95.

The author treats fabrics, stitches, and design together as an integrated whole in order to show the importance of the interaction of all these elements in creative stitchery. A variety of interesting and imaginative projects provides the context in which new stitches and techniques are introduced. The instructions are complete, step-by-step, and accompanied by photographs as well as line drawings.

CROSS STITCH PATTERNS. Thelma M. Nye, editor. Van Nostrand Reinhold, New York, 1973. 136 pages. illustrated. $4.95.

This book contains over a hundred charts of motifs and patterns drawn from the Balkans, ancient China, Denmark, and Peru, all of which can be worked in the normal cross-stitch and interpreted in countless ways and on materials of varying weaves with threads of varying thicknesses to produce different effects. The diagrams for each pattern are coded in terms of type of stitch and suggested color and are exceptionally clear. A small introductory section provides information on different types of cross-stitches and cross-stitching methods.

HANDBOOK OF STITCHES. by Grete Petersen and Elsie Svennas. Van Nostrand Reinhold, New York, 1970. 80 pages. illustrations, photographs. $3.95.

A sourcebook of embroidery stitches which covers archaic as well as better-known techniques. The material is presented in clear line drawings and black-and-white photographs which show the stitch repeated enough times to suggest the intrinsic pattern. The major drawback is the lack of verbal instruction and the absence of step-by-step format in the diagrams. This might make the going rough for novices, but experienced needlecrafters wishing to expand their stitch vocabulary will find this a useful book.

STITCHERY: ART AND CRAFT. by Nik Krevitsky. Van Nostrand Reinhold, New York, 1973. photographs, bibliography. $3.95.

This is primarily a visual compendium of inspiration themes drawn from Indian work, children's work, and natural forms. The emphasis is predominantly on children's work because the author feels that the child is fresh, spontaneous, unfettered by clichés and stereotypes, and therefore approaches this medium directly and with a frankness of expression. The adult, on the other hand, jaded by the bombardment of visual images encountered daily, feels inadequate as designer-craftsman and frequently resorts to the convenient.

BORDERS FOR EMBROIDERY. by Grete Petersen. Van Nostrand Reinhold, New York, 1973. 63 pages. illustrations. $3.95.

A sourcebook of decorative borders derived from a multitude of cultures, including Coptic, Scandinavian, Greek, French, and Japanese designs. Many of these borders can be useful in crafts other than embroidery. A good introductory section illustrated with very clear line drawings provides information on stitches, seams, fringes, tassels, and corner techniques for use on borders.

The bulk of this book consists of a glossary which lists the appropriate stitch and color suggestion for each design. The designs themselves are illustrated by line drawings, and the motif is repeated enough times to give a "feel" for each one. In all, 233 borders are covered, ranging from pictorial to three-dimensional illusionistic and geometric forms.

EMBROIDERY DESIGNS 1780–1820. Mildred J. Davis, ed. Crown Publishers, New York, 1971. 94 pages. illustrations. $7.50.

In this book, a collection of patterns derived from traditional motifs is presented in simplified line drawings. No instruction is given, and the only text supplied is a rather cursory historical introduction for a book concerned with historical pieces. Most of the designs are floral patterns used in borders, repeating fields, and the like. The lack of photographs to present the original, embroidered patterns is a grave deficiency.

EMBROIDERY MASTERWORKS: CLASSIC PATTERNS AND TECHNIQUES FOR CONTEMPORARY APPLICATION. by Virginia Churchill Bath. Henry Regnery Company, Chicago, Illinois, 1972. 225 pages. illustrations, photographs, bibliography. $15.00.

As the subtitle suggests, this book contains classic designs and techniques of European embroidery from the fourteenth to the twentieth centuries, drawn from the textile collection of the Art Institute of Chicago. Each piece is shown in a black-and-white photograph and then schematized in a diagram for easy design transfer, and each is accompanied by technical and historical data as well as advice for contemporary adaptation of the stitches. The concept behind this book is commendable, and it provides a means by which beautiful, classic embroidery can become a viable project for the moderately skilled needleworker. However, the scope of the book is by definition limited; it would have been nice if it could have covered designs from a broader range of sources.

LETTERING FOR EMBROIDERY. by Pat Russell. Van Nostrand Reinhold, New York, 1971. 160 pages. illustrations, photographs. $10.95.

The techniques used in embroidered lettering fall into two main categories: appliqué and stitchery. In appliqué lettering, the materials are fabrics of all types and the tools are a pair of scissors and a sewing machine or needle and thread. Stitched letters can be completely filled in with thread or have their shape and character determined by the stitch employed.

The author provides a great deal of information and examples of letter forms and patterns of alphabets which the knowledgeable embroiderer can use in whatever way he chooses. The inspirational quality of this book is heightened by beautiful photographs of historical embroidered letters.

ANCIENT PERUVIAN TEXTILE DESIGN IN MODERN STITCHERY. by Ellen Jensen. Van Nostrand Reinhold, New York, 1972. 64 pages. illustrations, photographs (some color), bibliography. $7.95.

The oldest Peruvian textile patterns yet discovered date from around 2000 B.C. This book supplies hundreds of authentic, preconquest Peruvian patterns ranging from abstract borders and fields to elegantly stylized animals. They are presented in color as finished works and as schematic patterns on black-and-white grids for easy transfer. Five pages of sewing hints contain suggestions for achieving the authentic look of the ancient Peruvian craftsmen.

Embroiderer's Guild of America
120 East 56 Street, Room 228
New York, N.Y. 10022

A group of men and women interested in the art of needlework. The purpose is setting and maintaining high standards of design, color, and workmanship in all kinds of embroidery and canvas work. The guild sponsors lectures, seminars, exhibitions, and field trips; offers examinations for teaching certificates, serves as an information source for individual needleworkers in the United States; offers lessons in all types of needlework from October to May; sells guild booklets, transfer designs, and charts; rents portfolios containing photos and specimens of needlework; maintains a comprehensive reference library; publishes *Bulletin*, quarterly.

PULLED THREAD EMBROIDERY. by Moyra McNeill. Taplinger Publishing Company, New York, 1972. 207 pages. illustrations, photographs, bibliography. $8.50.

Pulled work and drawn fabric are synonymous, but as drawn fabric is so often confused with drawn thread work, the author has chosen to use the term *pulled thread*. The effects of these two methods are vaguely similar, but the methods of execution are quite unalike. In pulled thread work the threads of the ground material are compressed by pulling the stitches tightly to form a pattern of holes. In drawn thread work threads are actually removed from the ground material, usually before any stitching is begun.

Pulled thread technique

Many people are deterred from trying pulled thread embroidery, thinking that it presents more difficulties than it actually does. There are one or two extremely complicated stitches in this technique, but the author sets out to prove how much can be achieved with a basically simple technique; although those who wish to pursue the craft to more complex procedures will find more than enough here to challenge them. There are a multitude of stitches and alternate "pullings" presented. Each is described and illustrated with a schematic line drawing of the stitches before pulling and a photo of the effect created by putting tension on the threads. The design section is quite good, the best part being suggestions for how the previously described stitches can be used together, and the worst part being the "contemporary" design suggestions.

This is a good book on an interesting craft and is suitable for a beginner. However, it would probably be a good idea to come to it with needlepoint or related experience to avoid strangulation with one's own threads.

AMERICAN CREWEL WORK. by Mary Taylor Landon and Susan Burrows Swan. Macmillan, New York, 1970. 192 pages. illustrations, photographs, suppliers list. $9.95.

The authors introduce their subject with a gallery of photographic examples of historical American crewelwork. The work is quite beautiful but the photographs unfortunately are only in black and white. The book then proceeds to a series of instructions and step-by-step diagrams for twenty-one crewel and four canvas embroidery stitches. Each stitch its accompanied by suggestions for how and where it may be used. These are followed by a series of projects, eyeglass cases, tablecloths, pillows and so on, which are decorated with crewel. A visual glossary of motifs suitable for working in crewel completes this volume.

The Bayeux Tapestry

Some think the Bayeux tapestry was made by Matilde, wife of William the Conqueror, after the Battle of Hastings. Others believe that it was executed by three Bayeux men in London who sent it as an offering to their native cathedral. Whatever the exact origin, the Bayeux Tapestry is one of the earliest specimens of needlework extant in a good state of preservation.

It is 214 inches long, 20 inches wide, and contains 530 figures who illustrate the variety of dress and custom of the time. The tapestry is divided into compartments, each highlighting an event leading up to the Battle of Hastings and, finally, the death of Harold.

Strictly speaking, the Bayeux Tapestry is not really a tapestry at all, but rather embroidery with crewel. The material is left exposed in many parts and the design is indicated with chain stitch.

PLEASURES OF CREWEL. by Jo Springer. Betty Crocker Home Library, 1972. 166 pages. illustrations. $8.95.

An illustrated glossary in this book gives step-by-step instructions for seventy-two stitches. Each stitch is coded (black dots in this case) to indicate difficulty of execution and is described in terms of function and possible problems that may be encountered. This is followed by a project section divided into beginner, intermediate, and

advanced categories. The projects in all three sections are interesting and some are quite beautiful. Each project has a complete list of materials, tools, stitches, colors, dimensions, hints, finishing information, and a line diagram of the design for transference. There is also an excellent and simply explained section on finishing.

A HANDBOOK OF AMERICAN CREWEL EMBROIDERY. by Muriel L. Baker. Charles E. Tuttle Co., Rutland, Vt. 1966. 67 pages. illustrations, bibliography. $4.75.

A fascinating subject which unfortunately receives a somewhat superficial treatment. The author presents a glossary of traditional American stitches, but the accompanying illustrations and textual instructions are unclear. The major failing of this book lies in the author's adaptations of motifs from old crewel pieces. Theoretically, this is a fine idea and the original works chosen are very beautiful. However, the author illustrates the motifs in a sketchy and informal manner that makes it virtually impossible for the reader to achieve authentic-looking patterns. Moreover, the descriptive text accompanying the motifs is too general in the specifications of color.

CREWEL EMBROIDERY MADE EASY. by Barbara C. McClennen. Doubleday and Company, Garden City, New York, 1972. 180 pages. illustrations, photographs, suppliers list. $5.95.

Although this book is intended for beginners, the format and presentation of the crewelwork methods, techniques, and stitches are confusing and most of the time unclear. The stitch glossary, while thorough in terms of quantity, is unsatisfactory, because the photographs are unclear and the descriptive text is almost always ambiguous. The usual sections on design, materials, finishing, and so on are not well organized or coordinated. This is unfortunate, because the author's tone is friendly and she obviously seeks to be helpful and informative. Somehow, it's not enough to overcome the shortcomings of organization.

Crewel pillow, Ruth Ross

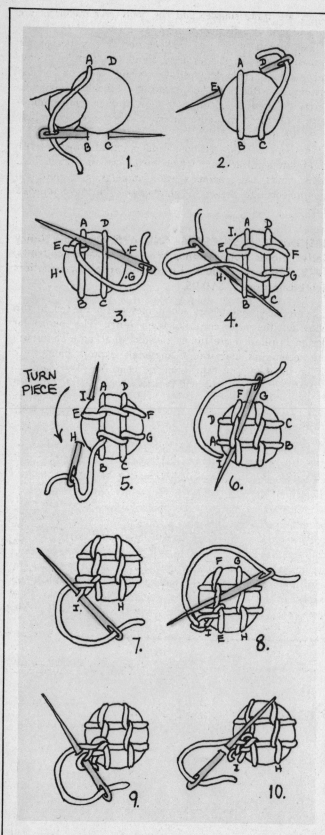

Shi Sha glass embroidery stitch

THE CRAFT OF CREWEL EMBROIDERY. by Erica Wilson. Charles Scribner's Sons, New York, 1971. 96 pages. illustrations, photographs. paperback edition $2.95.

This is an abridged version of Erica Wilson's fine book *Crewel Embroidery* (Scribner's, 1962). Either of these books is probably the best bet for crewel beginners. Every facet of the craft is covered clearly, simply, and without pretensions. Twenty-six basic stitches are covered in the stitch glossary, and applying patterns, notes on design, and finishing and blocking procedures are all fully explained in a terse yet informative style. The major difference between the condensed version and the original is the price and the former's lack of historical examples and color plates.

EMBROIDERY AND FABRIC COLLAGE. by Eirian Short. Charles Scribner's Sons, 1973. 130 pages. illustrations, photographs, suppliers list, bibliography. $12.50.

Fabric collage is understood to mean the application of pieces of fabric to a background, whether by gluing or sewing, and with little or no surface embroidery. Embroidery is used in its widest sense as the embellishment of a surface of fabric with some form of decoration carried out with a needle and thread. This takes into its realm patchwork and appliqué. In the author's view, No one method is considered superior to another; hand embroidery is not necessarily superior to machine embroidery or gold work better than quilting. The only criteria is that the method chosen is suitable and produces satisfactory results.

A thorough chapter on theoretical aspects of design clarifies the inspirational examples of functional and artistic embroidery presented in black-and-white photographs.

Indian Shi Sha embroidery

SMOCKING IN EMBROIDERY. by Margaret Thom. Drake Publishers, New York, 1972. 96 pages. illustrations, photographs, suppliers list. $5.95.

Many traditional embroidery methods have been developed and adapted to meet contemporary needs, but smocking is seldom incorporated in modern embroidered hangings and panels. Smocking's usefulness and popularity in clothing design seems to have hidden its possibilities as an exciting addition to free embroidery. The adaptability and textural qualities of smocking make it potentially a valuable asset to the embroiderer, and alteration in the scale and distortion of the basic geometrical structure of smocking present opportunities for the interpretation of ideas in fabric and stitchery too long unexplored.

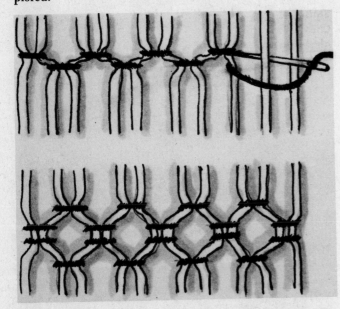

Basically, smocking is a way of controlling fullness. A number of different effects can be achieved from parallel rows of gathering stitches. When drawn tightly, the gathers form regimented lines of tubes; pulled slightly, they produce undulating curves; alternating rows, they form a honeycomb texture of cells and ridges. This last technique is the one most fully explored by Margaret Thom in her book, although all the traditional methods (including Canadian, English, and Italian varieties) are discussed and illustrated. Black-and-white photographs present examples of applied smocking techniques and feature articles such as bags, box covers, and umbrella cases. No instructions are given for these items, and it appears that the author wishes the smocker to derive specific methods from the discussion of technique.

APPLIQUE. by Evangeline Shears and Diantha Fielding. Watson-Guptill Publications, New York, 1972. 142 pages. illustrations, photographs, suppliers list, bibliography. $10.95.

Appliqué is the attachment of fabric, usually by sewing, to the surface of another piece of fabric. The basic tech-

niques are quite simple, and the tools and materials are common and usually inexpensive.

The authors point out that in choosing a design for appliqué work the shapes used should be simple, strong, and graphic. They demonstrate sewing and construction techniques with clear line drawings. Machine sewing is constantly used as an alternate technique to hand embroidery, but the basic embroidery stitches are thoroughly reviewed.

The book offers inspirational and practical projects (with step-by-step instructions) which encompass small household items, quilts, flags, banners, wall hangings, and more. All the projects are shown in photographs in the completed state.

DESIGNING IN STITCHING AND APPLIQUE. by Nancy Belfer. Davis Publications, Worcester, Massachusetts, 1972. 128 pages. illustrations, photographs, suppliers list, bibliography. $10.95.

Some basic embroidery techniques are presented in this book, but the major emphasis is on design. The sources for design inspiration are drawn mostly from "natural forms": the techniques and use of materials express biomorphic designs in a kind of expressionistic vein. Needleworkers interested in a "raw" look will find this book useful. The best feature of this book is an additional section at the end on soft objects and toys, which is imaginative and resourceful and which provides a nice supplement to the design suggestions that are the major theme of the book.

National Standards Council of American Embroiderers
5 Geyerwood Lane
St. Louis, Mo. 63131
A group that works to maintain and promote high standards in the art and craft of stitchery, embroidery, and needlework; to develop the practice of teaching the art; to educate persons interested in giving instruction; to provide a forum for an exchange of ideas, design, technique, and workmanship. It establishes seminars and correspondence courses, and conducts showings and exhibitions of quality work by professionals and amateurs. It also maintains a library, and publishes *Flying Needle*, triannually.

Embroidery Supplies

Arachne Webworks
2390 North West Thurman
Portland, Ore. 92710
brochure.
needlework supplies.

Berry's of Maine
20-22 Main Street
Yarmouth, Me. 04096
brochure $.10.
needlework frames, embroidery hoops.

Fredrick J. Fawcett, Inc.
129 South Street
Boston, Mass. 02111
catalog $1.00.
needlework supplies.

Harmony Acres Studio
Bag. 1550, St. Norbert
Manitoba ROG 2HO, Canada
brochure; samples, $.50.
needlework supplies.

Kay and EE Corporation of America
200 Fifth Avenue, Room 325
New York, N.Y.
brochure.
needlework and embroidery frames.

Joan Moshimer
North Street
Kennebunkport, Me. 04046
catalog.
needlework frames.

Naturalcraft
2199 Bancroft Way
Berkeley, Cal. 94704
Catalog $.50.
embroidery hoops.

Sears Roebuck and Company
4640 Roosevelt Avenue
Philadelphia, Pa. 19132
catalog.
embroidery and needlework frames.

Sun Spots
5906 Avenue N
Brooklyn, N.Y. 11234
catalog.
embroidery hoops.

Textile Crafts
856 Genesee Avenue
P.O. Box 3216
Los Angeles, Cal. 90028
catalog.
needlework supplies.

The Thread Shed
307 Freeport Road, Aspinwall
Pittsburgh, Pa. 15215
catalog.
needlework supplies.

The Weaver's Shop
King Street, Wilton, Salisbury
Wiltshire, England
catalog, samples $1.00.
needlework supplies.

Wool In Works
126 Orange Avenue
Suffern, N.Y. 10901
needlepoint catalog $1.00; yarn and fiber
    catalog $1.00.
needlework supplies.

Wool 'n Canvas Ltd.
306 82nd Street
Brooklyn, N.Y. 11209
brochure.
needlework supplies.

Enameling

SIMPLE ENAMELLING. by Geoffrey Franklin. Watson-Guptill Publications, New York, 1972. 103 pages. illustrations, photographs, suppliers list, bibliography. $7.95.

In simple enameling, the enamel is laid on a clean metal surface and is melted. It fuses with the metal at a temperature of approximately 1382 degrees F. Firing is usually done in a kiln, but may also be done over a torch flame, a technique useful for small jewelry pieces.

There are two types of enamel, opaque and transparent. Both are commercially available, already ground in the form of fine powder. This is fortunate, since grinding and preparing enamels are long and tedious processes. Opaque enamels do not allow any light to penetrate through them. They normally fire to a glossy finish; however, this can be varied by careful underfiring. Opaque enamels can be mixed to yield other colors. Transparent enamels allow light to pass through them and reflect the metal surface beneath them. The basis of all transparent enamels is flux, a clear, colorless enamel to which metal oxides have been added in order to obtain a colored but transparent appearance. They fire to a glossy finish, and it is not possible to underfire them as it is the opaque variety. They also do not mix well.

The basic enameling procedures commonly employed by beginners are presented and illustrated with simple and clear instructions. More sophisticated techniques are mentioned in passing and are not discussed in great detail. No projects are given, but a great number of photographs provides the craftsman with a feeling for the appearance of enameled objects.

METAL ENAMELING. by Polly Rothenberg. Crown Publishers, New York, 1969. 211 pages. photographs, suppliers list, bibliography, index. $7.95.

A thorough, instructional guide to the craft of enameling, providing techniques not generally found in other books. For example, the section on footed bowls has detailed instructions and step-by-step illustrations for soldering in the kiln and for enameling soldered pieces. The specific directions on the use of art glass in enameling should help the craftsmen who have found this process frustrating.

Enameling methods and projects progress from the simple to the most complicated, all presented with step-by-step instructions and illustrations. The projects are intended as guides for processes; they are not suggested as models for copying. Design inspiration is provided by photographs of the work of skilled craftsmen utilizing enameling techniques.

ENAMELING, PRINCIPLES AND PRACTICE. by Kenneth F. Bates. World Publishing Company, New York, 1972. 208 pages. illustrations, photographs, suppliers list, bibliography, index. $7.95.

Originally published in 1951, this book explains in a step-by-step format the various methods used to make enamels. The text is accompanied by well-drawn diagrams and clear photos. The author proceeds from the making of a simple tray to more complex designs in limoges, cloisonné, champlevé, and other techniques. The inclusion of numerous reproductions of historical works throughout the text provides the reader with a feeling for the fascinating tradition of this craft.

TEST FOR TRANSPARENT ENAMELS

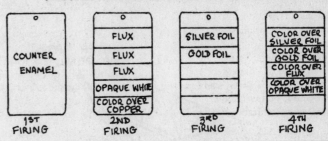

TEST FOR OPAQUE ENAMELS

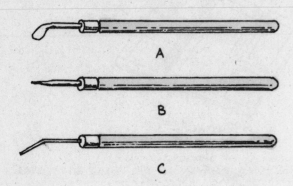

A   The spatula *is used for picking up moist enamel.*

B   The pointer *is for placing enamel and scratching lines.*

C   The spreader *is used for leveling the enamel.*

Immediately after removing from kiln, place bowl or plate on flat surface and put an old-fashioned flatiron on top of it. This will correct any warping of the enameled piece.

Traditional Enameling Techniques

Basse-Taille—A type of enameling making use of transparent enamels fired over a carved or chased metal surface.

Champlevé—A technique that uses transparent or opaque enamels fired into etched or carved areas, leaving the metal partly exposed.

Cloisonné—A type of enameling in which each color is separated by thin metal ribbons or wires.

En Résille—The method that uses finely ground colors fired into small depressions in crystal.

Grisaille—A type of enameling made by firing various thicknesses of white opaque enamel on a black opaque ground.

Limoges—A technique of enameling, originated in Limoges, France, that makes use of juxtaposed colors to cover the entire surface of the metal.

Plique-à-Jour—The method that uses transparent enamels suspended in small openings of metal, giving the appearance of stained glass windows.

Sgraffito—A technique in enameling whereby a linear motif is produced by scratching through one enamel to reveal a different colored ground underneath.

Steps in Cloisonné Enameling

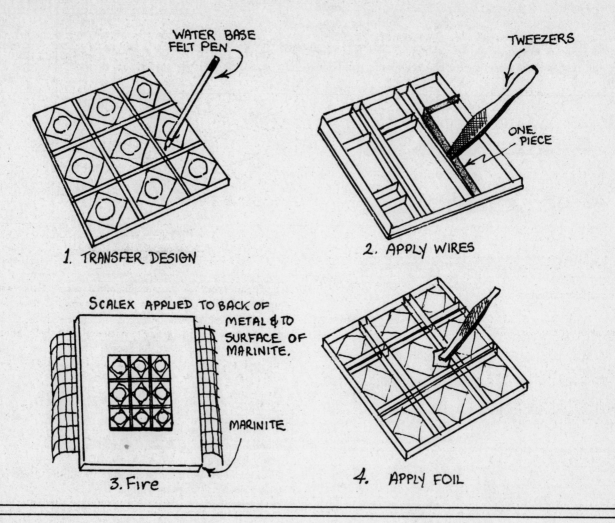

WATER BASE FELT PEN

1. TRANSFER DESIGN

TWEEZERS

ONE PIECE

2. APPLY WIRES

SCALEX APPLIED TO BACK OF METAL & TO SURFACE OF MARINITE.

MARINITE

3. Fire

4. APPLY FOIL

STEP BY STEP ENAMELING. by William Harper. Golden Press, 1973. 80 pages. illustrations, photographs, suppliers list, bibliography $2.95.

Basically, enameling is the process of applying a specially prepared glass to a metal and then fusing the two together through the use of heat.

This book is a step-by-step guide to working with the procedures and techniques of enameling. The tools required are simple, accessible, and reasonably priced. More sophisticated and expensive tools can eventually be acquired, but they aren't always necessary. The information presented is primarily concerned with the processes themselves, a most practical way for a beginner to learn. The processes are described and fully illustrated by photos and diagrams. They progress from the treatment of metal, including shaping, sawing, etching and the various methods of texturing, to complete information on enamels and how to apply them for different purposes through to the firing process.

Techniques include the traditional ones: limoges, cloisonné, basse-taille, champlevé, grisaille, plique-a-jour. Within the presentation of these techniques are projects that can be constructed as they are or employed as starting points for other work.

EXPERIMENTAL TECHNIQUES IN ENAMELING. by Fred Ball. Van Nostrand Reinhold, New York, 1972. 144 pages. illustrations, photographs, suppliers list, bibliography, index. $9.95.

A multitude of innovative and unusual techniques as well as a brief coverage of the basics.

The author introduces methods of pouring and squirting liquid enamel or an adhesive material that can be sifted with powdered enamel, "printing" with hands or crushed paper, spraying or sifting powder through templates, the use of metal inlays, iron filings mixed with enamel and then "arranged" with a magnet, overlays, textures produced by

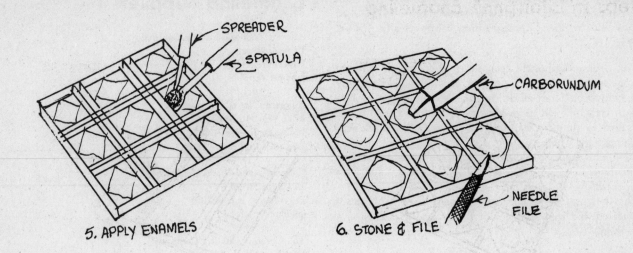

5. APPLY ENAMELS

6. STONE & FILE

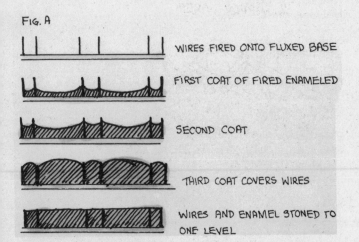

FIG. A

WIRES FIRED ONTO FLUXED BASE

FIRST COAT OF FIRED ENAMELED

SECOND COAT

THIRD COAT COVERS WIRES

WIRES AND ENAMEL STONED TO ONE LEVEL

1. Clean front of counterenameled base. Dust with flux and fire. When cool either position wires on base or transfer design as shown here.

2. Cloisonné wires being positioned. Apply binder along wire edges to fix to fluxed base.

3. Fire on marinite until flux is slightly molten. While hot, check that wire is securely fixed to base.

4. If foils are to be used, inlay at this point.

5. Fill cells with enamels—this should take three or four coats to accomplish. (Fig. A.)

6. Stone enamel and wire to the same level; refire to restore gloss. File and polish edges.

Source. STEP-BY-STEP ENAMELING. by William Harper.

water flooding, marbleizing, shaking, and swirling, and a variety of glazes that produce imaginative and often beautiful effects. All of these effects are depicted in a number of color photos which show the intricate color relationships in the objects.

An outstanding book for people who have some enameling experience and the bravery and imagination to try something new.

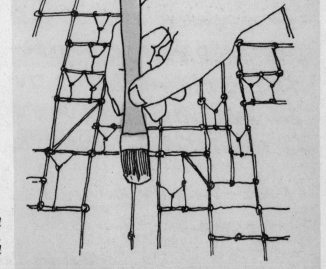

After enamel is applied to knotted string configuration and has dried, it is placed on prepared copper panels and fired. String burns out and enamel melts onto surface in knotted configuration.

THE CRAFT OF ENAMELLING. by Kenneth Neville. Transatlantic Arts, Levittown, New York, 1973. 156 pages. illustrations, photographs, bibliography, index. $6.95.

This book describes the techniques of enameling through the presentation of simple projects. It is intended primarily as a guidebook for teachers, but the text need not be limited to this function. The various traditional methods are described in simple, clear instructions and illustrated with line drawings. There is a lot of good technical information on materials and procedures as well as some interesting applications for enameled work to objects constructed with other media.

The designs for the projects themselves are a bit unsophisticated, but the discussion of the processes used is on a high level.

Sgraffito ashtray in green & tangerine enamel.

Fire ground coat of black enamel.

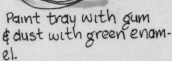

Paint tray with gum & dust with green enamel.

Lightly dust the edges with tangerine enamel.

WHEN DRY SCRATCH DESIGN THROUGH GREEN ENAMEL. GENTLY BLOW LOOSE PARTICLES & fire.

Sgraffito technique used to make ashtray

Enameling Suppliers

Allcraft Tool and Supply Company
Park Avenue
Hicksville, N.Y.
general supplies.

American Art Clay Company
4717 West 16 Street
Indianapolis, Ind. 46222
general supplies.

Carpenter and Wood Company, Inc.
15 Cedar Street
Providence, R.I. 02903
jeweler's enamels.

The Ceramic Coating Company
P.O. Box 370
Newport, Ky. 43072
leadless enamels.

Norbert L. Cochran
2540 Fletcher Avenue
Fernandina Beach, Fla. 32034
distributor for Schauer and Company of
    Vienna, Austria.
special enamels and supplies.

Kraft Corner
5842 Mayfield Road, Maryland Annex
Cleveland, O. 44124
general supplies.

Seaire
17909 South Hobart Street
Gardena, Cal. 90248
wire-brushed copper panels and shapes,
    special tools, racks, enamels, and other
    supplies.

Thomas C. Thompson
1539 Deerfield Road
Highland Park, Ill. 60035
general supplies.

Ludd Voella
11482 Pipeline
Pomona, Cal. 91766
kilns.

Western Ceramics Supply Company
1601 Howard Street
San Francisco, Cal. 94103
general supplies.

Fabric Decoration

THE HAND DECORATION OF FABRICS. by Francis J. Kafka. Dover Publications, New York, 1973. 198 pages. photographs, bibliography, index. paperback edition $2.75.

Textile decoration, according to Francis J. Kafka, is any method of applying color or design to a woven fabric. These methods stand apart from the technique of weaving in designs and patterns. The primary areas of textile decoration are:

Stenciling—The technique of applying dyes or pigments through a cut-out design or pattern.

Batik—A resist dyeing process in which the design is applied to the fabric with a material which will resist the action of the dye. After dyeing, the resist material is removed.

Block Printing—The method by which carved blocks of wood (or other materials) are used to carry paint or dye to the fabric and imprint them with design.

Tie-Dye—A resist method of dyeing in which the portions of fabric not to be colored are tied, sewn, or knotted before dyeing.

Freehand Painting—The freehand application of paint with a brush.

Silk Screen—Another stencil-type method, but one which allows greater control of color saturation and has a larger surface area potential.

Novely Decoration—The application of flock, raised decorations, etc.

The author presents the most basic techniques in all the above areas, but does not go into them in great depth. The instructions are good, and the retouched photos used to illustrate them can be read easily. However, the treatment of all methods is so simplistic a beginner would probably get the impression that not much can be done by the home craftsman to produce exciting decorated fabrics.

EXPLORING FABRIC PRINTING. by Stuart and Patricia Robinson. Charles T. Branford Company, Newton Centre, Massachusetts, 1972. 160 pages. illustrations, photographs (some color), suppliers list, bibliography, index. $8.75.

This is an excellent general source book on tie dye, batik, screen and block printing methods. The authors also include a very good section on dyeing techniques and recipes.

Each section contains enough information to enable a beginner to start working without much confusion. Instructions are illustrated with line drawings which provide a clear idea of the processes, and photographs of finished work provide the reader with an idea of what the result is of each process. Alternate tools and techniques are suggested and each section is followed up with an extensive bibliography.

This book is excellent for beginners who wish to try their hand at several fabric printing methods. However, people with experience in all of these techniques will probably find the information presented here of too elementary a nature.

BLOCK PRINTING ON TEXTILES. by Janet Erickson. Watson-Guptill Publications, New York, 1974. 168 pages. illustrations, photographs, index. $10.95.

This book provides a wealth of information, primarily on linoleum block printing. Techniques of making the block and printing are thoroughly discussed and illustrated with black-and-white photographs. There is a fine section on block printing for children and a chart of fabric characteristics.

Fortunately, lots of historical examples are included for inspiration, because most of the contemporary design pieces fall short in this area.

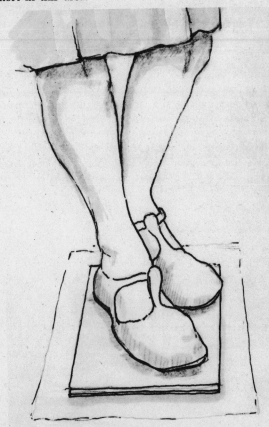

The simplest and most direct way to apply pressure in block printing

PRINTING ON FABRIC. BASIC TECHNIQUES. by Ellen Bystrom. Van Nostrand Reinhold, New York, 1971. 96 pages. illustrations, photographs, index. $4.95.

Negative shapes like these produce repeatable patterns that are easy to register. The straight lines and clear delineations make it simple to cut the shapes from linoleum.

Basic techniques of vegetable, linoleum, and cork block printing are presented through a series of projects. The instructions are given in a clear but general manner suitable for adaptation to the reader's own designs. Black-and-white photographs illustrate the steps in each procedure.

The major emphasis is on linoleum block techniques and, as such, this is a good book for beginners in that area.

The potato is cut away close to the pattern in order to place the print more accurately.

PRINTING FABRIC BY HAND: BEGINNING TECHNIQUES. by Gisela Hein. Van Nostrand Reinhold, New York, 1972. 117 pages. photographs. $4.95.

ROLLER MADE WITH WOOD & STRING

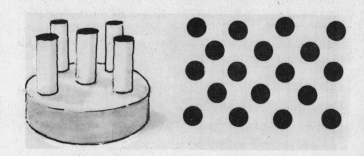

Dowel printing block and pattern

This is a good source for the fundamentals of block printing. Suggested techniques include fingerprinting; pototo, cork, felt, and clay stamps; string; wood; carved blocks and roller printing. Some of these techniques—such as the use of blocks with dowels and string glued to blocks—are quite innovative and produce interesting results.

All patterns and methods involve repeated patterns that are illustrated with black-and-white photographs and explained by an accompanying text.

Caution Note to Dyers

Certain dyestuffs, such as pigment dyes, contain small amounts of petroleum products or other inflammable solvents. Use them only in a well-ventilated room away from flames or cigarettes.

TIE AND DYE AS A PRESENT DAY CRAFT. by Anne Maile. Taplinger Publishing Company, New York, 1971. 181 pages. illustrations, photographs (some color). $6.50. paperback edition $2.95.

Way back in the 1960s, tie-dye clothes were all the rage. This book, originally published in 1963, fulfilled the need for a practical instruction book on this subject. Tie dye is still very popular today, and this fine book is still the place to look for information.

Tie-dye is a resist dyeing process consisting of the knotting, binding, folding, or sewing of certain parts of the cloth to prevent it from being dyed. The earliest records of tie-dye date back to 6th and 7th century Japan and

India. Traders on the ancient trade routes carried the dyed cloth as part of their merchandise.

In India tie-dye was known as "bandhana" work. This term became associated with any fabric decorated with little colored spots. The girls (bandahani) who tied the fabric grew the nails of their thumbs and forefingers very long in order to be able to pick up small points of the cloth to be bound. Tie dyeing is still being practiced as a folk craft in India and in other parts of the world as well.

Tie and Dye as a Present Day Craft presents a thorough treatment of this ancient craft. Twisting, coiling, knotting, binding, folding, rope tying, sewing techniques, ruching (oval and diamond patterns), and dyed backgrounds are described and illustrated. In addition to all the complete instructions for methods and processes, there are twenty-four pages of information on dyes and dyeing, making this book a must for tie dyers of all abilities.

TIE AND DYE MADE EASY. by Anne Maile. Taplinger Publishing Company, New York, 1971. 160 pages. illustrations, photographs, suppliers list. $9.95.

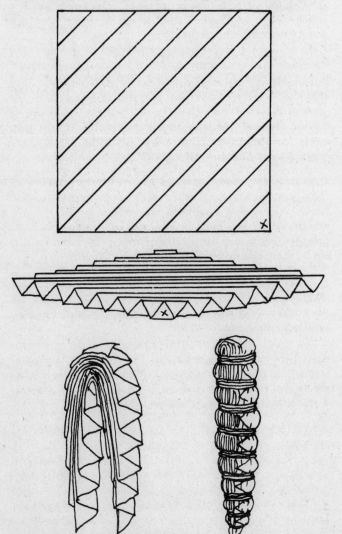

A method for tie-dye diagonal stripes

A hip version of *Tie and Dye as a Present Day Craft,* or, more accurately, a snappier presentation of the same material aimed at young people. There is no loss of clarity from one book to the other; in fact, the "Made Easy" version in many areas surpasses the original. There are more photographs of processes and finished articles, and a section on the use of tie-dye fabrics has been added. The inclusion of additional techniques and "right and wrong" diagrams makes this book especially appealing for beginners. Unfortunately, it is not available in paperback as yet, and the economical advantages of the first edition seem to outweigh the new touches introduced in the second.

TIE-DYE. by Sara Néa. Von Nostrand Reinhold, New York, 1972. 108 pages. illustrations, photographs (some color), index. $5.50. paperback edition $2.95.

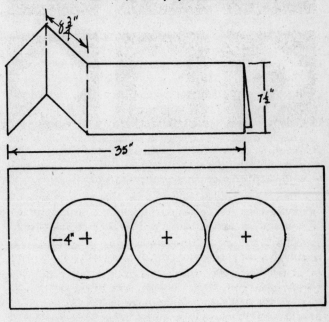

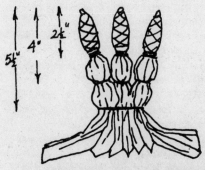

Size of material 15" x 35". Interlocking circles provide an interesting design, even on large pieces of work. Because of the particular way the material has been folded, a motif of radiating color is the pleasing result.

Following a rather comprehensive discussion of tie-dye techniques, dyeing, color mixing, equipment, and the basic folds and holds, the author presents an encyclopedia of sixty-two basic designs. Each design is accompanied by step-by-step illustrated instructions. The idea behind all this is to supply the craftsman with a vocabulary of design techniques which can be used freely in any combination. The possibilities of combination are increased by a discussion of multiple dyeing procedures.

All sixty-two designs are depicted in color photographs, which aids in a clear understanding of the cause and effect (technique and result) in tie dye. This is the most baffling aspect of the craft, and Ms. Néa's program clears up this issue in a simple and painless manner.

Glossary of Batik and Tie-Dye Terms

Acid dyes—Class of dyes especially formulated for use on protein fibers, silk, and wool.

Crackle—The fine, weblike network of lines over the surface of batiked cloth, caused by cracks made in the wax before dyeing.

Direct dyes—Group of dyes appropriate for use on cellulostic fibers, cotton, linen, and viscose rayon.

Discharge dyeing—Removal of color from cloth with bleach solution.

Dye bath—Proportionate mixture of dyestuff, water, and required additives needed to achieve coloration of the cloth.

Ikat—Resist dye technique in which certain predetermined sections of warp yarns are tightly bound as a protection from the dye. This is done prior to weaving.

Mordants—Chemical agents used to increase or promote dye absorption and fastness, used in most natural dyeing processes.

Overdyeing—Application of new dye on cloth initially dyed a different color.

Plangi—Malaysian term referring to different types of tie-dye techniques.

Resist—A substance, such as wax, or a method, such as tritik, which can be applied to protect predetermined portions of cloth from dye penetration.

Solvent—Commercially prepared solution used to dissolve wax, or for various related cleaning purposes.

Templates—Precut shapes which can be used as resists when applied to cloth with clamping methods.

Tjanting—Tool for applying wax. It consists of a reservoir to hold the hot wax, a spout through which the wax flows into the fabric, and a handle.

Tjap—Indonesian stamping tool used to apply intricate patterns of wax onto the cloth.

Tritik—Resist textile technique using different stitches sewn into cloth and gathered and fastened off to form a protection from the dye.

Wax formula—Proportionate combination of paraffin and beeswax used as a hot resist in batik process.

"Tie-Dye . . . The Great Color Explosion with Rit"
Best Foods Consumer Service Department
International Plaza
Englewood Cliffs, N.J. 07632

A free twenty-page booklet containing illustrated directions for tie dyeing jeans and T-shirts. Postcard requests only.

BATIK, ART AND CRAFT. by Nik Krevitsky. Van Nostrand Reinhold, New York, 1973. 92 pages. illustrations, photographs. paperback edition $3.95.

This pleasant pictorial story format reminiscent of '20s and '30s encyclopedias shows the traditional Javanese method of batik. The pictures and text describing the whole process from start to finish give the reader a good idea of how batik has been made in Java for over eight centuries.

Following the pictorial essay is a very cursory treatment of batik as it is practiced as a craft by contemporary Westerners. There is no hard information on dyeing, color, or alternate methods of wax application. However, there is a nice section on "Paper Batik," which is a good introduction to the craft for children.

About a third of the book is comprised of photographic examples of batik, some with accompanying descriptive text. These provide a good source of inspirational material for batik craftsmen.

BATIK, THE ART AND CRAFT. by Ila Keller. Charles E. Tuttle Company, Rutland, Vermont, 1966. 75 pages. illustrations, photographs. $5.80.

Batik is an Indonesian word which describes a form of resist printing obtained when hot wax is applied to the fabric. It probably originated somewhere in Asia, but it was developed to a high art after the 12th century in Java. Javanese Batiks are usually characterized by intricate patterns based upon natural forms.

Ila Keller gives a good deal of rich historical data on Javanese and other batiks illustrated by black-and-white photographs of the basic patterns and Javanese women at work. She explains the important place that batik holds in Javanese culture.

The book also gives the technique of modern batik practiced by craftsmen here in the United States, including instructions for several types of batik methods. Step-by-step photographs help to explain each process fully. Tie dyeing is also covered but not in any real depth.

Society of Batik Artists
c/o Astrith Deyrup
395 Riverside Drive
New York, N.Y.

This is a society of batik artists whose work has been presented to and approved by a jury. It presents batik exhibitions to the public, as well as lectures and demonstrations. They are planning to establish a library dedicated to batik sources.

Traditional Javanese batik pattern

BATIK. by Sara Néa. Van Nostrand Reinhold, New York, 1970. 96 pages. illustrations, photographs, index. $5.95. paperback edition $2.95.

This book provides some interesting alternatives for the application of wax. Instead of using the *tjanting*, or brush, the author suggests using a block method: cookie cutters, corks, jar tops, or shapes formed with pipe cleaners are first dipped into the wax and then pressed onto the fabric. Or, the stencil method: shapes are cut from Contact paper, or any self-adhesive paper, and placed over the fabric before the wax is brushed over it.

The author supplies some good information on the dyeing process, although the color combinations she suggests are a bit arbitrary and might tend to confuse some people. Otherwise, this is a good book for beginners.

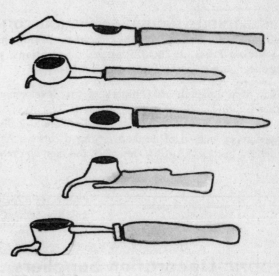

Tjanting tools

DESIGNING IN BATIK AND TIE DYE. by Nancy Belfer. Davis Publications, New York, 1972. 117 pages. illustrations, photographs (some color), suppliers list, bibliography. $9.95.

This very good book for serious fabric decorators contains a multitude of photographic examples of batiked articles. Oddly enough, though, while the traditional batiks are intricate and beautiful, the contemporary examples show a less interesting use of the technique.

Ms. Belfer describes the Javanese method of batik and the methods commonly employed by Western craftsmen. The procedures for waxing and dyeing are interlaced with a wealth of technical information, which on the one hand is good, but on the other hand is a little confusing. However, all the techniques are presented in an abbreviated, step-by-step format at the end of the method section. There is excellent information on all types of dyes, including all-purpose dyes, direct dyes, acid dyes, basic dyes, reactive or Procion dyes, and vat dyes. Alternative resist methods, starch paste, cold wax, and polymer emulsions are also discussed.

The section on tie dye is quite long and very good. The author thoroughly but simply discusses color considerations, folding techniques, use of solid templates, *ikat,* and *tritik.*

A HISTORY OF PRINTED TEXTILES. by Stuart Robinson. The M.I.T. Press, Cambridge, Massachusetts, 1970. 152 pages. illustrations, photographs (some color), index. $10.00.

The author discusses the developments in each craft from antiquity to 1970. Designers, craftsmen, and manufacturing companies are noted and briefly treated. The author includes information on economic and social factors associated with each craft, such as the practice of hymn singing to relax bound apprentices, and the influence of popular phenomena such as the Beatles on modern design.

PRINTED TEXTILES: ENGLISH AND AMERICAN COTTONS AND LINENS 1700–1850. by Florence Montgomery. The Viking Press, 1970. 379 pages. illustrations, photographs (some color), bibliography. $16.95.

This is a comprehensive history of the development of textile printing in England and America. The second half of the book consists of a catalog of chronologically arranged reproductions of decorative printed cottons. A book to delight historians, artists, designers and common readers.

Fabric Decoration Suppliers

Dyes for Batik and Dip-Dyeing

Aljo Manufacturing
116 Prince Street
New York, N.Y. 10012

Commercial Art Materials Company
165 Lexington Avenue
New York, N.Y. 10016

The Craftool Company, Inc.
1 Industrial Road
Woodridge, N.J. 07075

Fibrec, Inc.
2795 16th Street
San Francisco, Cal. 94130

Gothic Color Company, Inc.
727 Washington Street
New York, N.Y. 10014

For suppliers of aniline, cold water, natural, and Procion dye, refer to suppliers list in spinning and dyeing section.

Dyeing Tools and Equipment

Aljo Manufacturing Company
116 Prince Street
New York, N.Y. 10012
catalog.
tjanting tools, batik wax.

Dick Blick Company
P.O. Box 1267
Galesburg, Ill. 61401
catalog.
tjanting tools.

Stephen Blumrich
1200 Meadowview Road
Junction City, Ore. 97448
brochure; send stamped, self-addressed
envelope.
tjanting tools.

Craft Kaleidoscope
6412 Ferguson Avenue
Indianapolis, Ind. 46220
brochure.
batik wax.

Dharma Trading Company
1952 University Avenue
Berkeley, Cal. 94704
catalog; sample charge $.50.
batik wax.

Fibrec Inc.
2815-18th Street
San Francisco, Cal. 94110
catalog.
tjanting tools, batik wax.

The Handweaver
111 East Napa Street
Sonoma, Cal. 95476
catalog; samples $.50.
tjanting tools.

Walter Kircher
Alte Kasselerstrasse 24
Marburg-Lahn, Germany 3550
brochure.
batik frames.

Nasco Arts and Crafts
Nasco West
Fort Atkinson, Wis. 53538
Also P.O. Box 3837
Modesto, Cal. 95352
catalog.
batik frames.

Naturalcraft
2199 Bancroft Way
Berkeley, Cal. 94704
catalog $.50.
batik wax, tjanting tools.

Naz Dar Company
1087 North Branch Street
Chicago, Ill. 60622
catalog.
silk screen supplies.

Hazel Pearson Handicrafts
4128 Temple City Boulevard
Rosemead, Cal. 91770
catalog; samples, prices vary.
tjanting tools, batik wax.

Warp, Woof, and Potpourri
514 North Lake Avenue
Pasadena, Cal. 91101
tjanting tools, batik wax.

Flowers

In all places, then, and in all seasons
Flowers expand their light and soul-like wings,
Teaching us, by most persuasive reasons,
How akin they are to human things.
     —Henry Wadsworth Longfellow

THE DECORATIVE ART OF DRIED FLOWER ARRANGE-MENT. by Georgia S. Vance. Doubleday and Company, Garden City, New York, 1972. 194 pages. photographs (some color), index. $9.95.

In the first part of this book, the author explores the history of flower arrangements. Outstanding and characteristic arrangements from each decorative style are illustrated by reproductions of paintings, tapestries, prints, and photographs of the author's own arrangements. The text contains much information not strictly of historical interest but of practical value to modern arrangers as well. This is followed by a discussion of methods of flower preservation. The directions are clear and direct and are accompanied by many step-by-step photographs. The author also treats glycerin preservation of foliage and advises that stems not be placed in water before processing; that they be placed in solution as quickly as possible; that the leaves not be allowed to wilt before treating; that the level of solution be checked frequently to make sure that it covers the prepared part of stems; that the progress of the treatment be checked so that the plant can be removed as soon as the leaves have changed color. The book is completed by a concise guide to the best methods of preservation for 155 varieties of flowers and greens. This is a very complete and informative section and enhances the value of this already valuable guide for beginner flower craftsmen.

LILY-OF-THE-VALLEY (*Convallaria majalis*). Silica gel or sand; horizontal.
 The little bell-shaped flowers take on the appearance of parchment when dry. Silica gel: 2–3 days; "quick dry": 8–12 hours.

LOOSESTRIFE (*Lysimachia clethroides*). Sand or silica gel; horizontal.
 A narrow, goose-necked spiky white flower that is an attractive and interesting addition to mass arrangements. Silica gel: 2–3 days; "quick-dry": 8–12 hours.

LOVE-IN-A-MIST (Nigella). Sand; face-up.
 Charming little flowers enveloped in thin green lacy bracts. The blues dry a deeper blue and the whites often remain white. Adequate support is provided by the natural stem.
 The seed pod is quite attractive and should be picked and air-dried when well developed and of a good green color.

PLANT IT NOW, DRY IT LATER. by Harriet Floyd. Mc-Graw-Hill, New York, 1973. 231 pages. illustrations, photographs (some color), bibliography, index. $12.95.

The author classifies the plant-it-now, dry-it-later flowers according to the techniques by which they are dried. These fall into two basic assortments—the lazy flowers and the more-effort flowers. The lazy flowers are the enduring varieties, such as straw flower, immortelle, and statice, which require only a little drying in the air. The more-effort flowers are those like tulip, rose, and anemone; these require a more involved drying procedure. For this procedure, the author recommends the use of silica gel rather than sand or borax.

Mrs. Floyd has a great deal of information to impart, not only on drying flowers, but on planting them as well. However, the reader must be willing to meander through the chatty and anecdotal asides to which she is prone.

A Compote of Garden Flowers

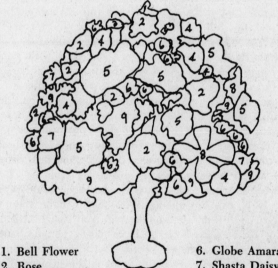

1. Bell Flower
2. Rose
3. Summer Phlox
4. Ranunculus
5. Anemone
6. Globe Amaranth
7. Shasta Daisy
8. Dogwood
9. Baby's-Breath filler
Foliage: Velvet leaves

Source: PLANT IT NOW, DRY IT LATER. by Harriet Floyd.

THE COMPLETE BOOK OF FLOWER PRESERVATION. by Geneal Condon. Prentice-Hall, Englewood Cliffs, New Jersey, 1971. 210 pages. illustrations, photographs (some color), index. $7.95.

Unlike many other flower driers, Geneal Condon does not like the silica gel method of preservation. She feels that the cost is prohibitive, especially in the active summer season, and that the composites are of irregular shape (as are sand's), which can cause blemishes on the petal surfaces. Moreover, it is a rapid-drying chemical and the flower cannot remain submerged for longer than one week. The faster the drying action, the greater the danger of burning or fading. After much experimentation, the author has come to the conclusion that the very best possible medium is sand from the Great Salt Lake. This is caused by buildup rather than erosion, which is the way most sand is formed. It is regular in shape and considerably heavier than other varieties of sand. Its alkaline content preserves many colors, particularly blues, lavenders, and purples. Of course, she rejects no method completely, recognizing that different flowers require different treatment.

This book contains very complete directions for all aspects of drying and storing plants, including vegetables and herbs. There is a teacher's manual for those who enjoy this craft enough to teach it, and an encyclopedia of flowers and the special treatments they require.

How to Dry Rose-Leaves or Any Other Single Flowers Without Wrinkling.

If you would performe the same wel in rose leaves, you must in rose time make choice of such roses as are neither in the bud, nor full blowne (for these have the smoothest leaves of all other), which you must especially cull and chuse from the rest; then take right Callis sand, wash it in some change of waters, and drie it thorowly well, either in an oven, or in the sunne; and having shallow, square or long boxes of four, five, or six inches deepe, make first an even lay of sand in the bottom, upon which lay your Rose-leaves, one by one (so as none of them touch other) till you have covered all the sand, then strowe sand upon those leaves, till you have thinly covered them all, and then make another laie of leaves as before, and so lay upon lay, Ec. Set this box in some warme place in a hot, sunny day, (and commonly in two hot sunnie dayes they will be thorow dry) then take them out carefully with your hand without breaking. Keepe these leaves in Jarre glasses, bound about, with paper, neere a chimney, or stove, for feare of relenting. I finde the red Rose leafe best to keepe in this manner; also take away the stalkes of pansies, stocke gilliflowers, or other single flowers, pricke them one by one in sand, pressing downe their leaves smooth with more sand laid evenly upon them. And thus you may have Rose leaves, and other flowers to lay about your basons, windows, Ec. all the winter long. . . .

Source: DELIGHTS FOR LADIES. by Sir Hugh Plat (1602).

DRIED FLOWERS FROM ANTIQUITY TO THE PRESENT. by Leonard Karel. Scarecrow Press, Metuchen, New Jersey, 1973. 184 pages. bibliography, index. $6.00.

A large portion of this book is devoted to a discussion of drying agents, and the author comes to the conclusion that silica gel is best for ordinary home use. He bases this opinion on its lightness, rapidity, ease with which it can be removed from most petals and stems, and ease with which it can be reconstituted, its freedom from external environmental variations in a sealed container. A chart of tabular data for silica drying comprises the second half of the book.

FLOWER PRESSING. by Peter and Susanne Bauzen. Sterling Publishing, New York, 1972. 48 pages. illustrations, photographs. $3.95.

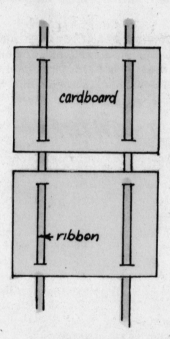

A collector's press should be the first piece of equipment for this craft. Take it along when gathering flowers.

In this book are tips on how to get the best results from pressed flowers. There are a number of easy-to-make projects—wall decorations, trays, bookends, and others—using pressed flower designs, and instructions for applying flowers to fiber glass, embedding flowers in polyester resin, and printing with flowers.

NEW CREATIVE DECORATIONS WITH DRIED FLOWERS. by Dorothea Schnibben Thompson. Hearthside Press, Great Neck, New York, 1972. 156 pages. photographs (some color), suppliers list, index. $7.95.

The author is known throughout the garden world for introducing silica gel processing several years ago in *American Home* magazine. In this book, she gives complete procedures for silica gel preservation and suggests ways to use the finished flowers in decorative projects such as dried flower hats, wedding bouquets, pin cushions, lamps, and so on. She also presents a way of preserving flowers so that they obtain a porcelain look. This is done by painting any fresh flower with Ceramix, a water base paint that gives a hard ceramic finish without firing, and by following the painting by the application of a clear glaze.

Ceramex is naturally of a puttylike consistency and must be placed in a small jar and heated in a saucepan full of water until it achieves a creamy consistency. The colors can be blended and shaded to obtain a natural look; when this is done, it is best to start with the lightest shade, and while it's still wet blend in the darker shades with a brush. Flowers with many petals (roses, carnations) should dry at least twelve hours before the glaze is applied. The author recommends this method as particularly appropriate for preserving especially cherished flowers, such as bridal bouquets and corsages.

DECORATING WITH PLANT CRAFTS AND NATURAL MATERIAL. by Phyllis Pautz. Doubleday and Company, Garden City, New York, 1971. 239 pages. illustrations, photographs (some color), suppliers list, bibliography, index. $8.95.

Bouquet of long-stemmed pine cone flowers

Step-by-step information on drying, pressing, and reconditioning flowers, as well as general gardening hints for the care of decorative houseplants, forcing branches, and prolonging the life of fresh-cut flowers. There are decorating ideas using dried vegetables, driftwood, and pinecones, and a chapter on making sachets and pomanders.

DESIGN FOR FLOWER ARRANGERS. by Dorothy W. Riester. Van Nostrand Reinhold, New York, 1971. 192 pages. illustrations, photographs, bibliography, index. $7.95.

This book is not for those with a casual interest in designing attractive centerpieces. The author, a professional sculptor, designer, and teacher, has written a book on design as it concerns all the arts but which focuses upon floral arrangements and sculpture as a core. The materials for flower arranging are treated as substances that can be perceived and consciously selected for their shape, color, size, and texture, and then as objects that can be abstracted as design elements. Designers learn to analyze their own work and to reevaluate and renovate when appropriate through the aid of textual instruction and photographic examples presented in the final chapter on critical evaluation.

Designs with Opposing Sizes and Shapes

A, B, C, illustrate dynamic balance by opposing sizes and shapes. Opposing forces are the result of thoughtful use of the planes and volumetric shapes of the various sizes. The balance is mostly a condition of weight, of finding the correct amount of supporting space.

It is important to remember that it is not solely the weight, but also the shape-interest of materials that exerts a force. A shape with an interesting contour will hold attention longer. If the large shape in A were serrated or changed into a more interesting free form, the shape would fall out of balance even though the size were unaltered.

The flower in B is so large that the leaf has assumed a pointy quality in relation to it. The added weight of a volumetric shape can be felt in C. The added weight of the bell-like flower requires the compensatory extension of the horizontal line.

Source: DESIGN FOR FLOWER ARRANGERS. by Dorothy W. Riester.

IKEBANA. by Linda M. Walker. Drake Publishers, New York, 1972. 141 pages. illustrations, photographs (some color), index. $6.95.

Moribana, or low bowl arrangement, is the style most accessible to beginners and together with Nagiere, or tall vase arrangement, forms the basis of instruction in most schools.

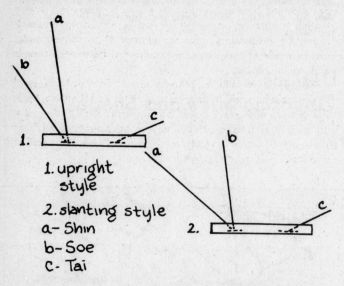

1. upright style
2. slanting style
a- Shin
b- Soe
c- Tai

Stems may be arranged in either upright or slanting styles in Moribana arrangements. The difference between these is in the angle from the vertical taken by Shin and Soe. Shin is 15° from the vertical, Soe is 45° and Tai 75° in the upright style. The angles from the vertical of Shin and Soe are interchanged in the slanting style so that Shin is 45°, Soe is 15°, and Tai remains at 75°.

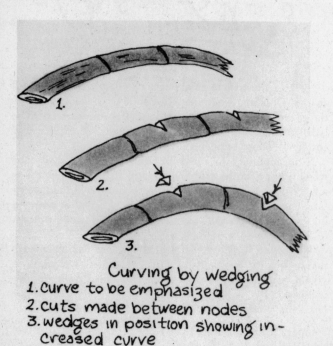

Curving by wedging
1. Curve to be emphasized
2. cuts made between nodes
3. wedges in position showing increased curve

A NEW WORLD OF FLOWER ARRANGEMENT. by Patricia Kroh. Doubleday and Company, Garden City, New York, 1969. 160 pages. photographs (some color), bibliography, index. $7.95.

The swollen buds of the plum blossom or the fallen branch of the sea grape covered with moss and lichens may not seem beautiful to the uninitiated, but the artist has an educated eye for beauty and he learns how to make these natural phenomena bring interest to his design.

To help educate the eye, the author presents a series of chapters containing advice on being creative the modern way, allowing floral design to reflect the mood of the times and the art of the times. There is also a special chapter written by Milton B. Freudenheim, Sr., on how to photograph flower arrangements, and a photo gallery featuring arrangements by guest artists from around the world.

THE ART OF ARRANGING FLOWERS, A COMPLETE GUIDE TO JAPANESE IKEBENA. by Shozo Sato. Harry N. Abrams, New York, 1971. 366 pages. illustrations, photographs (some color), index. $25.00.

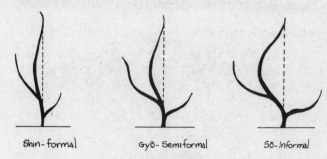

Shin- formal   Gyō- Semiformal   Sō- Informal

Out of print now, but certainly worth a trip to the library, this excellent book begins with the history and development of the flower-arranging art and its place in Japanese culture. Then the author introduces the reader to eleven basic styles of arrangement, and the tools, materials, methods, and vases needed for successful arranging. The pictures (which are exceptionally numerous and predominantly in color) and text explain how to keep flowers fresh, how to select and prepare both fresh and dried materials, and how to make the most effective use of them. It then proceeds to a series of twelve lessons in arranging in Moriban style. Special sections discuss advanced techniques and design, traditional and modern arrangements, and the setting of mood. An appendix contains hints for using plant and flower material from the garden and how to combine them and arrange them effectively.

BONKEI: THE CREATION OF TRAY LANDSCAPES. by Jōzan Hirota. Kodansha International, 1970. 128 pages. illustrations, photographs (some color). $7.95.

Bonkei, the creation of miniature landscapes, is thought to be one of Japan's oldest arts, dating back to the reign of Empress Suiko (554 to 628 A.D.). It is extremely versatile and can be made in many different forms—in trays, tables, and hanging pots—and from a diversity of materials, including artificial materials and moss. The author, however, is of a school which makes use only of living flora, for he believes that this is the only way the true beauty of nature can be expressed. He does make use of miniature houses, boats, and human figures though. The author's preference in this matter does not dissuade him from covering the full range of possibilities, and his discussion of tools, processes, materials, and design is quite thorough.

A Bonkei tray landscape

He stresses the importance of certain universal principles and harmonies which must be observed if authentic Bonkei is to be achieved. The scenes must follow a natural rhythm and this necessitates a close observation of nature, but observation alone is not enough: the final work must be true to nature but, at the same time, personal and individual.

FLOWERS FROM FEATHERS. by Michael and Pamela Woods. Drake Publishers, New York, 1974. 128 pages. illustrations, photographs, index. $7.95.

The basic similarity between the shape of a feather and that of a leaf or petal makes feathers an excellent as well as elegant choice for artificial flowers. Feathers, however, have their own characteristics and limitations which must be respected if successful flowers are to be produced. Every feather has its own curve which can be minimized or maximized by artificial means: the central vein, for example, can be made to curve more by running it between a thumb and scissor blade.

Feathers alone will not a flower make. They must be used in conjunction with other materials, such as Styrofoam balls for centers and pearl beads for stamens. The authors list all such additional materials at the beginning of each of their many flower projects, and note as well the number and variety of feathers required.

FEATHER PEONY

Materials
Approximately 9 grey goose coquilles, 2″ long
9 grey goose nagoires, 4″ long
teazel
glue

Procedure
The teazel forms the center of the peony and can be dyed if that is desired. The feathers are used in their natural state with all the fluff retained (1) and are attached by dipping the base into the glue and then into the teazel. Push the coquilles, curve inwards, into the sides of the teazel about halfway up. Allow the tip of the teazel to remain visible. (2). Push the nagoires into the lower part of the teazel. They too should curve inwards, but they should make a larger cup shape.

Source: FLOWERS FROM FEATHERS. by Michael and Pamela Woods.

Glass

But to shorten this comparison, I shall here set down the properties of glass, whereby any one may easily difference it from all other bodies.

'Tis a concrete of salt and sand or stones.

'Tis Artificial.

It melts in a strong fire.

When melted 'tis tenacious and sticks together.

'Tis ductile whilst red hot, and fashionable into any form, but not malleable, and may be blown into a hollowness.

'Tis friable when cold, which made our proverb, As brittle as glass. It only receives sculpture, and cutting, from a *Diamond* or *Emery* stone.

> —Antonio Neri, *The Art of Glass,* 1612.
> translated by Christopher Merret in 1662.

STAINED GLASS LAMPS. by Anita and Seymour Isenberg. Chilton Book Company, Radnor, Pennsylvania, 1973. 222 pages. photographs (some color), suppliers list, bibliography, index. $12.50. paperback edition $5.95.

America in the 1920s saw a boom of interest in stained glass lampshades. Though the idea was not solely that of Lewis C. Tiffany, he is generally recognized as the father of the stained glass lampshade and as its most productive designer. Tiffany's delicate creations were never really mass-produced by machines, but machines were developed by other companies to bend glass on Swedish steel molds and stamp out a line of shades. Brass channeling was form-fitted around these panels for strength, and the most popular glass seems to have been a rather bland caramel opalescent variety. The surge of excitment generated by Tiffany's creations was soon quenched by these less pleasing industrial reproductions and enthusiasm eventually turned to disdain. The once-prized objects began to be hidden in basements and attics. Careless storage resulted in broken or cracked panels which, due to the difficulties of replacement, were considered useless and sent out with the trash.

Today, more kindly treated shades have handsomely rewarded their owners, fetching anywhere from four hundred to nine hundred dollars at auctions. A number of businesses are actively engaged in reproducing old shades for an ever-growing market. These new, factory-made shades can be quite expensive, yet they lack the richness of the antiques or the originality of a handmade one. Many people are turning away from the production market lampshade to the home production of more personal and exciting shades. Thus far, this book is the most complete guide to detailed information dealing specifically with the making of stained glass lamps.

THE TECHNIQUE OF STAINED GLASS. by Patrick Reyntiens. Watson-Guptill Publications, New York, 1967. 192 pages. illustrations, photographs (some color), suppliers list, index. $15.00.

An excellent reference book for experienced stained glass craftsmen. Particular chapters cover the studio; cutting; techniques and methods of painting, staining, etching, plating, and enameling; firing, glazing; fixing; exhibition; extended use of antique and thin commercial glass; epoxy resin; dale de verre.

HOW TO WORK IN STAINED GLASS. by Anita and Seymour Isenberg. Chilton Book Company, Radnor, Pennsylvania, 1973. 237 pages. photographs (some color), bibliography, index. $12.50. paperback edition $5.95.

The Isenbergs' introduction is quite extensive, but not quite as good as Duval's. In addition to working techniques, there are chapters on selling, opening a shop, and repairing stained glass objects.

MAKING STAINED GLASS. by Robert and Gertrude Metcalf. McGraw-Hill, New York, 1973. 158 pages. photographs (some color), suppliers list, bibliography, index. $12.95.

Beginning with the history of stained glass, including classification of periods, styles, and types of windows, the book moves onward to a list of materials and tools for not only stained glass but glass painting and glass-making as well. The chapter "Evocative Techniques" presents a series of five projects which guide the student in working his own designs in stained and painted glass.

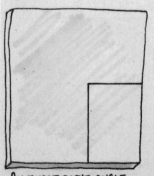

AN EXACT RIGHT-ANGLE CUT IS IMPOSSIBLE.

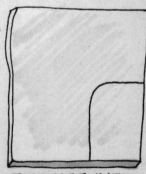

THE CORRECT WAY TO MAKE AN APPROXIMATE RIGHT-ANGLE CUT.

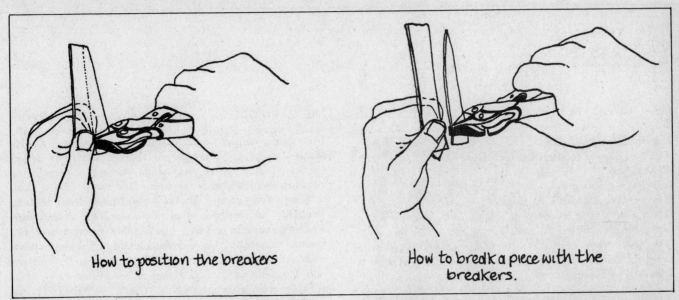

How to position the breakers

How to break a piece with the breakers.

STAINED GLASS CRAFT. by Jack W. Bernstien. Macmillan, New York, 1973. 118 pages. illustrations, photographs (some color), suppliers list, bibliography, index. $9.95.

Through the presentation of some basic projects (a modern "Tiffany" lamp, stained glass window, facet glass panel, stained glass mosaic) the author discusses the basic methods and techniques of the craft. The instructions for the projects are clear and well illustrated and are apt to appeal to beginners.

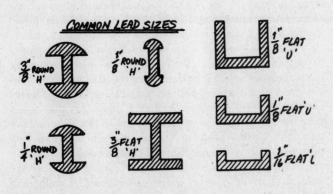

COMMON LEAD SIZES

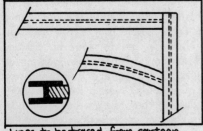

Lines to be traced from cartoon, with cutter.

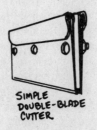

SIMPLE DOUBLE-BLADE CUTTER

CREATIVE STAINED GLASS: TECHNIQUES FOR UNFIRED AND FIRED PROJECTS. by Polly Rothenberg. Crown Publishers, New York, 1973. 96 pages. photographs (some color), suppliers list, bibliography, index. $4.95.

A good, clear introduction to glass techniques for beginners. The author also covers epoxy resin, bonded glass, fused glass, and glass painting. She even gives instructions for making a standing light box.

Stained Glass Club
482 Tappan Road
Northvale, N.J. 07647

A profit-making organization that sells materials and tools for beginning and advanced craftsmen in stained and leaded glass. Publishes *The Glass Workshop*, bimonthly.

Stained Glass Association of America
1125 Silmington Avenue
St. Louis, Mo. 63111

An association that assembles exhibits of native stained glass; sponsors four-year apprentice programs; holds competitions; compiles statistics. Publishes *Stained Glass Journal*, quarterly.

Glass Crafts of America
Grant Building
Pittsburgh, Pa. 15219

A group that sponsors research and tests. Maintains a library of twelve hundred volumes. Publishes *Bulletin*, weekly.

Recommended Design Books

ART DECO PATTERNS IN STAINED GLASS. by Glassworks, 4135 Olive Avenue, La Mesa, California. 162 pages. illustrations. paperback edition $4.95.

STAINED GLASS PATTERNS. by Nervo Art Stained Glassworks, Berkeley, California, 1973. illustrated. 140 pages plus patterns.

Interview

Elaine Tannenbaum operates a workshop/studio in the Chrysalis Gallery on Bleecker Street in New York City, where she teaches several beginning and advanced classes in stained glass. She has been experiencing a very positive response to her work lately and has exhibited in a number of shows and galleries. Her work has also been featured in several magazines, including *McCalls* and *Ladies Home Journal*. Stained glass is still a relatively new field for Elaine, who was an art teacher and printmaker before accidentally becoming involved with stained glass two years ago. Her rapid success also brought with it some problems and necessitated some decisions about how she was going to conduct herself in regard to her craft.

"I had to make a choice as to what I really wanted to do. Whether I wanted to wholesale or just work on a commission basis. I decided to work on a commission basis so now I don't make anything unless I'm hired by somebody."

Why this decision? Well, as Elaine sees it, "Primarily I'm an artist. I'm a craftsperson, but I'm also an artist and as an artist I enjoy making original designs. And as a craftsperson I enjoy working in stained glass. I have no interest in doing production work simply because then I might as well go into manufacturing and have a machine press it out. For me to do ten of one kind—well, first of all it's boring, it's tedious, and that was not my primary interest in pursuing stained glass. I was pursuing glass as a medium which offers me a whole other dimension to explore, which

I don't get in print-making. There you're working with shape and color, but it's flat. With glass I have an added quality of illumination, and when working in jewelry, it becomes more sculptural as well.

"The jewelry aspect of it to me was kind of fun because I initially got started in that just by playing around with seashells and wire and little bits of glass, trying to combine unusual materials. I like to combine things. I do some work with macrame in my pieces. I like to mix media and see how I can innovate, make things more unusual.

"I use flash glass for etching. That's two layers of glass which are hand-blown and fused. I etch through one layer to expose the other. I use Contact paper or wax as a resist. I use hydrofluoric acid which is very potent and worse than hydrochloric. Even the fumes are very dangerous so I wear a mask, rubber gloves, and work in a very well-ventilated place.

"There are two basic techniques in stained glass: the leaded technique and the Tiffany technique which Tiffany used in his lamps. Instead of using the traditional method of lead channels, Tiffany used copper foil and wrapped it around each individual piece of glass and then soldered them together. I use both methods according to what I'm trying to achieve. Very often the lead channel gives a more solid, heavy effect than you'd want on a delicate piece. Occasionally I use brass channel for delicate pieces, too.

"I'm working on an idea now, which hasn't been explored in stained glass—masks. I'm working on an African mask that combines etching and transparent stained glass, and I'm going to be adding feathers to it. Unfortunately, working on commission and teaching, I don't get that much time for my own work. Although I really like the teaching part of it. There's been such a resurgence of crafts, people who ordinarily would not think of themselves as having any artistic ability will attempt to learn a craft, whether it's stained glass, or pottery, or jewelry-making. I really like that because the fine arts have been so elitist.

"The initial problem with most people when they start out in stained glass is getting the right pressure for cutting properly. That's the hardest part because the foiling and leading techniques are fairly simple. But if you can't cut glass to your pattern, then your pieces won't fit and you won't have anything. I start my beginners out working on various cuts on pane glass. It's cheap and it's a good way to learn because plate glass doesn't have a back or a front the way stained glass does so they can cut on either side. And there are no air bubbles or imperfections so they can learn on a fairly easy kind of glass to work on and from there I give them stained glass so they can feel the difference."

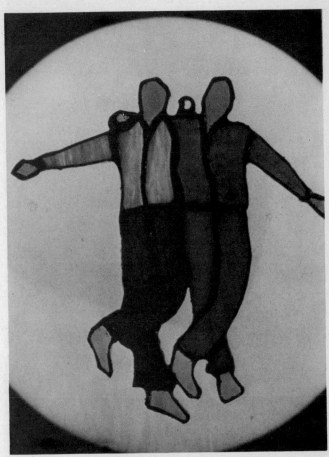

Photographic Cartoons

There has been an increasing use in recent years of photographic cartoons. The original sketch is blown up photographically to the right size of the cartoon. The photograph is then worked on in Indian ink, coloured perhaps, and serves as a basis to the cutline.

Superficially, this method has practically everything to commend it; but when it is examined, it does not really hold water. The objections are:

1. It is expensive.
2. It tends to distortion; using the best possible equipment there are always bound to be some distorted outlines and passages towards the periphery of the cartoon, however carefully the photographic work is done. This is less noticeable in small-scale work than in large-scale cartoons; but it is precisely the problems of large-scale cartooning to which photographic cartooning seems to be the answer.

I have found that the individual pieces of photo-enlarging are, each of them, slightly distorted; and this leads, when they are put together, to a very serious amount of distortion, which is corrected only with a very great deal of labour.

3. As well as exaggerating the good points of a sketch (which may look excellent as a sketch) it exaggerates the pitfalls, too. Mistakes of emphasis in the sketch are ludicrously exaggerated, and most of the time spent on photographic cartoon is time spent correcting the passages that appear to have gone wrong. Thus, the activity of manual cartooning, instead of being a positive statement on a large scale by the artist, with all its faults and drawbacks, is a negative one, because of all the corrections that have to be done to the photographs.

Added to this, a photographic cartoon always gives the impression of being a *small* thing that has, by some devious inflated means, illegitimately become large. Through some subtle means of cross-reference in the sub-conscious, it does not look right to be quite so big.

Source: THE TECHNIQUE OF STAINED GLASS. by Patrick Reyntiens.

WORKING WITH STAINED GLASS: FUNDAMENTAL TECHNIQUES AND APPLICATIONS. by Jean-Jacques Duval. Thomas Y. Crowell Company, New York, 1972. 132 pages. illustrations, photographs, suppliers list, index. $8.95.

The most thorough and responsible introduction to stained glass techniques, and techniques of laminated, painted, and slab glass.

Not Structural if in large sections

Weak joint Hard to put together too many leads converge at one point

Structural

In the meantime take the tin rods which you have cast, and anoint them over on both sides with wax, and rasping lead over the surface in all places to be soldered. Taking the hot iron, apply the tin to it in whatever places two pieces of lead meet and anoint with the iron until they adhere to each other. The legs being set up, arrange the grounds in the same manner, and of whatever color you wish, and so, piece meal, compose your windows. The window being finished and soldered on one side, turned upon the other, make it firm everywhere in the same manner by rasping and soldering.

> —Theophilus. *On Divers Arts*. Chapter XXVII, "Of Uniting Together and Soldering Windows."

KILN-FIRED GLASS. by Harriette Anderson. Chilton Book Company, Radnor, Pennsylvania, 1970. 185 pages. photographs (some color), suppliers list, bibliography, index. $12.50.

This offers basic step-by-step instructions for surface embellishment techniques using enamel powders, powdered glass glazes, frits (chemical compositions that act as flux),

Glass circle cutter

and laminated materials. Sections on sag molding and stained glass are also included but these techniques are not presented in sufficient detail to be useful.

THE ENCYCLOPEDIA OF WORKING WITH GLASS. by Milton K. Berlye. Oceana Publications, Dobbs Ferry, New York, 1968. 270 pages. illustrations, photographs, suppliers list, bibliography, index. $14.00.

This is a really complete survey of glass craft techniques. Everything from precision sandblasting to fiber glass is covered. Not all the sections discuss the subject matter in great depth, but enough information is given to satisfy general requirements. This is an excellent book for glass workers, but craftsmen in other fields who have any occasion to work with glass in any form will find this a ready reference.

COLORFUL GLASSCRAFTING. by Joseph H. Eppens-Van Veen. Sterling Publishing, New York, 1973. 112 pages. photographs (some color), suppliers list, index. $6.95.

This book offers a series of elementary projects that utilize a variety of simple but colorful techniques and a product named Glas-O-Past-X, an oil-base paint that can be fired to a high temperature and retain its color. Unfortunately, the author never reveals where Glas-O-Past-X can be obtained.

GLASSBLOWING: A SEARCH FOR FORM. by Harvey K. Littleton. Van Nostrand Reinhold, New York, 1972. 143 pages. illustrations, photographs (some color). $14.95.

In June 1959, at the Third Annual Conference of American Craftsmen, the potential of glass as a medium for craftsmen received official recognition. Today, there are more than fifty glass programs in American colleges and universities despite the fact that it was practically nonexistent as a craft or studio medium fifteen years ago. The glassblowing process, due to a general popular ignorance as well as the desire on the part of many workers and industrialists who viewed outside interest as a threat to their livelihood, was shrouded in an almost mystical secrecy.

The author has not provided a remedy, insofar as this is not a how-to instruction manual on the techniques of glassblowing, but it is a beautiful photographic exposition on this often-overlooked art. Practical roles are not overlooked, and many of the photographs are quite clear in the illustration of the techniques. These, however, are not of principal interest.

CREATIVE GLASS BLOWING. by James Hammesfahr and Clair L. Strong. W. H. Freeman and Company, San Francisco, California, 1968. 196 pages. illustrations, photographs (some color), suppliers list, bibliography, index. $9.00.

This is a great book on the flame-working method of glassblowing. The instructions are clear and beautifully illustrated. It should please beginners and old hands alike.

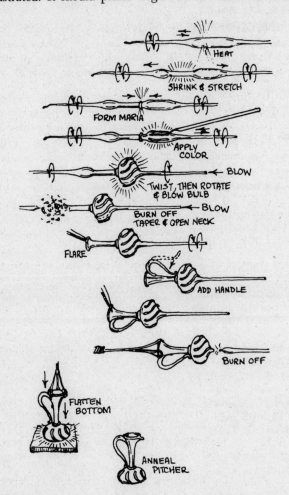

Making an ornamental pitcher

FLAMEWORKING, GLASSMAKING FOR THE CRAFTS-MAN. by Frederic Schuler. Chilton Book Company, Radnor, Pennsylvania, 1968. 131 pages. photographs (some color), suppliers list, index. $12.50.

This is a good book for beginners in the flame-working method. The author presents simple techniques geared to produce simple, bulbous forms. The color plates of this type of flame-worked object just add expense rather than inspiration to the book.

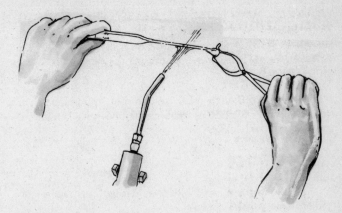

Pulling a point

GLASSFORMING, GLASSMAKING FOR THE CRAFTS-MAN. by Frederic and Lilli Schuler. Chilton Book Company, Radnor, Pennsylvania, 1970. 151 pages. illustrations, photographs (some color), suppliers list, bibliography, index. $12.50.

The second in a series on glassmaking techniques for craftsmen, this book concentrates on the glass-forming techniques involving the heating and softening of glass, but excludes flame-working and glassblowing which were covered in *Flameworking, Glassmaking for the Craftsman*, the first book of the series.

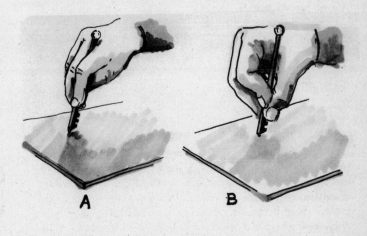

A *Eastern grip for cutting glass—pull*

B *Western grip for cutting glass—push*

Forming processes of sagging and laminating, using glass enamels and colors, and mold-fusing and mold-casting are discussed in terms of history, working techniques, properties of materials, and design considerations. Glass workers in all fields will find this a good source of useful technical information.

Magazines: Glass

Glass Workshop
482 Tappan Road
Northvale, N.J. 07647
Bimonthly. $4.00 a year.
  Official magazine of the Stained Glass Club.

Glass Art Magazine
P.O. Box 7527
Oakland, Cal. 94601
Bimonthly. $15.00 a year.
  Devoted to contemporary blown and leaded glass on an international and professional level.

Stained Glass Suppliers

CAME LEAD AND SOLDER

G. A. Avril Company
Langdon Farm Road and Seymour
  Avenue
Cincinnati, O.

Crown Metal Company
117 East Washington Street
Milwaukee, Wis. 53204

Gardiner Metal Company
4820 South Campbell Avenue
Chicago, Ill. 60632

Glassmasters Guild
52 Carmine Street
New York, N.Y. 10014

White Metal Rolling and Stamping Corp.
80-84 Moultrie Street
Brooklyn, N.Y. 11222

COPPER FOIL

Borden Chemical Company
Mystic Tape Division
1700 Winnetka Street
Northfield, Ill. 60093

Conklin Brass and Copper Company
324 West 23 Street
New York, N.Y. 10011

EPOXY RESIN

Benesco
40 North Rock Hill Street
St. Louis, Mo. 63119

H&M Plastics Corporation
129 South Street
Philadelphia, Pa. 19106

Permagile
101 Commercial Street
Plainview, N.Y. 11803

Resin Research
1989 Byberry Road
Huntingdon Valley, Pa. 19006

Thermoset Plastics, Inc.
5101 East 65 Street
Indianapolis, Ind. 46220

FLUX

Ruby Chemical Company
68 McDowell Street
Columbus, O. 43215

GALVANIZED STEEL BARS

Chicago Metallic Sash Company
4901 South Austin Avenue
Chicago, Ill. 60638

White Metal Rolling and Stamping Corp.
80-84 Moultrie Street
Brooklyn, N.Y. 11222

GLASS

Advance Glass Company
Grant and Decrow Avenues
Newark, O. 43055

S. A. Bendheim Company, Inc.
122 Hudson Street
New York, N.Y. 10013

Bienenfeld Industries, Inc.
1541 Covert Street
Brooklyn, N.Y. 11227

Blenko Glass Company
Milton, W.Va. 25541

Glassmasters Guild
52 Carmine Street
New York, N.Y. 10014

Kokome Opalescent Glass Company
P.O. Box 809
Kokomo, Ind. 46901

The Paul Wismach Glass Company Inc.
Paden City, W.Va. 26159

Leo Popper and Sons
143 Franklin Street
New York, N.Y. 10013

GLASS CUTTING TOOLS

The Fletcher-Terry Company
Spring Lane
Farmington, Conn. 06032

Glazier Hardware Company
1689 First Avenue
New York, N.Y. 10028
circle cutters.

Sommer and Maca
5501 West Ogden Avenue
Chicago, Ill. 60650

GLASS JEWELS AND NOVELTIES

S. A. Bendheim Company, Inc.
122 Hudson Street
New York, N.Y. 10013

Whitemore-Durkin Glass Company
Box 2065
Hanover, Mass. 02339

Glass Painting Suppliers

Aremco Products, Inc.
P.O. Box 145
Briarcliff, N.Y. 10510

L. Rausche and Company
2 Lister Avenue
Newark, N.J. 07105

Standard Ceramic Supply Company
P.O. Box 4435
Pittsburgh, Pa. 15205

Stewart Clay Company
133 Mulberry Street
New York, N.Y. 10013

Thomas C. Thompson Company
1539 Old Deerfield Road
Highland Park, Ill. 60035

White Metal Rolling and Stamping
   Corporation
80-84 Moultrie Street
Brooklyn, N.Y. 11222

GREASE AND RELEASE AGENTS

Famous Lubricants
124 West 47 Street
Chicago, Ill. 60609

GENERAL AND MISCELLANEOUS SUPPLIES

American Art Clay Company
4717 West Sixteenth
Indianapolis, Ind. 46222
enamels and related supplies.

S. Camlott-Lead Cutting Knives
520 Hollywood Avenue
Salt Lake City, Ut. 84105

Nitschke Products, Inc.
P.O. Box 104
Oak Park, Ill. 60303

The Stained Glass Club
482 Tappan Road
Northvale, N.J. 07647

Tepping Studio Supply Company
3003 Salem Avenue
Dayton, O. 45406

Whitemore-Durkin Glass Company
Box 2055
Hanover, Mass. 02339

Flame-working Suppliers

TORCHES

Bethlehem Apparatus Company, Inc.
Hellertown, Pa.

Eisler Engineering Co.
740-770 South 13 Street
Newark, N.J.

L. O. Bucher, Glassmaking Accessories
3874 Crescent Drive
Santa Barbara, Cal.

GLASS

Soft Glass
Conlon Glass Associates, Inc.
10 Bethpage Road
Hicksville, N.Y. 11802

*Borosilicate Glass and Soft or
   "Flint" Glass*
Corning Glass Works
Kimble Laboratory Glassware
Owens-Illinois Glass Company
(order through nearest dealer.)

ANNEALING FURNACES

Cress Electric Furnaces
Recco Equipment Company
323 West Maple Avenue
Monrovia, Cal. 91016

Wilt
Laboratory Glass Blowing, Inc.
860 Albany-Shaker Road
Lathan, N.Y. 12110

Glassblowing Suppliers

*Glass tubing and rod (in all sizes, kinds,
   and colors), kits for beginners, air
   compressors and related supplies*
Techno-Scientific Supply Company, Inc.
P.O. Box 191
Baldwin, N.Y. 11510

GLASS-WORKING TOOLS

Arthur H. Thomas Company
Vine Street at Third, P.O. Box 779
Philadelphia, Pa. 19105

Fisher Scientific Company
633 Greenwich Street
New York, N.Y. 10014

Techno-Scientific Supply Company, Inc.
P.O. Box 191
Baldwin, N.Y. 11510

ETCHING CHEMICALS

Fisher Scientific Company
633 Greenwich Street
New York, N.Y. 10014

GLASS FIRES AND GAS BURNERS

American Gas Furnace Company
Elizabeth, N.J. 07207

Techno-Scientific Supply Company, Inc.
P.O. Box 191
Baldwin, N.Y. 11510

GLASS-TO-METAL SEALS

Associated Engineering, Inc.
Glen Ridge, N.J. 07028

Jewelry

HANDICRAFTING JEWELRY: DESIGNS AND TECHNIQUES. by William E. Garrison and Merle E. Dowd. Henry Regnery Company, Chicago, 1972. 203 pages. illustrations, photographs, suppliers list, index. $12.95.

Believing that the best way to learn jewelry-crafting techniques is by doing, the authors open their book with the presentation of a band ring project. The instructions are easy to follow, and the beginner learns the technique of joint soldering by the time the ring has been completed. Subsequent chapters introduce new projects and techniques: cuff links teach sweat soldering and sawing, pendants and pins show how to mount round and oval stones, chains and catches demonstrate bending techniques, and so on. Later chapters feature variations of basic techniques and introduce principles of design and lost wax casting.

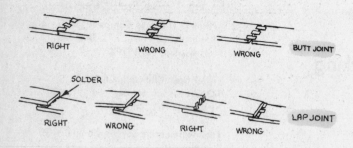

The end of the book is devoted to detailed explanations of tools, materials, coloring, and coating, and features appendixes of weights and thicknesses and a glossary of terms.

All instructions are simply stated and reinforced with understandable photographs and line drawings. The authors' learn-while-you-do approach seems to be a most pleasant and effective way of acquiring jewelry skills.

DESIGN AND CREATION OF JEWELRY, revised edition. by Robert von Neumann. Chilton Book Company, Radnor, Pennsylvania, 1972. 271 pages. illustrations, photographs, bibliography, index. $12.50. paperback edition $5.95.

This is an exceptionally good introduction to the procedures of the jewelry craft. It offers comprehensive coverage of materials and tools, as well as basic metalworking techniques and specialized techniques of metal-forming, and decoration. Simple directions are given for lost wax casting, niello, lamination, granulation, and inlay. An appendix sets forth charts on comparative weights, temperatures, fluid measures, surface speeds of wheels, ring sizes, melting points, and so on. There is also a section on design possibilities, amply supported by photographs.

MAKE YOUR OWN ELEGANT JEWELRY. by R. Boulay. Sterling Publishing Company, New York, 1972. 48 pages. illustrations, photographs (some color), index. $2.95.

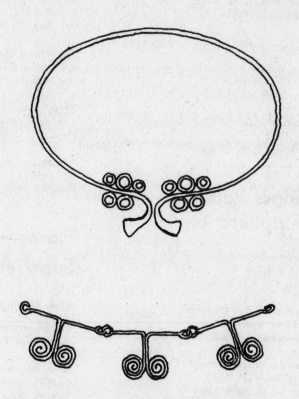

Two designs that can be realized only by soldering

Although it is a limited introduction to certain fundamental jewelry processes, this inexpensive book, however, is informative in its own way. It is divided into two categories of procedures, with corresponding projects for each— such as making jewelry from wires and rods, and making jewelry from sheet metal. The first section presents instructions for bending, hammering, and soldering; the latter for cutting, chasing, etching, and riveting with a hammer. There are several photographs of finished pieces, but there is no complete design section, and most of the design ideas presented are of a rather prosaic nature. However, the type of format used provides a good starting place for inexperienced metalworkers who would like to get a feel of jewelry techniques before committing themselves in a large way to the craft, and is also a good choice for teen-agers who want to create personalized jewelry.

The projects progress in difficulty and include more techniques as they go along. Starting with bent wire forms (to make bracelets and necklaces) and proceeding to sheet metal jewelry with and without soldering (for cuff links, earrings, rings, and pendants) and finally, to jewelry made by combining various methods, the beginner travels through all the most necessary jewelry techniques, and should gain enough familiarity with them to enable him to create his own, more sophisticated inventions.

Pendant made with buttonhead rivets

SIMPLE JEWELRY. by R. W. Stevens. Watson-Guptill Publications, New York, 1966. 96 pages. illustrations, photographs, suppliers list, bibliography, index. $1.95.

This book is an excellent introduction to jewelry made from copper and silver. Simple pieces are discussed in explicit step-by-step instructions, with line drawings for each step.

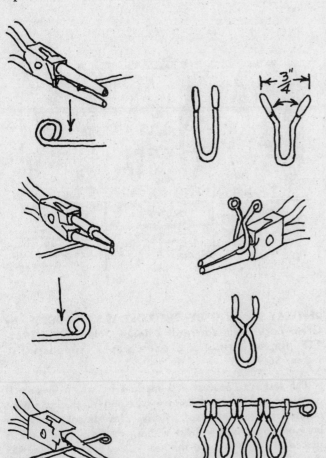

Riveting with A Hammer

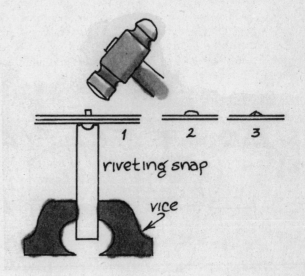

riveting snap

vice

With a planishing hammer or the flat face of a ball peen hammer, strike a smart vertical blow on end of projecting rivet. This will bulge it and hold the pieces firmly together. Do not hammer too hard, but hammer steadily from all sides so that the crushed metal expands and begins to round off. Continue hammering with care until you have shaped the end of the rivet into a pyramid with four sides.

Source: MAKE YOUR OWN ELEGANT JEWELRY. by R. Boulay.

JEWELRY. by Thomas Gentille. Golden Press, 1968. 96 pages. illustrations, photographs, suppliers list, bibliography, index. paperback edition $2.50.

A fine discussion of basic procedures, together here with information on a few simple tools, enables the reader to complete ten jewelry projects. These projects progress in logical sequence from a simple sawed pin to more complex pieces, such as a pendant with mixed metals and a gold pin with stone, and they have step-by-step directions with diagrams.

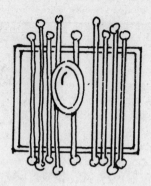

Design for gold pin with stone

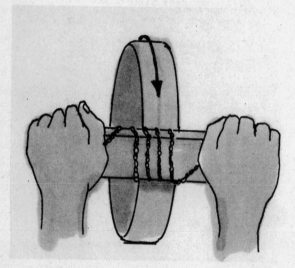

To secure chain for buffing, hold the ends tightly in your hands.

The book is profusely illustrated with black-and-white photographs of historical and contemporary work, which compensate for the rather weak design of the projects.

A section on advanced techniques includes enameling, electroforming, and lapidary. However, these receive a rather light treatment in comparison to the thorough coverage of the basics.

All in all, this is a fine book for beginners who wish a solid grounding in basic methods, but other sources might prove to be more fruitful for inspirational material.

JEWELRY: QUEEN OF CRAFTS. by William R. Sanford. Bruce, Beverly Hills, California, 1970. 196 pages. illustrations, photographs (some color), bibliography, index. $8.95.

A general introductory discussion of over forty jewelry techniques, this book is more like an extended glossary than an instruction manual.

CREATIVE CASTING. by Sharr Choate. Crown Publishers, New York, 1966. 213 pages. illustrations, photographs (some color), bibliography, index. $7.95.

A fine book on all the major methods of casting metals most commonly used by craftsmen and jewelry makers, this includes instructions for lost wax, replica, hollow core, sand, cuttlefish bone, and rubber mold methods of casting. The instructions are clear enough to enable beginners to cast any object desired without too much difficulty.

Especially interesting is the information given on replica casting, a method by which metal castings are made from any object that can be burned out in the furnace, thus leaving a pattern chamber free of ash residue. Particularly good choices for this method are: plants, marine animals, and insects. With this method, it's possible to make, for example, a real gold bug without meticulously constructing a model of it first.

The second half of this book concerns itself with finishing processes. There are sections on rough and fine finishing of castings (removal of sprues and vents, annealing, pickling, buffing, etc.), soldering, surface embellishment, electroplating, and enameling.

The book contains scores of hints, such as how to determine whether an oxidizing or reducing flame is appropriate for melting certain metals, and there is a multitude of black-and white photographs presenting finished cast objects.

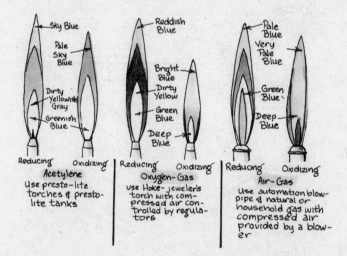

JEWELRY MAKING BY THE LOST WAX PROCESS. by Greta Pack. Van Nostrand Reinhold, New York, 1968. 113 pages. illustrations, photographs, suppliers list, index. $6.95.

The lost wax process is a method by which jewelry is cast in a mold formed from a wax pattern that has been encased in a plasterlike material (investment) that can bear up under intense heat without cracking. The mold is placed in a furnace, and the heat is slowly raised. The wax pattern melts and runs out of an opening left in the casing, leaving a mold into which molten metal can be thrown by

PATTERN

Wax patterns are made by:

1. carving
2. build-up
3. hand forming
4. mold reproduction

SPRUEING OR SET-UP

1. The sprue should be thicker than the heaviest part of the pattern.
2. The sprue should be attached to the heaviest part of the pattern
3. The sprue should be no longer than is absolutely necessary.

INVESTING

1. Weigh investment material and measure water according to manufacturer's recommendation.
2. Fill flask containing wax pattern a either vaccum or vibrate to remove air from the slurry.
3. Allow invested mold to air-dry for two hours or more before starting the burnout.

CLEAN-UP

1. Flasks containing gold or silver casting can be quenched in water 4 to 5 minutes after casting.
2. Fire scale and discoloration can be removed with acid pickle solution or with *Vigor* Solution.

BURNOUT

1. Place invested flask in furnace preheated. to 800°F. Hold at this temperature for one hour or until the wax has drained.
2. Raise temperature at the rate of 300°/400° per hour or until temperature of 1400°F is reached
3. Hold temperature at 1400°F for two hours or more
4. Drop temperature to that desired for casting.

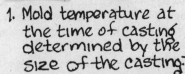

CASTING

1. Mold temperature at the time of casting determined by the size of the casting.
 * For example, delicate rings are usually cast into molds of aproximately 1000°F while molds for heavy rings are usually cast at about 700°F.
2. When vacuum-assist casting, the sprue should be about 25% larger than that used when casting with a centrifugal machine.
3. The weight of gold is 14 times that of wax.
4. The weight of silver and bronze is 9 times that of wax.

centrifugal force. The encased casting is then submerged in water; the investment disintegrates and releases the metal casting.

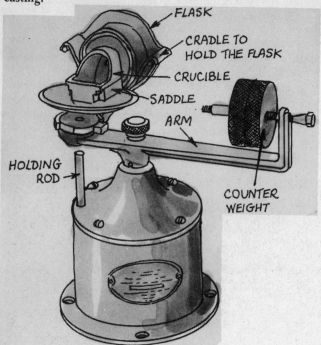

Centrifugal casting machine

All the materials and tools needed for casting jewelry in this manner are thoroughly enumerated and described in this book, as are the step-by-step procedures for the preparation of the metal, mounting and investing the pattern, casting, and finishing the resulting piece. The remainder of the book is comprised of fourteen projects, all of which follow the same casting procedure. There are step-by-step instructions for casting rings, brooches, pendants, a bolo tie slide, and earrings. The projects feature different stone settings, and require a variety of decorative techniques which are explained in separate sections on soldering, pickling, cleaning, and coloring.

PEBBLE COLLECTING AND POLISHING. by Edward Fletcher. Sterling Publishing Company, New York, 1973. 96 pages. illustrations, photographs (some color), index. $3.95.

This book offers information on selecting pebbles, on machinery and on jewelry findings. It contains good step-by-step instructions for polishing procedures.

COLLECTING AND POLISHING STONES. by Herbert Scarfe. Dufour Editions, Chester Springs, Pennsylvania, 1973. 88 pages. illustrations, photographs (some color), index. $5.75.

This is an excellent introduction to the craft of lapidary work. The author, recognizing that one of the difficulties that arises for the beginner is how to spot the sort of rocks that will polish successfully, presents a brief outline of the structural characteristics that will assist in the identification of three groups of rocks and minerals. He lists suitable and unsuitable stones and explains why they are classified as they are.

Although lapidary machines are available commercially, a chapter is devoted to the building of suitable machinery at home using basic manufactured components. Building equipment at home constitutes a considerable saving for the amateur lapidary who is unable or unwilling to commit himself to a large investment.

The basic skills of the craft itself are introduced in a section on how to cut a cabochon. This is a difficult process to learn from a book, but the instructions are well organized and clear and are assisted by excellent diagrams.

Those who don't care to get involved in lapidary but would like to be able to polish stones will derive great benefit from the hand polishing directions for flat and curved stones. The basic requirements are a graded powder abrasive and a polishing agent such as tin oxide or cerium oxide.

To polish a flat surface, for example, you would need: silicon carbide abrasive grits, grades 220, 320, and 500; tin oxide or cerium oxide; a small sheet of glass; a small sheet of Plexiglas; and a thick felt pad. Begin by applying ½ teaspoon of 220 grit on the surface of the glass and moistening with water. Press the stone firmly to the glass and rotate it steadily, distributing the grit over the entire surface of the plate. Reapply as necessary and periodically wash the stone in cold water to check progress. Continue grinding with circular clockwise and counterclockwise motions until the face of the stone is level and free from pits. Wash the stone and glass, and your hands, and apply 320 grit and dampen slightly. Repeat sanding procedure with moderate pressure. Wash the stone and score the surface of a thick sheet of Plexiglas with rough sandpaper. Apply 500 grit and continue as before, keeping the stone perfectly flat and checking progress throughout. The stone should achieve a flat surface and begin to show a dull luster.

When this condition has been obtained, it is time to polish with a thin paste made from the tin oxide and water. Dampen the felt pad slightly and apply the mixture with a soft brush. Rub the stone vigorously on the pad until friction dries up the moisture. When this occurs, speed up the polishing action but decrease the pressure. Continue applying paste as needed.

THE ART OF THE LAPIDARY, revised edition. by Francis J. Sperison. Macmillan, New York, 1961. 300 pages. photographs. $9.95.

In addition to the usual topics covered in a book of this kind, this book has illustrations not only of outstanding work of past and present artisans, but also of many original pieces designed and executed by the author. The book finishes with seven reference tables containing useful data.

Gemological Institute of America
11940 San Vincente Boulevard
Los Angeles, Cal. 90049

An educational organization of the jewelry industry, the institute conducts correspondence and resident courses in identification, grading, and appraising of diamonds and other gemstones, as well as instruction in commercial jewelry designing. It manufactures and sells gem testing and diamond grading equipment. It maintains a vast gemological library, awards certificates in various gemological fields, and publishes *Gems and Gemology* quarterly.

Magazines: Jewelry

Lapidary Journal
P.O. Box 2369
San Diego, Cal. 92112
Monthly. $5.75 per year.

GEMS AND MINERALS

Gemac Corporation
P.O. Box 808
Menton, Cal. 92359
Monthly. $4.50 a year. $.60 per single issue.
The official magazine for the American Federation of Mineralogical Societies. It offers articles on aspects of earth science as a hobby, but also contains some jewelry projects and gem cutting.

GEMS AND GEMOLOGY

Gemological Institute of America
11940 San Vincente Boulevard
Los Angeles, Cal. 90049
Quarterly. $3.50 a year. $1.00 per single issue.

Unsuitable Materials for Collecting and Polishing

1. Porous sandstone.
2. Granular sandstone.
3. Flaky shale, slate, mudstone, schist.
4. Veined sandstone.
5. Pitted or cracked pebbles.
6. Brick, concrete, earthenware, china.
7. Glass pebbles (unless they are loaded in the tumbler separately from everything else).
8. Overlarge pebbles or pebbles completely regular in size or shape.

Source: PEBBLE COLLECTING AND POLISHING. by Edward Fletcher.

JEWELRY, GEM CUTTING AND METALCRAFT. by William T. Baxter. McGraw-Hill, New York, 1950. 334 pages. illustrations, photographs, suppliers list, bibliography, index. $8.95.

This book provides a little bit about just about everything, presented in general terms but without line drawings.

The section on gem identification by amateurs is quite good and contains tables of gold and silver weights, hardness, sheet metal and wire sizes, and abrasive grit sizes. There are general instructions for making items such as bookends, letter holders, and agate-handled tableware, but also without working diagrams.

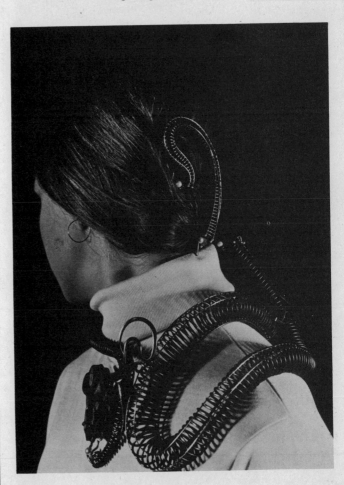

One-shoulder neckpiece/hairpiece combination #12, Lance Fredericks. Coiled bronze, fabricated 14k gold and sterling silver; conglomerate agate and pearls

THE JEWELER'S MANUAL. by Richard T. Liddicoat, Jr., and Laurence L. Copeland. Gemological Institute of America, 1967. 361 pages. illustrations, bibliography. $5.50.

A concise and comprehensive reference source for information and data pertaining to major types of jewelry merchandise, this book is designed with jewelers rather than craftsmen in mind. Nevertheless, it is an important source book for anyone working with gems and metals. There are sections on diamonds, colored stones, testing, property tables, gem lore, pearl testing and weighing, metal finding, jewelry and silver engraving. There is also some material on clocks, and some information about the Gemological Institute.

Mohs' Scale of Hardness

1. Talc (softest)
2. Gypsum
3. Calcite
4. Fluorite
5. Apatite
6. Orthoclase
7. Quartz
8. Topaz
9. Corundum
10. Diamond (hardest)

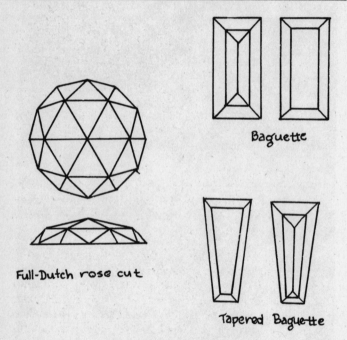

Baguette

Full-Dutch rose cut

Tapered Baguette

GEMSTONE AND MINERAL DATA BOOK. by John Sinkankas. Winchester Press, New York, 1972. 346 pages. $8.95.

This is a comprehensive collection of hard-to-find data, formulas, compounds, tables, tests, lapidary equipment, and so on. It also includes a special section detailing suitable methods for cleaning over a thousand species of minerals. Properties of gemstones are listed: hardness, density, refractive indices, fluorescence, Fraunhofer lines, and spectra. A section on chemicals and other useful materials used in lapidary work features workshop tips and safety precautions. Even serious craftsmen probably will never feel the need for a great part of the data contained in this book, but it can still serve as a handy, one-volume answer to just about every nonprocedural question that may arise.

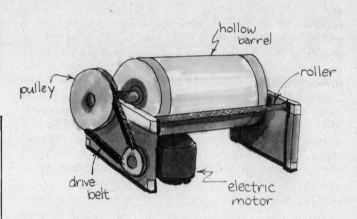

The working parts of a tumbler polisher

DICTIONARY OF GEMS AND GEMOLOGY. by Robert M. Shipley. Gemological Institute of America, 1971. 261 pages. $7.50.

A comprehensive glossary of gems written by the founder of the Gemological Institute of America, this book contains more than four thousand definitions of gems, gem materials, gem varieties, synthetics, biblical and historical gems, and incorrect and misleading terms. Definitions of gems include chemical composition, crystallography, physical and optical properties, and sources.

HANDBOOK OF GEMSTONE IDENTIFICATION, 17th edition. by Richard T. Liddicoat, Jr. Gemological Institute of America, 1972. 431 pages. illustrations, photographs. $11.95.

A practical guide to the identification of gemstones, the book explains in clear detail the various methods and mechanics of gem identification. Fundamental procedures and operations are presented in step-by-step instructions and illustrations.

GEMCRAFT: HOW TO CUT AND POLISH GEMSTONES. by Lelande Quick and Hugh Leiper. Chilton Book Company, Radnor, Pennsylvania, 1959. 179 pages. illustrations, photographs. $7.50. paperback edition $3.95.

The book includes instructions for cutting cabochons and faceting stones, but the outstanding features are the directions for sculpting gem materials, how to make mosaics and intarsia, and the list of necessary tools.

JEWELS OF THE PHARAOHS. by Cyril Aldred. Praeger Publishers, New York, 1971. 256 pages. illustrations, photographs (some color), bibliography, index. $15.00.

We found the noble mummy of the sacred king . . . numerous golden amulets and ornaments were upon his breast and a golden mask was over his face. . . . His coffin was embellished with gold and silver, both inside and out, and inlaid with precious stones. We collected the gold, together with the amulets and jewels that were about him and the metal that was on his coffin. . . . We retrieved the gold from the queen and her coffin . . . then we set fire to their coffins. . . . We divided the spoils. . . . There was 160 deben [about 31 pounds] of gold in all.

This is the actual testimony of an Egyptian tomb robber, Amun Pnufer, at his own trial in the time of Ramses IX (cir. 1124 B.C.). It is but one among many historical and modern examples of the ruthless plunder carried out through the centuries in Egypt.

Cyril Aldred brings together in this book Egyptian jewelry from museum collections around the world. He discusses the meaning, history, aesthetics, and, most interesting for craftsmen, the techniques employed in the making of these magnificent objects. His text is rather easy to read and is accompanied by excellent color plates. It offers a great deal of information and an even greater amount of inspiration to jewelry craftsmen interested in the accomplishments of their ancient predecessors.

Jeweler's Cements

DIAMOND CEMENT. Dissolve isinglass (very pure fish glue) in water to make thick paste; dilute with ethyl alcohol. Dissolve mastic resin in ethyl alcohol to form thick paste. Mix the two pastes thoroughly while warming the container gently. Use for cementing pearls or small stones into recesses.

ENGRAVER'S AND STONE SETTER'S CEMENT. Melt together burgundy pitch 2 pts./wgt., rosin 1.5 pts./wgt., beeswax 1.5 pts./wgt., and plaster of Paris 1 pt./wgt., to be added after the other ingredients have been melted and blended. Pour into cold water to solidify. Use for repoussé work.

Source: GEMSTONE AND MINERAL DATA BOOK. by John Sinkankas.

PRACTICAL GEMSTONE CRAFT. by Helen Hutton. The Viking Press, New York, 1972. 104 pages. illustrations, photographs (some color), suppliers list, bibliography, index. $8.95.

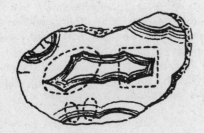

Pattern areas for cutting an agate

The book begins by giving background geological knowledge—how to identify rocks and recognize minerals from crystal systems. There is an alphabetical, descriptive listing of gemstones and decorative stones that are suitable for beginning and amateur lapidaries to work with and that do not require faceting. The author briefly describes fundamental lapidary equipment and then goes on to a well-presented lesson in cabochon cutting. The format proceeds step by step, and there are numerous clear line drawings and photographs. The last portion of the book contains ideas for using stones—in jewelry-making, simple settings, and so on. These topics are discussed briefly, and various findings are illustrated. The author also suggests other uses for polished and natural stones, such as casting in polyester resin and tile-making.

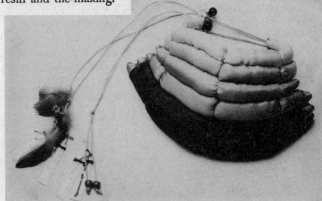

Stuffed taffeta collar, Marie Feinberg

GEM CUTTING IS EASY. by Martin Walter. Crown Publishers, New York, 1972. 96 pages. illustrations, photographs (some color), suppliers list, index. $4.95. paperback edition $2.95.

Until very recently, gem cutting was a closely guarded family secret; it is only in the last few decades that it has become a hobby practiced by amateurs. Many would-be rockhounds are discouraged and somewhat mystified by the machinery necessary for lapidary work; therefore the author presents an extensive and quite a good discussion of the basic tools. Beginners cannot be certain of the depth of their commitment to a new craft, and the author recommends purchasing a small B and I type of multipurpose machine that comes ready to use with the necessary accessories except for a ¼ horsepower electric motor which can be bought separately. He is also cognizant of the fact that most future gem cutters are not machinists, and so he supplies a few pointers on the care and feeding of lapidary machines.

The work itself begins with the cabochon cutting of quartz, the easiest and least expensive material to work on. Similarly, the first faceting is also done on clear white or smoky quartz. The instructions are not as clear as those in Mr. Scarfe's *Collecting and Polishing Stones* or Ms. Hutton's *Practical Gemstone Craft* book, and beginners might do well to start off with either of those books before moving ahead to Mr. Walter's instructions for faceting.

Interview

Maire Feinberg is a jewelry designer who lives and works in lower Manhattan. When asked about an almost "costume" effect to some of her more elaborate pieces, she admitted to a long-standing fascination with costume design, although her experience professionally has been limited to costuming a few dance performances. She claims to be a "compulsive collector," a trait that is responsible for the accumulation of her materials. **When I see things I really like I hate to throw them out. So, I started making things from them.** Despite a somewhat bizarre look to many of Maire's creations, she staunchly maintains that her things are absolutely made to be worn, though she does add that she herself doesn't know who would wear them.

When I start to make something, I think about it, draw it, and then go ahead and make it, allowing it to change along the way. But I never think of what it's for. I start out with the person's body, and that's the limitation—how it's going to fit the body—but never really its practical applications.

any of my things. They either tie or button around the neck, or something goes down the back so that there's some interest there, too.

Ear Feathers: My interest in feathers started when I was in Italy. There were places there where you could buy birds for dinner and people would pluck them on the way home and leave the feathers on the street. Once I picked some up, took them home, washed them and dried them, and fell in love with them. Sometimes I dye them. It took me a long time to give in and do that; I didn't want to ruin their integrity. Mostly, I leave them natural. They're very beautiful and have fantastic iridescences.

This is an ear piece. It attaches in the ear. The feathers are wrapped together as in fly fishing and they form a knot down at the bottom. The glass pieces have been taken off an old wastepaper basket. They're half mirror and half glass and they make a really beautiful sound. A lot of things I make have sound. When you walk along the sound adds another dimension. It's very pleasant.

Necklace: This is made of embroidery thread wrapped around jute and held together with brass wire. The wrapped pieces started as a way to lay the color on jute. Embroidery threads come in thousands of colors. The piece fastens in the back with a tie. I've never used conventional clasps on

Interlocking wedding set, Lance Fredericks

INVENTIVE JEWELRY-MAKING. by Ramona Solberg. Van Nostrand Reinhold, New York, 1972. 128 pages. illustrations, photographs. $8.95.

This is a book devoted to the making of inexpensive, expendable jewelry, humorous, spontaneous, and creative in its design concept and use of unusual materials. It is not a manual of jewelry techniques, and the preparation of materials is limited to simple processes such as sawing metal and wood, melting plastic, and bleaching bones. However, the basic techniques acquired here can be transferred to the more sophisticated methods of traditional jewelry-making.

Regardless of the cost of a piece of jewelry, the elements of good design and craftsmanship are still of paramount concern. The author devotes a chapter to design concepts, color, texture, and forms, and illustrates her points through numerous photographs. She also presents general procedural advice for stringing and attaching findings, using plastics, metals, furs, glass, paper, clay, and wood, and she provides a few step-by-step projects within each category. Her major objective, however, seems to be in getting the amateur jewelry maker awake to the possibilities all around for inexpensive, inventive jewelry, and the text contains many photographs that spark the imagination.

JEWELRY: FORM AND TECHNIQUE. by Michael D. Grando. Van Nostrand Reinhold, New York, 1970. 80 pages. illustrations, photographs, index. $5.95.

Dedicated to Carl Jung and the belief in jewelry-making as an art form rather than a craft, this book offers complete coverage of techniques in essay rather than step-by-step format, illustrated with examples of the author's rugged and startling creations.

Inedible Baker's Clay

Sunface made with inedible baker's clay

4 cups unsifted all-purpose flour
1 cup salt
1½ cups water

Combine ingredients in bowl. Mix thoroughly with hands. Add drops of water if dough is too stiff to handle. Knead dough on a board for about 5 minutes. Form into desired shapes. Preheat oven to 350° and bake on cookie sheet for one hour or longer depending upon size and thickness of pieces. Test for doneness with toothpick. Remove from cookie sheet with spatula. Cool on rack. When thoroughly cooled, decorate and paint. Spray with clear fixative to preserve.

● **This recipe must not be doubled or halved.**
● **The dough must be used within four hours or it will become too dry.**
● **Do not eat!**

Source: INVENTIVE JEWELRY-MAKING. by Ramona Solberg.

IDEAS FOR JEWELRY. by Ian Davidson. Watson-Guptill Publications, New York, 1972. 96 pages. illustrations, photographs (some color), suppliers list, bibliography, index. $7.95.

The author begins with a discussion of design and design sources. He recommends that the jeweler make models from cardboard, macaroni, and so on rather than attempt to translate three-dimensional effects into line drawings. He then moves on to a discussion of materials and their specifications, and tools and their uses. He explains how to link, anneal, rivet, and solder in general terms and without diagrams.

ORGANIC JEWELRY YOU CAN MAKE. by Carson I. Ritchie. Sterling Publishing Company, New York, 1973. 48 pages. illustrations, photographs, suppliers list, index. $2.95.

Many people who are unable to afford higher priced gems and jewelry materials have turned from unattractive and poorly designed imitations to genuine inexpensive natural materials.

The author arranges his projects in order of materials, since each material requires some special handling before it can be turned into jewelry. Many of the items are simple, such as the pinecone pendant which is made from cones picked before they are open, dried thoroughly in a well-ventilated cupboard, rubbed with wax polish or sprayed with artist's fixative, and then have bell caps epoxied onto them. Others, like the delicate and lacy mother-of-pearl brooches, require more skill and thought. Note: Many of these more complicated projects assume a familiarity with basic shop techniques (such as sawing, polishing, drilling).

Feather necklace, Carol Sloane

BODY JEWELRY, INTERNATIONAL PERSPECTIVES. by Donald J. Willcox. Henry Regnery Company, Chicago, 1973. 226 pages. photographs (some color). $14.95.

This is a book of interviews with close to fifty artists from all over the world. There are also photographs of the artists' work, which, while differing in terms of materials and techniques, all share the spirit of experimentation, unconventionality, and fun.

Feather necklace, Carol Sloane

CONTEMPORARY JEWELRY: A STUDIO HANDBOOK. by Philip Morton. Holt, Rinehart and Winston, New York, 1970. 308 pages. illustrations, photographs (some color). $9.95.

The author begins with the principles of design, an analysis of jewelry use, and a survey of jewelry in history. He then moves on to the practical problems and procedures of jewelry-crafting, offering advice on making layouts, cutting, hammering, casting, and finishing. He even gives information on problems of cost and marketing. His treatment is quite thorough, but this cannot really be considered a beginner's handbook. Most of the methods require sophisticated equipment and a reasonable level of proficiency.

Findings

Abbey Materials Corporation
116 West 29 Street
New York, N.Y. 10001

Allcraft Tool and Supply Company
22 West 48 Street
New York, N.Y. 10036
catalog $1.00.

American Handicraft Company
1110 Mission Street
San Francisco, Cal.

Anchor Tool and Supply
231 Main Street
Chatham, N.J. 07928

Bead Game
505 North Fairfax Avenue
Los Angeles, Cal. 90036

C. E. Marshall Company
Box 7737
Chicago, Ill.

C. W. Somers and Company
387 Washington Street
Boston, Mass. 02108

Evans Finding Company, Inc.
55 John Street
Providence, R.I.

George Sassen
350 West 31 Street
New York, N.Y. 10001

Hagstoz and Son
709 Sansom Street
Philadelphia, Pa. 19106

Jewelart, Inc.
7753 Densmore Avenue, Department CW
Van Nuys, Cal. 91406
116-page catalog, $.10.

Karlan and Bleicher, Inc.
136 West 52 Street
New York, N.Y. 10019

Krieger and Dranoff
44 West 47 Street
New York, N.Y. 10036

Myron Tobac
23 West 47 Street
New York, N.Y. 10036

Newall Manufacturing Company
139 North Wabash Avenue
Chicago, Ill.

Northeast Bead Trading Company
12 Depot Street
Kennebunk, Me. 04043

William J. Orkin, Inc.
373 Washington Street
Boston, Mass.

R and B Artcraft Company
11019 South Vermont Avenue
Los Angeles, Cal. 90044

Sam Levin
236 West 26 Street
New York, N.Y. 10001

Sy Schweitzer and Company
P.O. Box 431
East Greenwich, R.I. 02818

Wildberg Brothers
635 South Hill Street
Los Angeles, Cal.
Also 742 Market Street
San Francisco, Cal.

Metal Suppliers

Allcraft Tool and Supply Company
22 West 48 Street
New York, N.Y. 10036
catalog $1.00.

American Handcraft Company
1110 Mission Street
San Francisco, Cal.

Anchor Tool and Supply Company
231 Main Street
Chatham, N.J. 07928

C. R. Hill
2734 West 11 Mile Road
Berkeley, Mich. 48072

Eastern Smelting and Refining Corporation
107 West Brookline Street
Boston, Mass.

Goldsmith Brothers Smelting and
    Refining Company
58 East Washington Street
Chicago, Ill.

Handy and Harman
850 Third Avenue
New York, N.Y. 10022
catalogs: "Silver for the Craftsman"; "An
    Introduction to Carat Gold for the
    Hand Craftsman."

Hauser and Miller
4011 Forest Park Boulevard
St. Louis, Mo.

Hoover and Strong, Inc.
119 West Tupper Street
Buffalo, N.Y. 14201
suppliers of fine-quality gold at reasonable prices.

Myron Tobac
23 West 47 Street
New York, N.Y. 10036

Patterson Brothers
15 Park Row
New York, N.Y.
copper, brass, and bronze.

R and B Artcraft Company
11019 South Vermont Avenue
Los Angeles, Cal. 90044

Revere Copper and Brass, Inc.
230 Park Avenue
New York, N.Y.

Riverside-Alloy Metal Division
H. K. Porter Company, Inc.
1021 Stuyvesant Avenue
Union, N.J.

Silvercraft Suppliers
P.O. Box 282
Rosemead, Cal. 91770
sterling and fine silver, sheet wire.

Southwest Smelting and Refining
Company
P.O. Box 2010
Dallas, Tex.

T. B. Hagstoz and Son
709 Sansom Street
Philadelphia, Pa. 19106

T. E. Conklin Brass and Copper
54 Lafayette Street
New York, N.Y. 10013

Wildberg Brothers
635 South Hill Street
Los Angeles, Cal.
Also 742 Market Street
San Francisco, Cal.

Wildent Corporation
2330 Beverly Boulevard
Los Angeles, Cal. 90057
carat golds.

William Dixon, Inc.
32 East Kinney Street
Newark, N.J.

Jewelry Materials and Supplies for Casting

Abbey Materials Corporation
116 West 29 Street
New York, N.Y. 10001

Alexander Saunders and Company
95 Bedford Street
New York, N.Y.

Casting Supply Company
107 Elmwood Avenue
Providence, R.I.

Casting Supply House
62 West 47 Street
New York, N.Y.

The Cleveland Dental Manufacturing
Company
Cleveland, O.

Craftools
1 Woodbridge Road
Woodridge, N.J.

Denton Precision Casting Company
665 Eddy Street
Providence, R.I. 02901

Dick Ells Company
908 Venice Boulevard
Los Angeles, Cal. 90015

C. R. Hill Company
2734 West 11 Mile Road
Berkeley, Mich. 49072

The Jelrus Company, Inc.
136 West 52 Street
New York, N.Y.

Kerr Dental Manufacturing Company
6081-6095 12th Street
Detroit, Mich.
wholesale only; will supply names and
addresses of local distributors.

S. S. White Dental Manufacturing
Company
55 East Washington Street
Chicago, Ill.

Custom Casting Services

Ala Casting Company
71 Fifth Avenue
New York, N.Y. 10003

Avnet Shaw Art Foundry
91 Commercial Street
Plainview, N.Y. 11803
specializes in fine sculpture casting in
bronze, stainless steel, and other metals
for professional and amateur artists.

Billanti Casting Company
64 West 48 Street
New York, N.Y. 10010
custom casting in lost wax process.

Casting Supply House Inc.
62 West 47 Street
New York, N.Y. 10036

Conrado Casting
49 West 47 Street
New York, N.Y. 10036

Dick Ells Company
908 Venice Boulevard
Los Angeles, Cal. 90015

Gesswein
235 Park Avenue South
New York, N.Y. 10006

Magic Circle Corporation
P.O. Box 22027
Seattle, Wash. 98122
custom casting in precious metals, brass,
and bronze; in most cases, casting is
done on a fixed fee basis plus cost of
metal, tools and hard to find items.

Romanoff Rubber Company
153-159 West 27 Street
New York, N.Y. 10001

Technical Specialties International, Inc.
487 Elliott Avenue West
Seattle, Wash. 98119

Tools (general jeweler's)

Abbey Materials
116 West 29 Street
New York, N.Y. 10001

Allcraft Tool and Supply
22 West 48 Street
New York, N.Y. 10036

Anchor Tool and Supply
231 Main Street
Chatham, N.J. 07928

C. R. Hill Company
2734 West 11 Mile Road
Berkeley, Mich. 48072

C. W. Somers and Company
387 Washington Street
Boston, Mass. 02108

Northeast Bead Trading Company
12 Depot Street
Kennebunk, Me. 04043

William Dixon, Inc.
32 East Kinney Street
Newark, N.J.

GENERAL LAPIDARY
(*Rough material, Machines,
Supplies, etc.*)

Ace Lapidary Supply
6015 Sepulvedo Boulevard
Van Nuys, Cal.
custom slabbing and polishing, all supplies.

Allen Lapidary Equipment Manufacturing Company
P.O. Box 75411
Oklahoma City, Okla. 73107
cabochon combination machines.

Arrow Profile Company
P.O. Box 38
St. Clair Shores, Mich. 48080
manufacturers of Sapphire faceter; publishes a monthly information sheet, *The Facetier.*

Baskin and Sons, Inc.
732 Union Avenue
Middlesex, N.J. 08846

Beacon Engineering
Rothsay, Minn. 56579
manufacturers of Beacon Star grinding units, saws, tumblers, vibrating laps, and recirculating pumps.

Brad's Rock Shop
911 W. Nine Mile Road
Ferndale (Detroit), Mich. 48220
lapidary equipment and materials.

Covington Engineering Corporation
112 First Street
Redlands, Cal. 92373
one of the largest and oldest firms supplying grinding equipment, saws, tumblers, slab, polishers, drills, spheremaker, lapping units, faceters, tuptype multipurpose units, grinding wheels, saws.

Diamond-Pro, Unlimited
P.O. Box 25
Monterey, Cal. 91752
sintered diamond tools.

Earth Treasures
Box 1267
Galesburg, Ill. 61401
manufacturers of B and I.

Fundy Rocks and Minerals
RR 3 Street, Stephen
New Brunswick, Canada
cabochon slabs in agate and other minerals.

Geode Industries
106-108 West Main
U.S. Highway 34
New London, Ia.
vibratory tumblers and lapidary equipment.

Gillman's
Hellertown, Pa. 18055

Henry B. Graves Co.
1190 South Old Dixie H'way
Delray Beach, Fla. 33444
Graves faceter.

Grieger's, Inc.
1633 East Walnut Street
Pasadena, Cal. 91109

Highland Park Manufacturing
Division of Musto Industries
12600 Chadron Avenue
Hawthorne, Cal. 90205
grinding equipment, saws, vibrating laps, belt sanders, faceting units; will refer you to closest dealer.

Hillquist
1545 North West 49 Street
Seattle, Wash. 98107
amateur lapidary equipment.

Francis Hoover
12449 Chandler Boulevard
North Hollywood, Cal. 91607
unusual stones, cut and rough material.

Hoover and Strong
111 West Tupper Street
Buffalo, N.Y. 14201
electroplating equipment.

Lapidabrade
8 East Eagle Road
Havertown, Pa. 19038

Lee Lapidaries
3425 West 117 Street
Cleveland, O. 44111
Lee faceter.

M.D.R. Manufacturing Company
4853 North West Jefferson Boulevard
Los Angeles, Cal. 90016
M.D.R. Master II faceter; publishes a two-volume compendium of most popular facet cuts and how to cut them.

M. K. Diamond Products
Highland Park Manufacturing
12600 Chadron Avenue
Hawthorne, Cal. 90025
suppliers of some of the finest lapidary equipment.

Murray American Corporation
15 Commerce Street
Chatham, N.J. 07928
tumbling materials.

Nogalee Manufacturing Company
435 Grand Avenue
Nogalee, Ariz. 85201
producers of automatic cabochon grinder.

O'Brien's
1116 North Wilcox
Hollywood, Cal. 90038
equipment for amateur.

Plummer's Minerals
4720 Point Loma Avenue
San Diego, Cal. 92107
stones, cut and rough materials.

Raytech
P.O. Box 84A
Stafford Springs, Conn. 06076
diamond compounds, Ray-Tilt Gem Maker, diamond saws.

Jack V. Schuller
P.O. Box 420
Park Ridge, Ill. 60068
diamond compounds, diamond laps.

Scott-Murray Manufacturing Company
Box 25077
Northgate Station
Seattle, Wash. 98125
excellent six-sided all-rubber tumblers and tumbling machines.

Shipley's Mineral House
Gem Village
Bayfield, Colo. 81122
lapidary equipment and supplies.

Stanley Lapidary
503-F South Grand Avenue
Santa Ana, Cal. 92705
Ultra-Tech faceter.

Technicraft Lapidaries
2248 Broadway
New York, N.Y. 10024

3-M Company
Building 224-55
3-M Centre
St. Paul, Minn. 55101
lapidary machines, diamond blades, disks, belts, grits.

Universal Lapidary Division
495 West John Street
Hicksville, N.Y. 11801

William Munz
P.O. Box 639
Nome, Ak. 99726
suppliers of Alaska nephrite jade.

Knitting and Crochet

She seeketh wool, and flax,
and worketh willingly with her hands.
—*Proverbs* 31:13

101 WAYS TO IMPROVE YOUR KNITTING. by Barbara Abbey. The Viking Press, New York, 1969. 61 pages. illustrations. $2.00.

This is not a manual of knitting how-tos, but rather a collection of suggestions for materials, methods, and techniques that will help the knitter avoid the common pitfalls of knitting and develop good knitting habits. The author provides hints for buying needles: they should be precision tapered, although technically you can knit on wooden dowels. Procedure: When you need a gauge, never use a pliable measure or hold the swatch in your hand, and never let another person work your swatch, nor should you work a swatch for anyone else.

The suggestions for working knitted pieces are accompanied by good diagrams and elucidate many instructions for neckline division, picking up stitches, and neckline shaping. For example, the main points to remember about picking up stitches are: pick up the necessary number according to the instructions. If no instructions are given, pick up according to your gauge and do not get too close to the edge. To determine the number to be picked up, measure the edge where the stitches are to be taken, multiply the number of inches by the gauge used in the body of the sweater, and use the results obtained for the number of stitches. If, for example, one edge of the V on a V-necked sweater measures 10 inches, and you have worked the body on an 8-inch stitch gauge, pick up about 80 stitches along the edge.

KNITTING WITHOUT TEARS. by Elizabeth Zimmerman. Charles Scribner's Sons, New York, 1971. 120 pages. illustrations, photographs, bibliography, index. paperback edition $3.95.

The "opinionated knitter" shares some of her opinions with knitters already acquainted with the rudiments of the craft. She reviews fundamental techniques and offers some new ways to cast on, presenting everything with her own particular slant.

Have you been struggling to knit tightly in order to make your work look neat? Forget it. Are you a habitually tight knitter? Try to kick the habit. The author admits that loose knitting tends to make stitches uneven, but so what? If you wanted the look of a machine-made sweater you would buy

one way to purl

A better way to purl

one. Anyway, she muses, a few washings will do wonders for an erratically knit sweater, so relax—and have fun!

THE COMPLETE BOOK OF KNITTING. by Barbara Abbey. The Viking Press, New York, 1972. 231 pages. illustrations, photographs, index. $12.95.

This book contains two hundred patterns, plus a comprehensive treatment of the basic stitches and procedures of knitting, and even gives eight diffrent ways to cast on. The written text is adequate, but the diagrams are small and unclear and take a lot of puzzling over before they can be comprehended. This is a shame, because otherwise the book is quite good. Perhaps the amateur knitter rather than the raw beginner would benefit by the information the author has to give.

ADVENTURES IN KNITTING. by Barbara Aytes. Doubleday and Company, Garden City, New York, 1968. 179 pages. illustrations, photographs. $5.95.

A brief section of general instructions intended as a memory refresher for the suddenly bewildered knitter is the extent of the technical, how-to information of this book. The adventures are directed toward the knitter who is at least an advanced beginner. The 106 patterns presented by the author are arranged in order from simple to complex, with enough variety in each category to keep the slightly experienced, average, and advanced knitter happy in their own territory.

Many of the stitch patterns, such as eyelet chevron and Battersea are quite ancient; others, such as Bows in Rows, were designed for this collection.

The patterns are varied and range from prosaic to beautiful; they can also be adapted for garments other than the somewhat dated and uninteresting ones supplied by the author.

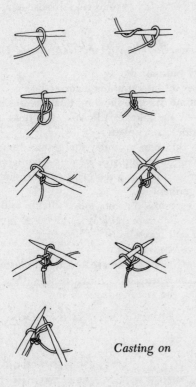

Casting on

GOLDEN HANDS COMPLETE BOOK OF KNITTING AND CROCHET. Random House, 1973. illustrations (some color), photographs (some color), index. $10.00.

An excellent source of both beginning how-to information and attractive, contemporary patterns. The step-by-step instructions are accompanied by multicolored diagrams and photographs and are exceptionally clear and easy to follow. Each new technique is reinforced by a project which allows the new knitter to have fun while learning.

In addition to a large selection of projects, from baby booties to evening gowns, the book contains a wide variety of stitch patterns and motifs encompassing styles from Aran knitting to Irish lace.

Each project contains standard finishing details and directions, and a guide as to whether or not the yarn can be pressed.

During the Middle Ages, a man was apprenticed to a guild for six years before he could become a master knitter. He would spend the first three years learning the fundamentals of knitting, and the next three studying the techniques of other countries. After his six years were over, he was given thirteen weeks in which to create and complete a woolen shirt, a pair of woolen socks with Swedish clocks, and an original and intricately designed carpet. These he submitted for examination to the masters of the guild, who would then decide if he could become one of them.

KNITTING MADE EASY. by Barbara Aytes. Doubleday and Company, Garden City, New York, 1971. 194 pages. illustrations, photographs. $4.95. paperback edition (Pocket Books, New York, 1971) $.95.

The first five chapters of this book offer instructions for the basic stitches of knitting. Each chapter is followed by directions for simple items which can be made using only the knowledge of knitting previously acquired. These reinforcing projects are a good idea not only because they allow the beginner to practice new skills, but also from the point of view of morale. Learning can often be discouraging unless the novice can see some immediate results.

The second half of the book features projects of greater complexity, but the designs are rather uninspired, and the youthful knitter probably would not want to create any of the garments suggested.

Unfortunately, the instructions for the stitches are accompanied by poor photographs, and the steps involved in any one operation are not clear. Beginners who would like to turn out simple items as they go along might want to use this book with a better manual of techniques.

Terms and Abbreviations Found in British Print But Not Usually Found in U.S. Print

British	American
Plain Intake	—K 2 tog
Purled Intake	—P 2 tog
Pull over one-Take in	—SKP
Sl and b-Slip and Bind	—SKP
Take in with 3 sts	—Sl 1, K2 tog, and psso (SK2togP)
Wool forward (wl fwd)	—yarn over; *or,* yo; *or,* O
Plain intake taken from behind	—K2 tog from the back (K2togb)
Make 1 (M 1)	—increase, either yarn over or pick up 1 st from between 2 sts
Stocking Stitch (S.S.)	—Stockinette Stitch
Welt	—a finish as applied, either ribbing or Quaker Stitch

Source: THE COMPLETE BOOK OF KNITTING. by Barbara Abbey.

KNITTING DICTIONARY, revised edition. compiled by *Mon Tricot* and translated by Margaret Hamilton-Hunt. Crown Publishers, New York, 1972. 162 pages. illustrations, photographs (some color). $3.95. paperback edition $1.98.

In this book, nine hundred stitches, patterns, and definitions are arranged in alphabetical order. This means that the instructions don't appear in the order they would ordinarily. For example, instructions for knitting various types of buttonholes appear before instructions for casting on.

The dictionary is quite complete and provides a valuable reference source for experienced knitters.

KNIT, PURL AND DESIGN. by Annette Feldman. Harper and Row, Publishers, New York, 1972. 146 pages. illustrations, photographs, index. $7.95.

This book offers a friendly discussion of elementary knit design. The author works sample problems for an afghan, a sweater with ribbed waistline, and a man's jacket. The major portion of the book consists of patterns, all of which note their stitch multiple. The third division, a knitter's guide, explains about gauge and ways of determining the number of stitches that must be cast on. It contains illustrated instructions for casting on, knitting, purling, and other basic operations. Knitting on four needles and knitting on a round needle are just briefly noted, as is finishing information.

MARY THOMAS'S KNITTING BOOK. by Mary Thomas. Dover Publications, New York, 1972. 356 pages. illustrations, index. paperback edition $2.50.

This is a reissue of a 1934 edition in the style of the time, which some may find amusing and others annoying. The diagrams are small but fairly clear, and the instructions and scope are remarkably thorough. Countless patterns are presented, including faggot stitch patterns and lace. Also there are instructions for making seamless garments and accessories; a chapter on pattern making; another on sundries, including the tambour stitch, eyelet embroidery, and filet darning; a chart of French knitting terms; and a texture index featuring suggested uses for textured patterns. It is a complete reference library in itself for the amateur knitter who desires to increase stitch and pattern knowledge.

KNITTING. by Marjorie Collins. Drake Publishers, New York, 1974. 96 pages. illustrations, photographs (some color), index. $6.95.

This is a book designed with the beginner in mind. It presents a good introduction to standard yarn and needles, although it fails to really clarify basic stitching techniques. The diagrams are inadequate and do not follow each step in the written instructions. However, the pattern instructions provide an excellent start for new knitters. They are very clear and list all materials at the beginning. On the other hand, the selection is quite limited and contains only patterns for a baby's cardigan, suit, and trousers; a child's dress; a teen-age dress and beret; a man's sweater; and a basic sweater and skirt (which are not illustrated).

AMERICA'S KNITTING BOOK. by Gertrude Taylor. Charles Scribner's Sons, 1968. 289 pages. illustrations, photographs, index. $9.95.

This book offers a comprehensive and clear introduction to the fundamentals of knitting, including step-by-step instructions and diagrams on how to knit, how to follow pattern directions, and how to finish and block. The author demonstrates how a pattern can be adapted, and what changes should be made in any pattern before starting work. Also featured are chapters on knitting for infants and children, knitting with sequins and beads, and knitted accessories.

What Makes So Many Hand-Knits Look Homemade

1. Baggy bottom ribbing
2. Sleeves set into armhole incorrectly
3. Bound off stitches showing in the seams at the shoulder
4. "Picked up stitches" leaving big holes or where the two sides aren't even
5. Skirts that cup in under the seat or tummy
6. Knitting on wrong size needles—too large needles give a hard texture, also too large needles give a sleazy look to a garment
7. Seams made with long loose stitches will have gaps
8. Stitches improperly woven together in the Kitchener stitch will leave holes
9. Pig eye buttonholes
10. Ribbon facings that are too tight causing the sweater front to draw, or, ribbon facings that are too loose causing the sweater front to sag.

Source: AMERICA'S KNITTING BOOK. by Gertrude Taylor.

KNIT TO FIT: A COMPREHENSIVE GUIDE TO HAND AND MACHINE KNITTING AND CROCHET. by Ida Riley Duncan. (revised, enlarged edition of *The Knitter's Bible*.) Liveright, New York, 1970. 254 pages. illustrations, photographs, index. $8.95.

A one-volume edition of a forty-nine-lesson correspondence course given by the author's Progressive School of Knitting Design. At the outset, the author states uncategorically that no matter what the reasons may be for undertaking this course, proper development depends upon the reader becoming style-conscious, figure-conscious, color-conscious, and personality-conscious.

The course is designed for an experienced knitter who wishes to diagram and chart his own fashions. Diagramming is the drawing of each part of a garment—back, front, sleeves, etc.—and charting is the putting in of necessary figures for the shaping of each part. Shaping by hand and machine are pretty much the same process, except that the hand knitter can use both straight and circular needles, whereas only very expensive knitting machines have circular knitting.

The author insists that the garment should be designed the best way possible and then altered to suit the particular machine. The important thing for a designer is to get away from the cheaper machine look, even when this involves assisting the machine by hand.

The patterns in this book range from bikinis to fitted weskits, and each section contains a knitting problem, the answer to which is fully charted at the back of the book. In addition to the instructions for pattern design and "scientific knitting," the author devotes a chapter to operating a knitting shop.

MARY THOMAS'S BOOK OF KNITTING PATTERNS. by Mary Thomas. Dover Publications, New York, 1972. 320 pages. illustrations, index. paperback edition $3.00.

This reprint of the 1943 sequel to *Mary Thomas's Knitting Book* features 297 stitch patterns, with descriptions of the difficulties and uses of each. It is an excellent encyclopedia with the characteristic Thomas touch.

THE COMPLETE BOOK OF PROGRESSIVE KNITTING, revised edition. by Ida Riley Duncan. Liveright, New York, 1971. 384 pages. illustrations, photographs, index. $6.95. paperback edition $2.75.

This book begins with a history of knitting and an excellent discussion of different yarns and their suitabilities for a variety of items. The author is not concerned with teaching the fundamentals of knitting but, rather, the fundamentals of garment knitting. She presents information of a technical nature on the elements of construction, materials, and design and insures the success of each garment by listing a formula that should be followed. She also presents fashion information on color and design to suit the individual complexion and body type.

The Stocking and the Garter

The gartered stocking has always been a feature in the Heraldic devices of knitting guilds. This is because it symbolized the knitters' warp and weft, not because it had any connection with their occupation—they might knit gloves, hats, coats, or trousers, either in addition to or without knitting stockings at all.

Source: MARY THOMAS'S BOOK OF KNITTING PATTERNS, by Mary Thomas.

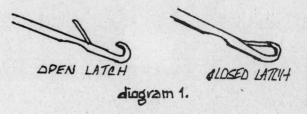

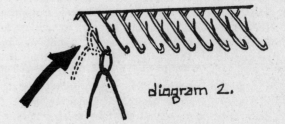

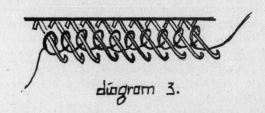

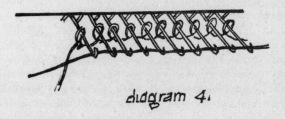

Casting on using a knitting machine

Interview

Susan Toplitz has been knitting since she was four. She was taught by her grandmother, "one of those old European ladies, didn't speak any English but she sure knew how to knit." Susan regarded knitting as a hobby, something she did in her spare time. It is only recently that knitting has become a profession for her. She earned her Bachelor of Fine Arts degree in crafts—pottery, woodworking, and so on; knitting was not part of her academic curriculum.

For a long time, fiber—any of the fiber crafts but especially weaving—has been considered crafts, but knitting and crochet have only recently been accepted. Even in places like the Museum of Contemporary Crafts they haven't really accepted it; they still don't want to get involved with it but they are. They still don't like to admit that it's a craft. It's like the exhibit they had on quilts. They're finally getting around to saying these quilts are a craft. They're no longer household items people made out of necessity. They're something of beauty.

I think all the crafts go through phases. Crochet is very big now—it has been for a while—and knitting is going through a lull. A lot of younger people are doing crochet. It's much simpler to do and you can just pick it up and work on it. Most people learn the techniques of knitting from someone older and they don't think of it as a young person's craft. It's a strange way of thinking, but most people consider crochet as something that can be very creative, something you can do without a pattern, something you can make sculptural, you can make different shapes and sizes out of crochet; but knitting they think of only as clothing, and it's very difficult to get them out of that.

I teach creative knitting. That is, instead of following a pattern, I teach people to figure out how to make their own sweaters or dresses (most people are interestd in learning how to knit clothing). I teach them shaping and using yarns together, mixing yarns to get different textures, and using things they wouldn't ordinarily use, like package twine.

A lot of older people take my course. People who know how to knit but are afraid of getting away from a pattern. They just say, "I can't do it." It's not hard. It's just common sense, which unfortunately many people seem not to have. It's also more fun. I could never work from a pattern any more. I've probably even forgotten how to use one. I'm so used to writing up my own instructions and reading my own Greek.

I worked for *Ladies Home Journal Needlecrafts* for a year and one of the functions I had was answering the obscene phone calls and letters we'd get from people saying, "What happened to the rest of the instructions?" and "You made a mistake." Ninety-nine percent of the time it wasn't the fault of the magazine; people just didn't read it right. If you think in terms of shapes instead of a pattern, you won't run into those problems even if you want to use a pattern.

You can learn to knit from a book, if it's a well-done book. I'm very visual and I can learn anything from looking at a picture, but if I have to read a lot of copy, forget it! The only book I ever really use is Barbara Walker's *Second Treasury of Knitting Patterns*.

I don't think anyone is using knitting to its fullest potential. Mary Walker Phillips' pieces are certainly the most outstanding, but I'd like to see her progress into something more sculptural, more three-dimensional. I haven't been doing any sculptural forms right now. I've been thinking about it and maybe about applying for a grant. The sweaters have been bringing me sort of an income so I really don't have the time to do sculptural pieces. I have hundreds of ideas, but it's a matter of getting the time and being financially set.

I get my income from teaching knitting and embroidery and I sell designs for sweaters to magazines. I don't sell sweaters to retail stores any more because I found that it just wasn't worth it. I sold some to Bendel's and by the time I deducted for my yarns I made thirty dollars for a week's work while they were making seventy dollars.

Some people are just too stupid to know how to sell a sweater. They always ask me, "Well, how did you get started in magazines? How did you get your foot in the door?" If they can't figure that out—I mean, I made a phone call and made an appointment! If you're not aggressive enough, you're not going to be able to sell. Also, most people don't know who their audience is. Just because a certain store sells handmade sweaters doesn't mean that your type of handmade sweater should be sold there. A store might carry very sleek, sophisticated garments and you might be making some far-out, sculptural clothes that would do better in Greenwich Village.

A lot of people are unrealistic in their pricing demands. You really have to give your work a thorough examination and you really have got to be honest. There's a certain average, a certain amount that people will pay. A sweater done on large needles with very thick yarn will sell for less than one done on very tiny needles with extrafine yarn because there's a substantial difference in the amount of time required to complete it. But a craftsperson will never get paid back for the work they do. Lots of people don't realize that and they're putting two-hundred-dollar price tags on a sweater. Nobody is going to spend that much. These people have got to start being realistic and thinking about how much they can get, not how much they'd like. They have to get paid back for the materials of course and *some* of their time, but a craftsperson will never really get paid back for *all* the time they put in.

Knitted pillow, Susan Toplitz

STEP-BY-STEP KNITTING. by Mary Walker Phillips. Golden Press. 95 pages. illustrations, photographs (some color), suppliers list, bibliography. $2.50.

The instructions presented and the accompanying diagrams are quite good and the book contains an ample number of projects. However, the major problem of the book is that it is incomplete. There is no information on changing colors (except row by row), blocking, or finishing.

CREATIVE KNITTING: A NEW ART FORM. by Mary Walker Phillips. Van Nostrand Reinhold, New York, 1971. 119 pages, illustrations, photographs (some color), suppliers list, bibliography, index. $10.95.

In this book, knitters and other craftsmen are called to an awareness of knitting as an independent art style. Knitters must divest themselves of the long-accepted convention of developing someone else's designs and begin to see knitting as a promising and new experience in creative expression.

Ms. Phillips attempts to encourage knitters to apply their basic skills in new, more innovative directions by emphasizing the ways to alter, combine, and experiment with traditional stitches to achieve totally new results. She presents easy-to-follow instructions and explicit diagrams for many of the more unconventional stitches such as horizontal stitches, plaited basket, bell frilling, and lace diadem patterns. The elementary steps of knitting are not described. Particular attention is paid to the various yarn-over techniques and methods of increasing and decreasing for open lacework.

Creative knitting admits the use of many untraditional materials such as leather, fiber glass, straw, and silk. Most conventional knitters are unfamiliar with the vagaries of

using such fabrics, and so the author discusses the use of experimental materials as well as recommending ways of knitting and combining yarns. Special materials also require fastidious blocking, and Ms. Phillips devotes a chapter to this subject, which, though important in any type of knitting, is crucial in creative knitting.

This book is full of photographs featuring Ms. Phillips' creations. These are not only pleasant to look at but they offer a learning experience as well. The author assists the reader in analyzing the pictures so that the progressions of pattern and stitch are clearly visible.

THE CRAFT OF CABLE-STITCH KNITTING. by Barbara G. Walker. Charles Scribner's Sons, New York, 1971. 128 pages. photographs. paperback edition $2.95.

A glossary of terms and abbreviations, the book also contains photographs and instructions for a number of cables and cable-stitch patterns, which differ from cables in that they are intended primarily for use all over a fabric rather than in isolated panels. These are all reprinted from the cable sections in the author's previous books, *A Treasury of Knitting Patterns* and *A Second Treasury of Knitting Patterns*, and are useful because they provide a complete guide to the subject in one inexpensive volume.

There is also a special section on designing fisherman sweaters, a task which the author demonstrates is not nearly as difficult as many people seem to think. All that need be done is to find the number of stitches needed to reach halfway around the wearer's body by taking the gauge of a cable swatch, or the average of several different swatches, and multiply it by the inches across the front or back of the sweater. Then the knitter should select the patterns desired and mark off the panels on graph paper beginning with the center. The designer may choose as many cables as he wishes until the stitch allotment has been fulfilled, but he must keep in mind that at least one knit stitch must be inserted between panels to set them off.

KNITTING FROM THE TOP. by Barbara G. Walker. Charles Scribner's Sons, New York, 1972. 160 pages. illustrations, photographs (some color), index. $9.95.

The author asserts that knitting from the top is as easy as conventional knitting because it assures a perfect fit with a minimum of calculation. Length measurements are the trickiest part of knitwear, and designers may plan the upper portion of a garment to fit a body shaped differently from that of the potential wearer. If the upper portion of a garment is too long or too short, no matter how carefully the lower portion has been figured out, the look of the finished piece will be wrong. When knitters begin at the top, the neck or waist portion on which the whole garment hangs, and on which all other measurements depend, is already there and can be tried on at any time.

Knitting from the top can also increase the life of any article because it enables the knitter to make easy renovations necessitated by a growing spurt or change in fashion.

Ms. Walker believes that a knitter's primary objective should be to clothe the body and not to solve mathematical equations, and her directions reflect this opinion. The rambling and digressive approach she takes is motivated by the desire to help the reader understand not just what to do, but why it should be done.

CHARTED KNITTING PATTERNS. by Barbara G. Walker. Charles Scribner's Sons, New York, 1971. 289 pages. illustrations, photographs (some color), index. $14.95.

Charting is frequently used for all sorts of patterns in Europe but only for the Fair Isle type of color knitting in America. Americans seem to rely primarily upon the written word, not always a very practical approach. Charting is an efficient way to convey knitting directions, especially for long and complicated patterns requiring a great deal of space to write out. Moreover, a chart is actually easier to use, at least according to Ms. Walker. It can be deciphered at a glance and gives to the knitter a pictorial idea of what the finished work will look like. Charting is also an aid to the knitter who wishes to design his own fashions or alter a preconceived design; an entire garment with every stitch in place can be charted on a large sheet of graph paper. Each square of the graph is used to represent one stitch. If the gauge on a particular sweater is eight, then eight squares on the chart would equal one inch. In this way, any part of the garment can be measured long before yarn touches needle. Similarly, shaping can be represented by widening or narrowing the chart at the appropriate heights, determined by counting squares vertically.

Reading a chart is not difficult, but it does take some getting used to, and knitters familiar with reading patterns might justifiably argue that it's not worth the time. However, the author provides a complete list of general symbols, symbols for increases and decreases, and an additional key for charting cable stitches. The cable stitch has been notorious for its incomprehensibility in charting systems, because there are more than a hundred possible ways of working a cable crossing, and any system is hard pressed to spread itself over them all. The author offers a new system designed to solve some of the old problems by making a picture of the cables. Knit ribs are outlined, and when they cross each other, the outlines show where the cabled stitches go, how many over, and in what direction.

In addition to offering instructions on the reading and construction of knitting charts, the book features over 350 original patterns and chart notation for their execution.

Knitted lace sampler tablecloth, Barbara G. Walker
Photo by Werner P. Brodde

SAMPLER KNITTING. by Barbara G. Walker. Charles Scribner's Sons, 1973. 178 pages. illustrations, photographs (some color). $9.95.

Sampler knitting is a very visually interesting form of knitting because it presents different combinations of patterns and/or colors within the framework of a single knitted article.

This book presents over a hundred new patterns designed by the author which can be used to make any number of knitted articles. The inclusion of the knitting patterns, how-

Knitted lace sampler bedspread, Barbara G. Walker
Photo by Werner P. Brodde

A SECOND TREASURY OF KNITTING PATTERNS. by Barbara G. Walker. Charles Scribner's Sons, New York, 1970. 398 pages. photographs (some color), bibliography, index. $15.00.

This is a continuation of the work begun in the first *Treasury* and probably the best, most inclusive pattern reference volume there is.

Knitted mosaic sampler afghan—original design in the new mosaic technique created by Barbara G. Walker

ever, is only a means to the author's real goal: to teach basic principles of knitting geometry so that the reader can create and not just copy. Sampler knitting allows anyone who can knit, purl, increase, decrease, make a yarn-over, and use a cable needle to achieve a truly personal expression of creativity.

A TREASURY OF KNITTING PATTERNS. by Barbara G. Walker. Charles Scribner's Sons, New York, 1968. 301 pages. photographs, index. $10.00.

The author presents over five hundred patterns, accompanied by photographs and descriptive text giving information about origin and history, use, and some helpful hints for working. All of the patterns can be done by anyone who can knit, purl, make a yarn-over, and use a cable needle. Even someone unfamiliar with pattern knitting can gain experience on some of the simpler patterns, such as the knit-purl combinations, before moving ahead to the more complex color changes, fancy textures, and lace and eyelet patterns.

I could name a hundred crocheters for every knitter I know.

—Susan Toplitz

ADVENTURES IN CROCHETING. by Barbara Aytes. Doubleday and Company, Garden City, New York, 1972. 244 pages. illustrations, photographs. $7.95.

Brief instructions for a few basic stitches are given but there are no accompanying diagrams, so they are virtually useless for a beginner. The major portion of the book consists of one hundred patterns for crochet and selected projects. The projects themselves are not particularly exciting; the usual run of covered coat hangers, three styles of slippers, and rather old-fashioned blouses. An additional chapter suggests ways of using leftover yarn to make flower gift wrap decorations.

Crocheted pillow, Pamela Veley

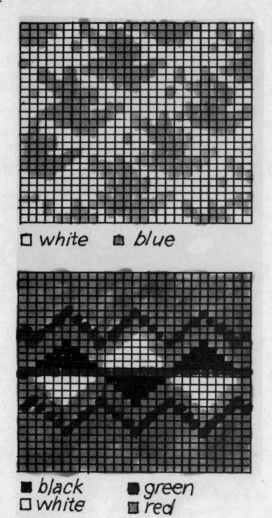

□ white ▪ blue

▪ black ▪ green
□ white ▪ red

Colored jacquard patterns

CREATIVE CROCHET. by Nicki H. Edson and Arlene Stimmel. Watson-Guptill Publications, New York, 1973. 143 pages. illustrations, photographs. $10.75.

This book is inspirational in its revelations about the amazing things crocheters can do in textural and three-dimensional forms. Some of the works pictured are sculptural, some tapestrylike, and some are funny, like the outfits for animals and the great coats for potentates. All this and clear diagrams, too!

NEW DESIGN IN CROCHET. by Clinton D. Mackenzie. Von Nostrand Reinhold, New York, 1973. 144 pages. illustrations, photographs (some color), bibliography, index. $9.95.

This is an excellent source for both technical and inspirational material. The many photographs not only illustrate points of text, but encourage the reader to see the tremendous potential of this craft. There are no projects to make, and the objects depicted are art objects, not clothing or household items.

The section on materials is exceptionally good; photographs are used to demonstrate the effects produced by the use of different fibers.

The author supplies concise instructions and clear diagrams for stitching procedures. The techniques are presented according to the degree of difficulty most novices have in mastering them, rather than in more conventional arrangement. Thus, the slip stitch is introduced after the triple triple crochet stitch. There is detailed informaton on gauging, shaping, and finishing, and a chart of comparative British-American terminology since these vary in many instances. The American single crochet, for example, is called the double crochet in England. In addition to demonstrating the traditional methods and techniques of crochet stitchery, the author offers a number of alternative approaches. These are the result of his experience in handling modern materials and materials that may be employed in the creation of more avant-garde crochet pieces but not ordinarily associated with the craft.

Mon Tricot Knit and Crochet
c/o Paris-Match, Inc.
22 East 67 Street
New York, N.Y. 10021
Monthly. $12.00 a year. knit and crochet patterns.

Knitting and Crochet Suppliers

Check your yellow pages for the nearest supplier. Look under needlework or art needlework. Or contact the following companies for mail orders.

Al Rodriguez
736 Sutter Street
San Diego, Cal. 92103
brochure.
handmade crochet hooks.

Arachne Webworks
2390 North West Thurman
Portland, Ore. 92710
brochure; yarn samples $.35.

J. Hyslop Bathgate and Company
Victoria Works
Galashiels, Scotland TD1 1NY 2642
catalog.

Black Sheep Weaving and Craft Supply
318 South West Second Street
Corvallis, Ore. 97330
catalog $.75.

Boutique Margot
26 West 54 Street
New York, N.Y. 10019
brochure.

Briggs and Little Woolen Mills Ltd.
Harvey Station
New Brunswick, Canada
catalog.

Cambridge Wools Ltd.
Box 2572
Auckland, New Zealand
brochure.

Clicking Needles Studio
104 Fifth Avenue
New York, N.Y. 10011
catalog.

Colonial Woolen Mills, Inc.
6501 Barberton Avenue
Cleveland, O. 44102
catalog; sample charge $.50.

Conlin Yarns
P.O. Box 11812
Philadelphia, Pa. 19128
catalog; samples $.50.

Contessa Yarns
P.O. Box 37
Lebanon, Conn. 06249
brochure $.25.

Craft Yarns of Rhode Island
603 Mineral Spring Avenue
Pawtucket, R.I. 02862
catalog.

Creative Handweavers
P.O. Box 26480
Los Angeles, Cal. 90026
catalog; sample charge $2.00. undyed, unbleached wool available.

Dharma Trading Company
1952 University Avenue
Berkeley, Cal. 94704
catalog; sample charge $.50.

Edgemont Yarn Service
RR 2, Box 14
Maysville, Ky. 41506
brochure.

Eskimo Yarns, Inc.
81 Essex Street
New York, N.Y. 10002
catalog; samples $.50.

Frederick J. Fawcett, Inc.
129 South Street
Boston, Mass. 02111
catalog $1.00.

Gager's Handcraft
3516 Beltline Boulevard
St. Louis, Minn. 55416
catalog $1.00.
knitting frames.

Gallagher Spinning and Weaving Tools
318 Pacheco Avenue
Santa Cruz, Cal. 95060
catalog.
handmade crochet hooks.

Greentree Ranch Wools
Countryside Handweavers
163 North Carter Lake Road
Loveland, Colo. 80537
brochure; samples, prices vary.

Handcaft Wools
Box 378
Streetsville, Ontario, Canada
catalog; samples $.50 to $3.00.

Handspun Wool
P.O. Box 132
Monroe, Ore. 97456
catalog; samples $.50.

The Handweaver
111 East Napa Street
Sonoma, Cal. 95476
catalog; samples $.50.

Harmony Acres Studio
BAG. 1550
St. Norbert, Manitoba, ROG 2HO, Canada
brochure; samples $.50.

Harrisville Designs, Inc.
P.O. Box 51
Harrisville, N.H. 03450
catalog $.25.

Henry's Attic
81 Park Terrace West
New York, N.Y. 10034
catalog $.25.
undyed, unbleached wool available.

House of Kleen
P.O. Box 265
Hope Valley, R.I. 02830
Catalog: Samples $.35.

J. L. Hammett Company
Hammett Place
Braintree, Mass. 02184
catalog.
knitting frames.

Kessenich Looms and Yarn Shop
7463 Harwood Avenue
Wauwatosa, Wis. 53213
catalog.

KM Yarn Company
18695 Wyoming Avenue
Detroit, Mich. 48221
catalog.
undyed and unbleached wool available.

Macrame and Weaving Supply Company
63 East Adams Street
Chicago, Ill. 60603
catalog $.50.
undyed, unbleached wool.

The Makings
2001 University Avenue
Berkeley, Cal. 94704
catalog.

Metallic Novelty Yarns, Inc.
252 Marion Street
Brooklyn, N.Y. 11233
samples, prices vary.

Naturalcraft
2199 Bancroft Way
Berkeley, Cal. 94704
catalog $.50.

Needleart Guild
2729 Oakwood North East
Grand Rapids, Mich. 49505
catalog $.50.

Northwest Handcraft House, Ltd.
110 West Esplanade
North Vancouver, British Columbia,
Canada
catalog; sample cards $.50 to $2.00.

The Ohio Wool Growers Association
3900 Groves Road
P.O. Box 27068
Columbus, O. 43227
Newsletter.
undyed, unbleached wool available.

Old Mill Yarn
P.O. Box 115
Eaton Rapids, Mich. 48827
brochure; samples.

Osma Gallinger Tod
319 Mendoza Avenue
Coral Gables, Fla. 33134
brochure.
handmade knitting needles.

Robin and Russ Handweavers
533 North Adams Street
McMinnville, Ore. 97128
catalog; samples $1.75.

School Products Company, Inc.
312 East 23 Street
New York, N.Y. 10010
catalog.

The Sheep Village
2005 Bridgeway
Sausalito, Cal. 94965
yarn samples $.25.

Small Fortune
145 East Main Street
Tustin, Cal. 92680
catalog.

Starlet Yarns, Inc.
114-10 Rockaway Boulevard
Rockaway Park, N.Y. 11694

Stavros Kouyoymoutzakis
166 Kalokerinou Avenue
Iraklion, Crete, Greece
catalog.
undyed, unbleached wool available.

Straw Into Gold
5550 College Avenue
Oakland, Cal. 94618
catalog.
fiber samples $1.00 plus stamped self-
addressed envelope.

Studio Yarn Farms, Inc.
10024 14th Avenue South West
Seattle, Wash. 98146
catalog.
knitting machines.

Suma
P.O. Box 9273
Berkeley, Cal. 94709
catalog; samples $1.00.

Sutton Yarns
2654 Yonge Street
Toronto, Ontario, Canada
catalog.

Texere Yarns
9 Peckover Street
Bradford, Yorkshire, England BDI 5BD
catalog; samples $1.00.

Textile Crafts
856 North Genesee Avenue
P.O. Box 3216
Los Angeles, Cal. 90028
catalog.
handmade crochet hooks.

William Condon and Sons Ltd.
P.O. Box 129
Charlottetown, Prince Edward Island,
Canada
catalog.
undyed, unbleached wool available.

Yarn Box
P.O. Box 7342
Little Rock, Ark. 72207
catalog $.25.

Lace-making

There is still some distinction between Machine-made and Hand-made Lace. I will suppose that distinction so far done away with that, a pattern once invested, you can spin Lace as fast as they now do thread. Everybody then might wear not only Lace collars, but Lace gowns. Do you think that, when everybody could wear them, everybody would be proud of wearing them? A spider may perhaps be rationally proud of his own cobweb, even though all the fields in the morning are covered with the like, for he made it himself; but suppose a machine spun it for him? Suppose all the gossamer were Nottingham made? If you think of it, you will find the whole value of Lace as a possession depends on the fact of its having a *reality* which has been the reward of industry and attention. That the thing is itself a price—a thing everybody cannot have. That it proves by the look of it, the ability of the maker; that it proves by the rarity of it, the dignity of its wearer—either that she has been so industrious as to save money, which can buy, say, a piece of jewellery, of gold tissue, or of fine Lace—or else that she is a noble person, to whom her neighbors concede as an honour the privelege of wearing finer dress than they. If they all choose to have Lace too—

if it ceases to be a price, it becomes, does it not, only a cobweb? The real good of a piece of Lace, then, you will find, is that it should show first that the designer of it had a pretty fancy; next, that the maker of it had fine fingers; lastly, that the wearer of it has worthiness or dignity enough to obtain what it is difficult to obtain, and common sense enough not to wear it on all occasions.

—John Ruskin

LACE AND BOBBINS: A HISTORY AND COLLECTOR'S GUIDE, by T. L. Huetson. A. S. Barnes and Company, Cranbury, New Jersey, 1973. 186 pages. illustrations, photographs, bibliography, index. $6.95.

Pillow, or bobbin lace is made by the weaving and plaiting of a number of threads. Originally the threads were hand held, but this was often difficult and restricted the size and quality of the lace. Spools were soon developed which alleviated the problem of hand shortage. These were commonly made of bone and gave rise to the term "bone lace." A spangle (a ring of flat glass beads) was attached to the end of the shank of the bobbin. Its function was to give the bobbin a little extra weight and increase the tension on the thread to prevent the bobbin from rolling out of place. Hundreds of bobbins were needed for a large piece of lace. Each bobbin had to remain in place while the others were woven around pins.

This interesting book explains the process of pillow lace making, discusses the evolution of the lace industry in Europe, and describes the functions and decorative aspects of the tools of the trade. Most of the spools were handsomely decorated with designs, inlays, and inscriptions, and are now valued as collector's items. Many examples of antique lace and bobbins are reproduced in black-and-white photographs, and inscriptions are transcribed. These inscriptions endow the bobbins with a very human quality and reveal aspects of their maker's personality. There are many different types of inscriptions, but the sentimental appear to have been particularly popular. These were made by the young woman's beau and presented to her as a love token.

Bobbin Inscriptions

- Love me now love me for ever
- I like my love to well to leave her
- If you are ready I am willing for to give the clak [clerk] a shilling
- I love Susy yes I do
- Harts united must live contented
- George Boyce Mary Devricks sweet hart 1859
- Name the day
- Whisper soft to me my lovely dear
- Give me a kiss for a token

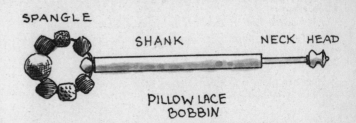

SPANGLE   SHANK   NECK HEAD

PILLOW LACE BOBBIN

A HISTORY OF HAND MADE LACE. by Emily Jackson. Tower Publications, New York, 1972. 243 pages. photographs. $17.50.

Anyone involved in lacework should find this an important and fascinating account. The tradition of lace-making is as complex and beautiful as many of the lace objects made in the past. Even the book itself, which traces in anecdotal fashion the history of lace from the earliest Egyptian times to the late nineteenth century, becomes a compelling historical document all its own. The present edition is a facsimile of the original 1900 publication, and the prose style and opinions voiced by the author reflect the societal conventions of the time, a time when the innovations of the Industrial Revolution were threatening the values and traditions of the past. The author herself is fearful for the survival of the lace-making industry in nineteenth-century England, and she enumerates the industry's value for her contemporary society as follows:

Briefly, the advantages of the lace industry for [19th century] England are these:

1. Women need not leave their homes in order to do the work.

2. In a properly organised lace school the girls are well cared for and protected while learning the industry.

3. Perfect hygienic conditions and personal cleanliness are essential for the lace-maker.

4. There is plenty of scope for individual effort and distinction, a stimulating consideration, which puts the lace-worker on a superior footing to the woman who merely works a machine.

5. The work is so light that the most delicate woman or girl can undertake it.

6. Mastery of the technical details is so easy that in lace-making countries, such as Belgium and Italy, children of seven or eight years commence to learn the "stitches."

7. Every woman newly employed in lace-making is one taken from the great army of women who, in earning their living, encroach upon those trades and professions which have hitherto been looked upon as the monopoly of men.

LACE AND LACE MAKING. by Marian Powys. Charles T. Branford Company, Newton Centre, Massachusetts, 1953. 219 pages. illustrations, photographs, index.

This book is out of print now, but it's worth a trip to the library. It contains a comprehensive listing of lace varieties, accompanied by photographs and descriptive text, and a good historical section on ecclesiastical lace, decorative lace, and costume lace, also accompanied by numerous photographs.

A small section is devoted to making lace (bobbin, embroidered net, point de Venise, point de gaze, and tape lace). The instructions are general and assume experience with needlework and lace-making. However, the photographs are clear and give a good idea of the various techniques being described.

HAND MADE BOBBIN LACEWORK. by Margaret Maidment. Charles T. Branford Company, Newton Centre, Massachusetts, 1954. 184 pages. illustrations, photographs, index. $12.50.

Another out-of-print book that is a storehouse of information, this describes the stitches of various pillow laces in a manner clear enough to allow a student with ambition and patience to get under way. Because this is a reissue of an earlier publication, the photographs and diagrams might appear a bit outdated, but they are informative and well suited to the text.

Lace

The word *lace*, derived from the Latin word *laqueus*, means "noose" or "snare." Laces are open, airy products which can be created by several different techniques, each producing certain effects and correspondingly different uses. There are five basic methods of producing lace: the bobbin method of weaving numerous threaded bobbins; the needle-point method of fastening net, cords, and tapes with needle and thread; the knitted method; the tatted method; and the crocheted method. Each technique requires an individual set of instructions, stitches, patterns, and equipment.

LACE MAKING. by Eunice Close. Charles T. Branford Company, Newton Centre, Massachusetts, 1970. 112 pages. illustrations. $2.95.

Many people who are competent knitters and crocheters regard lace-making as a skill beyond their ability. Accord-

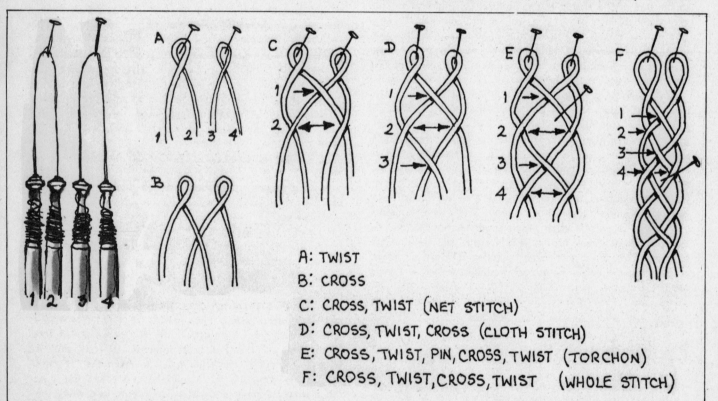

A: TWIST
B: CROSS
C: CROSS, TWIST (NET STITCH)
D: CROSS, TWIST, CROSS (CLOTH STITCH)
E: CROSS, TWIST, PIN, CROSS, TWIST (TORCHON)
F: CROSS, TWIST, CROSS, TWIST (WHOLE STITCH)

MAKING BOBBIN LACE. by Osma Gallinger Tod. Osma Tod Studio, Coral Gables, Florida, 1970. 14 pages. illustrations, photographs.

BOBBIN LACE STEP BY STEP. by Osma Gallinger Tod. Osma Tod Studio, Coral Gables, Florida, 1969. 35 pages. illustrations, photographs. $4.00.

Both these little pamphlets are modest instruction guides to the art of bobbin lace-making. The basic stitches, patterns, and techniques are explained simply and illustrated

with diagrams. *Making Bobbin Lace* is essentially an introduction to lace-making, and *Bobbin Lace Step by Step* presents more advanced techniques.

Neither book supplies design material, because their primary function is technical instructions; they are probably the only recent information available on this craft.

Ordering information may be obtained by writing the **Osma Tod Studio, 319 Mendoza Avenue, Coral Gables, Florida.**

ing to Eunice Close, however, nothing could be further from the truth. "If you can manipulate a pair of knitting needles," she says, "then you can certainly handle a set of bobbins." This may be true, but you would never believe it by looking at the instructions in this book. These are quite confusing and do not follow the format of the text in step-by-step fashion. The author has taken on a noble challenge in presenting information on bobbin lace; however, this exacting craft needs a sharp focus and clear, simple explanation.

bobbin lace pillow

Extensive Smuggling Operations Uncovered in France

In the beginning of the 19th century, what was perhaps the most ingenious and systematic order of smuggling known to the world was carried on between France and Belgium. France at that time was using much Belgian lace and smugglers discovered that dogs could be used to serve their purposes. Dogs were raised in France. They were well fed, petted, and made extremely happy; then, they were taken across the frontier into Belgium, where they were starved and otherwise ill-treated. After a short time of such abuse, the skins of larger dogs were fitted to the dogs' bodies and the intervening spaces were filled with lace and sewn up. The dogs were allowed to escape and naturally headed straight for the old home across the frontier in France where they had led such a good life and where they were relieved of their contraband. The French Custom House at last got wind of this enormously successful method of evading duties and between 1820 and 1836 many hundreds of such smuggler dogs were destroyed.

Source: A HISTORY OF HAND MADE LACE. by Emily Jackson.

International Old Lacers
c/o Mrs. Marguerite Gill
60 Kingston Street
Lawrence, Mass. 01843

This is a group of lace collectors and makers who seek to promote interest in fine old laces and preserve them for posterity. Members study the history of the craft, make lace, and hold exhibitions. The group maintains a slide library of laces and publishes *International Old Lacer's Bulletin*, a bimonthly publication.

CREATIVE LACE MAKING. by Harriet U. Fish. Sterling Publishing Company, New York, 1972. 48 pages. illustrations, photographs. $2.95.

This book is concerned with hairpin lace, a form of crocheted lace employing six basic stitches: loop, yarn-over, chain, single crochet, double crochet, and half double crochet, which are stitched onto a type of loom (the hairpin fork).

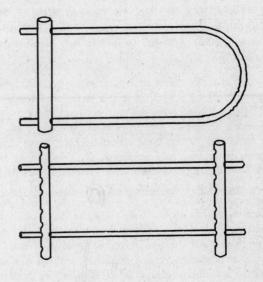

Hairpin fork and hairpin crochet flame or fork.
In the Victorian period, when hairpin lacemaking was at its peak, the ladies actually used their large bone hairpins for frames. Hairpin frames are available in knit and weaving shops where crochet hooks and yarn-type materials are bought.

The book provides information on materials, tools, and gives instructions for the basic stitches. However, a person desiring to make hairpin lace probably should have some familiarity with crochet techniques before attempting the projects presented here. These include a wall hanging, throw pillow, string grocery bag, poncho, and shawls. These are all presented with construction detail diagrams and photographs of the finished article.

Lace-Making Suppliers

E. Braggins & Sons Ltd.
26/36 Silver Street
Bedford, United Kingdom
brochure.
lacemaking supplies.

Magnolia Weaving
2635-29th Avenue, West
Seattle, Wash. 98199
catalog.
lace bobbins.

The Makings
2001 University Avenue
Berkeley, Cal. 94704
catalog.
lace bobbins.

Robin and Russ Handweavers
533 North Adams Street
McMinnville, Ore. 97128
catalog; samples $1.75.
lace bobbins.

School Products Company, Inc.
312 East 23 Street
New York, N.Y. 10010
catalog.
lace bobbins and pillows.

Osma Gallinger Tod
319 Mendoza Avenue
Coral Gables, Fla. 33134
brochure.
lacemaking supplies.

Leather

MODERN LEATHER DESIGN. by Donald Willcox. Watson-Guptill Publications, New York, 1969. 160 pages. illustrations, photographs, suppliers list, bibliography, index. $12.50.

An extensive discussion of leather tools and equipment, with many hints for selecting proper ones, together with a comprehensive chapter on dyeing, finishing, and the care and cleaning of leather comprises over half this book.

The remainder of the book contains chapters on sandals, moccasins, handbags, and garments, with lots of information on procedural possibilities and variations, but no diagrams to help the reader visualize the steps. The author also explores the advantages of leather as an artist's material, advantages the author believes to be those of a "pure form material"; that is, a sculptural material that allows for a minimum in aesthetic and technical limitations and over which the artist can exercise a maximum amount of control and have a maximum amount of freedom of expression.

The final chapter is devoted to suggestions for opening a leather shop, selling leather designs, and merchandising. (Mr. Willcox recommends that leather be displayed against earthy materials such as word, cork burlap, and hemp.)

LEATHER CRAFTSMANSHIP. by J. W. Waterer. Praeger Publishers, New York, 1968. 121 pages. illustrations, photographs, bibliography, index. $10.00.

Fashionable footwear of the 14th century

Neither a textbook nor a history book, this book is aimed at outlining the development of leather craftsmanship from very early times and how it spread into many fields of use, each with its own particular technical requirements and different skills, and yet joined by a "community of interest in fundamental mastery of materials, methods, and tools."

The author begins by providing the reader with a brief, nontechnical explanation of what leather is and how it's made, followed by glossaries of many different types of leathers, descriptions of processes, and tools. This information is provided with a view toward establishing a basis of understanding so that there can be full appreciation of the achievements in the various fields. Throughout are a number of beautiful black-and-white photographs of historical examples, many of which trace the development of leather products up to the present.

Magazines: Leather

Make It with Leather
P.O. Box 1386
Fort Worth, Tex. 76101
$6.00 a year.
  Step-by-step patterns and instructions.

The Craftsman
The Leather Craftsman, Inc.
Box 1386
Fort Worth, Tex.
bimonthly. $3.50 a year.
  Devoted to hand leather processes as done by sandal makers of the old West. How-tos for making and decorating useful leather items.

Weekly Bulletin of Leather and Shoe News
183 Essex Street
Boston, Mass.
$8.00 a year.

CONTEMPORARY LEATHER: ART AND ACCESSORIES—TOOLS AND TECHNIQUES. by Dona Z. Meilach. Henry Regnery Company, Chicago, 1971. 185 pages. illustrations, photographs (some color), suppliers list, index. $10.00.

Leather has traditionally been used by artists and craftsmen only in the most limited ways. This book is intended to stimulate interest in leather as an expressive, decorative, and functional medium. Traditional and nontraditional approaches are explored in order to encourage new, individual expressions of creativity. The author has chosen to gloss over well-known techniques and techniques that are amply covered elsewhere in order to devote more time to other possibilities, such as knitting, macrame, jewelry, and collage.

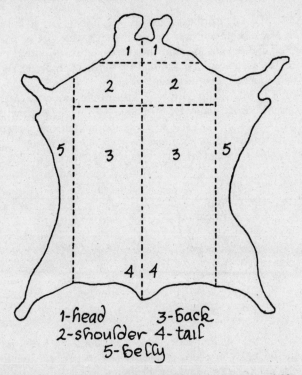

1-head   3-back
2-shoulder 4-tail
5-belly

GETTING STARTED IN LEATHERCRAFT. by Maria M. di Valentin. Collier, 1972. 96 pages. illustrations, photographs (some color), suppliers list, bibliography, index. paperback edition $2.95.

This is an elementary introduction that is by no means comprehensive or in depth, but it is clearly presented. There are a number of projects, starting with a simple fold-over leather eyeglass case and progressing to a pair of soft leather shoes, most of which are not very exciting.

A FIRST BOOK OF LEATHER WORKING. by Paul Villiard. Abelard-Schuman Limited, New York, 1972. 126 pages. photographs, index. $7.95.

This is a book on how to work leather, not how to make things from leather. The author believes that if a beginner learns to master the methods of working, he can apply these skills to the making of whatever article he desires.

The reader is introduced to the different types of leather, and told what to look for when examining hides and what types are best suited to what purposes. The author cautions that for really fine work, good leather is essential, and the craftsman grade, the economy grade, and the custom tooling designations are applied to leathers that are less than top quality and serviceable only as practice pieces. To be suitable for tooling and carving, leather should be bark tanned or water tanned.

Chapters with procedural photographs are devoted to stitching—saddle, whipstitch, and buttonhole; tooling, the easiest method of decorating the surface of leather, which entails nothing more than tracing a design on dampened leather and strengthening each line with modeling tools; modeling, which is also called repoussé or embossing, and which is an extension of plain tooling in that, after tooling, certain portions of the design are modeled by raising the leather from the back with a ball-ended tool; incising, a popular European method in which traced lines are cut in with a knife rather than with a modeler; carving, which is widely used to embellish western saddles and animal trappings; hammering methods, which utilize punches to put designs into leather; stenciling, appliqué, and patchwork; and Venetial lacquer, the most technical kind of leatherwork and one with which very few people in the United States are familiar—it involves the gilding of certain portions of leather designs (tooled, modeled, or incises) which are then covered with a transparent lacquer, oil colors, or dyes.

Organizations

Tanners Council of America
411 Fifth Avenue
New York, N.Y. 10016

New England Tanners Club
Box 371
Peabody, Mass. 01960

WORKING WITH LEATHER. by Xenia Ley Parker. Charles Scribner's Sons, New York, 1972. 159 pages. illustrations, photographs (some color), index. $8.95.

This is an elementary introduction to leatherworking techniques, primarily those encountered in working with soft leathers. However, there is a brief discussion of tooling and an equally brief discussion of dyeing.

The latter part of the book contains a series of twelve projects, none of which is outstanding.

Sewing Leather and Suede

Leather and suede are not any more difficult to sew than fabric. In fact, sometimes they are even more manageable, since they do not slip under the presser foot.

When sewing leather on a machine, make sure that the machine is free from oil. Use a leather-point needle. This is designed specifically for this purpose and the wedge point makes a clean cut and thus, a uniform stitch in the leather.

1. Use a size 11 needle for lightweight leathers, kidskin, fine capeskin, and sheer suedes.
2. Use a size 14 needle for medium-weight leathers, garment suede, capeskin, lambskin.
3. Use a size 16 needle for heavyweight leathers, heavier capeskin, lambskin, or multiple layers.

Test the length of the machine stitch on a scrap of leather and adjust if necessary. Generally, 7–10 stitches per inch are used. Sheer suedes and soft leathers may use as many as 12 stitches per inch. Use 7–8 stitches per inch on heavy leathers. A few more stitches per inch will improve the appearance of topstitched leather.

Leather and suede are thicker and spongier than fabric and thus require less pressure when sewn. Check the pressure regulator and loosen it if necessary.

Check the upper tension. If the thread is too loose and forms loops on the bottom of the seam, tighten the tension. Loosen the tension if the thread breaks or forms loops on the top of the seam.

Use a roller-presser foot or a Teflon-coated foot, especially for topstitching.

Use one of the following threads:

1. Silk thread (its elasticity and tensile strength make it especially good for sewing on leather).
2. Subsilk (a mercerized cotton which is chemically treated to increase its strength and receptivity to dyes).
3. 2- or 3-ply heavy-duty mercerized or Dual Duty thread.
4. Texturized nylon thread (it's elastic, but some synthetic threads pick up lint and sometimes fray).

Source: **HOW TO SEW LEATHER, SUEDE AND FUR, revised edition. by Phyllis W. Schwebke and Margaret B. Krohn. Collier, 1974. 151 pages. illustrations, photographs, suppliers list, bibliography, index. paperback edition $2.95.**

Sandal Making

MATERIALS

cobbler's hammer and anvil
cutting tools
edge beveler
skive
slot and oval drive punches
needle-nose pliers
rasp
awl
clinching nails
beeswax
contact cement
neat's-foot oil
Scotch tape
water
dyes
sanding and buffing wheel

PROCEDURE

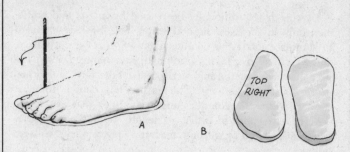

A. Make a cardboard pattern by tracing around each foot. Mark beginning and end of the arch, the spot between big toe and second toe, and the placement of side strap one third the distance from the end of the heel. Indicate right or left and top side on each.

B. Transfer pattern to the upper sole cowhide. Allow about ¼″ extra edge for working. This will be trimmed later. Use the cut top sole to make the bottom sole pattern, but remember to reverse the bottom sole or you will be left with two negatives that won't fit together.

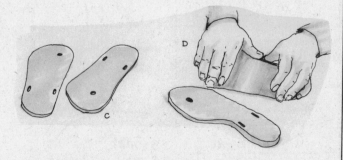

C. After all four soles have been cut, punch the strap and toe holes in the top soles. Place these far enough in from the edge to allow for trimming and finishing and for the nails to hold in the strap. Mark shape of the arch with awl or pencil. If you place the straps in the correct location toward the back end of the arch, they will prevent the heel straps from slipping. Straps are not put in until after the soles are laminated and molded. Laminate the top and bottom soles with contact cement and place the roughened flesh sides together. Lay a strip of Scotch tape from the edge to each strap hole before gluing. This will produce an unglued path so that the straps can later be placed without first having to pry open and tear the leather layers. Glued soles must dry at least 24 hours before molding.

D. Dip the dried, laminated soles in warm water for 5 to 10 mins., depending upon how pliable you want it to be for bending and pushing. Hold sole as shown, using arch mark as guide. Place thumbs along the edge to be curved and work the wet leather until it conforms to the arch shape. Curve the end of the heel and bend up the top slightly. Allow the soles to dry at least 24 hours and then test the arch for comfort. Remold if necessary and dry thoroughly. Rub or dip the soles in neat's-foot oil to restore oils lost in the wetting. Do any preliminary dyeing, edge beveling, and sanding before putting in the straps.

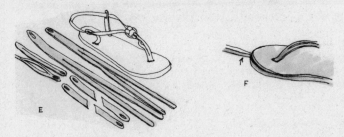

E. Use latigo or 4 to 6 ounce top or full grain cowhide rubbed with neat's-foot oil to make straps. Strip them from the hide with a stripper, paper cutter, or shears. They should be about ½" wide and 2 to 3" longer than necessary. Make necessary slits and punches where straps will slip through one another.

F. Open the path between the soles where the tape is and pull each strap through beyond the edge of the sandal. Pry open the path with a screwdriver if you have mistakenly glued the soles completely together. When all straps are through, skive the ends. Try the sandal and fit straps to foot. Cobble, or nail, soles and straps together. If a minimum of nails are used and the straps stretch, the nails can be easily removed, the straps adjusted, and cobbled again.

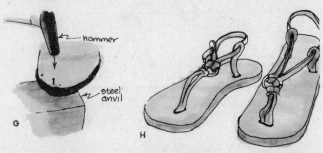

G. To cobble, use a triangular-shaped pointed clinching nail a little longer than the thickness of all leathers because the end is bent over when it is hammered against the anvil. Brass and steel nails can be obtained in ⅜" to 1¼" lengths. Use a ⅝" brass nail here and nailed from the bottom to the top of the sole. Punch a starting hole with your awl, set the nail in, and hammer, holding the top of the sole against a hard iron anvil (a piece of pipe or gear can serve as a substitute anvil). During the hammering, the nail tip will bend over and back into the top sole and thus, will not protrude or poke into your foot. Cobble all strap areas. Some sandalmakers cobble all around the sole from top to bottom at 1" intervals.

H. Finish sandals by trimming off any excess edge. Take care not to trim too close to the strap holes and the cobbler's nails. Bevel top and bottom edges if you like. Immerse sandal in neat's-foot oil for about 10 minutes. Finish edges by more beveling; sanding; waxing; burnishing with beeswax, water, or saddle soap, and buffing. The

sandals should not be worn for more than three or four hours the first few days.

Source: CONTEMPORARY LEATHER: ART AND ACCESSORIES—TOOLS AND TECHNIQUES. by Dona Z. Meilach.

LEATHERCRAFT BY HAND. by John Faulkner. Walker and Company, New York, 1973. 217 pages. illustrations, photographs, suppliers list. $8.95.

This book contains information on how to choose hides, how to calculate the amount of leather needed for any project, how to select tools, how to care for leather, as well as clear diagrams for lacings and stitching. There are lots of useful tips, such as how to adapt patterns for leatherwork, even how to duplicate your favorite wardrobe items in leather. If, for example, you have a favorite vest that you'd like to reproduce in leather, just lay it front side down on brown paper and trace one side (this will be used to trace the other side later). Trace as far as the side seams. Trace the back as one piece, even if this means eliminating a center seam. Add ⅜ inch seam allowance and cut out the pieces. Cut out the second front piece.

The author also provides a number of projects—boleros, a smock, a watchband, moccasins, a patchwork coverlet, and more—all quite nice and clearly presented.

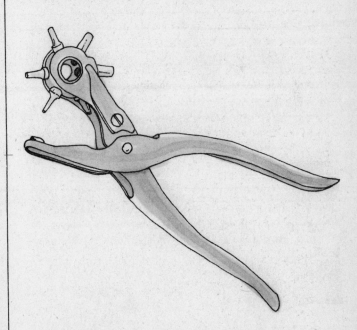

A revolving punch, one of the most important tools for making leather garments. This one has six rotating punch tubes. A good punch has threaded, replaceable tubes which are numbered from #00 to #5.

Zig-zag stitch

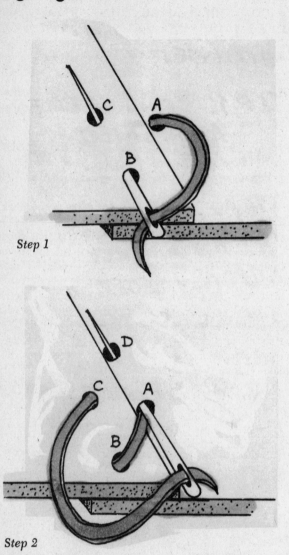

Step 1

Step 2

This is the most versatile of the simple stitches. It makes a very sturdy seam and is also good for stitching around appliques.

Step 1: Bring needle up at A. Insert at B and emerge at C.
Step 2: Re-insert needle at A and emerge at D. This completes a V-shaped stitch.
Step 3: Repeat stitching pattern on both sides of seam.

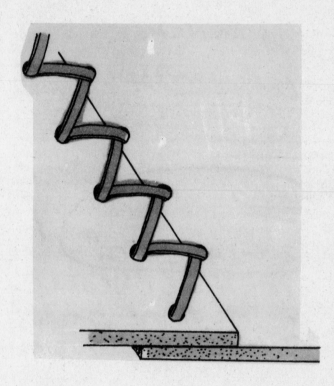

Step 3

CRAFT MANUAL OF NORTH AMERICAN INDIAN FOOTWEAR. by George M. White. Mission Valley News, St. Ignatius, Montana. 71 pages. illustrations. $1.95 (postpaid).

This book offers step-by-step instructions for stitching and assembling about forty design patterns for traditional-looking American Indian footwear.

SADDLERY AND HARNESS MAKING. by Paul H. Hasluck. British Book Center, 1972. illustrations. $7.50.

First published in 1904, this is still one of the few, if not the only, textbook on the subject. It is a mine of information that even includes a hansom cab harness.

Leather-Suppliers

ANTELOPE

R. G. Leather Company, Inc.
127 Spring Street
New York, N.Y.

Risedorph, Inc.
140 West 8th Avenue
Gloverville, N.Y.

BELT LEATHER

A. C. Products Company
422 Hudson Street
New York, N.Y.

Adams Tanning Corporation
118 Street
Newark, N.J.

Arrow Leather Company
39 West 32 Street
New York, N.Y.

Berman Leather Company
103 South Street
Boston, Mass.

Dermaton Leather Company
291-297 New Jersey Railroad Avenue
Newark, N.J.

Farkash, Inc.
114 East 25 Street
New York, N.Y.

National Supply Company
28 Washington Street
Haverhill, Mass.

Virginia Oak Tannery, Inc.
Luray, Va.

Williams Industries
213 Wilson Avenue
Newark, N.J.

BUCK

Beggs and Cobb
179 South Street
Boston, Mass.

Button's Buckskins
West Danville, Vt.

Creative Leather Workshop
Box 1495
Prudential Central Station
Boston, Mass. 02199

Daier Leather Company
5 Beekman Street
New York, N.Y.

Legallet Tanning Company
1099 Quesada Avenue
San Francisco, Cal.

Rueping Company
Fond du Lac, Wis.

BUFFALO

C and P Leather Company
222 Verona Avenue
Newark, N.J.

Essex Tanning Company
148 River Street
Haverhill, Mass.

Renar Leather Company
68 Spring Street
New York, N.Y.

CABRETTAS

A. C. Lawrence Leather Company
Peabody, Mass.

Bill Levine Corporation
17 Cleveland Place
New York, N.Y.

Crown Leather Finishing Company
422 North Perry Street
Johnstown, N.Y.

Feuer Leather Corporation
160 Broadway
New York, N.Y.

Leather's Best
120 Wall Street
New York, N.Y.

R. G. Leather Company
127 Spring Street
New York, N.Y.

Tandy Leather Company
P.O. Box 79
Fort Worth, Tex.

Walter Loeber Company
3108 West Meinecke Avenue
Milwaukee, Wis. 53208

CALF

Barette and Company
49 Vesey Street
Newark, N.J.

C. A. Andres and Company
386 Park Avenue
New York, N.Y.

F. C. Donovan
Riverview Industrial Park
Needham Heights, Mass.

Louis I. Silverman, Inc.
729 Atlantic Avenue
Boston, Mass.

Ohio Leather Company
Girard, Ohio

R. A. Rubin Company
684 Broadway
New York, N.Y.

Victory Tanning Corporation
23 Upton Street
Peabody, Mass.

CALF SUEDE

A. C. Products
422 Hudson Street
New York, N.Y.

Bill Levine Corporation
17 Cleveland Place
New York, N.Y.

Globe Leather Corporation
432 Park Avenue
New York, N.Y.

Hunt-Rankin Leather Company
134 Beach Street
Boston, Mass. 02111

Hyman Zeitlin Company
79 Walker Street
New York, N.Y.

Walter Loeber Company
3108 West Meinecke Avenue
Milwaukee, Wis. 53208

CAPESKINS

Coey Tanning Company
Wartrace, Tenn.

David Ungar Corporation
154 West 27 Street
New York, N.Y.

Donnell and Mudge
151 Canal Street
Salem, Mass.

Liberty Dressing Corporation
17-29 Burr Street
Gloversville, N.Y.

Steinberg Brothers
443 Park Ave. South
New York, N.Y.

COLT AND HORSE

John A. Dauer Leather Company
100 Gold Street
New York, N.Y.

John Flynn and Sons
80 Boston Street
Salem, Mass.

Legallet Tanning Company
1099 Quesada Avenue
San Francisco, Cal.

Weil and Eisendrath Company
2221 North Elston Avenue
Chicago, Ill.

CORDOVAN

Horween Leather Company
2015 Elston Avenue
Chicago, Ill.

Steinberg Brothers
443 Park Ave. South
New York, N.Y.

A. L. Gebhardt Company
226 North Water Street
Milwaukee, Wis. 53202

J. P. Fliegel Company
P.O. Box 505
Gloversville, N.Y.

Sax-Crafts
1101 North 3rd Street
Milwaukee, Wis. 53203

EMBOSSED GRAINS

Armour Leather Company
1113 Maryland Avenue
Sheboygan, Wis.

Hallmark Leather Company
46 North Central Street
Peabody, Mass.

Keystone Leather
81 Spring Street
New York, N.Y.

Superior Tanning
1244 West Division Street
Chicago, Ill.

GARMENT LEATHER

Berman Leather Company
103 South Street
Boston, Mass.

Blackhawk Tanners
1000 West Bruce Street
Milwaukee, Wis.

Coey Leathers
Wartrace, Tenn.

Gebhardt and Company
226 North Water Street
Milwaukee, Wis.

Hyman Zeitlin and Company
79 Walker Street
New York, N.Y.

Independent Leather Corporation
315 South Main Street
Gloversville, N.Y.

MacPherson Brothers
730 Polk Street
San Francisco, Cal. 94109

Tandy Leather Company
P.O. Box 79
Fort Worth, Tex.

Thiele Tanning Company
123 North 27 Street
Milwaukee, Wis.

KANGAROO

American Guild of Kangaroo Tanners
1405 Statler Building
Boston, Mass.

Mullins, Towbridge and Company
210 South Street
Boston, Mass.

William Amer Company
215 Willow Street
Philadelphia, Pa.

OSTRICH

Dreher Leather Manufacturing Corporation
42 Garden Avenue
Newark, N.J.

PIGSKIN
C and P Leather Company
222 Verona Avenue
Newark, N.J.

Hallmark Leather Company
46 North Central Street
Peabody, Mass.

Harvey-Mallis Leather Company
386 Park Avenue South
New York, N.Y.

Wolverine World-Wide, Inc.
Rockford, Mich.

RAWHIDE

Griess-Pleger Tanning Company
Waukegan, Ill.

National Rawhide Manufacturing Company
1464 West Webster Avenue
Chicago, Ill.

REPTILE

Beggs and Cobb, Inc.
171 Madison Avenue
New York, N.Y. 10016

Cedamar International
24 Commerce Street
Newark, N.J.

Hagen Company
386 Park Avenue
New York, N.Y. 10016

Redi-Cut Reptile Company
60 Warren Street
New York, N.Y.

SHARK

Ocean Leather Company
42 Garden Street
Newark, N.J.

SHEEPSKIN

Adams Tanning Corporation
118 Adams Street
Newark, N.J.

Chicago Tanning Company
1508 West Cortland Street
Chicago, Ill.

David Ungar Corporation
154 West 27 Street
New York, N.Y.

Globe Tanning Corporation
432 Park Avenue South
New York, N.Y.

Homer Bear and Company
225 West 34 Street
New York, N.Y.

MacPherson Brothers
730 Polk Street
San Francisco, Cal. 94109

Morris Feldstein and Sons
215 Water Street
Brooklyn, N.Y.

Sirois Leather, Inc.
73 Lowell Street
Peabody, Mass.

Walter Loeber Company
3108 West Meinecke Avenue
Milwaukee, Wis. 53208

Weil and Eisendrath Company
2221 North Elston Avenue
Chicago, Ill.

SOLE LEATHER

Berman Leather Company
103 South Street
Boston, Mass.

Charles L. Hardtke
3320 West Hopkins
Milwaukee, Wis.

Virginia Oak Tannery, Inc.
Luray, Va.

Wisconsin Leather Company
1830 South 3rd Street
Milwaukee, Wis.

WOVEN LEATHERS

Arrow Leather Company
39 West 32 Street
New York, N.Y.

Ouimet Welting Company
Brockton, Mass.

Shain and Company
179 South Street
Boston, Mass.

DEERSKIN

Deerskin Products
Little Delaware Route 28
Delhi, N.Y. 13753

Walter Loeber Company
3108 West Meinecke Avenue
Milwaukee, Wis. 53208

LAST MAKER'S SUPPLIES

Brockston Last Corporation
4 Capen Street
Stoughton, Mass.

Compo Industries, Inc.
125 Roberts Road
Waltham, Mass.

Robert Last Corporation
341 Taylor Street
Manchester, N.H.

Vulcan Corporation
6 East 4 Street
Cincinnati, Ohio

United Shoe Machinery Corporation
140 Federal Street
Boston, Mass.

DYES AND PIGMENTED COLORINGS

Behlen and Brothers, Inc.
10 Christopher Street
New York, N.Y. 10014
Behlen's aniline stains—wood stains applicable to leather.

Fezandie and Sperrle, Inc.
103 Lafayette Street
New York, N.Y. 10013
leather and batik dyes.

Fiebing Chemical Company
516 2nd Street
Milwaukee, Wis. 53202

Magi Dyes Company, Inc.
Linden, N.J. 07063

Master Chemical Company
27 Brandston Street
Boston, Mass. 02100

Omega Leathercraft Products Company
Fort Worth, Tex. 76100
Also Los Angeles, Cal. 90052

BUCKLES AND FINDINGS

Allens Manufacturing Company
89 Shipyard Street
Providence, R.I.

American Jewelry Finding Company
10 West 47 Street
New York, N.Y.

American Shoe Specialties Company
318 West 39 Street
New York, N.Y.

American Specialty Hardware
Chattanooga, Tenn. 37400

Bernard Abrams, Inc.
52 West 39 Street
New York, N.Y.

D. W. Tool and Findings Corporation
52 Salem Street
Providence, R.I.

Eastern Findings Corporation
19 West 34 Street
New York, N.Y.

E. E. Weller Company
253 Georgia Avenue
Providence, R.I.

Felch-Anderson Company
248 Toronto Avenue
Providence, R.I.

General Fashions
Suite 957, Marbridge Building
47 West 34 Street
New York, N.Y.

Gordon Shoe Findings
2 McRaw Street
Roslindale, Mass. 02131

Handy Ormond Manufacturing Company
50-05 47th Avenue
Woodside, N.Y.

Lynn Buckle Manufacturing Company
721 Washington Street
Lynn, Mass.

Nailhead Creations, Inc.
20 West 31 Street
New York, N.Y.

North and Judd Manufacturing Company
New Britain, Conn.

Orville Leather Hardware Company
228 West Chestnut Street
Orville, O. 44667

Precision Buckles, Inc.
231 Georgia Avenue
Providence, R.I.

Star Buckle Company
3721 Chestnut
Philadelphia, Pa. 19104

Trinity Buckle Company
P.O. Box 5169
Santa Monica, Cal. 90405

United Shoe Ornament Company
35 Tripoli Street
Cranston, R.I.

Waterbury Buckle Company
Waterbury, Conn. 06702

FINDINGS

Allcraft
22 West 48 Street
New York, N.Y. 10038

Tandy Leather
P.O. Box 79
Fort Worth, Tex.

CEMENTS AND GLUES

Barge Cement
100 Jacksonville Road
Towaco, N.J. 07082

Borden Chemical Company
New York, N.Y. 10000
Elmer's Glue-All.

DuPont de Nemours and Company
Wilmington, Del. 19898
Duco Cement.

Franklin Glue Company
Columbus, O. 43207
Franklin Liquid Hide Glue.

Master Chemical Company
27 Bradston Street
Boston, Mass. 02100

Petronio Shoe Products
1447 McCarter Highway
Newark, N.J. 07100
Petronio Glue.

Sandord's Elephant Glue
Bellwood, Ill. 60104

Tandy Leather
P.O. Box 79
Fort Worth, Tex.

U. S. Plywood Company
2305 Superior Street
Kalamazoo, Mich. 49003

TOOLS—MANUFACTURERS AND/OR DISTRIBUTORS

A. C. Products
422 Hudson Street
New York, N.Y. 10014

Allcraft
22 West 48 Street
New York, N.Y. 10038

Anchor Tool and Supply Company
12 John Street
New York, N.Y. 10038

Boin Arts and Crafts Company
91 Morris Street
Morristown, N.J.

C. S. Osborne
Harrison, N.J. 07029
all leatherworking for shoemakers and craftsmen.

Henry Westpfal and Company
4 East 32 Street
New York, N.Y. 10016

H. K. Kauffman and Sons Saddlery Company
139-141 East 24 Street
New York, N.Y. 10010

J. C. Larson Company, Inc.
7330 North Clark Street
Chicago, Ill. 60626

MacPherson Leather Company
100 South Los Angeles Street
Los Angeles, Cal. 90052

Russo Leather and Finding Company
1460 East 4 Street
Los Angeles, Cal. 90052

Sax Arts and Crafts
207 North Milwaukee
Milwaukee, Wis. 53202

Tandy Leather
P.O. Box 79
Fort Worth, Tex.

United Shoe Machinery
104 Federal Street
Boston, Mass. 02109
complete line of tools available at shoe and leather findings companies.

William Dixon, Inc.
32-43 Kinney Street
Newark, N.J.

X-Acto Precision Tools, Inc.
48-41 Van Dam St.—Department 25
Long Island City, N.Y. 11100

Macrame and Knotting

MACRAME MADE EASY. by Eunice Close. Macmillan, New York, 1973. 88 pages. illustrations, photographs, index. paperback edition $3.50.

During the Victorian Period in England, macrame was one of the "accomplishments" that all young ladies were supposed to possess. The craft suited the overornate Victorian tastes very well and was used to edge blinds, cover mantels, and probably was applied to any other flat surfaces found in the drawing room. Macrame and many other crafts suffered for its Victorian overuse when tastes changed in the first half of this century and it virtually disappeared from the scene. Recently, macrame has come back very strongly and is one of the most popular of modern crafts. Its uses and techniques are ever expanding.

Macrame Made Easy is a fine introduction to this craft for beginners. The first half of the book explains simply

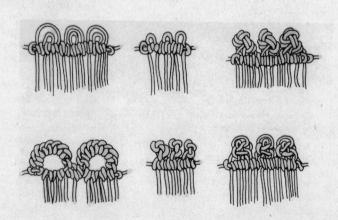

Decorative borders formed by various methods of knotting on

and directly the basic knots, the construction of knot chains and bars, decorative borders made by various knotting on techniques, and other useful construction practices. The second half is taken up with various macrame projects which utilize the newly acquired skills. The projects begin with simple belts and headbands, and progress to such items as wall hangings, lampshades, and a vest, jacket, and evening shawl constructed in macrame functioning as a kind of alternative to crochet work.

The outstanding feature of this book is a chapter on fine macrame, a technique often excluded from introductory manuals. It uses threads to create delicate lace patterns. The book also supplies instructions for making a doily, lace mat, and an exquisite lace collar.

MACRAME ACCESSORIES: PATTERNS AND IDEAS FOR KNOTTING. by Dona Z. Meilach. Crown Publishers, New York, 1972. 96 pages. illustrations, photographs. $4.95. paperback edition $2.50.

This book offers a multitude of designs, projects, and advanced knotting techniques for old hands at macrame. The author utilizes primarily the clove hitch and the square knot which she varies and combines to form an incredible number of pattern arrangements and to make a variety of objects. The knots, if they are familiar to the reader, can be read without difficulty from the photographs that present them.

A great many articles are pictured in black-and-white photographs and are accompanied by just enough descriptive text to allow for construction. Some of these items, such as the belt for shy hot pants wearers, are quite unusual. Others, such as the pot hangers and table coverings, are more traditional. Whatever it is you're looking for, be it sandals, jewelry, or handbags, you name it she's got it. Knot on!

MACRAME, CREATIVE DESIGN IN KNOTTING. by Dona Z. Meilach. Crown Publishers, New York, 1971. 212 pages. illustrations, photographs, suppliers list, bibliography, index. $7.95.

This could have been a fine book for beginners, but the instructions and illustrative photographs are just not clear enough to avoid confusion. Many of the photographs used to illustrate specific procedures are sloppily retouched. This was probably an attempt on the part of the author to clarify otherwise ambiguous prints and make them more readable, but it seems to have backfired and left the reading of the knots even more unclear.

People who have experience with macrame should find information and inspiration in the multitude of works (especially the three-dimensional ones) by contemporary craftsmen. These works are described and analyzed in terms of their structure and design. The author also presents at least a score of variations and combinations of knots and knotting techniques accompanied by photographs and texts which are much clearer than in the elementary sections.

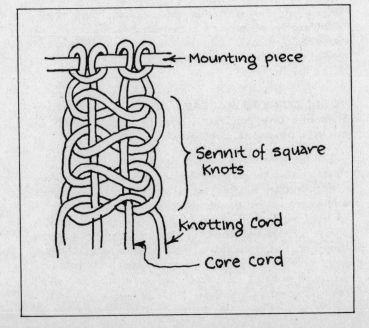

Mounting piece

Sennit of square Knots

Knotting cord

Core cord

COLOR AND DESIGN IN MACRAME. by Virginia I. Harvey. Van Nostrand Reinhold, New York, 1971. 104 pages. illustrations, photographs (some color), bibliography, index. $7.95.

This excellent book is intended for experienced knotters who are concerned with the possibilities of texture and design inherent in the knotting process itself. The author is not interested in presenting information on how to tie basic knots, but rather, in the way these knots can work together. She explains her concepts by showing diagrams of each knot and its variations, and then a field of knots repeated in a photograph brilliantly illustrates the resultant textural effect.

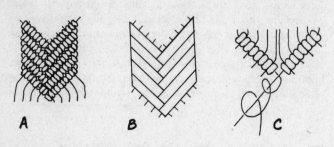

A and B   Adjacent parallelogram

C   Beginning a parallelogram

Combining these knot "fields" yields motifs and patterns which can then be employed to design imaginative pieces. The finished object has a structure much like that of a grammar: each element is a significant part of the whole. The section on diagonal motifs is an outstanding example of the author's artistry. These clearly show how the nature of the material and the configuration of knot patterns suggest structure.

About half of this book is devoted to a discussion of color, and every example is illustrated by a large full-color photograph. There is no theoretical presentation of color

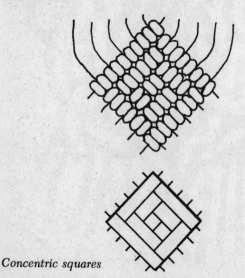

Concentric squares

science, but in this case that's an attribute as the author has evidently digested available material on the subject and feeds it back through beautiful multicolored macrame pieces, which ultimately are more instructive.

There is also a section on three-dimensional work and additional pieces that use unique form, texture, and material combinations to achieve imaginative designs.

GRADED LESSONS IN MACRAME, KNOTTING, AND NETTING. by Louisa Walker. Dover Publications, New York, 1896. 254 pages. illustrations, photographs. paperback edition $2.00.

This is an easy-to-follow collection of exercises in knotting. Each lesson is directed toward a particular age group or skill level, and the aim is clearly stated at the beginning of each lesson as are the necessary materials.

This book would probably make a good teacher's manual and there are many good suggestions for classroom projects.

THE MACRAME BOOK. by Helene Bress. Charles Scribner's Sons, New York, 1972. 274 pages. illustrations, photographs, suppliers list, bibliography, index. $12.50.

This is a really comprehensive guide for beginning as well as advanced macrame enthusiasts. Every aspect of the craft is covered thoroughly. The basic knots are presented with step-by-step illustrated instructions, and the more advanced combinations of knots and techniques, including addition of beads, bangles, and buckles, are described thoroughly and illustrated by means of both drawings and photographs. There is complete coverage of beginning and ending work and a full chapter devoted to unique techniques such as twining, wrapping, and rya. The inspirational quality of this book is enhanced by a chapter on historical work, contemporary work, and wall hangings, and a final chapter on combining macrame with other crafts is inventive and extremely useful for people with multicraft ability.

Projects per se are not presented; however, a diligent craftsperson should have the confidence and know-how needed to carry out any macrame undertaking with the aid of this fine book.

VOGUE GUIDE TO MACRAME. edited by Judy Brittain. Stein and Day Publishers, Briarcliff Manor, 1973. 80 pages. illustrations, photographs. $6.95.

The introductory chapters of this book constitute a good, clear presentation of macrame basics. Following the technical instruction is a bevy of extremely handsome projects, each illustrated by a photo and accompanied by a text describing the method of construction. The projects include a vest, a cashmere shawl, an evening bag, a rug, and a hammock. Unfortunately, a beginner, or even a knotter of some experience, is bound to have problems with these projects, problems that some simple, schematic diagrams would have remedied.

Interview

One thing that worries me is that I don't know anything about the life expectancy of jute. It may not be in the buyer's mind but it's really in my mind a lot. I don't want to cheat anyone. If someone spends a thousand dollars for something it should last a good long while. There's a lot of research I've got to do yet. I'm sure there must be something I can spray that wool with or treat that jute with to make sure that it won't disintegrate as I fear that it will do.

Unless I'm just experimenting and having a good time I usually do a drawing, a very basic one, but I do sketch it. It's just the form; I know by now that certain knots are going to produce effects that will be dimensional or non-dimensional, so I don't need to figure that out in advance.

My pieces that I like I feel are organic, there's a presence and it's natural.

I think people are trying to get away from the "plastic" sort of thing, and they're willing to spend money. A lot of organizations and corporations that used to buy art are switching over to crafts.

Carol Beron is a practitioner of the knotting arts who lives and works in New York City.

I used to teach art, and really my field is drawing and painting. I went to live in Israel for two years; I had just started to learn macrame at the time and I saw they didn't really have it there. I went into business with a dress factory. I had a small macrame factory of my own and we combined cloth and macrame on a mass production level.

For my own pleasure while in Israel I combined macrame with Arab embroidery. I felt they should be together since the origins of macrame are Arabic, too.

I took a short course in macrame, about four lessons. The knots are really very easy. After that it's what you do with them that counts.

I use the same principles I used in painting except that this is more tactile.

I really want to work completely three-D, very large pieces, but for that I need a loft.

There's no armature on any of my work. That's the thing I'm most proud of.

I use a lot of rope and jute and wool from the Gaza Strip.

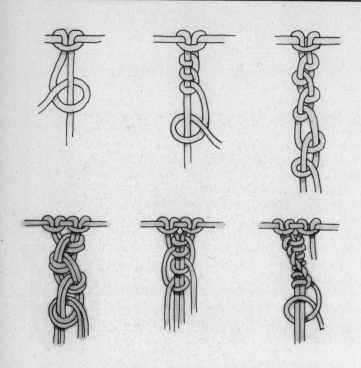

Half hitch variations

There are hundreds of projects from head- and hatbands to dog leashes, as well as a multitude of square knot and square knot related sennit braids and mats.

This book was originally published in 1949 by the Cornell Maritime Press, and the format betrays a dated quality. Photographs and information are placed far apart, and consequently the instructions are confusing. However, veteran knotters looking for standard and esoteric patterns and methods will find this an excellent reference tool.

BIG-KNOT MACRAME. by Nils Strom and Ander Enestrom. Sterling Publishing Company, New York, 1971. 48 pages. photographs, index. $2.95.

This book includes twelve projects which use simple knots tied with relatively heavy rope. All the projects create functional articles requiring a minimal assortment of tools.

Mat from four-ply turk's head knot

Instructions are step-by-step and photograph-illustrated, and they provide a good starting place for novice knot tiers. It is not, however, a good book for macrame enthusiasts wishing to learn how to do traditional decorative knot work.

KNOTS: USEFUL AND ORNAMENTAL. by George Russell Shaw. Macmillan, New York, 1972. 194 pages. illustrations. paperback edition $2.95.

A facsimile of the 1924 edition, this book features hand-drawn and -lettered pages. It contains step-by-step instructions for every conceivable knot, including Celtic knots, temple ornaments, and belt buckles.

PRACTICAL MACRAME. by Eugene Andes. Van Nostrand Reinhold, New York, 1971. 118 pages. illustrations, photographs, suppliers list. $7.95. paperback edition $3.95.

A series of projects that increase in difficulty and sophistication form the basis of this book. This can be a fine idea for learning a craft, but the author should first give a clear account of the basic techniques. *Practical Macrame* lacks this necessary requirement.

The basic knots are shown finished in huge line drawings, but the procedure for knotting is illustrated by step-by-step photographs in which the hands of the person doing the knotting dwarf the knot, which is constructed of yarn of a very small diameter and dark color.

The projects themselves are rather nice. They include belts, a hat, purses, vests, and a slightly weird knotted bikini. The instructions are terse but clear. Unfortunately, the text and the illustrations don't seem to work together and might make things a bit confusing.

SQUARE-KNOT HANDI-CRAFT GUIDE. by Raoul Graumont and Elmer Wenstrom. Random House, New York, 1971. illustrations, photographs, index. paperback edition $3.95.

Although intended for beginners, this book offers a wealth of knotting and macrame techniques and projects that are actually more suitable for experienced knotters.

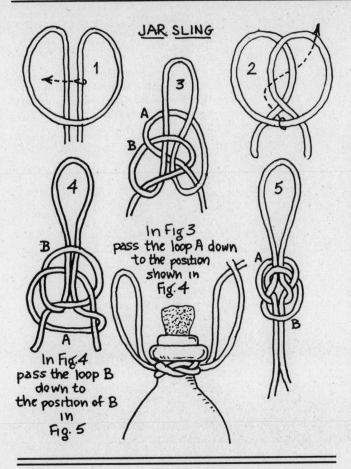

JAR SLING

In Fig 3 pass the loop A down to the position shown in Fig. 4

In Fig. 4 pass the loop B down to the position of B in Fig. 5

ENCYCLOPEDIA OF KNOTS AND FANCY ROPE WORK. by Raoul Graumont and John Hensel. Cornell Maritime Press, Cambridge, Maryland, 1952. 690 pages. illustrations, photographs. $15.00.

This is an excellent "last word" in knotting books, containing more knots than anyone will probably ever need or use in a lifetime.

THE ASHLEY BOOK OF KNOTS. by Clifford W. Ashley. Doubleday and Company, Garden City, New York, 1944. 260 pages. illusrations. $16.95.

Those really involved with knotting will probably be enthralled by Ashley's incredible compendium of 3,900 knots. The instructions are not as clear nor the diagrams as easy to read as in the *Encyclopedia of Knots and Fancy Rope Work*, but the book is comprehensive and has a certain salty charm all its own.

KNOTS AND SPLICES. by Percy W. Blandford. Arco Publishing Company, New York, 1967. 79 pages. illustrations. paperback edition $.95.

This is an excellent and inexpensive first book of knotting. The eighty knots presented are explained well and illustrated with clear diagrams.

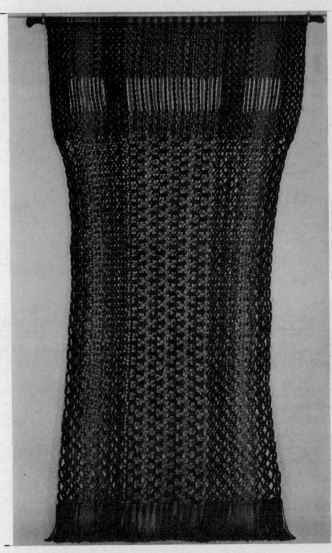

Wall hanging, Terri Fredericks

HANDBOOK OF KNOTS. by Raoul Graumont. Cornell Maritime Press, Cambridge, Maryland, 1954. 194 pages. illustrations. $2.00.

A collection of 428 knots diagramed and explained. Those with a bit of experience will have an easier time of it than complete greenhorns, but anyone can make it with perseverance.

Macrame, Carol Beron

Macrame Suppliers

American Handicrafts Company
1110 Mission Street
San Francisco, Cal.
catalog.

Arachne Webworks
2390 North West Thurman
Portland, Ore. 92710
catalog.

Bead Game
505 North Fairfax Avenue
Los Angeles, Cal. 90036
catalog.

Black Sheep Weaving and Craft Supply
318 South West 2nd Street
Corvallis, Ore. 97330

Boin Arts and Crafts
87 Morris Street
Morristown, N.J. 07960
catalog.

Colonial Woolen Mills
6501 Barberton Avenue
Cleveland, O. 44102
catalog.

Contessa Yarns
P.O. Box 37
Lebanon, Conn. 06249
brochure $.25.

Craft Kaleidoscope
6412 Ferguson Avenue
Indianapolis, Ind. 46220
brochure.

Creative Fibres, Inc.
1028 East Juneau Avenue
Milwaukee, Wis. 53202
catalog $1.00.

Dharma Trading Company
1952 University Avenue
Berkeley, Cal. 94704
catalog; sample charge $.50.

Dick Blick Company
P.O. Box 1452
Church Street Station
New York, N.Y. 10008
catalog.

Edgemont Yarn Service
RR 2, Box 14
Maysville, Ky. 41056
brochure.

Fetty-Nielson, Macrame Looms and
  Cords
P.O. Box 1511, Wedgewood Station
Seattle, Wash. 98115
brochure.

Hammett and Company
Hammett Place
Braintree, Mass. 02184
catalog.

The Handcrafters
1 West Brown Street
Waupun, Wis. 53963
brochure $.50.

Hazel Pearson Handicrafts
4128 Temple City Boulevard
Rosemead, Cal. 91770
catalog.

Jean Malsada, Inc.
P.O. Box 767
Roswell, Ga. 30075
catalog.

Kristine Eckert
1430 Montrose Avenue
Dayton, O. 45414
catalog; sample $.50.

Lemco
P.O. Box 40545
San Francisco, Cal. 94149
catalog.

Lily Mills, Handweaving Department
P.O. Box 88
Shelby, N.C. 28150
catalog; samples $.25 per card.

Macrame and Weaving Supply
63 East Adams Street
Chicago, Ill. 60601
catalog $.50.

Macrame Studio
3001 Indianola Avenue
Columbus, O. 43202
catalog $.50.

Magnolia Weaving
2635-29 Avenue, West
Seattle, Wash. 98119
catalog.

The Mannings
RD #2
East Berlin, Pa. 17316
catalog; samples $.50.

Nasco Arts and Crafts
Fort Atkinson, Wis. 53538
Also P.O. Box 3837
Modesto, Cal. 94704
catalog $.50.

Naturalcraft
2199 Bancroft Way
Berkeley, Cal. 94704
catalog $.50.

Northeast Bead Trading Company
12 Depot Street
Kennebunk, Me. 04043

Nylon Net Company
7 Vance Avenue
P.O. Box 592
Memphis, Tenn. 38101
catalog.

Owl and Olive Weavers
4232 Old Leeds Lane
Birmingham, Ala. 35213
samples $1.00. deducted from orders of
$10.00 or more.

P. C. Herwig Company, Inc.
264 Clinton Street
Brooklyn, N.Y. 11201
catalog; samples $.50.

Peoria Arts and Crafts Supplies
1207 West Main Street
Peoria, Ill. 61606
catalog $.50.

Reeves Knotique
2510 Rambling Court
Riverside, Cal. 92504
catalog $.75.

Robin and Russ Handweavers
533 North Adams Street
McMinnville, Ore. 97128
catalog; samples $1.25.

Seaboard Twine
49 Murray Street
New York, N.Y. 10013

Some Place
2990 Adeline Street
Berkeley, Cal. 94703
catalog; samples $.50.

Textile Crafts
856 North Genesee Avenue
P.O. Box 3216
Los Angeles, Cal. 90028
catalog.

The Unique
21½ East Bijou
Colorado Springs, Colo. 80902
catalog; sample charge $1.00, complete
portfolio, $8.00.

Valley Handweaving Supply
200 West Olive Avenue
Fresno, Cal. 93728
brochure; samples $.50.

Warp, Woof and Potpourri
514 North Lake Avenue
Pasadena, Cal. 91101
catalog; sample charge $.50.

The Weaver's Corner
P.O. Box 560125
Miami, Fla. 33156
catalog; samples $.50.

The Weaver's Place
12490 Black Forest Road
Colorado Springs, Colo. 80908
samples $.50–$1.00.

Yellow Springs Strings
P.O. Box 107
68 Goes Station
Yellow Springs, O. 45387
catalog.

Metal

CREATING WITH METAL. by K. E. Granstrom. Van Nostrand Reinhold, New York, 1967. 92 pages. illustrations, photographs. $4.95.

A sound grounding in tools and technique is essential to successful metalworking. *Creating with Metal* presents the basic methods and tools for a variety of metalworking techniques, including: joining, polishing, etching, chasing, raising, smithing, and forging. These techniques are discussed and illustrated as they appear in the construction of useful and decorative articles.

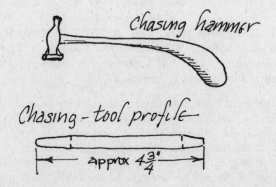

Chasing is a mechanical embellishment of the metal surface. Using chasing tools, decorative patterns are pounded into the metal.

The instructions, for the most part, are concise, simple, and amply clarified by black-and-white photographs. Such simplicity can have its drawbacks, however; a beginner, or even a person with some metalworking experience, would probably get the impression that the techniques are as easy as they look in the pictures. A great deal of experience is required before a successful raising, chasing, or forging operation can be accomplished. The reader unaware of this might be tempted to despair at the thought of an ineptness that really can't be helped. A few hints and encouraging words, plus the use of a step-by-step format and some simpler projects, would be a welcome addition, as would the inclusion of some historical or inspirational material.

SILVERSMITHING. by Robert Goodin and Phillip Popham. Oxford University Press, London, 1971. 128 pages. illustrations, photographs, suppliers list, bibliography, index. paperback edition $5.00.

This little English book covers the usual areas of smithing: forming, joining, casting, and surface embellishing. The text is informative but not sufficiently detailed for beginners. The descriptive photographs are exceptionally clear, but unfortunately few in number.

The Worshipful Company of Goldsmiths

The Worshipful Company of Goldsmiths is the present day successor of the medieval craft guild in London. It has been in existence since the twelfth century and in 1179 was fined 45 marks by King Henry II for having formed itself before receiving his Royal Charter. The Company, which is a great charitable and educational foundation, still encourages high standards in its craft. The hallmark (the word originally meant the mark of Goldsmiths' Hall, London) still guarantees the purity of English gold and silver. It still tests the nation's coinage at the annual Trial of the Pyx at Goldsmiths' Hall, it still 'binds' or enrolls apprentices, it gives scholarships at suitable art schools, it arranges lectures and discussions at the Goldsmiths' Hall and elsewhere, it stages exhibitions, and makes films and filmstrips about the craft, which are available on loan or for sale. It acts in the interests of the whole craft and industry with which it has always been closely associated and is not connected with any individual trade form or association. Despite its proud history and respect for the past, the Company has not neglected the future. It owns the largest collection of modern works in Great Britain, to which additions are continually being made.

Source: SILVERSMITHING. by Robert Goodin and Phillip Popham.

METAL TECHNIQUES FOR CRAFTSMEN. by Oppi Untracht. Doubleday and Company, Garden City, New York, 1968. 509 pages. illustrations, photographs, suppliers list, bibliography, index. $19.95.

The big one, the Bible of metalworking techniques, this book is as indispensable to the metal craftsman as any one of his tools.

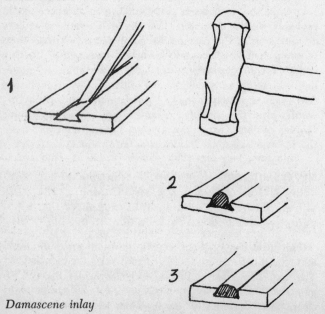

Damascene inlay

Every aspect of metal surface decoration, metal fabrication, and finishing is covered here. The physical and mechanical characteristics of everything from aluminum to zinc are discussed, as are all of the common and most of the obscure tools used for metalworking.

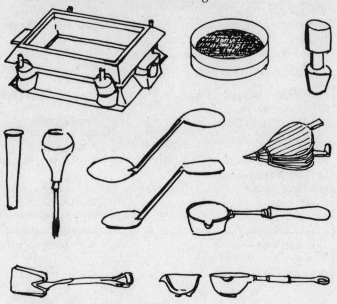

Sand casting tools and materials

Name it and it's here in detail—smithing (silver and pewter), forging, welding, cold metal spinning, soldering (fifty pages on this alone), casting, electroplating and electroforming, polishing and grinding, coloring, and more—all illustrated with photographs and diagrams.

Almost forty pages are devoted to useful charts and tables, listing such things as U.S. standard ring sizes, melting points, and silver and gold wire forms.

One of the nicest features is the inclusion of hundreds of photographs of historical and contemporary metal-crafted items.

For beginners however, this is a silly book to buy, because it's expensive and because a smaller and less inclusive text would serve their needs better. For serious metalworkers, who know they are going to stick with the craft, this is an excellent all-around source book.

METALSMITHING FOR THE ARTIST-CRAFTSMAN. by Richard Thomas. Chilton Book Company, Radnor, Pennsylvania, 1960. 173 pages. illustrations, photographs, bibliography, index. $7.50.

Metalsmithing encompasses a large range of skills, from engraving and carving to die cutting and embossing. For this fine book, Richard Thomas has decided to restrict the field of interest to joining (soldering and riveting), forming (raising, forging, and casting), surface treatment (buffing, polishing, and coloring with chemicals), and general shop information (tools and techniques).

The most complete section is that on raising. Six methods of raising are discussed and presented with step-by-step instructions and really clear photographs. The other material covered is somewhat less comprehensive, although the soldering and general shop information sections are also quite good.

There are no projects as such, because the author feels that the successful design of an object is a personal achievement and a "mystical" province that shouldn't be invaded. However, some remarkable historical pieces are included for inspiration.

CREATIVE GOLD AND SILVERSMITHING. by Sharr Choate with Bonnie Ciecil De May. Crown Publishers, New York, 1970. 298 pages. illustrations, photographs, bibliography, index. $8.95.

This is a rather good all-around source book on smithing techniques aimed at the jewelry-making crowd. Hundreds of helpful hints on all aspects of jewelry related techniques are included. There are complete sections devoted to rings,

---

Dutch Raising to Form a Hemisphere

1. Place a flat metal disk at an angle against the T-stake. With a 1½ lb. cross-peen hammer, strike the portion projecting above and drive to the horizontal plane.
2. The angle is increased.

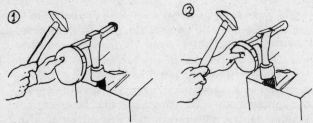

3. Work progressively to the center of the piece. Hold the hammer at the butt for added leverage.
4. Use a heavy rawhide mallet to work out irregularities in the surface. Hold the work parallel to the horizontal surface of the stake.

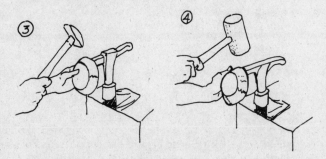

5. Continue working towards the center with the cross-peen hammer (annealing might be necessary at various stages of the raising).
6. Use rawhide mallet again for "bouging" (removing surface irregularities).

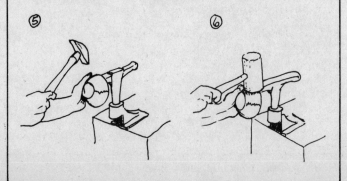

7. When the center is reached the angles are removed by working the piece over a mushroom vertical stake. Again, a rawhide mallet is used.
8. Once a hemispherical shape is attained, the work is planished (surface irregularities are removed).

Source: METALSMITHING FOR THE ARTIST-CRAFTS-MAN. by Richard Thomas.

---

mountings and findings, appliqué, inlay work, stone inlay, and channel work. The section on engraving, one of the more difficult decorating techniques to master, is rather good, as is that on electroplating and electroforming.

Lots and lots of good, clear illustrations help in demonstrating techniques and tools, and fifteen pages' worth of tables and charts is an additional feature.

INDIAN SILVERSMITHING. by W. Ben Hunt. Collier Books, 1972. 160 pages. illustrations, photographs, suppliers list, index. paperback edition $4.95.

Sometime between 1850 and 1870, the Navajo Indians learned the more sophisticated techniques of European silversmithing from the Mexican *plateros* (silversmiths). This art spread from the Navajos to the Zunis and other smaller tribes of the Pueblo group. Many of the objects made by the Indians were endowed with religious significance, and therefore they were well crafted and highly prized by their owners. Most of the silverwork done today by the Navajo is made for the commercial market; the traditional forms have been retained, but the craftsmanship and original power and beauty have almost been lost.

Squash blossom motifs

This book offers the craftsman a series of silver-crafted projects, some of which, like the *keto* (a Navajo armguard to protect the wrist and arm when shooting with bow and arrow) are authentic; others, like the saltcellar or silver watchband, have adapted the techniques and design motifs of the Indian but are obviously not traditional items. The

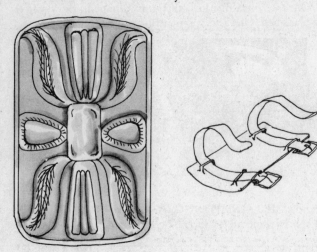

Keto design and armband detail

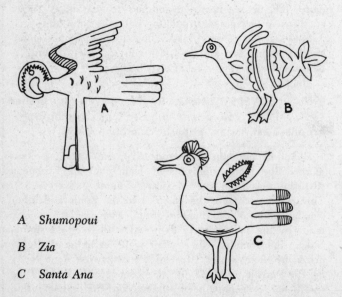

A   *Shumopoui*

B   *Zia*

C   *Santa Ana*

Indian pottery motifs adopted for pins

instructions are extremely clear and well illustrated with line drawings and photographs. The tools required for these projects are relatively simple, and the author suggests alternative handmade tools to use for many of the techniques. The motifs used are all authentic, and the objects and jewelry are quite beautiful, making this an extremely fine book for silversmiths who wish to broaden their design vocabulary while enhancing their wardrobe and surroundings.

COPPERCRAFT AND SILVER MADE AT HOME. by Karl Robert Kramer and Nora Kramer. Dover Publications, New York, 1971. 175 pages. illustrations, photographs, suppliers list. $5.50. paperback edition $3.00.

This book was written not only for beginning metalworkers, but for people who have no craft experience in any field.

The procedures given for each of the projects are simple and the directions are precise. The projects themselves—and they include nameplates, a pin and earring set, a silver salt spoon, and copper plates—are supposed to have actually been made in ordinary home kitchens with simple equipment and by amateurs of all ages. The designs employed in these projects are a bit unsophisticated; however, it is the learning process rather than the finished product that is emphasized here.

Ore smelting, from a Japanese print

Interview

Lance Fredericks is a silversmith and teacher at the Lexington School for the Deaf in Jackson Heights, New York.

Five percent—and that's all—of the people we call "deaf" can't hear at all. Ninety-five percent have some residual hearing and with a good hearing aid can hear to augment their vision. They have, from my experience, far better visual sensitivity than a fully hearing person does; they have it developed. I thought that would lend itself well to any craft area, and specifically metal, since I personally believe that a lot of the technical skills required for metalwork are visually oriented. For instance, when you're planishing a raising, it's important to have daylight; it's important that you position yourself so that the light reflects off your piece so that you can put a uniform surface on it. Now, I work, simply because of the way I receive sensory input, auditorily and visually. If I hear a "ping" that's wrong, I know I haven't got my work positioned properly on the stake, but it's not impossible to do that totally visually because the same thing I'm responding to aurally, I've found I can respond to tactilely. When I hear a "ping" I can feel the same thing with my fingers. These kids are able to respond and pick up by vision and taction what they're being deprived of in audition.

There are a lot of things I feel can be offered to hearing-impaired children through this kind of a class, both in its ability to acquaint them with sensory input they don't normally respond to—such as taction, and hopefully, directing some of these kids into a field they never before would have approached. However, I'm not out to prepare any child for an apprenticeship. This course is used by me as an enrichment, not as a vocational training. If a kid has no desire to go to college, or he hasn't the money or the ability, and he sees that he has an aptitude for metalwork and his parents see it, too, and he says to himself I really better buckle down and work after school if possible and see how far I can get, then I'm more than happy to work with him. I have one student now where this is the case. But on the whole, deaf education has been too much geared in the past along vocational lines.

I have an arrangement with the school whereby I maintain my shop at the school and keep all of my metalsmithing equipment at school and the students use my tools under my supervision. In this way the school has a minimum outlay of funds.

There are people in the school who are just dumbfounded by the results of this program. When I put up an exhibition of the kids' work they think that I did it all myself, and these are people who work with the hearing-impaired every day! So it is the kids themselves who are the greatest salesmen for the program, which is beginning to move on its own; I don't have to push it so hard any more, and I'm able to get back and devote more time to my own work.

Salt and pepper #2, Lance Fredericks

Originally I made the transition from painting to metalwork because I thought that painting was nonfunctional. When I was going through school everything was *function*. I think I have been forced into that so much that my own bent now is toward the nonfunctional. However, I haven't completely given the other up yet. I like to make functional items that are definitely beautiful as nonfunctional objects.

Altar set: chalice, paten, candlesticks, cruets; Lance Fredericks

Once you prove yourself as competent you gain the right to question.

There are certain basic things to have if you want to do metalwork. There are about six basic pairs of pliers which are the first six you'll find in any catalog. And an excellent planishing hammer is a necessity and you have to keep it well. You have to grind the sharp edge it comes with and you have to take off the protective coating. You have to take a piece of polishing paper and a piece of leather and you have to keep a mirror finish on it at all times. A planishing hammer is only used to hit precious metal; it's never used to hit steel and it's never used for chasing.

There's one way to get around the expense of silver and that's to use copper. Copper tends to be a little more malleable, a little softer. If you want a true representation of the workability of silver use brass. Use the same gauge for raising, say, eighteen gauge, and you'll cut down tremendously on cost while learning.

The people who sit at home with their precut pieces of copper and their fifty-dollar kilns, turning out little charms, have contributed to tearing down the craft I'm trying to build up.

Pentapus pumping punchbowl, Lance Fredericks

I do a lot of business with Allcraft. They tend to be retail-oriented and the people there are knowledgeable. Dixon in New Jersey is really good for any custom jobs; if you want a hallmark made, go there. Hoover and Strong in Buffalo is great for gold—fast, and the goods are well labeled. The best thing to do is to write everybody. Get all the catalogs you can and price lists and shop around that way.

METALWORK AND ENAMELLING. by Herbert Maryon. Dover Publications, New York, 1971. 335 pages. illustrations, photographs, bibliography, index. paperback edition $3.50.

When the Queen of England invested Herbert Maryon with the Order of the British Empire, she asked him what he spent his time upon. "Well, Ma'am,' he answered, "I am a sort of back room boy at the British Museum."

This backroom boy has produced a book, now in its fifth edition (it was originally published in 1912), that is a solid source for metalwork and its allied crafts. Some tools and technique references are dated, but basic information on soldering, gem setting, chasing, repoussé, inlay, enameling, casting, and general construction is quite complete and useful.

Instructions for methodology are illustrated with line drawings, and photographs of historical metalwork are provided in a section at the end of the book along with a discussion of their techniques.

Gold Immersion Bath Without Electric Current

1 gallon water
3 ounces sodium cyanide
½ ounce sodium or potassium gold cyanide
2 ounces sodium bisulfite
2 ounces caustic potash

Heat solution to 180° F. and maintain this temperature throughout plating process. Suspend article by a thin copper wire and immerse in solution. Article should not be held in solution more than a few seconds as prolonged immersion adds no thickness to the deposit. Once the article is covered with a thin gold plating, it acts as a solid gold article and the deposit ends. Gold immersion deposits are quite thin and less durable than those of regular gold plating baths.

The gold in this immersion bath formula comes from the sodium or potassium gold cyanide in the solution. It is gradually diminished with use and should be replenished. In fact, some amount is removed each time an article is taken from the bath. This is called *drag-out*. This loss can become expensive, but it can be reduced by dipping the article into a container of clean distilled water immediately upon removal from solution. This water can be saved and used to replenish the bath when necessary, thereby returning to the solution what it has lost.

Source: METAL TECHNIQUES FOR CRAFTSMEN. by Oppi Untracht.

MODERN PEWTER, DESIGN AND TECHNIQUE. by Shirley Charron. Van Nostrand Reinhold, New York, 1973. 143 pages. illustrations, photographs, suppliers list, bibliography, index. $9.95.

Modern pewter is a bright, shiny, nontarnishing metal. The old, dark pewter was adulterated with lead, a practice now illegal.

Pewter—the old pewter, that is—was used by the Greeks, Romans, Chinese, and Japanese over two thousand years ago. In the Middle Ages England arose as the pewter center of the world. Strong guilds were organized which governed the craftsmanship of pewter objects and also the social and moral life of the pewtersmith. Pewter was used extensively in English households for over five hundred years. Everything from ale mugs to bedpans was crafted from it.

The alloy pewter has varied in composition through the ages, but tin has always been the major component. Most early pewter contained lead, and this caused the metal to become dark with age. The lead alloy was used because it was less expensive and easier to work than other tin alloys. During the guild era, pewter was graded according to its lead content. The best quality contained tin, copper, or antimony, and a little bismuth.

Pewtersmithing reached its height in America in the period between 1750 and 1850. Since the tariffs on raw tin were very high (Britain was the major supplier), much of the production of pewtersmiths was recycled back into the melting pot. This is the reason for the scarcity of antique American pewter today.

Modern pewter contains about 92 percent tin, 6 percent antimony, and 2 percent copper. It's a beautiful, useful, easily worked metal. Shirley Charron's book is an excellent introduction to the ways of crafting this metal. She discusses raising, soldering, shaping, and polishing as they arise in the course of making a series of elegant pewter objects—bowls, dishes, candlesticks, and coffee pots to name just a few. All techniques are clearly illustrated with black-and-white photographs.

With the price of silver climbing out of sight these days, the author is performing a valuable service in pointing out that pewter has aesthetic as well as economic advantages as an alternative metal.

METALWORKING. by Oscar Almeida. Drake Publishers, New York, 1971. 288 pages. illustrations, photographs, suppliers list, bibliography, index. $6.95.

This is a small encyclopedic text that covers the whole spectrum of the craft from heat treatment of steel to turning pieces on an engine lathe. The treatment of all the subjects is rather cursory, but the book's inclusive nature makes it a good choice for general craftsmen who want to know a little about a lot.

REPOUSSAGE: THE EMBOSSING OF METAL. by Yves Meriel-Bussy. Sterling Publishing Company, New York, 1970. 48 pages. illustrations, photographs. $2.95.

Repoussage is the technique of hammering out metal in hollow forms from the reverse side.

This book does not really deal with the traditional techniques of this craft, because extremely thin metal sheets are used in the projects. The necessity of hammers and repoussage tools is thus eliminated. The author suggests using wooden clay modeling tools and metal-tipped styluses to emboss the surface of thin copper, aluminum, or tin sheet.

The projects are presented in order of difficulty, and range from a simple medallion plaque to complicated, stylized animal forms and mobiles. The design motifs are rather unsophisticated, but the techniques are simple and rewarding, making this a perfect children's rainy day activity book.

TINCRAFT. by Lucy Sargent. Simon and Schuster, New York, 1972. 200 pages. illustrations, photographs (some color), suppliers list, index. $9.95.

Don't throw out that tin can! says Lucy Sargent. Recycle it into a pair of beautiful Mexican candlesticks, or a flower basket, a bird feeder, a colonial lantern. Remaking tin cans into useful and decorative objects is a brilliant solution to an environmental problem. The annual tin can consumption in America averages 389 per person.

This book is written in a clear, friendly style. The instructions for the various projects are easy to follow, and the construction diagrams are exceptionally good. The tools required for this craft are simple and inexpensive; the techniques are uncomplicated and easy to master. Yet all the projects have a high-quality look, not what might be expected from tin can constructions. One of the nicest is a bonbon basket made entirely from a Portuguese sardine can! For ornaments and jewelry, Lucy Sargent favors the Campbell's soup can (I seem to remember a fellow named Warhol who liked them, too).

METAL. by John Hack. Van Nostrand Reinhold, New York, 1972. 88 pages. illustrations, photographs. paperback edition $2.95.

This book is concerned mostly with objects made from metal wire, such as earrings, necklaces, pins, salad spoons, and an umbrella stand.

The instructions for metal wire-working techniques are adequate, but the superficial treatment of other techniques (raising, soldering, and surface embellishment) makes it almost impossible for a novice metalworker to construct any of the given projects that utilize these techniques.

EARLY AMERICAN METAL PROJECTS. by Joseph William Daniele. McKnight Publishing Company, Bloomington, Illinois, 1971. 144 pages. illustrations, photographs, suppliers list. $9.32.

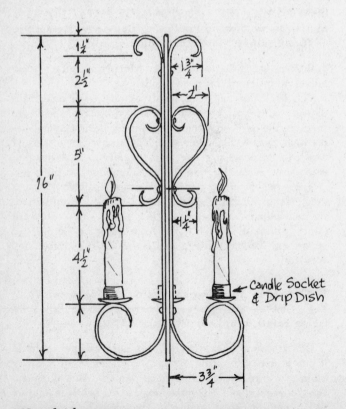

Masacksick sconce

A book of projects based upon replicas of Early American objects. Each project is presented with plans, step-by-step "cook book" type instructions, and construction diagrams. The projects are depicted in their finished state by black-and-white photographs, and all of them look quite authentic.

Belt buckle of fabricated and oxidized brass, Thomas Della Marica (age 14)

GOLD, ITS BEAUTY, POWER AND ALLURE, revised edition. by C. H. Sutherland. McGraw-Hill, New York, 1969. 196 pages. illustrations, photographs (some color), bibliography, index. $8.95.

An interesting historical account of gold, goldsmithing, and coinage systems, both ancient and modern, this book has numerous photographs, both black-and-white and color, depicting objects made of gold from all over the world and from all periods.

Egyptian goldsmiths at work, showing different stages in process and control. Detail from a tomb painting at Beni Hassan, early second millennium, B.C.

PROJECTS IN GENERAL METALWORK. by M. J. Ruley. McKnight Publishing Company, Bloomington, Illinois, 1969. 80 pages. illustrations, photographs, bibliography. text edition $5.28.

This book offers thirty-five vocational high school type projects—everything from a garden trowel to an all-purpose

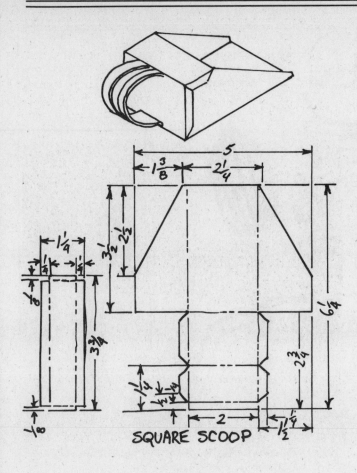

SQUARE SCOOP

scoop. The projects are presented with layout plans and step-by-step instructions. All of them are useful and look like a lot of fun to make.

EARLY AMERICAN IRONWARE. by Henry J. Kauffman. Charles E. Tuttle Company, Rutland, Vermont, 1967. 166 pages. illustrations, photographs, index. $10.00.

This is a thoroughly documented historical panorama, depicting the importance of ironware in the lives of our ancestors. The author describes not only what was made, but also how it was made, exploring all the crafts concerned. Separate chapters are devoted to blacksmiths, whitesmiths (tin or white metalworkers), farriers (shoe smiths who also treated diseases of the horse), edge toolmakers, cutlers, locksmiths, gunsmiths, nailers, wheelwrights, and tinsmiths. The text is accompanied by hundreds of photographs and illustrations depicting the objects made and the techniques employed in making them. It is a good informational and inspirational book.

AMERICAN COPPER AND BRASS. by Henry J. Kauffman. Thomas Nelson, Nashville, Tennessee, 1968. 288 pages. illustrations, photographs, bibliography, index. $12.50.

THE AMERICAN PEWTERER, HIS TECHNIQUES AND HIS PRODUCTS. by Henry J. Kauffman. Thomas Nelson, Nashville, Tennessee, 1970. 158 pages. illustrations, photographs, index. $10.00.

A HISTORY OF AMERICAN PEWTER. by Charles F. Montgomery. Praeger Publishers, New York, 1973. 246 pages. illustrations, photographs, bibliography, index. $17.50.

Bed warming pan construction

Name That Tool

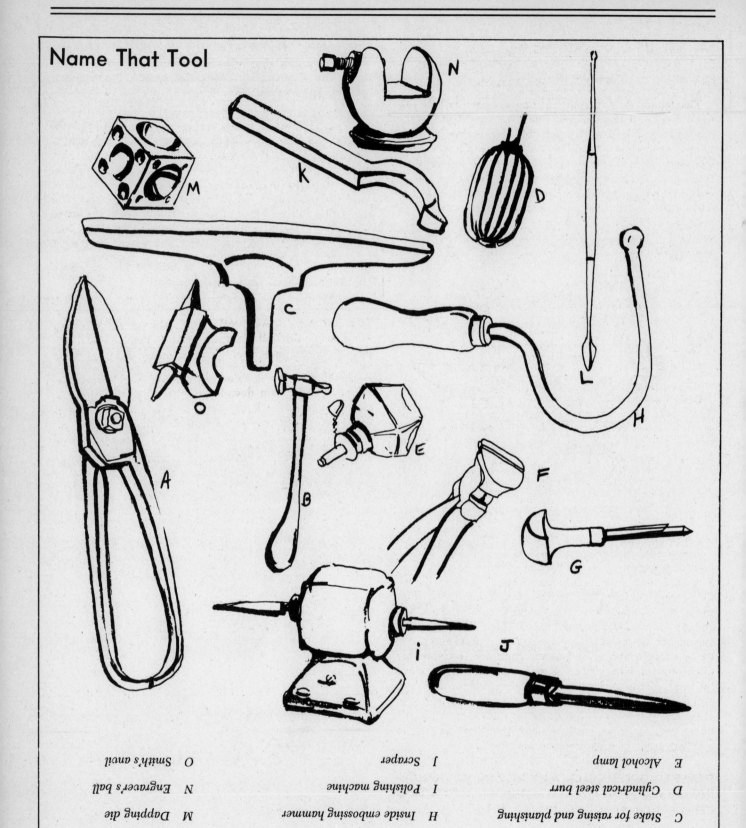

A   Silversmith's shears
B   Chaser's hammer
C   Stake for raising and planishing
D   Cylindrical steel burr
E   Alcohol lamp

F   End cutters
G   Graver with half round head
H   Inside embossing hammer
I   Polishing machine
J   Scraper

K   Inside metal stamp
L   Wax carver
M   Dapping die
N   Engraver's ball
O   Smith's anvil

THE ART OF BLACKSMITHING. by Alex W. Bealer. Funk and Wagnalls, New York, 1969. 425 pages. illustrations, bibliography, index. $10.00.

The smith was revered by the ancients because he worked with all four elements—fire, air, earth, and water. His bellows controlled the air; his primary metal, iron, came from deep within the bowels of the earth; and water was essential to cool his iron and temper his red-hot steel. Hephaestus, Vulcan, and Thor were mythological smiths endowed with magical powers; their art, spanning over 6,000 years, is still being practiced today by craftsmen all over the world.

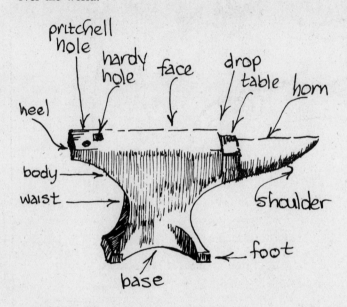

If you want to know how to make an eighteenth-century iron hinge, or how a muzzle-loading rifle barrel was welded, *The Art of Blacksmithing* has the answers. If you would like to set up a blacksmith shop, this book describes and illustrates the equipment and techniques, both modern and ancient, of working iron by hand. There is a wealth of information on the history of this craft, useful for the collector of wrought iron as well as the craftsman. Included are discussions of how kitchen utensils and tools were made by hand, of the intricate methods used to form arms and armor, and of the special tools and techniques of the decorative iron worker. On the most practical level, however, the instructions for using tools and smithing techniques may be a bit too general for beginners to use.

DRAKE'S MODERN BLACKSMITHING AND HORSESHOE-ING. by J. C. Holmstrom. Drake Publishers, New York, 1971. 114 pages. illustrations, index. $4.95.

This little book is full of helpful hints to the practical blacksmith who must make and repair most of his own tools. However, the instructions are very general and rarely illustrated. The sections on shoeing and horse diseases are interesting and perhaps useful to people living out in the backwoods.

How to Repair a Flopping Plow

When a plow is flopping or going everywhere so that the owner don't know what is the matter, the fault should be looked for first in the beam. If the beam is loose the plow will not run steady, but the reason for this trouble, in most cases, is in the share. If the point has too little "suction," and the edge of the share is too much rolling, the plow generally acts this way. To remedy this, sharpen the share, set the point down, and the edge of the lay from the point all the way back to the heel, and the plow will work right.

Source: DRAKE'S MODERN BLACKSMITHING, AND HORSESHOEING. by J. C. Holmstrom.

THE VILLAGE BLACKSMITH. by Aldren A. Watson. Thomas Y. Crowell Company, New York, 1968. 125 pages. illustrations, bibliography, index. $6.95.

The blacksmith was no mere shoer of horses. He was the maker of tools, barn door hinges, andirons, sled runners, wagon springs, door latches, pots and pans, harnesses, and hardware. In his pre–mass production village smithy, he made by hand nearly every metal object then in common use.

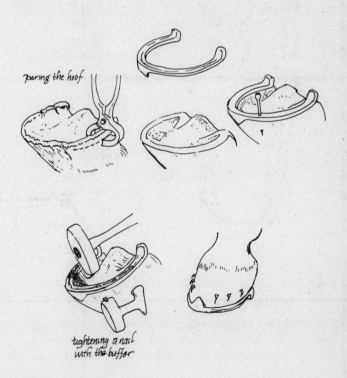

Shoeing a horse

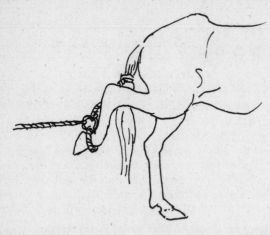

A horse that was a "kicker" could be restrained by lashing him up in a rope tied to his tail and looped around his hind feet. The harder the horse tried to kick, the harder he pulled on his own tail.

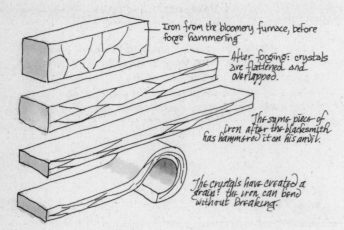

Iron from the bloomery furnace, before forge hammering

After forging: crystals are flattened and overlapped.

The same piece of iron after the blacksmith has hammered it on his anvil.

The crystals have created a grain: the iron can bend without breaking.

Forged iron

This profusely illustrated book discusses the tools, techniques, and cultural importance of the village blacksmith in the era of horse-drawn transportation. Craftsmen interested in smithing will find Aldren Watson's book a wonderful, inspirational survey.

THE MODERN BLACKSMITH. by Alexander G. Weygers. Van Nostrand Reinhold, New York, 1974. 96 pages. illustrations, photographs. paperback edition $4.95.

The utilization of salvaged steel material is a contemporary phenomenon. The present "economy of waste and obsolescence" has created an abundance of high-quality steel from scrapped cars and heavy mechanical and industrial equipment. This gives the modern blacksmith excellent material at almost no cost.

principles in use of hammer & body motions, & body stance

hammer is above head at start

⊙shoulder joint

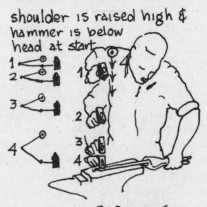

Right

shoulder is down & stationary, all muscles & joints are at maximum use.

shoulder is raised high & hammer is below head at start

Wrong

shoulder does most of work, arm & wrist are less active

Today's blacksmith must learn to do by himself what the old-time blacksmith and his helper did as a team. Therefore, the author proposes to teach a sense of resourcefulness that will allow for the invention, improvisation, and construction of whatever may be needed to reduce the handicap of working alone.

Mr. Weygers' love for this craft is borne out by his excellent presentation of the techniques of blacksmithing. Six hundred illustrations demonstrate how the various procedures and alternative procedures are executed.

This is a great book for beginning blacksmiths and an even better one for old hands.

1ˢᵗ heat

2ⁿᵈ heat

3ʳᵈ heat

heading plate

anvil hardy hole

Upsetting a rod end to form a bolt end ∼

Metal Suppliers

For suppliers of:
Metalworking Tools
Materials and Supplies for Casting
Custom Casting Houses
Metals (Precious, Copper, Bronze, and White Metal)
refer to jewelry section suppliers list.

PLATING

Auromet Corporation
199 Canal Street
New York, N.Y.

B and D Polishing and Plating Corporation
1575 York Avenue
New York, N.Y. 10028
gold and silver plating.

Davis-K Products Company
135 West 29 Street
New York, N.Y.
gold solutions and salts.

Franklin Plating and Polishing Company
630 South Sixth
Columbus, O.

Hill Cross Company, Inc.
393 Pearl Street
New York, N.Y. 10038

Hoover and Strong, Inc.
111 West Tupper Street
Buffalo, N.Y.
electroplating.

Sel-Rex Corporation
(subsidiary of the Meaker Company)
75 River Road
Nutley, N.J.
plating equipment.

PEWTER SUPPLIERS

Golden Metal Industries
50 Taylor Drive
East Providence, R.I. 02916

J. C. Boardman and Company
86 Hartford Turnpike
South Wallingford, Conn. 06492

Meriden Rolling Mills
Meriden, Conn.

White Metal Rolling and Stamping Corporation
80 Moultrie Street
Brooklyn, N.Y. 11222

Mosaics

MAKING MOSAICS. by John Berry. Watson-Guptill Publications, New York, 1966. 104 pages. illustrations, photographs, suppliers list, bibliography, index. $2.50.

Mosaic making is traditionally a process of producing pictures or patterns by cementing together small pieces of stone, glass, etc. Almost any material that is permanent and reasonably light in weight can be used in mosaic as *tesserae* (the Latinized Greek word meaning "four cornered," it refers to the discreet units of mosaic).

cutting tesserae

This book, originally published in England, is a really fine introduction to the art of making mosaics. All the basic aspects of the processes are covered: collection and construction of tesserae, construction of supports, and a step-by-step discussion of the direct and indirect methods of applying materials to mosaic adhesive. A series of simple projects is presented, which further illustrates mosaic techniques. The projects include a coffee table, a nameplate, a lamp base, and a clever and instructive paper mosaic.

MODERN MOSAIC TECHNIQUES. by Janice Lovoos and Felice Paramore. Watson-Guptill Publications, New York, 1967. 169 pages. illustrations, photographs, suppliers list, bibliography, index. $9.95.

Contemporary mosaic makers still employ two traditional methods: the direct and indirect techniques.

The direct method involves the direct setting of the *tesserae* in the cement, sand, glue, or whatever material is used. Rough sketches can be followed, or more experienced craftsmen may work spontaneously.

The indirect, or reverse, method is so called because the design is first drawn on paper and then the *tesserae* are pasted onto this same paper. The whole thing is then turned upside down into the wet binding material, the paper is peeled off, and the design appears in the reverse of the original. This procedure has been used for over 500 years.

These techniques, along with a host of modern ones, are presented with explicit instructions in this book. Sand casting (reverse method using sand to hold the tesserae), found object mosaics, wood mosaics, nail mosaics, three-dimensional mosaics, and simple mosaic techniques for children are discussed in great detail and profusely illustrated with black-and-white photographs of the processes and finished objects.

MOSAIC TECHNIQUES. by Mary-Lou Stribling. Crown Publishers, New York, 1966. 244 pages. illustrations, photographs, suppliers list, bibliography, index. $7.95.

To meet diversified interests, the material presented in this book goes beyond traditional concepts of mosaics, and includes guidance for experimentation and design, ways of making unusual materials and original forms, as well as detailed directions for specific projects.

THE MOSAICS OF JEANNE REYNAL. text by Dore Ashton, Elaine De Kooning, and others. George Wittenborn, New York, 1964. 111 pages. photographs (some color).

This is an excellent inspirational book on the work and techniques of an innovative and highly respected artist, Jeanne Reynal. Her primary concern was, and still is, to detach the mosaic from its static mural tradition. Furthermore, she is determined that her own mosaics were to be fresh works of art, not translations of painting. The extent of her success is portrayed in the numerous black-and-white and color photographs in this interesting and inspiring book.

MOSAIC HISTORY AND TECHNIQUE. by Peter Fischer. McGraw-Hill, New York, 1971. 152 pages. illustrations, photographs (some color), bibliography, index. $12.95.

This is a beautiful and complete historical survey of the techniques and design motifs of the mosaic art.

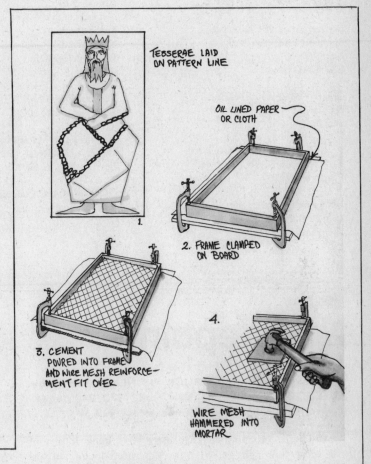

TESSERAE LAID ON PATTERN LINE

OIL LINED PAPER OR CLOTH

1.

2. FRAME CLAMPED ON BOARD

3. CEMENT POURED INTO FRAME AND WIRE MESH REINFORCEMENT FIT OVER

4.

WIRE MESH HAMMERED INTO MORTAR

MOSAIC MAKING. by Helen Hutton. Von Nostrand Reinhold, New York, 1966. 136 pages. illustrations, photographs, suppliers list, bibliography, index. $7.95.

This is a fine introduction to the techniques of mosaics for beginners. A discussion of the basic methods is followed by a series of didactic projects presented in illustrated, step-by-step format.

After the traditional techniques have been presented, the author goes on to offer a number of alternative mosaics—stained glass mosaics, pebble mosaics, mosaics using homemade ceramic tesserae, mosaics using stones, flints, and fossils, seed and bark mosaics, wood and paper mosaics. There is also practical information on mortar mixes, carpentry, water-proofing and more.

Beginners will find the discussion of the direct and indirect methods of construction extremely clear and easy to follow.

5.

DESIGN TRACED THROUGH WITH TAILOR'S WHEEL (ONLY ABOUT $\frac{1}{8}$ OF PATTERN IS TRACED AT A TIME.)

6.

MORTAR CUT CLOSE TO PATTERN LINE IN ORDER TO FACILITATE ADDING NEW MORTAR WHEN THIS SECTION HAS DRIED.

General Mosaic Supplies

Avalon Manufacturing Corporation
128 Middleton Street
Brooklyn, N.Y.

Bergen Arts and Crafts, Inc.
Shetland Industrial Park
Box 689
Salem, Mass.

Creative Merchandisers, Inc.
285 Jacoby Street
San Rafael, Cal.

Economy Handicrafts, Inc.
47-11 Francis Lewis Boulevard
Flushing, N.Y.

Immerman's Crafts, Inc.
16912 Miles Avenue
Cleveland, O.

Korsin, Inc.
1500 Cortland
Chicago, Ill.

Latco Products
3371 Glendale Boulevard
Los Angeles, Cal.

Leo Popper and Sons
143 Franklin Street
New York, N.Y. 10013

Magnus Craft Materials, Inc.
108 Franklin Street
New York, N.Y. 10013

The Mosaic Arts Company
Pittsburgh, Pa.

The Mosaic Shop
3522 Boulevard of the Allies
Pittsburgh, Pa.

Mosaic Workshop
8426 Melrose Avenue
Los Angeles, Cal.

Stewart Clay Company
133 Mulberry Street
New York, N.Y.

Tepping Studio Supply Company
3517 Riverside Drive
Dayton, O.

Needlepoint

THE NEW YORK TIMES BOOK OF NEEDLEPOINT. by Elaine Slater. Quadrangle, New York, 1973. 248 pages. illustrations, photographs (some color). $17.50.

Although comparatively expensive, this book is one of the most thorough guides to certain needlepoint stitches for the beginner. People who generally have difficulty learning needlework on their own, and who have money enough to spend on this book and an additional one to fill in lacking information, will probably benefit greatly from the author's approach. She has chosen to connect the theory and practice of needlepoint by a common thread, the sampler. Nine stitches: the brick, old Florentine, Hungarian point, upright gobelin encroaching, oblong cross with back, Hungarian ground, mosaic, basketweave, and continental, are used in a twenty-five-square sampler. Each stitch receives full chapter coverage, in which the needle movements for each row of canvas are described and illustrated with clear multicolored drawings. There are suggestions for how and where to use the stitch under discussion. Ms. Slater also shows the common errors that might be made by the beginning needlepointer, a very instructive feature.

There is not too much general information on materials aside from what's needed for completion of the sampler, and there is a similar lack of adequate finishing and blocking instructions. However, the purpose behind this book seems to be to teach the stitches as clearly and completely as possible, and persons seeking additional information on other needlepoint necessities will have to look elsewhere.

NEEDLEPOINT. edited by Susan Sedlacek Lampton. Sunset Books, Menlo Park, California, 1972. 80 pages. illustrations, photographs. paperback edition $1.95.

Probably the most difficult and confusing aspect of needlepoint for beginners is exactly how to stitch in the design on canvas. The second most difficult aspect is the finishing process. This inexpensive book deals with the basic methods of needlepoint with special emphasis on these two problem areas. One section, "Learning the Basic Needlepoint Stitch," presents an exhaustive step-by-step treatment of how and where to start stitching, how to move to the next row, how to stitch in background areas, and how to end a length of yarn. The text is full of helpful pointers and is accompanied by clear photographs of each step. Nine basic stitches, including a bargello variation, are presented in the same manner. The section on finishing discusses thoroughly making a pillow from start to finish, mitering corners, mounting a canvas piece on a support, boxed edges, and tassels and framing.

Sixteen projects are presented with patterns, step-by-step instructions, and finishing details. These projects include an eyeglass case, a belt, watchbands, coasters, and a handbag.

All in all, this book offers the beginner terrific value from the standpoint of both price and content.

CREATIVE CANVAS WORK. by Elsa S. Williams. Van Nostrand Reinhold, New York, 1971. 64 pages. illustrations, photographs. $6.95.

This is a short book containing short but clear sections on all topics of needlepointing. There is an especially nice treatment of stitch uses—what stitches are appropriate for certain patterns—and good border suggestions.

NEEDLEPOINT FOR THE WHOLE FAMILY. by Nina Mortellito. Walker and Company, New York, 1973. 192 pages. illustrations, photographs, suppliers list, bibliography. $12.95.

If any book is going to turn a bumbling beginner into an accomplished ace needlepointer, it's this one. Nina Needlepointer (as she is known to the trade) gives general information on everything from mesh size to the fine points of shading. Her stitch glossary not only gives standard needlepoint scheme diagrams, but also diagrams order and position of each successive stitch for right- and left-handed workers. Thirty-three stitches in all are explained in this way.

CANVAS EMBROIDERY. by Diana Springall. Charles T. Branford Company, Newton Centre, Massachusetts, 1969. 192 pages. illustrations, photographs, bibliography. $12.00.

The first half of this book is taken up with designs. Again, as with many British books (this one was originally published in England by B. T. Batsford,) the design inspiration for needlework is derived from "natural sources." Unfortunately, when British needlepointers use nature as their source, they seem to be compelled to create abstract designs by a kind of expressionistic technique. Moreover, they neglect to make would-be needleworkers sufficiently aware of the difficulties inherent in dealing with motifs of this type and the fact that only a handful of painters and sculptors have been truly successful in creating abstract work from so-called natural forms.

The remainder of the book is comprised of a stitch glossary that contains 138 different stitches. The stitching process is not described but only illustrated by schematic line drawings and very unclear photographs of the finished stitches.

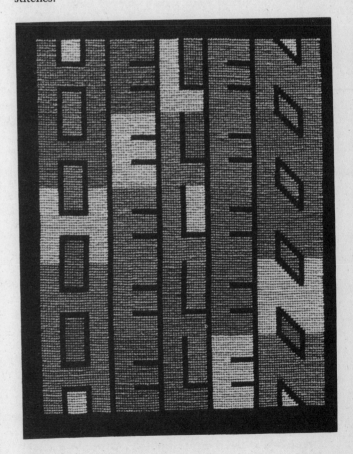

"Helen," 14" x 18" 10-mesh-to-the-inch canvas, 3 ply tapestry yarn; Helen Yrisarry

The projects section is organized in a kind of family togetherness structure with special items for mom and dad, sister and brother, the whole family. A nice touch. Finishing the projects shouldn't cause too much difficulty, because Nina's finishing section is very clear and inclusive. The blocking operation is illustrated by step-by-step photographs.

With all these good features, the lack of a strong design section is unfortunate, but not fatal. This is still an excellent book for left- and right-handed moms, dads, brothers, and sisters.

Interview

It was a hot and sunny Monday in August when the cab from the suburban train station stopped before the well-manicured acreage of the corner house. I walked around to the back, unlatching the wooden gate as I had been instructed, and was greeted by my cousin Kathy and her husband Eric who were sunning themselves poolside. The sunlight played upon the ceramic surfaces of the two temple dogs that stood guard over the shallow end and I looked longingly toward the unused sliding pond. As I shook hands with Eric, my distinctive shade of urban drab was all too apparent. Stumbling over a discarded tube of Coppertone I cursed my stupidity and lack of swimsuit and headed for the air-conditioned house. I was inside only a few minutes when I heard the sound of the electric garage door open and knew Aunt Ruth was home. She emerged carrying several bags of groceries. These, I later learned, contained our lunch—a feast of fried chicken from the Poultry Mart, potato pancakes, applesauce, chicken salad, farm fresh tomatoes, rye bread, and more Coca-Cola than in Sammy Davis's wildest dreams. We exchanged a few pleasantries but wasted no time in laying the spread and getting down to cases.

Deborah Lippman: First of all, when did you start needle-pointing? How long have you been doing it?

Ruth Ross: I've been doing it all my life, since I was about fourteen, fifteen, because Mr. Barrak—did you know the Barraks on East Fifth Street? Well, his sister was a home economics teacher at Evander Childs High School and they used to do these projects, and so she'd bring material home and we would all sit and she would teach us. We'd do it on graph paper first and then transpose it ourselves to the canvas.

Deborah Lippman: I remember you were doing a lot of knitting for a while and not much needlepoint—

Ruth Ross: Well, then I used to needlepoint. I started knitting later, after Barbara was born.

Deborah Lippman: It seems that now you don't knit any more, you only needlepoint.

Ruth Ross: I'm knitting your mother a sweater, wait till you see. I also crochet. I'm making an Irish lace bedspread for Stacy.

Deborah Lippman: Oh, so I guess needlepoint isn't your number one overriding passion.

Ruth Ross: I love them all. I couldn't tell you which one I like best.

Deborah Lippman: Do you prefer needlepoint or bargello, or do you like one for some things and another for other things?

Ruth Ross: I like to combine. Like, a border will be bargello, but the middle will be needlepoint. Then I like to use the different mediums—the metallic threads, the silk threads, the mercerized threads—to combine them with the wool, with the Persian yarns for different effects. You can see that in my sampler. The border on that is bargello. A lot of those are embroidery stitches that I applied to canvas. You can see, here I used a daisy stitch, here's a leaf stitch, this is Hungarian, that's rya or turkey stitch. . . .

Deborah Lippman: What are all these different-looking stitches?

Ruth Ross: Those are weaves. I just do them as I go along. I like to modify and invent new stitches when it seems right.

Deborah Lippman: I notice that you like to work with gradation of color. Do you encounter many difficulties in that? Is it hard to find a dye lot in the real world that matches up with the color in your head?

Ruth Ross: It gets tricky. Now, in the Vasarely Op painting I did I had one color I used three times, but the grid was different—the grid is the stitch where I boxed it out—and so each one looks different and actually it's from the same hank of wool. You can't take anything for granted. Very often you'll see a purple and you'll think, "This is just great," and you put it next to the one you're using and it turns out that even though it's a purple, it's blue against yours. I need a plum, and I thought I found one, but when I put it next to the other colors I'm using, it looked red.

Deborah Lippman: Do you have any canvas preferences?

Ruth Ross: I don't like working on a white canvas unless I'm using a white thread. I like a sort of beige, it's darker than a beige actually.

Deborah Lippman: How come?

Ruth Ross: White, if you use a dark color, no matter how heavy you make your stitch, seems to come through. I don't know, maybe it's just a quirk of mine, but I enjoy working on the natural canvas better than on a stark white canvas.

Deborah Lippman: You seem to use more basketweave than anything else. Reason?

Ruth Ross: If you use a continental it pulls your canvas out of shape. Then, in the blocking, it has to be pulled back together. Mine, even when it's not blocked, it looks perfect.

Needlepoint sampler, Ruth Ross

Deborah Lippman: What do you like the least?
Ruth Ross: I don't like working on those printed patterns.
I got this one and it's very pretty, but I just don't enjoy working on it at all. I like to figure out my own. I like changing things and using different textures and seeing a design take shape as I go along.

At this point, we went out to take some pictures and to play with Kathy's newborn daughter. As the day began drawing to a close, I collected my equipment, thanked Aunt Ruth for her time and the provisions she sent back for Paul, and with a light heart and a heavy shopping bag headed back toward the Great Neck Station.

NEEDLEPOINT FOR EVERYONE. by Mary Brooks Picken and Doris White. Harper and Row, Publishers, New York, 1970. 215 pages. illustrations, photographs (some color), suppliers list, bibliography. $12.50.

This is a good, basic introduction to needlepoint fundamentals that features special chapters on recreational and rehabilitation therapy; samplers, mottoes, and monograms; men and needlepoint; and needlepoint and interior design.

NEEDLEPOINT DESIGNS FROM AMERICAN INDIAN ART. by Nora Cammann. Charles Scribner's Sons, New York, 1973. 84 pages. illustrations, bibliography. $9.95.

This book presents twenty needlepoint projects derived from Indian motifs originally used on baskets, bowls, boxes, or clothing and not executed in stitchery. The designs were culled from the work of Indian tribes of the Southwest, the Great Plains, and the northwest and eastern woodlands. The author's adaptations are quite clever and, for the most part, the translation of materials is successful. Each project includes instructions for stitches, materials and tools, color

Needlepoint design adapted from southwest Indian ceramic bowl

suggestions, and finishing. A clear glossary of stitches is also included at the end of the book.

COMPLETE GUIDE TO CREATIVE NEEDLEPOINT. by Jo Bucher. Creative Home Library Books, Des Moines, Iowa, 1972. 324 pages. illustrations, photographs, suppliers list. $8.95.

The outstanding feature of this book is that 218 stitches are beautifully illustrated and explained in full detail. Each stitch receives a step-by-step treatment and is illustrated by clear line drawings (including one of how the stitch looks repeated to form a field). Also included is an excellent section on needlepoint techniques that covers two-size canvas method, cording, tassels, pompons, and so on; and a very good section on finishing, mostly as applied to specific objects. As usual, there is a chapter devoted to materials and tools, this one rather extensive.

SAMPLERS FOR TODAY. by Cecile Dreesman. Van Nostrand Reinhold, New York, 1972. 160 pages. photographs. $12.50.

In the past, children would learn their alphabet by embroidering letters with simple cross stitch patterns. Later, they might be taught more complicated openwork and the finer execution of a variety of stitches. Older children regarded sampler making not only as an exercise, but as a proof of talent, competence, neatness, and discipline.

Some of the samplers made by children in the later part of the seventeenth century through to the early part of the nineteenth century contained heavily moralizing verses, the likes of which would send present-day educators and psychologists into a frenzy. Among the examples noted by Cecile Dreesman in her excellent discussion of samplers old and new is one embroidered by a fourteen-year-old Welsh girl in 1839 containing the following sentiments:

> There is an hour when I must die
> Nor can I tell how soon twill come
> A thousand children, young as I
> Are called by death to hear their doom.

Needless to say, such verses are hardly in tune with contemporary taste, and the author provides a number of new and provocative suggestions for the construction of samplers with a more modern flavor.

THE NEW WORLD OF NEEDLEPOINT. by Lisbeth Perrone. Random House, New York, 1972. 143 pages. illustrations, photographs (some color). $8.95.

This is the new world of repeatable patterns, generally handsome, useful, and applicable to a variety of specific projects.

A knowledge of the basics and some of the fancier stitches is really required, and the author notes difficulty of execution for each design. On the whole, it is a good source book for avid needlepointers.

Where There's Hope There's Needlepoint

NEEDLEPOINT. by Hope Hanley. Charles Scribner's Sons, New York, 1964. 58 pages. illustrations, photographs, suppliers list, bibliography. $7.95.

This is a good method book for beginners, containing schematic line drawings and photos of fifty-five stitches.

NEW METHODS IN NEEDLEPOINT. by Hope Hanley. Charles Scribner's Sons, 1966. 96 pages. illustrations, photographs, bibliography. $6.95.

The new method is that of using the binding stitch for finishing needlepoint projects. The author explains how this stitch, which was originally used to cover the selvage in strip needlepoint rugs, along with other needlepoint techniques, can be used in thirteen projects of increasing difficulty.

The information presented here is valuable for beginners and other needlepointers who are put off by finshing the fruits of their labors.

NEEDLEPOINT IN AMERICA, 1600–1900. by Hope Hanley. Charles Scribner's Sons, New York, 1969. 160 pages. illustrations, photographs (some color), bibliography. $10.00.

The author traces the origins of American needlepoint, which were essentially derived from English sixteenth- and seventeenth-century work, and follows the subsequent development in the American colonies. Embroidery at that time was considered a necessary part of the education of young ladies and was included in the school curriculum as well as taught by private teachers who actively competed for students.

Needlepoint became a real craze with the introduction of Berlin work in the nineteenth century and women of all ages stitched away their leisure time. Printed patterns with colors clearly marked were sold, copied, and traded. Gaudy examples of work done with the new, bright "Berlin colors" abounded and everything in the home, from footstools to flytraps, was a possible target for needlepoint decoration.

This book, beautifully illustrated with black-and-white and color photographs, presents the designs, materials, and tools used throughout the reign of American needlepoint. There is also a look at some long-lost techniques, and instructions for a dozen archaic stitches.

NEEDLEPOINT RUGS. by Hope Hanley. Charles Scribner's Sons, New York, 1971. 115 pages. illustrations, photographs, suppliers list, bibliography. $7.95.

Using needlepoint techniques for making rugs requires special attention to details of construction, tools, materials, and design. Hope Hanley clearly points out all of the possible contingencies in this book.

The stitches employed should not span too much canvas at one stroke for that will hasten wear. Stitches that distort the canvas should also be avoided. A good rug stitch doesn't have more wool on the back of the canvas than on the front. Twenty-six stitches useful in rug-making are presented with diagrams and instructions as well as discussion of where and when they should be used. The author also considers possibilities of canvas size and methods of joining, border techniques, blocking, and finishing (including fringes and tassels).

This book should be used by people with a little needlepoint experience; however, a clever and ambitious beginner could probably cut a rug without too much difficulty.

THE ABC'S OF NEEDLEPOINT. by Hope Hanley. Charles Scribner's Sons, New York, 1973. 96 pages. illustrations, photographs, suppliers list, bibliography. $6.95. paperback edition $2.95.

This is a beautifully written book for beginners. It covers the basic questions asked by novices about materials, the mechanics of starting a canvas, and the basic stitch. There is a simple explanation of the principles of design and color and how they can be applied to needlepoint, a glossary of twenty fancy stitches and notation as to which canvas is most appropriate for each, and basic tips for finishing, blocking, and so on.

NEEDLEPOINT SIMPLIFIED. by Jo Ippolito Christensen and Sonie Shapiro Ashner. Sterling Publishing Company, New York, 1972. 48 pages. illustrations, photographs. $3.50.

The basic idea behind this book is to learn the craft of needlepoint while making simple projects. The first projects are suitable for children and adult beginners and become progressively more sophisticated as they draw toward the end.

THE FINE ART OF NEEDLEPOINT. by Muriel B. Crowell. Thomas Y. Crowell Company, New York, 1973. 128 pages. illustrations, photographs (some color). $10.00.

The bulk of this book is taken up with twenty projects that employ all the popular needlepoint stitches. Each project is presented along with a photograph of the unworked canvas design, a photograph of the finished product, and clear line illustrations of each stitch used. The projects are sophisticated and sufficiently explained to allow even those with minimal experience to complete them.

NEEDLEPOINT STITCHERY. by Margaret Boyles. Macmillan, New York, 1973. 158 pages. illustrations, photographs (some color). $12.95.

This book offers an all-around good treatment of needlepoint fundamentals. It has with an especially good section on adapting designs to needlepoint, and recommendations for which stitch to use for different sections of any needlepoint piece.

NEEDLEPOINT DESIGN: A HOUSE AND GARDEN BOOK. by Louis J. Gartner, Jr. William Morrow and Company, New York, 1970. 191 pages. illustrations, photographs (some color), suppliers list, bibliography. $15.95.

At last, a book that offers real honest-to-goodness ways of adapting designs and motifs to needlepoint stitchery, instead of simply showing natural forms and leaving it up to the reader to use his "imagination" and "creativity" to develop and transfer an original design. It is an excellent source of reliable transfer methods, as well as basic information on materials, supplies, and fundamental needlepoint techniques. The bulk of the book, however, is devoted to showing how the use of photostats, felt markers, and acrylic paints can be used for the unworked canvas design. There are also at least six chapters devoted to design sources usually not covered by most needlecraft books, such as contemporary paintings, old engravings, photographs, wood grain, and animal skins.

ADVENTURES IN NEEDLEPOINT. by Wilhelmina Fox Feiner. Doubleday and Company, Garden City, New York, 1973. 116 pages. illustrations, photographs (some color), bibliography. $9.95.

This book is a woman's odyssey through the pitfalls and pleasures of needlepointing. The author presents the most widely used methods and stitches and illustrates them with good, clear black-and-white photographs (color photographs for finished projects). Her chatty, personal style helps to explain the techniques of designing original needlepoint motifs, choosing the proper stitches, making borders and fringes, and finishing.

PLEASURES OF NEEDLEPOINT. by Inman Cook and Daren Pierce. Betty Crocker Home Library, Universal Publishers and Distributors Co., New York, 1972. 136 pages. illustrations, photographs (some color). $5.95.

The book offers the usual sections on needlepoint basics, but it also provides an exceptionally clear presentation of stitches, featuring both a standard schematic representation and a photograph next to it with exactly the same number and position of stitches. There are also lots of nice projects, illustrated in color and accompanied by suggestions for canvas size, stitches, and yarn color.

NEEDLEPOINT BY DESIGN. by Maggie Lane. Charles Scribner's Sons, New York, 1970. 114 pages. illustrations, photographs (some color). $8.95.

This book introduces the author's "unique" method of transferring a design to canvas. Actually, the design is transferred in the needlepointer's head. She suggests that you mark off grid lines on the canvas corresponding to the grid lines of the design—a good method for simple designs and for people who are good at counting and keeping track of numbers in their head.

The main feature of the book is a collection of twenty-four generally pretty, Orientally inspired designs presented by schematic grid diagrams and accompanied by information on color, stitch, size, and finishing touches.

MORE NEEDLEPOINT BY DESIGN. by Maggie Lane. Charles Scribner's Sons. New York, 1972. 150 pages. illustrations, photographs. $10.00.

This book gives another twenty Orientally inspired designs fully illustrated in color and with grid schema and construction information. The major change from the first book is that the first project presented here is a checkerboard that actually functions as a sampler for sixty-four different stitches, a very novel and clever idea that is not only didactic, but rather beautiful as well.

For Southpaws Only!

LEFT-HANDED NEEDLEPOINT. by Regina Hurlburt. Van Nostrand Reinhold, New York, 1972. 64 pages. illustrations. paperback edition $2.95.

What does a left-handed needlepoint lover who was advised by the best needlework shops in the country to hold a book up to the mirror do? She teaches herself slowly

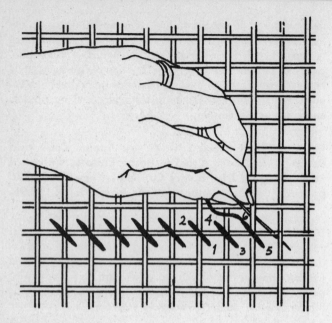

Continental stitch

and painfully and then writes a book based on her experiences so that others will not have to tread the same path. Regina Hurlburt, the left-hander in question, supplies outstanding illustrations for twenty-five stitches done from a left-handed point of view. Each illustration contains not only the ordinary needlepoint schema for stitches, but also has a prominently drawn left hand stitching away at the canvas.

DESIGNS FOR BARGELLO. by Nikki Scheuer. Doubleday and Company, Garden City, New York, 1973. 144 pages. illustrations, photographs (some color), suppliers list. $9.95.

This is a collection of sixty-two original patterns derived from various historical and cultural sources. Each pattern project is classified as to difficulty and contains information on color, stitch, and technique. The patterns themselves are quite beautiful and are shown partially finished in black and white on the page opposite the instructions, and again, completely finished, in a color photograph.

The instructions are clear but assume a reasonable familiarity with needlepoint techniques, and in order to use this book to full advantage, some experience is preferable.

The author's adaptations of design sources are almost always very clever and imaginative and provide interesting original designs for needlecrafters.

BARGELLO, FLORENTINE CANVAS WORK. by Elsa S. Williams. Van Nostrand Reinhold, New York, 1967. 64 pages. $6.95.

This book offers page after page of knockout Florentine canvas work patterns (fifty-five in all) accompanied by stitch and color information. It is geared toward the experienced bargello practitioner.

BARGELLO AND RELATED STITCHERY. by Charles Barnes and David P. Blake. Hearthside Press, Great Neck, New York, 1971. 245 pages. illustrations, photographs. $8.95.

The book has an inadequate stitch glossary that neglects to inform beginners about changing rows, an often traumatic occasion for the new worker. The projects, however, and there are lots of them, are quite beautiful and range from book covers to vests and tank tops. Each project lists materials, stitches, suggested colors, and finishing information.

A NEW LOOK AT BARGELLO: THE FLORENTINE NEEDLEPOINT STITCH. by Carol Cheney Rome. Crown Publishers, New York, 1973. 80 pages. illustrations, photographs. $4.95.

The author begins by schematizing seven "filler stitches" to be used by themselves to form a decorative field or background. She then presents eleven "new-old" Florentine patterns, four border designs, and a selection of "new" Florentine patterns, as well as a large section on rendering representational (pictorial) patterns in bargello.

The book assumes a competent knowledge of needlepoint techniques, and as an advanced manual, it doesn't have enough design information to inspire a veteran stitcher. It is also flawed in that the schema in stitch diagrams are unclear when related to accompanying photos.

Bargello pillows, Ruth Ross

FOUR WAY BARGELLO. by Dorothy Kaestner. Charles Scribner's Sons, New York, 1972: 93 pages. photographs (some color), bibliography. $9.95.

For most bargello patterns, stitching is worked vertically. This book sets out to expand the possibilities of bargello by working it in four directions at once. In other words, a kaleidoscope effect in which the origin of the design is at the center. Since bargello is primarily decorative and does not lend itself easily to pictorial modes as does tent stitch work, this four-way method is most applicable.

The four-way procedure is presented in a multitude of patterns. Each one is described in terms of the color of the yarn used, the stitches employed, and the problems encountered. Color photographs illustrate the effect of the completed work.

There is also a very complete section on materials and bargello stitching theory.

BARGELLO PLUS. by Mira Silverstein. Charles Scribner's Sons, 1973. 90 pages. illustrations, photographs. $9.95.

This book is written neither for beginners nor for experienced needlepointers. It has no consistent theme and includes a little of everything. The major problem is that the project instructions are tentative and often incomplete, and the design graphs are almost always separated from the photographs and instructions for the finished pieces.

BARGELLO MAGIC: HOW TO DESIGN YOUR OWN. by Pauline Fischer and Anabel Lasker. Holt, Rinehart and Winston, New York, 1972. 150 pages. illustrations, photographs (some color), suppliers list, bibliography. $12.95.

This is a very beautiful book featuring fifty-eight bargello patterns illustrated by color photographs and completely described in terms of material, technique, color, and potential problems of execution. The patterns are preceded by a good section on the general technique of bargello, necessary tools, and materials.

FINISHING AND MOUNTING YOUR NEEDLEPOINT PIECES. by Katharine Ireys. Thoms Y. Crowell Company, New York, 1973. 232 pages. illustrations. $10.00.

After spending what usually amounts to a good deal of time and money on the process of needlepointing, most people would like the canvas to be finished and mounted without disaster. This book is devoted solely to the avoidance of such disasters and deals exclusively with poststitching operations: how to conquer the problems of finishing and the high cost of having it done professionally.

There are general directions for blocking, finishing edges, lining, and mitering corners, but the major emphasis is on ways to finish forty different kinds of home furnishings: pillows, rugs, luggage racks, book covers, even golf club bonnets. The process of finishing each object is illustrated in step-by-step line drawings.

Needlepoint Bicycle Seat Cover

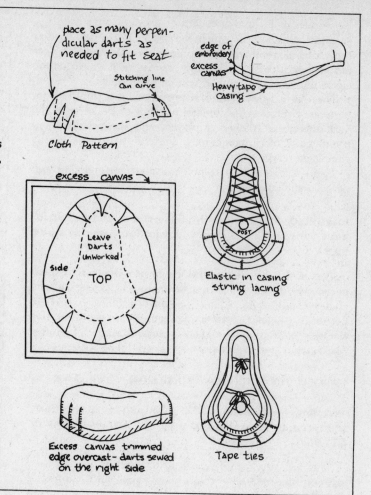

place as many perpendicular darts as needed to fit seat

Stitching line can curve

Cloth Pattern

edge of embroidery

excess canvas

Heavy tape casing

excess canvas

side

Leave Darts Unworked

TOP

Elastic in casing string lacing

POST

Excess canvas trimmed edge overcast – darts sewed on the right side

Tape ties

MATERIALS

Canvas to accommodate the cloth pattern and 1½ inches excess canvas (bicycle seats vary in size and shape, so it's best to make a cover for a specific seat).
Heavy tape for edge casing
½ yard strong elastic
Strong thread or string for fastening the cover (to prevent slipping)
Yarn of your choice

Bind the canvas. Embroider, leaving dart areas unworked. Block, using your pattern as a guide. Cut away binding and all but 1 inch of the excess canvas. Sew darts together on right side (sew down into excess canvas). Overcast edges to prevent fraying. Fit cover on seat, checking room between seat and underlying metal parts. It is probably small in front and wider in back. If necessary, trim canvas down to ½ inch near elastic in casing. Fit cover again; pull up elastic quite tight. Lace back and forth under the seat with string to assure firm fit or attach ties around metal parts.

Source: FINISHING AND MOUNTING YOUR NEEDLE-POINT PIECES. by Katharine Ireys.

Needlework

Come hyder to me, sone, and loke wheder
In this purse ther be any croise or crouche,
Sauf needle and threde and thermel of lether.
—John Taylor, *The Praise of the Needle*, 1640

YARN—THE THINGS IT MAKES AND HOW TO MAKE THEM. by Carolyn Meyer. Harcourt Brace Jovanovich, New York, 1972. 128 pages. illustrations. $5.50.

This is one of the best, clearest introductions to macrame, knitting, crochet, and weaving. It is intended for children, but there is no reason why confused adults cannot benefit from its simplicity. The author gives instructions for fundamental knitting stitches (garter, stockinette, seed, fancy ribbing) and techniques of shaping and finishing. She then presents projects utilizing what has been learned. These include a pair of mittens and a poncho. The crochet section also features instruction in basic stitches and techniques

(single, double, crocheting in the round, and making granny squares). From the macrame section, beginners will learn the half knot, square knot, half-hitch, double chain, double half-hitch, horizontal half-hitch, crossed diagonal double half-hitch. The weaving section presents instructions for simple weaving on homemade frames.

None of the crafts is presented in great depth, and there are no design or inspirational accompaniments. However, the fundamentals are explained explicitly enough to allow for the making of practical and attractive items that both children and adults can enjoy.

ENCYCLOPEDIA OF NEEDLEWORK, revised edition. by Therese De Dillmont. Joan Toggitt, Ltd., New York, 1971. 788 pages. illustrations, photographs (some colors). $9.50.

First published in 1921 to fill a need for a one-volume

complete needlework reference book, this encyclopedia has continued to enjoy an unrivaled position of comprehensiveness up until today. Virtually every needle art, including macrame, lace-making, and netting, is represented. Instructions are detailed, but the accompanying diagrams are not clear enough to satisfy the requirements of inexperienced needleworkers. However, it is a volume that no serious needlecrafter should be without.

STITCHERY, NEEDLEPOINT, APPLIQUÉ, AND PATCHWORK: A COMPLETE GUIDE. by Shirley Marein. Viking Books, New York, 1974. 207 pages. illustrations, photographs, bibliography, index.

An excellent historical section featuring examples of antique and contemporary needlework introduces the reader of this book to modes of embroidery. The "how-to" information is presented step by step and accompanied by photographs and diagrams. The instructions are concise and informative, but they presuppose a familiarity with needleworking in general. It is geared more toward the stitcher who is acquainted with only one or two sewing techniques and desires a wider range of knowledge than the beginner coming in cold.

THE WORK OF OUR HANDS: JEWISH NEEDLECRAFT FOR TODAY. by Mae Shafter Rockland. Schocken Books, New York, 1973. 258 pages. illustrations, photographs, index. $10.00.

Instructions for a few of the basics of crewel, needlepoint, and patchwork—just enough to enable the beginner to create any of the numerous projects provided by the author. The experienced needleworker wishing a more individual form of expression will find a rich source of inspiration in Ms. Rockland's survey of tradition in Jewish art, symbols, and colors which can be used in the creation of secular objects, such as guitar straps, pillows, and tablecloths as well as the ritualistic items like yarmulkas, tallis bags, and challah covers. The ritual use and history of each object is thoroughly explained and the author even throws some light on lesser known subjects. For instance, did you know that King David was a Gemini?

WOMAN'S DAY BOOK OF AMERICAN NEEDLEWORK. by Rose Wilder Lane. Simon and Schuster, New York, 1963. 208 pages. illustrations, photographs (some color), index. $12.50.

In typical Old World needlework, each detail is a particle of the whole; no part of the design can stand alone, whole and complete in itself. The background is solid, the pattern is formal, and the border encloses all.

American women smashed that rigid order to bits. They discarded borders and frames. They made the details create the whole and they set each detail in boundless space, alone, independent, complete.

This book contains information on American needlecrafts from embroidery and patchwork to rug-making and candlewicking. Each of the thirteen chapters contains interesting

historical information as well as specific projects, such as a needlepoint shell motif from Martha Washington's chair cushion. Projects are presented by concise instructions and good diagrams, and each chapter contains a generous number of color photographs showing examples loaned by museums.

McCALL'S NEEDLEWORK TREASURY. by the editors of McCall's *Needlework and Crafts* magazine. Random House, New York, 1965. 396 pages. illustrations. $8.95.

The book offers general instructions for embroidery, quilting, rug weaving, knitting, crochet, tatting, handloom weaving, netting, knotting, and braiding, presented in step-by-step format and clear line illustrations. Each craft has accompanying projects which range in difficulty from moderately easy to highly difficult. The book was originally published in 1950; consequently, the projects are somewhat dated.

THE DICTIONARY OF NEEDLEWORK: AN ENCYCLOPEDIA OF ARTISTIC, PLAIN, AND FANCY NEEDLEWORK. by Sophia Frances Anne Caulfield and Blanche C. Saward. Arno Press, New York, 1972. 528 pages. illustrations. paperback edition $3.95.

This facsimile of an 1882 edition contains over eight hundred illustrations and an alphabetically organized dictionary of terms. It is not actually an instruction manual, although some instructions are given. Frequently, however, the procedural diagrams are difficult to discern unless one has had some previous experience. For those who are in the know, this compendium makes interesting reading from a historical standpoint as well as supplying a means for creating the sort of items you may remember your grandmother doing.

ANCHOR MANUAL OF NEEDLEWORK, third edition. Charles T. Branford Company, Newton Centre, Massachusetts, 1968. 499 pages. photographs, index.

This is a complete manual of needlecrafts including macrame and a variety of lacework. Unfortunately, some of the instructions are presented as photographs rather than line drawings, and it is difficult to see exactly what is taking place.

Some of the practical information, such as that about sewing machines, is somewhat dated, as are a few of the clothing projects. On the whole, however, most of the examples are of work of classic appeal and very beautiful.

GOOD HOUSEKEEPING NEW COMPLETE BOOK OF NEEDLECRAFT. by Vera P. Guild. Hearst Books, New York, 1971. 548 pages. $8.95.

The crafts covered here are sewing, embroidery, quilting, smocking, needlepoint, rug-making, knitting, crochet, tatting, netting, macrame, and hand-weaving. This is probably the best book of its type, supplying exceptionally detailed technical information, information on materials and tools, and construction details for all crafts. The embroidery section is surprisingly complete for such a general book and features imaginative use of gingham as a base material for cross-stitching. The knitting and crochet section is the best of all the needlecraft compendia and the general sewing section is similarly excellent.

> To all dispersed sorts of ARTS and TRADES,
> I writ the needles prayse (that never fades)
> So long as children shall be got or borne,
> So long as garments shall be made or worne,
> So long as Hemp or Flax or Sheep shall bear
> Their linnen woollen fleeces yeare by yeare:
> So long as Silk-wormes, with exhausted spoile,
> Of their own Entrailes for mans gaine shall toyle:
> Yea till the world be quite dissolv'd and past;
> So long at least, the Needles use shall last.
>
> —John Taylor, *The Praise of the Needle*, 1640

THE REINHOLD BOOK OF NEEDLECRAFT. by Jutta Lammer. Van Nostrand Reinhold, New York, 1972. 296 pages. illustrations, photographs. $12.95.

This book includes instructions for embroidery, crochet, knitting, tatting, weaving, rug knotting, appliqué, patchwork, decorative machine stitching, macrame, and finishing.

All sections feature very clear line drawings (usually of each step) and photographs of finished stitches and projects. There are also additional sections on the care of handmade garments, motifs for embroidered letters, and designs for quilts.

PATCHCRAFT: DESIGN, MATERIALS, TECHNIQUE. by Elsie Svennas. Van Nostrand Reinhold, New York, 1972. 96 pages. illustrations, photographs (some color), index. paperback edition $2.95.

Although this is not a comprehensive manual of basic instructions, it is a good source for a variety of ideas and for new uses for patchwork. Beginners are advised to think in terms of basic shapes for fabric patches from geometric to irregular. The instructions are rather general and the diagrams are few, but most of the projects are of simple design and do not require explicit information. A majority of the projects are particularly suitable for working with children.

MOUNTING HANDICRAFT: IDEAS AND INSTRUCTIONS FOR ASSEMBLING AND FINISHING. by Grete Kroncke. Van Nostrand Reinhold, New York, 1970. 96 pages. illustrations, photographs. $4.50.

The author presents this book as a supplement to other books on handicraft procedures. The instructions are intended as general guidelines rather than something that should be followed literally, since there are so many possibilities for combining materials, projects, and techniques. The suggestions offered in this book can be adapted by the

craftsman to suit individual needs.

The author is concerned primarily with finishing and assembling needlecraft-related articles. The instructions are accompanied by extremely clear drawings (by Grete Petersen, another Reinhold star) and black-and-white photographs that illustrate techniques and projects. The projects themselves are quite specific—finishing in cords and fringes; pillow construction; handbags; purses, and so on—but the techniques are general enough to make this a continually useful book for the needleworker.

OLD NEEDLEWORK BOXES AND TOOLS: THEIR STORY AND HOW TO COLLECT THEM. by Mary Andere. Drake Publishers, New York, 1971. 184 pages. illustrations, photographs, bibliography, index. $5.95.

For many centuries, tools as simple as needles and pins were difficult to come by and therefore received great care and respect. Reasons of both safety and convenience motivated women to carry their sewing equipment with them, and, as early garments had no pockets, work tools were attached by chains or cords to the waistbands of both men and women. Medieval ladies wore needlecases, some of which were very elaborate, suspended from their girdles. It

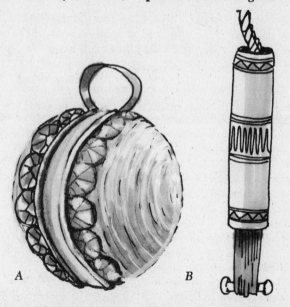

A Round pincushion covered with green silk and silver thread. It is from the period of William and Mary, and was worn suspended from the waist, contained in a circular silver mount.
B Early bone needlecase

was not until the late seventeenth and early eighteenth centuries that the needlework box came into its own.

In this book, the author succinctly reviews the history of these polished wood needlework boxes and tables and the often exquisite tools they housed, from their simple beginnings in Anglo-Saxon times up until their eventual establishment as a quasi art form. The book describes and illustrates a great many varieties of needlework boxes and tools in order to help would-be collectors with their identifica-

How to Make a Pillow

MATERIALS:
1 foam block, 17¾″ x 17¾″ x 2⅜″
1 piece of material, 24″ x 24″ for cover front
1 piece of material, 19½″ x 19¼″ for cover back

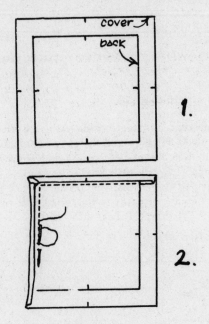

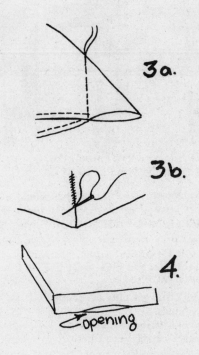

PROCEDURE:

The front of the cover must be large enough to stretch down over the 2⅜″ sides of the foam block. The size of the cover is determined by adding the thickness of the foam block to each side, or 17¾″ plus 4¾″, and adding two seams, each ¾″ or a total of 1½″. The material will then measure 24″ x 24″ and that is what should be cut (17¾″ + 4¾″ + 1½″).

The back of the cover should measure 17¾″ plus the seam allowance of ¾″, or 19¼″ for each side, after cutting.

FINISHING:

The drawings illustrate the most important steps in finishing. Mark both pieces of the material at the middle of the edges on all four sides (1). With a dot, mark all four corners on the front cover. These dots show where the corners of the nylon block will come.

The pieces of material are put together with right sides facing (2). Put straight pins in the four marking points and baste together from corner to corner. Sew seams with a machine. The extra material will cause corners to stand out like cones. Leave an opening on one side large enough to insert nylon foam block (4). Two different ways of making these corners are shown in Fig. 3. A shows how to sew the corner from dot to the corner of the back piece. Figure ¾″ seam allowance and cut off the rest. B shows how to sew the corner from the outside after the block has been inserted. Cut off some of the material and turn it from the mark at the top down to the corner of the back piece and overcast together as close to invisibly as possible.

Position the seams as inconspicuously as possible when you insert the foam. Finish the opening of the cushion with invisible stitches.

Source: MOUNTING HANDICRAFT. by Grete Kroncke.

---

tion, care, and repair. It is, however, a subject that is often of interest to anyone involved in the craft of needlework.

THE HISTORY OF NEEDLEWORK TOOLS AND ACCESSORIES. by Sylvia Groves. Arco Publishing Company, New York, 1973. 136 pages. illustrations, photographs. $10.00.

Gradual improvements in the skill of craftsmen, changing customs, and the invention of new and more elaborate techniques over the centuries led to the production of ever more delicate and complicated tools. The author traces their development from simple Anglo-Saxon sewing boxes to the mass of Victorian paraphernalia in detailed description and illustrations. The objects are quite beautiful and display great imagination in construction and function; they are of great interest to anyone concerned with the history of needlework itself.

Bronze hemmingbirds, c. 1800. These birds were used clamped to the table; their beaks were spring loaded to grip fabric.

Magazines: Needlecraft

Better Homes and Gardens Crafts and Sewing
Special Interest Publications
Magazine Division of Meredith Corporation
1716 Locust Street
Des Moines, Ia. 50336
annual. $1.35.

Good Housekeeping Needlecraft
Hearst Publications
959 Eighth Avenue
New York, N.Y. 10019
semiannual. $.75 per single issue.

Ladies' Home Journal Needlecraft
Downe Publications
641 Lexington Avenue
New York, N.Y. 10022
semiannual. $1.25 per single issue.

all of the above feature patterns, book reviews, special features.

Woman's Day Needlework Ideas
Fawcett Publications, Inc.
Fawcett Building
Greenwich, Conn. 06830
quarterly. $.95 per single issue.
also craft ideas for weaving and macrame.

Old Time Needlework Patterns and Designs
Box 428
Seabrook, N.H. 03874
semiannual. $2.00 a year.

Crafty Ideas
Crafty Ideas, Inc.
Evansville, Wis. 53536
quarterly. $4.00 a year. $1.25 per single issue.
needlecrafts and other crafts.

Netting

NET MAKING. by Charles Holdgate. Emerson Books, Buchanan, New York, 1972. 136 pages. illustrations, photographs. $5.95.

This book originally was planned for teachers and their students, but it should be of great interest to anyone wishing to learn the craft of net making.

Net making is a very old and interesting skill. It requires simple, inexpensive tools and materials. The author teaches the basic techniques through very good step-by-step instructions, and then presents variations and more advanced techniques in various net projects. Elementary projects include the making of a bottle bag and a woven scarf; more advanced projects feature a hammock, a basketball net, and a crab pot. The author suggests that beginners follow the instructions precisely in order to avoid confusion and to learn the basic principles, but advanced netters may vary as they will.

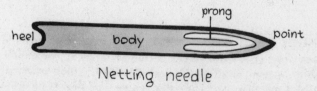

Netting needle

Netting needles are string holders, usually made of flexible but durable plastic. They can be obtained from suppliers of craft materials and some anglers' shops, or from the manufacturer: Linen Thread Company, Blue Mountain, Alabama 63201. (from Net Making by Charles Holdgate)

The author, a headmaster at a boys' school, has taught a course in net making to nine-, ten-, and eleven-year-old children and has brought all his practical experience to bear upon his presentation of the fundamentals of netting and thus make it possible for children and adults of all ages to learn this craft.

NETMAKING. by P. W. Blandford. Brown, Son, and Ferguson, Glasgow, Scotland, 1969. 104 pages. illustrations, index.

This little British book is a comprehensive guide to this specialized craft. Several chapters devoted solely to technique cover all aspects of net making. The instructions for the various knots, meshes, and net configurations are illustrated with line drawings that correspond to the step-by-step presentation of the text.

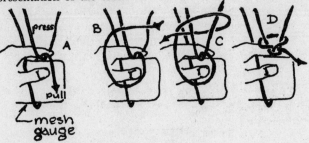

Steps in forming a mesh (first variation)

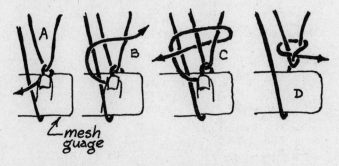

Steps in forming a mesh (second variation)

A beginner using this book would soon become a good net technician, but would probably be hard put to utilize his knowledge in making useful articles. There is a section on "Things to Make," but only the instructions for making a hammock seem to be adequate.

KNOTTING AND NETTING: THE ART OF FILET WORK. by Lisa Melen. Van Nostrand Reinhold, New York, 1973. 88 pages. illustrations, photographs. $4.95.

Filet embroidery is done by embroidering simple stitches (darning, cloth, wheels, and loop) on square or diamond mesh net. The most arcane aspect of the whole process is the making of the net itself, but Lisa Melen maintains that this is actually quite simple and requires only simple tools. She gives step-by-step instructions for making square, diamond, and round nets, for stretching (a process not unlike blocking), and for embroidering. The instructions are illustrated by large clear photographs at every stage of the procedure. There are also reproductions of historical and contemporary work, a nice, inspirational feature. The last few pages of the book contain fourteen patterns that can be used singly or in combination to produce handsome designs.

Paper

PAPER AS ART AND CRAFT. by Thelma Hartley and Lee Scott Newman. Crown Publishers, New York, 1973. 308 pages. illustrations, photographs (some color), suppliers list, bibliography, index. $9.95. paperback edition $4.95.

This excellent adult approach to paper potentials begins with the history of paper and paper processes, and follows that with a paper vocabulary including methods of description. Paper is commonly sold in terms of weights based upon five hundred sheets, but different types of paper are weighed in different sizes. Book sheet paper is based upon 24- by 36-inch sheets, while writing paper is based upon 17- by 22-inch sheets. As a result, 20-pound book paper is much lighter than writing paper described as the same weight.

The authors discuss tools and their appropriate uses, glues and adhesives and paper possibilities—bending crumpling, wading, folding, pleating, weaving, twisting, puncturing, tearing, cutting, curling, scoring, surface treatments, stands, and fasteners. There is also a chart of papers, containing weights, characteristics, texture, color, and uses, and a similar chart for adhesives.

Diagrammatic and photographic instructions as well as a tremendous number of inspirational pictures are presented in all the chapters—collage, bookbinding, decoupage, paper sculpture, and decorating paper, which includes stamping, printing, stenciling, batik, tie-dye, silk-screen, and painting. There are simple, colorful, cutout folk designs and kites, and sophisticated procedures for making life-size papier-mâché figures.

Kinds of Adhesives

Adhesive	Characteristics	Uses
Duco cement	flexible, waterproof	all-purpose
glue sticks	very tacky, often very strong	good for adhering tabs and for small areas
epoxy	clear, exceptionally strong, comes in two parts that must be mixed and used immediately	makes paper permanent
LePage's Original Glue	natural base, very strong, resists climatic changes	general paperwork
library paste	strong but nonpermanent	temporary paperwork
Metylan cellulose paste	inexpensive, dissolves in water	papier mâché, collage
mucilage	amber color, tacky, syrupy consistency	cardboard, woodwork
plastic glaze (Mod Podge, Art Podge)	white, dries clear, strong	protects paper surfaces, acts as a finish over papier mâché, etc.
polyvinyl acetate (Elmer's, Sobo, Duratite, etc.)	white, dries clear, strong	for small areas, especially those under tension, used in decoupage and papier mâché
rubber cement	transparent, quick drying, easy to remove excess	for temporary and permanent bonds, good for large areas

Source: PAPER AS ART AND CRAFT. by Thelma Hartley and Lee Scott Newman.

PAPER PLAY. by Michael Grater. Taplinger Publishing Company. New York, 1972. 278 pages. illustrations, photographs (some color). $9.95.

Mechanism for blinker toy

The key word in this book is play, but with a definite purpose behind it. The author is concerned with shapes, and since he is talking about paper, he is concerned with cut rather than drawn shapes. The ability to draw is a specialized skill, but everyone has the ability to see, to look at shapes, and thereby to discover some of the ways in which paper can be manipulated.

Mr. Grater begins by setting up simple exercises to increase the reader's awareness and help him in his more sophisticated work later on. Simple squares are cut and other shapes placed upon them to illustrate the effects of size and placement. Similar exercises of varying complexities are performed which take the reader through discoveries about pattern, color, shape, and movement.

PAPER SCULPTURE. by Alan Allport. Drake Publishers, New York, 1971. 85 pages. illustrations, photographs. $5.95.

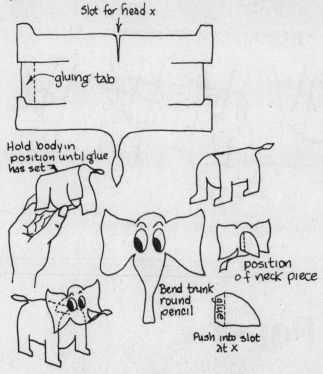

The early sections of this book are written with parents or teachers in mind, but there is no reason why an adult cannot amuse himself by carrying out the simple paper sculptures outlined there. The elementary chapters are primarily devoted to the construction of simple animal models, but the principles learned from this are prerequisites for the more advanced models, which include everything from a three-dimensional pub-sitting dart player to a palace guard complete with fur-trimmed cape and gold braid.

PAPER CUTTING. by Brigitte Stoddart. Taplinger Publishing Company, New York, 1973. 96 pages. illustrations, photographs (some color), suppliers list. $6.50.

Paper cutting is a craft that appeals to child and adult

alike. It is economical, and requires no equipment except a small dissecting type of scissors, a packet of assorted gummed paper, a packet of assorted plain paper, an X-Acto knife, paste, and a compass. With these you can make anything from simple paper-doll chains to complex multicolored panels utilizing layer upon layer of tiny, separately shaped slivers of paper.

The author presents a great many illustrations showing different paper-cut items. These are largely inspirational; and there are no diagrammatic instructions for projects. However, basic hints for paper-cutting techniques are supplied.

Simple Techniques of Paper Cutting

Internal spaces—Whenever it is necessary to make a hole as a starting point for cutting out an internal space, do not use the points of the scissors unless the part to be cut out is very large. It is too easy to make a small slip with the scissors and spoil the whole work. Instead, place the paper on several layers of newspapers and make the initial incision with an Exacto knife or guarded razor blade.

With silhouettes, internal spaces can only occur where shapes overlap or just touch one another. Overlapping shapes should be fully drawn first, as in the illustration, so that a long blade of grass, for example, remains quite straight although partially covered by a leaf.

Source: PAPER CUTTING. by Brigitte Stoddart.

THE PAPER BOOK, 187 THINGS TO MAKE. by Don Munson and Allianora Rosse. Charles Scribner's Sons, New York, 1972. 176 pages. illustrations, photographs. $8.95. paperback edition $3.95.

This is a book of diagrams and instructions for projects primarily of the party favor-holiday ornament variety. Some of the diagrams are unclear and sloppily done (some diagrams referred to in the text are omitted).

FORMS OF PAPER. by Hiroshi Ogawa. Van Nostrand Reinhold, New York, 1971. 114 pages. illustrations, photographs. $8.95.

This is predominantly a beautiful photographic exploration into the quintessence of forms paper can be given.

A small section at the end of the book presents diagrams, instructions, and suggested uses for the paper forms depicted in the photographs.

SCULPTURE IN PAPER. by Ralph Fabri. Watson-Guptill Publications, New York, 1966. 165 pages. illustrations, photographs (some color), index.

This book offers a thorough discussion of basic forms, techniques, sketching designs, details, and finishing touches, not only for paper sculpture in three dimensions, but also for relief and mobiles. The author reviews possibilities of marketing sculptures for commercial, promotional devices, and decorations. The mass production of paper sculpture requires some modifications in procedures; for example, all parts should be attached to each other with the help of die-cut tongues, paper hooks, and slots.

This is an excellent introduction to a fun pastime that has great possibilities for elementary and secondary school teachers. These are possibilities of which the author is not unaware—he dedicated his book to all the education majors in his art courses at City University of New York.

ALL KINDS OF PAPERCRAFTS. by John Portchmouth. The Viking Press, New York, 1973. 128 pages. illustrations, photographs, bibliography, index. $8.95.

This is a book of processes and possibilities, rather than a manual of step-by-step instructions for projects. The author emphasizes the paper itself, its characteristics and suitabilities. He offers suggestions for the use and effect of various types of paper. Tissue, for example, becomes very transparent when pasted to a surface, but loses this effect when dry. However, the author discloses that this clear appearance of tissue can be retained if it is struck down with a polyurethane varnish rather than paste.

There is a good general section on main procedures and techniques. Each process—using paper flat, using paper in relief, and using paper for modeling—contains complete lists of tools and materials, notes on beginning and carrying out a work, supporting illustrations, and suggested themes. Aside from illustrating textural points, many of the photographs are inspirational in nature.

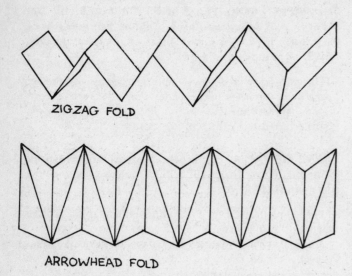

ZIGZAG FOLD

ARROWHEAD FOLD

Zig-Zag Fold: Lay a sheet of paper flat. Fold a strip upwards from near edge at right angles to the sides and press out to form a sharp crease. Turn sheet over and fold again up the new side. Continue in this manner, turning the sheet before making each new fold.

Arrowhead Fold: Lay sheet of paper flat. Make zig-zag fold and press out. Fold shape diagonally across from two of the corners and press out to a sharp crease. Open up sheet. Accentuate creases so that they face alternate ways.

Source: ALL KINDS OF PAPERCRAFTS. by John Portchmouth.

FLOWER MAKING FOR BEGINNERS. by Priscilla Lobley. Taplinger Publishing Company, New York, 1971. 87 pages. photographs. $5.95.

The author presents illustrated instructions for twenty basic techniques of making paper flowers, along with advice on copying from nature. She then presents ten flower patterns beginning with the easiest, such as tissue pompons, and progressing to more complicated varieties, such as morning glories.

The text supplies some good advice not found elsewhere. For example, the author, realizing that florists are often reluctant to sell their wire, provides alternatives which can be purchased in most hardware stores. Galvanized wire, easily obtained, is a good substitute. Thick wire (#14 to #16) should be used for the main stems of large flowers like poppies, lilies, or sunflowers; average thickness (#16 to #18) for smaller stems; and thin wire (#20) for petals and leaves. Another good choice is cotton-covered wire. This is quite fine (#20 to #30) and comes in green and white. It is often used for making hats and can be found at most large department store notions counters under the name of millinery wire.

Blossoms without perfume that neither grew nor faded.
—Henry Vaughan, in tribute to Mary Delany

Mary Delany was a member of an upper-class British family. In 1774, at the age of seventy-four, she began making "paper mosaics." She worked on these until her death in 1784, leaving behind thousands of intricate paper flowers cut from hand-watercolored paper.

Making a daisy

Materials:
thin crepe paper: mauve or white for petals, yellow for stamens, dark green for center and stems
stem wires, 16 or 18 gauge, 10" long
reel wire

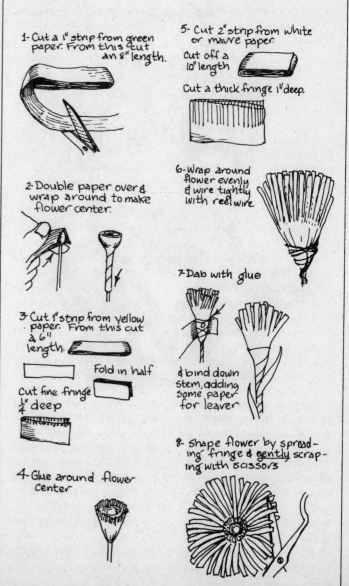

1- Cut a 1" strip from green paper. From this cut an 8" length.

2- Double paper over & wrap around to make flower center.

3- Cut 1" strip from yellow paper. From this cut a 6" length. Fold in half. Cut fine fringe 1/4" deep

4- Glue around flower center

5- Cut 2" strip from white or mauve paper. Cut off a 10" length. Cut a thick fringe 1" deep.

6- Wrap around flower evenly & wire tightly with reel wire

7- Dab with glue & bind down stem, adding some paper for leaves

8- Shape flower by spreading fringe & gently scraping with scissors

PAPER FLOWER DECORATIONS. by Pamela Woods. Taplinger Publishing Company, New York, 1972. 88 pages. illustrations, photographs (some color). $8.95.

This book describes how to make thirty-nine flowers and leaves. Entries are arranged according to five main methods of assembly: disc, strip, separate-petal, combination, and multiflower.

COLLAGE, MONTAGE AND ASSEMBLAGE: HISTORY AND TECHNIQUE. by Norman Laliberte and Alex Mogelon. Van Nostrand Reinhold, New York, 1972. 80 pages. photographs (some color). $8.95.

This is a photographic gallery of art objects, some by famous, now-dead artists (Picasso, Juan Gris, Kurt Schwitters, Diego Rivera), but it is largely devoted to more contemporary work.

CONTEMPORARY DECOUPAGE. by Thelma R. Newman. Crown Publishers, New York, 1972. 214 pages. illustrations, photographs (some color), suppliers list, bibliography. $7.95.

The author is all in favor of breaking some of the traditional practices that would keep decoupeurs from combining painted elements with cut paper, working in relief, or combining dissimilar materials. She pleads for thoughtful and deliberate use of decoupage as a form that requires artistry and attention to design, the basic principles of which she discusses at length and illustrates by means of photographs showing the effects of size, balance, and color.

Traditional decoupage techniques are thoroughly discussed and illustrated in a chapter which concludes with a decoupage clinic. In this clinic the author states various maladies, the reasons for their occurrence, and the most successful cures. If, for instance, you find a bloom or cloudiness on the surface of your decoupage, you can look it up in the clinic and find that it might have been caused by the original mixture of the varnish. The remedy is to wash the surface with warm water and detergent. Let it dry and wax it. What happens when cracks appear? Well, they might have been caused by shrinkage of the film or because the undercoat is not thoroughly dry. Let it dry out completely and then continue varnishing. If it's an old piece, sand away the wax with #0000 steel wool and revarnish until the cracks disappear. Sand again and wax.

There is also a list of materials for basic and advanced processes, and a chart of finishes containing their main components, what they are soluble in, compatibilities, characteristics, drying time, and mode of application.

Instructions are given for methods of lining and covering boxes, using Oriental themes, special processes for applying decoupage to glass and acrylic (with and without gesso), as well as individual recommendations for using decoupage on metal, cork, ceramic, and papier-mâché. The author also presents a special chapter on exotic techniques, such as how to lift printing inks from paper and transfer them to the surface of your choice, and how to make polyester embedments.

Canterbury Bell

You will need: Duplex Crepé, teazels, stem and binding wires, stem binding.

Cut five 3″ long petals and five 2¼″ long petals in the shapes shown in (1) and (2). (Make sure the grain of the crepe paper is running up the petals.) Mold petals by cupping centers and rolling up edges over a pencil (3). Leave teazle head on stem and bind large petals around stem so that they encircle it once, with the rolled tips overlapping each other and making a complete ring if possible (4). Bind small petals around large ones, so that color on the upper surface matches that on the lower surface of large petals. Cover base of petals and stem (5).

Source: PAPER FLOWER DECORATIONS. by Pamela Woods.

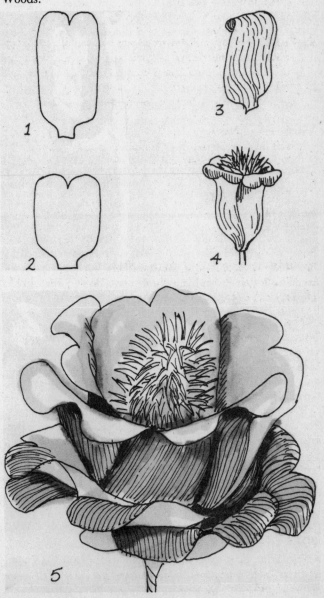

THE CRAFT OF DECOUPAGE. by Patricia Nimrocks. Charles Scribner's Sons, New York, 1972. 128 pages. illustrations, photographs. $3.95.

This is an excellent introduction to decoupage from both the historical and practical approaches. The author discusses ways of re-creating the look of eighteenth-century and Victorian decoupage as well as techniques of modern decoupage. Many of the problems often encountered by beginners are settled in question-and-answer sections, and there is a quick reference chart on how to prepare and apply decoupage to various items, such as previously painted metal wastebaskets, unglazed ceramic surfaces, and so on. There are numerous projects for beginners, featuring step-by-step instructions for making shadow pictures, baskets, and other decorative items.

The author's slant is quite traditional and she does not approve of bringing fabrics, real flowers, butterflies, etc., into the decoupage process. She is also in favor of the decoupeur coloring his prints, and she presents detailed information on how to go about this, including an extensive listing of an eighteenth-century palette. However, even though tradition-oriented, the author does include instructions for unusual techniques not found elsewhere. Among these are instructions for using mother-of-pearl, which can be prepared quite easily by soaking the shell in hot water for ten minutes and then cutting the thin layer of mother-of-pearl to the desired shape with decoupage scissors.

DECOUPAGE, A NEW LOOK AT AN OLD CRAFT. by Leslie Linsley. Doubleday and Company, Garden City, New York, 1972. 95 pages. illustrations, photographs (some color). $3.95.

The author of this book feels that decoupage is a traditional craft and should not have a contemporary emphasis. She also believes that it is possible to achieve a creative new look without losing the traditional feeling. The book contains lots of friendly advice, especially on the subject of materials—Ms. Linsley seems particularly concerned about the reader's pocketbook. She also devotes a page or two to the debunking of some common fallacies, such as the glue fallacy. She uses Elmer's right from the jar and applies her varnish soon afterward, not waiting for the glue to dry over night. The whole trick, she says, is to apply the design firmly, pat it down, and wipe off the excess glue.

There is quite a bit of information in this book, but it's not as concentrated as in others; the author is prone to digressions about junkyard finds and other decoupage adventures.

THE SUNSET BOOK OF PAPIER MÂCHÉ. by the Sunset editorial staff with William J. Shelley and Barbara Linse. Lane Magazine and Book Company, Menlo Park, California, 1973. 79 pages. illustrations, photographs (some color). $1.95.

The Chinese invented paper more than a thousand years ago. They also began to experiment with ways of shaping and molding it into functional boxes by tearing it into pieces and mixing it with glue. However, interest in the craft lay dormant in western Europe until it was revived in 18th century France. Papier-mâché has remained a popular material for all sorts of decorative and functional items, and today it is even being regarded as a viable medium for art objects.

This book discusses various kinds of papier-mâché and presents a number of recipes for making it. Instructions are given for a variety of projects, most of which would be especially good to do with children. There is also a section devoted to making objects from paper mash, a claylike material made from bits of paper that have been soaked in paste. These include a number of household items, such as a baroque mirror frame, a bowl of fruit, and a clock housing. A chapter on finishing techniques presents instructions and information on finishes, paints, antiquing, and other basic finishing procedures.

DECORATIVE TREASURES FROM PAPIER MÂCHÉ. by Alice Shannon. Hearthside Press, Great Neck, New York, 1970. 158 pages. illustrations, photographs (some color), index. $6.95.

This book is a collection of projects divided categorically into matching bath accessories, items for bedroom and boudoir, boxes, jewelry, trays, bowls, baskets, simple figures, and Christmas ornaments. Most projects require only a simple cut-paper papier-mâché, although a few here and there do use a mash mixture or an armature. Most, like the simple bracelet that follows, require few materials to complete and little attention to problems of design.

DESIGN IN PAPIER-MÂCHÉ. by Carla and John B. Kenny. Chilton Book Company, Radnor, Pennsylvania, 1973. 190 pages. illustrations, photographs (some color), index. $12.50. paperback edition $4.95.

Papier-mâché mermaid table support

Using newspaper, paper bags, corrugated cardboard, chipboard, and discarded cartons, the authors present basic techniques of constructing a wide assortment of decorative and functional objects. Some of these are quite simple and are made by applying torn bits of newspaper to a form.

This is done with a mixture of white glue diluted with water. Like most people who experiemented with papier-mâché as children, the authors used, for a time, a paste made from flour and water. However, they found that making their own paste was a waste of time, and more than that, bugs often liked the taste of their finished products.

Objects that require modeling are generally armatured structures upon which the authors apply a mash made from paper pulp to which is added whiting, white glue, linseed oil, and oil of wintergreen or oil of cloves. Whiting (calcium carbonate) is a white powder sold in paint stores. It acts as a filler in mash and makes the finished work denser and more solid. Linseed oil makes mash more workable and the finished pieces heartier. It is sold in paint stores in either raw or boiled form. Either works just as well and the raw is cheaper. Any plain white synthetic resin glue will work as a binder. The oil of wintergreen or oil of cloves acts as a preservative and keeps the mash from going sour too quickly. A pint of mash uses about four sheets of newspaper (full size), 2 tablespoons whiting, 1 tablespoon linseed oil, and two drops oil of wintergreen or oil of cloves.

The authors are helpful, providing patterns and photographs for a great many items that may or may not appeal to everyone's sensibilities.

CREATIVE PAPIER MÂCHÉ. by Betty Lorrimar. Watson-Guptill Publications, New York, 1972. 104 pages. illustrations, photographs (some color), bibliography, index. $7.95.

This book offers some general guidelines for working with papier-mâché and a few simple projects. It is primarily a gallery of photographs of papier-mâché sculpture, jewelry, hats, and other items made by young children.

PAPIER-MÂCHÉ ARTISTRY. by Dona Z. Meilach. Crown Publishers, New York, 1971. 211 pages. photographs (some color), index. $7.95.

The first part of this book deals with materials, procedures, and approaches, and gives step-by-step instructions for placing papier-mâché over objects, over an armature, and in a mold. Procedures have been simplified and broken down into four steps: applying the paper, sealing, decorating, and finishing.

As the author goes over the fundamentals, she presents many papier-mâché projects wth how-to and finished photographs as well as a number of inspirational examples worked along the lines being discussed.

The second half of the book contains many photographs of papier-mâché sculptures. For many years, papier-mâché was not considered a good medium for serious artists, probably because it was mistakenly assumed to be very perishable. In recent years, however, papier-mâché sculptures have been appearing more regularly in museums and art galleries. Polyurethane, polymers, and other such chemicals have contributed to the versatility and resistance of this medium. The author discusses the virtues of papier-mâché art and points out pertinent technical and constructional details of the objects she presents.

There are also chapters on papier-mâché plaques, furniture, and home decorating, and a special section on papier-mâché by and for young children, containing numerous project suggestions.

CHINESE KITES: HOW TO MAKE AND FLY THEM. by David Jue. Charles E. Tuttle Company, Rutland, Vermont, 1967. 51 pages. illustrations (some color). $3.50.

This book offers a general discussion of kite flying, historically and sociologically, followed by notes on making kites, general techniques, and nine colorful kite designs with instructions for fabrication.

Hawk Kite

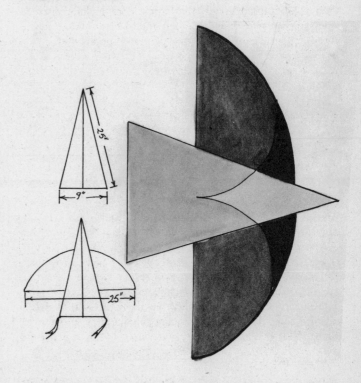

1. Construct triangular shaped frame. Attach centerpole.
2. Measure down 8″ from top on each leg and mark. Center 30″ bamboo strip across the marks on side opposite centerpole. Tie at the three intersections. Measure down about 9″ and mark. Cut a 40″ length of string. Tie on the tip of the crosspiece. Notch the bamboo slightly so that the string won't slip. Bend the tip inward until the string will stretch horizontally to the marks on the frame. Make two turns with the string around leg, centerpole, and leg (both turns should be upward from the point of intersection). Bend the other tip of the

crosspiece inward until the string stretches horizontally to it. Tie string with a bow knot on the notched tip. Do not clip excess string.

3. Check the frame for symmetry. The distance from the wingtip to the frame should be equal on each side, and the curve of the wingtips should be the same on each side. Correct any unevenness in curve by shaving the inner surface of the bamboo in any too-rigid areas. Adjust the distance from the wingtips to the frame by slipping the string at the turns. It may be necessary to re-adjust the length of string to achieve desired curvature.

4. Check and adjust balance of frame. Convert bowknot at wingtip to a square knot. Clip off excess string at wingtip. Glue all joints and string turns.

5. Cover side opposite centerpole with rice paper and decorate it as you will.

6. Attach bridle. Attach 2 15″ crepe-paper tails by gluing them to the rear surface at the lower corners.

KITES. by Clive Hart. Praeger Publishers, New York, 1967. 196 pages. illustrations, photographs (some color), bibliography, index. $12.50.

Beautiful and comprehensive, this book is a classic in the field.

In 1844, Colladon was experimenting with self-releasing "messengers" which traveled up the line of the kite and dropped a parachute when they struck the kite's bridle. He decided to try it with a full-sized dummy, complete with umbrella, boots, and chair. The dummy weighed 15 lbs., but it rose to a height of about 200 yards, much to the amazement of the onlookers. A coach load of late comers arrived on the scene, and unaware of the dummy's true character, thought they were watching a feat of astounding bravery being performed by a dauntless youth.

Source: KITES. by Clive Hart.

KITES. by Wyatt Brummitt. Golden Press, Western Publishing Co., Racine, Wisconsin, 1971. 120 pages. illustrations (some color), photographs, index. paperback edition $1.50.

This is an inexpensive and excellent basic introduction to kites.

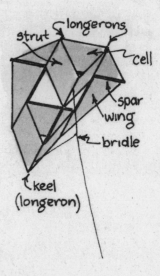

American Kitefliers Association
P.O. Box 1511
Silver City, N.M. 88061

The only real organization of kite fliers in the world, this group represents forty states and nine foreign countries. They publish a quarterly magazine, *Kite Tales*, which contains many articles of interest on building and flying kites as well as advertising for many different sorts of kites, probably the biggest selection anywhere. Membership costs $10.00 per year, which includes a subscription to the magazine.

GETTING STARTED IN KITEMAKING, revised edition. by Leslie and H. M. Hunt. Macmillan, New York, 1971. 84 pages. illustrations, photographs (some color), bibliography, index. $2.95.

This is a good, inexpensive introduction to kite making. It contains hints on accessories, decorations, flying, and other useful information. Construction details are given as they arise in the course of twenty-five projects. To avoid repetition, more construction details are given for the first group of kites—plane surface kites—than for the remainder.

This book is designed as a guide for making and flying moderate-size kites and is not intended to be professional. Certain aspects, such as knots and lashings, do not receive the treatment an expert would demand. The main idea is to let people see that kite making is easy and kite flying is fun. Not all the kites are designed for their aerodynamic advantages. Some are better than others, but they all fly and will ascend without too much difficulty.

Repairing loose hinges

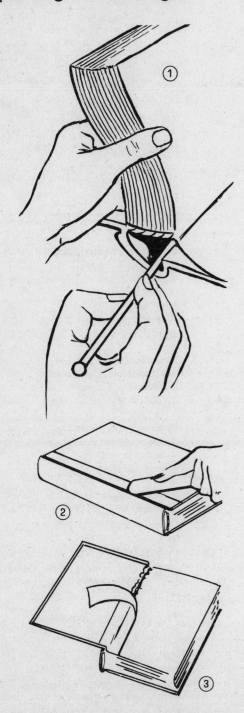

YOU WILL NEED: 1. Bind-Art Adhesive. 2. Wax Paper. 3. Knitting Needle. 4. Bone Folder. 5. Hinge Tape.

1. If hinge is loosened from cover, a knitting needle may be dipped into the Bind-Art bottle and then worked into the torn areas of the hinge by rolling the needle into damaged areas (Fig. 1). Be careful not to glue cover to spine. Place a piece of wax paper the full length of the hinge on the inside of the cover before closing the book to keep the adhesive from sticking to the end sheet.

2. Close the book and use a bone folder to crease the hinges as shown in Fig. 2.

3. If hinge is partly broken or torn, reinforce with white paper hinge tape. (Fig. 3).

Knitting needle can be used for working glue into weakened hinges or hinges that have separated from the case. They are also used to place in the hinge after repairs are completed as shown in the illustration. Weights are left on overnight.

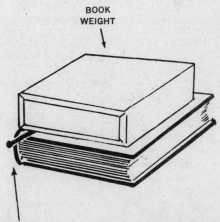

BOOK WEIGHT

KNITTING NEEDLE (OR CUT COAT HANGER)

From Modern Simplified Book Repair, *Bro-Dart Book Service, 1609 Memorial Avenue, Williamsport, Pa. 17701.*

THE GREAT INTERNATIONAL PAPER AIRPLANE BOOK. by Jerry Mander, George Dippel, and Howard Gossage. Simon and Schuster, New York, 1967. 128 pages. illustrations, photographs. paperback edition $2.95.

If we knew what it was we would learn, it wouldn't be research, would it? Or so went the advertisement for *Scientific American's* international paper airplane competition.

The twenty winners of this competition are immortalized in the pages of this book. Each is photographed in full-page aeronautical glory followed by a tear-out pattern for imitations.

The materials required for airplane-making are few and the hours of pleasure are long. It's a great book for **kids**, too.

HOW TO MAKE AND FLY PAPER AIRPLANES. by Ralph S. Barnaby. Bantam Books, New York, 1970. 83 pages. illustrations. paperback edition $.75.

The winner of the Great International Paper Airplane Contest tells all.

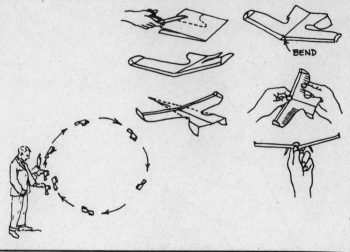

Paper Suppliers

Aiko's Art Materials Import
714 Wabash Avenue
Chicago, Ill. 60611
oriental art supplies, collage kits. sample book of Japanese handmade paper $4.00 plus $.50 handling.

Andrews-Nelson-Whitehead
7 Laight Street
New York, N. Y. 10013
exotic and handmade papers.

Aquabee
P.O. Box 10-16-100 Eighth Street
Passaic, N.J. 07055

Bienfang Paper Company, Inc.
P.O. Box 408
Metuchen, N.J. 07840
general selection.

Boins Arts and Crafts Company
91 Morris Street
Morristown, N.J. 07960
Also 75 South Palm Avenue
Sarasota, Fla. 33577
general selection.

CCM: Arts and Crafts, Inc.
9520 Baltimore Avenue
College Park, Md. 20740
general selection.

Central Art Supply Company
62 Third Avenue
New York, N.Y. 10013
general selection.

Charles T. Bainbridge's Sons
20 Cunberland Street
Brooklyn, N.Y. 11205
general selection.

Crystal Craft Art Tissue Company
Middletown, O. 45042
tissue paper.

David Davis
530 La Guardia Place
New York, N.Y.
exotic and handmade papers.

Dennison Manufacturing Company
Framingham, Mass. 01701
Scorasculpture, crepe paper, and Duplex crepe.

Dick Blick
P.O. Box 1267
Galesburg, Ill. 61401
general selection.

Economy Handicrafts, Inc.
47-11 Francis Lewis Boulevard
Flushing, N.Y. 11361
general selection.

J. L. Hammett Company
Boston, Mass. 02114
Also Lynchburg, Va. 24502
Lyons, N.Y. 14489, and
Union, N.J. 07083
general selection.

Joseph Torch
147 West 14 Street
New York, N.Y. 10011
general selection.

DECOUPAGE PRINTS AND MATERIALS

Boins Arts and Crafts Company
91 Morris Street
Morristown, N.J. 07960
Also 75 South Palm Avenue
Sarasota, Fla. 33577

Connoisseur Studios, Inc.
Louisville, Ky. 40207
paper tole prints and decoupage supplies.

NASCO
Fort Atkinson, Wis. 53538
general selection.

Paperchase Products, Ltd.
216 Tottenham Court Road
London W.1, England
handmade and exotic papers.

Pyramid Paper Company
310 Morgan Street
Tampa, Fla. 33602
general selection.

Riverside Paper Corporation
Appleton, Wis. 54911
Dubl-hue two-tone paper.

Rupaco Paper Corporation
62 Kent Street
Brooklyn, N.Y. 11222
general selection.

Technical Papers Corporation
729 Boylston Street
Boston, Mass. 02116
tableau-block printing paper.

Three Arts Materials Group, Inc.
375 Great Neck Road
Great Neck, N.Y. 11021
Acta sewable paper.

PAPIER-MACHE

Activa Products, Inc.
7 Front Street
San Francisco, Cal. 94111
Celluclay instant papier-mâché.

Riverside Paper Corporation
Appleton, Wis. 54911
Decomache.

QUILLING

Labelon Corporation
10 Chapin Street
Canandaigua, N.Y. 14424
Pottery Paper.

American Handicrafts Company
Tandy Corporation
P.O. Box 791
Fort Worth, Tex. 76107
Cerami Paper.

KITE MATERIALS SUPPLIERS

Kyte House
Richardson, Tex. 75080
   Sells kite plans for about $2.00 each. catalog "Kyte Lines" on request.

Go Fly a Kite Shop
1613 Second Avenue
New York, N.Y.
   Mail order suppliers. price list on request.

BOOKBINDING MATERIALS AND EQUIPMENT

Craftool Company, Inc.
1 Industrial Road
Woodridge, N.J. 07075

School Products Company
312 East 23 Street
New York, N.Y. 10010

Talas Division of Technical Library
   Service
104 Fifth Avenue
New York, N.Y. 10011

Plastics

PLASTICS: FOR ARTISTS AND CRAFTSMEN. by Harry B. Hollander. Watson-Guptill Publications, New York, 1972. 224 pages. photographs, suppliers list, index. $14.95.

Technological breakthroughs in the field of plastics have opened a vast area of supplies and techniques for the craftsman. However, he may find himself frustrated and confused as well as intrigued by the profusion of new and wonderful products at his disposal. This book provides a much-needed and explicit guide to a variety of plastic materials and the many alternate ways of employing them in the creation of both useful and decorative objects.

The processes are discussed in the context of generalized projects which are presented with clear step-by-step instructions and black-and-white photographs. The projects and processes include: casting polyester panels and reliefs; gelatin molds for polyester; polyester and fiber glass sculpture; nonglare polyester coating for graphic and photographic prints; dyeing, bleaching, and painting; plastic batik resist; epoxy metal jewelry; epoxy enameling; "stained glass" reliefs with epoxy; epoxy metal casting; making silicone rubber molds; and polyurethane foams.

Each topic is covered thoroughly, and many plastic works constructed by contemporary craftsmen and artists are presented to illustrate the effects achieved with each process.

An incredible glossary of plastics materials and techniques plus an excellent section on fire and health problems add the finishing touches to this very useful manual for craftsmen and artists both novice and knowledgeable.

PLASTICS AS AN ART FORM. by Thelma R. Newman. Chilton Book Company, Radnor, Pennsylvania, 1969. 338 pages. illustrations, photographs (some color), bibliography, index. $12.50.

Despite Ms. Newman's disclaimers, this volume has really been superceded by her far superior *Plastics as a Design Form*. *Plastics as an Art Form* was published a number of years ago and therefore is lacking some of the newer and more exciting new materials featured in the later volume. The artists highlighted here also reflect the outdated quality of the text insofar as they are primarily working with traditional motifs in plastic rather than experimenting and innovating in the way that the contemporary *Design* artists are.

PLASTICS AS A DESIGN FORM. by Thelma R. Newman. Chilton Book Company, Radnor, Pennsylvania, 1972. 348 pages. illustrations, photographs (some color), suppliers list, bibliography, index. $17.95.

Literally thousands of contemporary designs in every available plastic material are presented in this excellent book. For the most part, construction information for home workshop craftsmen is limited to acrylic. However, the how-to hints are extremely complete: bending, blow molding, vacuum forming, cementing (techniques with four different types of solvents and glues are illustrated), and general cutting and shaping procedures are well detailed.

The sections treating other materials and processes present designs in which the construction is more suited to industrial techniques, but the wealth of visual material provides inspiration for working in other, more manageable materials.

This is an expensive book, but it provides a great deal of information on the properties of various plastic materials and, more importantly, how these properties can be exploited for unique, imaginative designs. The author is especially sensitive to the properties of light reflection and refraction in cast plastic and illustrates this in a number of photographs.

Serious craftsmen should profit by a familiarity with the information presented here, which makes this a very valuable book to have in the workshop.

Modern Plastics
Fulfillment Manager
P.O. Box 430
Hightstown, N.J. 08520
Monthly. $10.00 a year.

This is a technically oriented publication covering the latest plastic products, manufacturing, and engineering. Included in the subscription price is the annual *Modern Plastics Encyclopedia*, the most comprehensive text available on up-to-date plastic happenings. It comes out every October and consists of a summary of the year's trends in plastic, information on polymer science, a textbook of fundamental plastics, a directory of 3,600 companies, and reference data on plastic properties and characteristics.

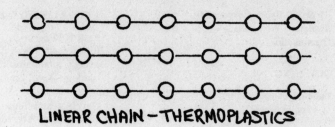

LINEAR CHAIN — THERMOPLASTICS

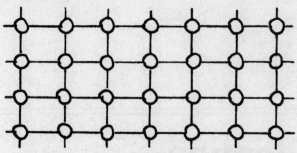

CROSS-LINKING CHAIN, THERMO-SETTING PLASTICS

CREATIVE PLASTICS. by David Rees. The Viking Press, New York, 1973. 112 pages. illustrations, photographs, suppliers list, bibliography, index. $8.95.

This book offers techniques and some sample projects for a variety of plastic materials. Unfortunately, none of the techniques is explained fully, and sometimes the information given is misleading or just wrong.

There are some strange applications for the materials discussed. For example, the section on expanded polystyrene (Styrofoam) demonstrates how the material can be used as a pattern for sand casting aluminum objects, and that's all the author uses it for. In speaking about casting and embedding with polyester resin, he says not a word on glass or rubber molds or commercial spray pattern releases.

CREATIVE PLASTICS TECHNIQUES. by Claude Smale. Van Nostrand Reinhold, New York, 1973. 124 pages. illustrations, photographs, suppliers list, index. $6.95.

Claude Smale adapts industrial techniques to craft work in this small but informative book. Readers, however, should be familiar with the basic techniques of forming and fabrication, as the material covered involves somewhat sophisticated tools and processes, requiring experience and a good working knowledge of all kinds of plastics. The techniques discussed are presented with generalized instructions on methods and equipment.

Among the topics discussed are thermoforming acrylic; welding polyethylene, vinyl, and acrylic; PVC (hot and cold dipping); foams and other expanded plastics; polyester reinforced with glass; casting and embedding polyester; and vacuum forming. Some subjects are covered in more detail than others, but all are well illustrated with diagrams and lots of photographs of interesting objects made with the technique in question.

The sections devoted to explanation of the properties and characteristics of different plastic materials are quite informative and should be of use to craftsmen working in this field.

CREATING WITH FLEXIBLE FOAM. by A. De Brouwer. Sterling Publishing Company, New York, 1971. 48 pages. illustrations, photographs, index. $2.95.

This is a nice little book for children on how to carve animals out of polyurethane soft foam.

PLASTICS FOR THE CRAFTSMAN. by Jay Hartley Newman and Scott Newman. Crown Publishers, New York, 1972. 214 pages. photographs (some color), suppliers list, bibliography, index. $7.95. paperback edition $3.95.

There are basically two types of plastics: thermoplastics and thermosetting plastics. Thermoplastics are hard and rigid at normal room temperatures but become soft and malleable when heated. This group includes acrylic and styrene. While the material is soft it can be formed into a desired shape and this shape will be retained when the plastic cools. Thermosetting plastics, on the other hand, can only be shaped once. Initially, these plastics are often liquid and cure at room temperature after the addition of a catalyst. This is called polymerization and it is a chemical process in which the molecules become tightly linked to produce a rigid state. Polyester and epoxy resins and some of the liquid foams are of this type.

This book provides projects and basic information utilizing both varieties of plastic. The instructions are clear and well illustrated but somewhat inadequate. The authors assume a great deal of skill and experience with tools and general shop and craft practice that not all craftsmen have. General information on drilling, buffing, using solvent, heat forming, mold making, and other such procedures particularly relevant to plastic work cannot be taken for granted. Also, and most critically, there is a lack of emphasis on safety precautions. Very great care must be taken when working with all plastics to prevent unsafe conditions. Fumes from polyester and epoxy resins, for example, are extremely toxic.

The projects, for the most part, are pleasant but mundane, and the instructions are so explicitly geared for them that it would be difficult to "take off" on them or to improvise using the principles employed therein.

Information on how to use plastics, supplies, instructions, technical services, and more available from: **Polyproducts Corporation, Order Department 12, 13810 Nelson Avenue, Detroit, Mich. 48227.**

WORKING WITH PLASTICS. by George Gashzner. Drake Publishers, New York, 1971. 60 pages. illustrations, photographs. $4.95.

This is a fairly good manual of plastic techniques for those with a knowledge and degree of skill in using hand and power tools. Almost all types of plastics are covered, but the major emphasis is on working with cast acrylic sheet (Plexiglas).

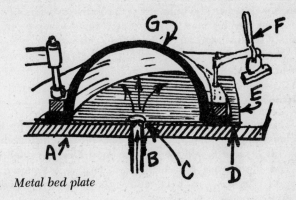

A   *Metal bed plate*

B   *Air inlet*

C   *Baffle*

D   *Rubber seal*

E   *Clamping ring*

F   *Toggle clamp*

G   *Hot acrylic inflated to require shape*

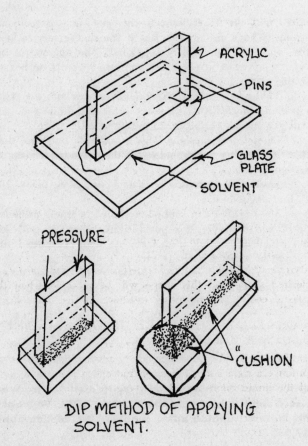

DIP METHOD OF APPLYING SOLVENT.

Cutting, drilling, cementing, and finishing receive thorough treatment. Heat forming and blow and vacuum molding are also presented, but they are not really covered in a complete, useful manner.

MILLICENT ZAHN'S ACRYLIC. by Millicent Zahn. Van Nostrand Reinhold, New York, 1973. 96 pages. illustrations, photographs, suppliers list. $8.95. paperback edition $4.95.

Millicent Zahn, queen of the plastic giftware trade, presents a multitude of attractive and interesting projects using acrylic (Plexiglas) plastic. About half the projects are functional, and the other half decorative. A clear plastic coffee table with a built-in terrarium is one of the better

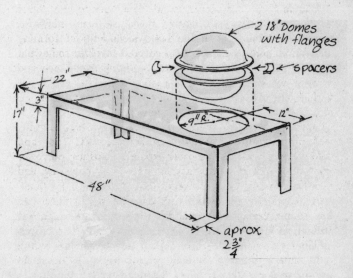

Table with built-in terrarium

functional items. The bulk of the decorative articles is composed of jewelry made with precast acrylic shapes and a variety of small and large sculptures. There are many hints on acrylic fabrication and finishing, though the information on heat forming is a bit sparse.

WORKING WITH PLEXIGLAS

This booklet of more than 42 pages is published by the Rohm and Haas Company (P.O. Box 14619, Philadelphia, Pa. 19134) and is sold for $1.00 by most Plexiglas retailers.

This inexpensive introduction to Plexiglas techniques is one of the best available and belongs in every plasticrafter's workshop or library.

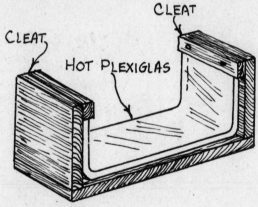

Jig for U-shaped bend

SETTING IN CLEAR PLASTIC. by Katharina Zechlin. Taplinger Publishing Company, New York, 1971. 72 pages. illustrations, photographs. $4.95.

Embedding objects in polyester resin can be an enjoyable hobby, or a valuable aid to scientists who wish to preserve specimens for further study. This book is chiefly concerned with the simple techniques of embedding, but it also suggests lines of experimentation that readers might like to follow up.

The instructions for a variety of embedment project suggestions and general procedures are very clear and well illustrated, and also are very thorough in the area of safety and health hazards. Chemical proportions, preparation of objects for embedment, various mold materials, and finishing are covered in depth.

FIBERGLASS, PROJECTS AND PROCEDURES. by Gerald L. Steele. McKnight Publishing Company, Bloomington, Illinois, 1962. 159 pages. illustrations, photographs, suppliers list, bibliography, index. text edition $6.64.

This is an excellent introduction to the use of fiber glass for students and craftsmen. It contains many functional, household type projects, each stressing a different process of fiber glass laminate construction. Instructions are simple (the author states that each project has been made by eighth-graders), clear, and illustrated in a step-by-step format.

Cautions When Using Polyester Resins

1. *Good ventilation.* Work with windows open, or try to make sure that air in workroom or studio is changed by exhaust fan at least 6 times per hour. Industrial health experts maintain that the styrene vapor from polyester resins should not be in greater concentration than 100 PPM [parts per million] when one is exposed to the resin throughout the day.

2. *Do not smoke.* This is not only dangerous because polyesters are generally flammable, but because it is also a good way to get polyester resin in your mouth.

3. *Wear gloves when possible.* Resin is sticky, irritating, and difficult to remove from the hands without the use of solvents which are flammable and tend to dry skin. Also, when using fiberglass, gloves are a must!

4. Remove fiberglass cuttings and fibers from clothing and body with masking tape; blowing off the glass needles may cause them to land in pores and bloodstream. This could kill you.

5. *Accelerators in their pure state are explosive when mixed with the MEK-Peroxide catalyst.* There is really no reason to have any around, but if you do, be sure to keep the two chemicals widely separated. The amount of accelerator present in the polyester resin presents no hazard in this respect.

6. *Thoroughly mix all ingredients needed into the resin, especially the MEK-Px.* If you do not mix these well, you will get uneven curing or no curing at all.

7. *Do not over catalyze.* This is wasteful, but more than that, it will alter the properties of the polyester if taken to extremes.

8. *Store resin in coolest area available.* Store below 70° F. Freezing is best.

9. *Store MEK-Px in cool place.* This is a strong oxidizing agent and therefore is a possible fire hazard if spills are not wiped up. Put all trash from use with polyester resins outside in a metal garbage can.

10. *Keep containers of polyester resin covered except when pouring.* Not only will this keep out dirt, but it will help resin to last longer.

Source: PLASTICS: FOR ARTISTS AND CRAFTSMEN. by Harry B. Hollander.

CRAFTS IN POLYESTER RESIN. by Herbert Scarfe. Watson-Guptill Publications, New York, 1973. 96 pages. illustrations, photographs, suppliers list, bibliography. $7.95.

This is a good, straightforward presentation of basic embedding and molding techniques. It includes a nice section on jewelry made with wire and polyester resin. The book is recommended for teachers and younger craftsmen.

1. WAX — MOLD

2. MIX RESIN PLUS CATALYST

3.

COVER

4.
FIRST LAYER SHALLOW & LEVEL

5. SPECIMEN HUNG BY WIRE FROM SUPPORT & TOUCHING FIRST HARDENED LAYER.

6.
2ND LAYER
1ST LAYER

7. REMOVE THREAD & SUPPORT

8. FINAL LAYER
2
1

Embedding an inorganic object

GETTING STARTED IN PLASTICS. by Nancy M. Lang. Macmillan, New York, 1972. 95 pages. photographs, bibliography, index. paperback edition $2.95.

This book is a good, simple introduction to casting polyester resin and making embedments. The properties, procedures, and safety precautions for polyester are covered in well-illustrated instructions for a variety of molding techniques. Acrylic and Styrofoam are also discussed, but in a very superficial way.

Plastic paperweights and tabletop sculpture are the typical suggested uses for the techniques presented. These are less than exciting, but beginners will be able to get the feel of the medium through this book and go on to more sophisticated projects and methods.

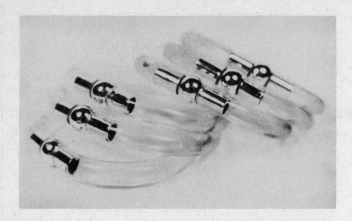

Vinyl and silver bracelets by Hotcakes, Peter and Maire Ksiezopolski

Plastic Suppliers

Manufacturers usually do not sell small amounts but will be happy to send you product information. When inquiring of manufacturers about the sale of small quantities, ask them for their nearest retailer in your location.

ADHESIVES FOR PLASTICS

Adhesive Products Corporation
1660 Boone Avenue
Bronx, N.Y. 10460
many different adhesives.

Columbia Cement Company
159 Hanse
Freeport, N.Y. 11520
Quik Stik, rubber cement for urethane foam.

Eastman Chemical Products, Inc.
Chemicals Division
Kingsport, Tenn. 37662
Eastman 910, an exceptionally strong glue.

Guard Coating and Chemical Corporation
58 John Jay Avenue
Kearney, N.J. 07032
cements for acrylics, Mylars, nylons, styrenes, PVAs, PVCs, epoxies, and polyesters.

Rezolin Division of Hexcel Corporation
20701 Nordhoff Street
Chatsworth, Cal. 91311
cements for epoxy, acrylic, and polyester.

Schwartz Chemical Company, Inc.
50-01 Second Street
Long Island City, N.Y. 11101
solvent cements.

CATALYSTS

May be obtained at outlets for polyester resin. Or write:

Lucidol Division
Wallace and Tiernan, Inc.
1740 Military Road
Buffalo, N.Y. 14817

Reichold Chemicals, Inc.
RCI Building
White Plains, N.Y. 10602
MEK peroxide.

COLOR

May be obtained from all jobbers of polyester resin.

Chempico Pigments and Dispersions Company
P.O. Box 203
South Orange, N.J. 07079
polyester color pastes.

Ferro Corporation
Color Division
Cleveland, O. 44105

Patent Chemical, Inc.
335 McLean Boulevard
Paterson, N. J. 07504

Plastics Molders Supply Company, Inc.
75 South Avenue
Fanwood, N.J. 07023

FILM

E. I. du Pont de Nemours and Co., Inc.
Wilmington, Del. 19898
Mylar film.

FINISHES

Ditzler Automotive Finishes
Detroit, Mich. 48204
acrylic lacquer for spray coating.

PPG Industries, Inc.
1 Gateway Center
Pittsburgh, Pa. 15222
Durethane 600 elastomeric lacquer and Durethane 100 elastomeric lacquer thermosetting enamel, both for use over urethane foam.

FOAM CUTTING MACHINES

Dura-Tech Corporation
1555 North West First Avenue
Boca Raton, Fla. 33432
Hot-wire cutters.

POLISHING EQUIPMENT

The best polishing equipment for acrylic can be purchased at jewelry suppliers.

STRIP HEATERS

Briscoe Manufacturing Company
Columbus, O. 43216
Briskeat RH-36 heating element.

Electric Hotpack Company, Inc.
5083 Cottman Street
Philadelphia, Pa. 19135

General Electric Company
1 Progress Road
Shelbyville, Ind. 46176

MASKS AND TAPES

Borden Chemical Company
369 Madison Avenue
New York, N.Y. 10017
clear Mylar tape.

J. L. N. Smythe Company
1300 West Lehigh Avenue
Philadelphia, Pa. 19132
Clearmask.

Spraylat
1 Park Avenue
New York, N.Y. 10016
Spraylat—a water-soluble latex that can be brushed on. dries in 45 minutes and may be peeled off when dry.

3M Company
St. Paul, Minn. 55101
masking paper and protective tape.

MOLD MATERIALS

Adhesive Products Corporation
1660 Boone Avenue
Bronx, N.Y. 10460
s-t-r-e-t-c-h-y vinyl.

Dow Corning Corporation
Midland, Mich. 48640
RTV silicone Silastic.

General Electric Company
1 River Road
Schenectady, N.Y. 12306
RTV silicone.

PAINT FOR PLASTICS

Glidden Company
11001 Madison Avenue
Cleveland, O. 44102
Glidden acrylic sign finishes.

Keystone Refining Company, Inc.
4821-31 Garden Street
Philadelphia, Pa. 19137
Grip-Flex.

Wyandotte Paint Products Company
P.O. Box 255
Norcross, Ga. 30071
Grip-Flex and Grip-Mask.

FIBER GLASS

Burlington Glass Fabrics
1550 Broadway
New York, N.Y. 10018

Western Fibrous Glass Products
739 Bryant Street
San Francisco, Cal. 94107

SOLVENTS

National Solvent Corporation
3751 Jennings Road
Cleveland, O. 44109

Shell Chemical Company
110 West 51 Street
New York, N.Y. 10020
acetone.

Union Carbide Company
Chemicals and Plastics Division
270 Park Avenue
New York, N.Y. 10017

TOOLS AND CHEMICALS

Rohm and Haas
Tools for Plexiglas
P.O. Box 14619
Philadelphia, Pa. 19134

RELEASE AGENTS

Dow Corning
Midland, Mich. 48640
silicone release paper.

Price Driscoll Corporation
75 Milbar Road
Farmingdale, N.Y. 11735
general-purpose mold releases for epoxy
and polyester resins.

RESINS

Acme Resin
1401 Circle Avenue
Forest Park, Ill.

Ain Plastics
65 Fourth Avenue
New York, N.Y. 10003

Allied Chemicals
Plastics Division
40 Rector Street
New York, N.Y.

American Acrylic Corporation
173 Marine Street
Farmingdale, N.Y. 11735

American Cyanamide Company
Plastics and Resins Division
Wallingford, Conn. 06492
Laminac polyester resin.

Cadillac Plastics and Chemical Company
15841 Second Avenue
P.O. Box 810
Detroit, Mich. 48234

Glidden Company
Baltimore, Md. 21226
"Glidpol" polyester resin.

Industrial Plastics
324 Canal Street
New York, N.Y. 10013

Koppers Company, Inc.
Tar and Chemical Division
Koppers Building
Pittsburgh, Pa. 15219

Mobau Chemical Company
Penn-Lincoln Parkway West
Pittsburgh, Pa.

Model Craft Hobbies
314 Fifth Avenue
New York, N.Y. 10001

Polyproducts Corporation
13810 Nelson Avenue
Detroit, Mich. 48227
suppliers of a complete line of resins,
foam systems, fillers, reinforcements,
mold materials, and related equipment.

PPG Industries
Coatings and Resins Division
1 Gateway Center
Pittsburgh, Pa. 15222
Selectron polyester resin.

Reichold Chemicals, Inc.
RCI Building
White Plains, N.Y. 10602
Polylite polyester resin.

World of Plastics
1129 South Elmora Avenue
Elizabeth, N.J. 07202

SHEETS AND FINDINGS (Mail Order)

Arizona
Cadillac Plastic and Chemical
2625 University Drive
Phoenix, Ariz. 85034

Arkansas
Cope Plastics
2000 East 17 Street
Little Rock, Ark.

California
Cadillac Plastic and Chemical
1531 State College Boulevard
Anaheim, Cal. 92806

Corth Plastics
725 Delaware Street
Berkeley, Cal. 95071
Also 532 Howland Street
Redwood City, Cal. 94063

Port Plastics
180 Constitution Drive
Menlo Park, Cal. 94025
Also 8037 Slauson Avenue
Montebello, Cal. 90640

Terrell's Plastics
3618 Broadway
Sacramento, Cal. 95817

Colorado
Plasticrafts
2800 North Speer
Denver, Colo. 80211

Regal Plastic Supply Company
3985 South Kalamath
Englewood, Colo. 80116

Connecticut
Commercial Plastics
100 Prestige Park Road
East Hartford, Conn. 06108
Also 463 Boston Post Road
Orange, Conn. 06477

Florida
Commercial Plastics
2331 Laura Street
Jacksonville, Fla. 32206
Also 3801 North West Second Avenue
Miami, Fla. 33127

Faulkner Plastics
4504 East Hillsborough Avenue
Tampa, Fla. 33601

Georgia
Commercial Plastics
334 North Avenue, North West
Atlanta, Ga. 30318

Illinois
Cope Plastics, Inc.
111 West Delmar Avenue
Godfrey, Ill. 62035

Iowa
Cope Plastics
714-66th Avenue South West
Cedar Rapids, Ia. 52404

Van Horn Plastics
8000 University Avenue
Des Moines, Ia. 50311

Maryland
Alman Plastics of Maryland
6311 Erdman Avenue
Baltimore, Md. 21205

Michigan
Alman Plastics of Michigan
2882 36th Street, South East
Grand Rapids, Mich. 49058
Also 26004 Groesbeck Highway
Warren, Mich. 48090

Missouri
Cope Plastics Missouri
6340 Knox Industrial Drive
St. Louis, Mo. 63139

New Jersey
Almac Plastics of New Jersey
171 Fabyan Place
Newark, N.J. 07112

New Mexico
Regal Plastics
3019 Princeton North East
Albuquerque, N.M. 87106

Almac Plastics
47-42 37th Street
Long Island City, N.Y. 11101

Industrial Plastics
324 Canal Street
New York, N.Y. 10013
They have no catalog, but will mail order
if specific requests are made.

Mail Order Plastics
55 Lispenard Street
New York, N.Y. 10013

North Carolina
Commercial Plastics
731 West Hargett Street
Raleigh, N.C. 27611

Ohio
Almac Plastics of Ohio
30 North Summit Street
Akron, O. 44308

Dayton Plastics
2554 Needmore Road
Dayton, O. 45414

Oklahoma
Cope Plastics
105 North East 38th Terrace
Oklahoma City, Okla. 73105

Plastic Engineering
6801 East 44 Street
Tulsa, Okla. 74145

Ted's Hobbies Unlimited
11122 East Admiral Place
Tulsa, Okla.

Pennsylvania
Commercial Plastics
2022 Chateau Street
Pittsburgh, Pa. 15233

Rohm and Haas
P.O. Box 14619
Philadelphia, Pa. 19134

Puerto Rico
Commercial Plastics
Avenida Fernandez Juncos 635
San Juan, Puerto Rico 00902

Rhode Island
Commercial Plastics
920 Broadway
East Providence, R.I. 02974

Tennessee
Norrell, Inc.
721 Scott Street
Memphis, Tenn. 38112

Texas
Commercial Plastics
2200 Vantage Street
Dallas, Tex. 75207

Quilting

QUILTING. by Averil Colby. Charles Scribner's Sons, New York, 1971. 212 pages. illustrations, photographs, bibliography, index. $12.50.

A small ivory figure housed in the British Museum provides evidence suggesting that quilted garments have been worn as early as the 1st Dynasty in Egypt. The figure presents a king wearing the Crown of Upper Egypt and wrapped in a mantle which bears carved patterns charac-

teristic of quilted fabric. The mantle hangs stiffly, not in the soft folds of single thickness material. There must, of course, be some doubt as to the actual nature the textile represented, although the workmanship is of fine quality and the face of the figure is believed to be an accurate portrait of the king.

The earliest extant example of quilting is a carpet which was found on the floor of a warrior-chief's tomb in 1925. It is now in the possession of the Soviet Union and has

A figure wearing a jack, from a fifteenth century Hans Memling painting

been dated somewhere between the first century B.C. and the second century A.D.

Averil Colby has thoroughly researched the long history of the quilt and in her book presents a fascinating and scholarly account of its development up until modern times. This book is not so much a practical manual of technique as a thoughtful consideration of the varieties and vagaries of quilting. The precocious beginner may be able to derive enough how-to information from the descriptions and illustrations of tools and equipment and the four brief appendixes which contain terse instructions for stuffed quilts, cord quilting, flat quilts, and wadded quilts; but this is really not the book's strong point. More experienced quilters will probably benefit on a practical level from the large selection of patterns, many of which can be used as templates and which Ms. Colby describes in both comparative and historical contexts.

QUILTS AND COVERLETS. by Jean Ray Laury. Van Nostrand Reinhold, New York, 1970. 128 pages. illustrations, photographs (some color). $9.95.

Quilt makers today are recapturing the spirit and essence of Early American quilts. At last we can look forward to exciting designs. Gone, thank goodness, are the rows upon rows of obese, sunbonneted girls in pale green and lavender. Traditional designs no longer meet our needs. Creativity and inventiveness make it possible to modify and rejuvenate the old approaches and techniques. Systems of construction in quiltmaking are strong, durable, and beautiful. If we can retain the structural integrity of the traditional quilt and add to it a contemporary approach in color and design, we will achieve a quilt which merges past and present.

The author combines the spirit of modernity with comprehensible instructions for fabrication both by hand and

machine using traditional and new synthetic fibers. The design suggestions and photographic examples are of an original and highly exciting nature.

ONCE UPON A QUILT: PATCHWORK DESIGN AND TECHNIQUE. by Celine Blanchard Mahler. Van Nostrand Reinhold, New York, 1973. 96 pages. illustrations, photographs (some color), suppliers list. $8.95. paperback edition $4.95.

This is a nice, clear introduction to beginning patchwork. Information on machine quilting is supplied, though the author doesn't seem overly enthused about it. She does not offer information on pattern modification for sewing machines as Ms. Gutcheon does in her book, *The Perfect Patchwork Primer*, and simply recommends that the quilter not attempt to sew traditional curved patterns other than by hand.

The book features sixteen traditional patchwork patterns drawn on actual-size graph paper for easy transfer; these provide an excellent opportunity for the inexperienced quilter to get right to work. The patterns were chosen for historical value and adaptability to today's homes as well as for the degree of ease or difficulty which they present. The author also offers suggestions for other decorative uses for patchwork.

At your quilting, maids, don't dally,
Quilt quick if you would marry,
A maid who is quiltless at 21
Never shall greet her bridal sun!

—Devon Rhyme

AMERICAN PIECED QUILTS. by Jonathan Holstein. The Viking Press, New York, 1973. 94 pages. photographs (some color), bibliography. $5.95.

A brief historical text introduces this collection of eighty-four quilts, but the main purpose of this book is for looking, not for reading. The author chose each quilt not for the quiltmanship involved in its making, but rather for the "visual statement" it makes.

. . . Our interest is in the images the quilts form, and not in their stitches; many are in poor condition, have some machine work in them; or, indeed, exhibit a level of workmanship which would be unacceptable to those interested mainly in fine craftsmanship.

The planning of a quilt required a great many aesthetic decisions, and within the framework of the technique each woman had complete freedom to exercise her individual creativity. In effect, as the author would have it, she "painted" with fabrics. The photographs he presents attest to the outstanding artistry of many of the creators, and anyone involved in quilting, abstract, or op art should find this a rich storehouse of inspiration.

Patchwork and applique in an entirely free design. Center medallion of appliqued figures of human forms and birds. This quilt was found in New Jersey and was traditionally made by a Civil War veteran. A descendant of his tells the following story: The quilt was made by a wounded, discharged Union soldier toward the end of the Civil War in order to soothe his shattered nerves. He could not escape entirely the effects of the war: his quilt has silhouette figures of armed soldiers on horseback and afoot, marching grimly around an intermediate border; and in the central group, foot soldiers surround women who appear to be offering refreshments on trays. Their outlines recall the trademark figure on the box of a well-known brand of chocolate. This trademark was adopted by the manufacturers in 1780 and had its origin in a contemporary French painting called "La Chocolatière." Crescent moons, hearts, and fat complacent doves may have been introduced to the militant picture to humor a wife or sweetheart.

The applique stitchery is meticulously even, the quilting entirely adequate.

Many of the textiles in this quilt are much older than the Civil War period; many are fine early copperplates. Probably of New Jersey origin, as it was found in that state.

Photo courtesy of Shelburne Museum

AMERICAN PATCHWORK QUILTS. by Lenice Ingram Bacon. William Morrow and Company, New York, 1973. 190 pages. photographs (some color), bibliography, index. $16.50.

This is a chatty, anecdotal history and appreciation of the art of quilting, accompanied by beautiful color photographs of the quilts and interesting gossip about the people who made them. The author gives no instructions for how to make the quilts, but she does offer advice on their care and cleaning.

PATCHWORK FOR BEGINNERS. by Sylvia Green. Watson-Guptill Publications, New York, 1972. 103 pages. illustrations, suppliers list, bibliography, index. $7.95.

The beginning patchworker may feel a quilt too ambitious an undertaking right off, so the author suggests smaller articles, such as cushions, boxes, belts, and toys, as a means of whetting the enthusiasm and increasing the confidence of more timid novices. No specific instructions for the various items are included, but there are photographs of the finished products, and most are simple enough to be figured out independently by the reader.

Patchwork demands precision and accuracy in the making, and unless a seamstress is quite proficient, the fabrics from which a quilt is constructed should be of a firm, even weave that will crease and seam well and that will not fray. Therefore, the author devotes several pages to fabric characteristics and the way in which various fabrics can be employed to create a patchwork of character and individuality. She recommends that beginners restrain themselves and limit their fabric to cotton until they have attained a sense of confidence about their work. The author presents the standard geometric shapes and patterns accompanied by instructions and diagrams which are clear and easy to use. On the whole, this book is an adequate, though not outstanding, first step for beginners on the road to patchwork.

PIECED WORK AND APPLIQUE QUILTS AT SHELBURNE MUSEUM. by Lilian Baker Carlisle. Hobby House Press, Riverdale, Maryland, 1967. 99 pages. photographs. paperback edition $4.50.

This is a catalog of the outstanding pieces in the Shelburne collection discussed in a descriptive text and featured in black-and-white photographs. Send $4.50 and $.25 postage to the Shelburne Museum, Shelburne, Vermont 05482.

THE STANDARD BOOK OF QUILTING AND COLLECTING. by Marguerite Ickis. Dover Publications, New York, 1949. 273 pages. illustrations, index. paperback edition $3.00.

This is a reprint of a 1949 edition containing a history of quilt making and information for the hobbyist-collector. The author has not limited her field to patchwork quilts; and she discusses many different quilt types. She gives general procedural information as well as specific instructions for forty quilts. Several templates are presented but she also explains how to make full-size patterns from pictures, small designs, or enlargements of the more than 140 block patterns illustrated. This is not one of the glamorous books, but it contains solid information at a reasonable price.

THE PERFECT PATCHWORK PRIMER. by Beth Gutcheon. David McKay Company, New York, 1973. 266 pages. illustrations, suppliers list, index. $9.95.

The author writes for the modern quilt maker with the hope and expectation that some of the best of the quilt making tradition is still to come. She writes sympathetically, yet unromantically, about the development of quilting in America and the situations of the women who made it— all with a view toward establishing a relationship between past and present so that the place of tradition within the craft of the contemporary quilter can be determined.

The outstanding feature of Ms. Gutcheon's handling of the subject is the information she gives about quilting on the sewing machine. Sewing quilts by machine necessitates certain changes in some of the traditional patterns which were designed before mechanized sewing was possible and which cannot be sewn with straight seams. Some of the patterns simply cannot be adapted, and when this is the case the author notes it. Others can and have been adapted, and several examples of modified, straight-seamed versions of historic patterns are presented. All of the two hundred patterns can be worked by hand if that is preferred, so the traditionalist can still benefit from Ms. Gutcheon's advice. The patterns have been reduced and thus cannot be used as templates. The author suggests transferring them onto graph paper.

The section on selling quilts contains a bit more practical and realistic advice than is found in most other books, and the author makes some suggestions for the use of patchwork in other things besides quilts.

The basic contribution of this book to the library of patchwork manuals is in its modernistic approach, the information it has to share about machine quilting, and the use of modern fabrics. The instructions are sometimes difficult to understand because the presentation is not step-by-step but rather a collection of easygoing and freehanded alternatives that are intriguing but often confusing to the beginner.

POLLY PRINDLE'S BOOK OF AMERICAN PATCHWORK QUILTS. by Alice I. Gammell. Grosset and Dunlap, New York, 1973. 238 pages. illustrations, photographs (some color). $12.50.

At the age of eight, Alice Gammell finished her first quilt. Now, eighty-one-year-old grandmother Alice shares with the world her techniques, memories, and oldest patterns.

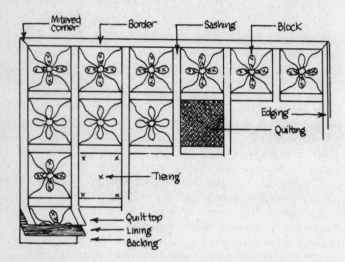

Parts of a quilt

The author is not lacking in helpful hints. For instance, if you use a paper pattern, try sandpaper. It's thick enough so that the pattern can be reused again and again without being cut down, and when laid face down on the material, sandpaper adheres without pins. She also offers simple, step-by-step instructions and supplies fifty pattern-templates for quilt design and borders, plus complete yardage requirements and simple instructions on how to calculate yardage for other projects. All the instructions are for the type of quilting Alice Gammell grew up with (hand-stitched), and the existence of the sewing machine is virtually ignored. However, those with time to spare and a desire to make traditional patchwork quilts with the unique hand-sewn quality that is their hallmark, would do well to make the acquaintance of Polly Prindle.

QUILTMAKING: THE MODERN APPROACH TO A TRADITIONAL CRAFT. by Ann-Sargent Wooster. Drake Publishers, New York, 1972. 160 pages. illustrations, photographs (some color), bibliography, index. $8.95.

A nice feature of this book is the quilting dictionary in the front. This enables the reader to turn back quickly for a concise definition of a forgotten term or procedure.

The author has a friendly style and the book is readable and full of interesting historical anecdotes. The author reviews modern quilting methods and supplies advice for quilting layers and applying appliqué on a sewing machine. She also provides clear directions for the use of trapunto, a technique often glossed over by other manuals. The major drawback with this book, at least from this beginner's point of view, is its layout. It is almost impossible to find continuous, step-by-step instructions, and the author offers little advice in the way of helpful hints or encouragement.

The somewhat "arty" applications for quilting featured in the photographs may offer inspiration to experienced quilters who are so inclined; a special interest of the author appears to be quilt-sculpture.

Although England, greedy for revenues, originally outlawed the manufacturing of cloth in the colonies, by 1640 people were actively encouraged to produce textiles. Each family was required by law to engage a full-time spinner. These spinners were usually children or unmarried women and so the name spinster entered our vocabulary.

Quilting Co-ops

Cabin Creek Quilts of Eskdale, West Virginia. A co-op formed by a VISTA worker to provide a source of income to women in an economically depressed area.

Mountain Artisans, West Virginia

Peach Blossom Exclusives, Tazewell County, Virginia

Freedom Quilting Bee, Alberta, Alabama. One of the earliest.

QUICK AND EASY QUILTING: HOW TO MAKE HOME AND FASHION ACCESSORIES WITHOUT A FRAME. by Bonnie Leman. Hearthside Press, Great Neck, New York, 1972. 191 pages. illustrations, photographs, index. $6.95.

No frame quilting offers many advantages aside from the obvious one of saving space. It enables quilting to join the ranks of the portable needle arts and thereby become a pleasant and restful diversion during the course of a busy day, rather than something for which a special time and place must be set aside. Even more important, when the quiltmaker is not limited by the frame, more methods and techniques of quilting open up, such as machine quilting.

Lap quilting requires certain modifications in procedure. For instance, when a quilt is made on a frame the stitches are usually begun on one side of the quilt and as the work progresses the finished section is rolled under. Frameless stitching begins in the center and moves outward to the perimeter so that any unevenness can be worked out towards the edges.

The author presents a number of "quilt as you go" patterns which can be executed with a variety of techniques and employed in a number of different quilts or quilted objects. Most of the projects involve prepieced blocks which are afterward quilted on a machine to form puff quilts. The patterns, which are presented as templates, are adequate though not outstanding in design, but the concept of the book is laudable and it opens up quilting to those who might not have had either time or space to try it before.

Jules and Harry Sleeping, by Susan Zucker. Color print quilted on satin (pillow fabric fake quilted cotton chintz).

THE MOUNTAIN ARTISANS QUILTING BOOK. by Alfred Allen Lewis. Macmillan, New York, 1973. 179 pages. illustrations, photographs (some color), index. $12.50.

This book offers comprehensive instructions on the basic techniques of patchwork, a selection of quilting patterns, and examples of traditional and contemporary applications for patchwork in the creation of quilts, toys, pillows, clothing, and place mats. The step-by-step photographs for procedures and the clear written instructions are excellent. In addition to the practical knowledge contained in this book is the story and flavor of the West Virginia cooperative from its organization to its reception by the world of high fashion. The author explains the techniques used by the Mountain Artisans, a combination of the new (many of the items are sewn in whole or in part on the sewing machine) and the traditional (most of the women cannot remember a time when quilting was not a part of their lives), joined together in perfect harmony to create patchworks prized as collector's items. Not the least interesting aspect of the book is the sense of the quilters themselves, women like Mrs. Blanche Griffith of Sod for whom quilting is more than an occupation or pastime.

The gift for quilting is like the gift for music. You have to love it. It's *borned* in you. You have to want to create

Indian Hatchet

Material Estimate: Allow extra for seams to make these blocks 11″ square. 28 pieced blocks set together with alternate plain squares will yield a quilt top about 77″ x 88″, 7 blocks wide by 8 blocks long. It requires a total of 8 yards—3⅓ yards light, 2 yards dark, and 2⅔ yards white for plain blocks.

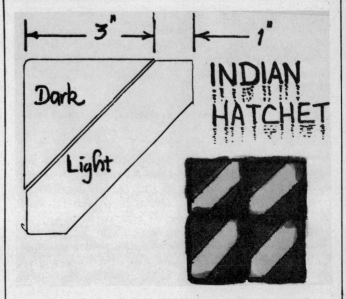

Should be laid accurately on the true bias with threads running parallel to the right angle sides. Seams may or may not be allowed additional to the sizes given here. Some quilters prefer to make their cardboard patterns to the cutting line, others prefer to mark around and cut a larger seam which they then sew back to the line. If pencil lines are drawn on the wrong side of the fabric, they act as a guide which assures accuracy when the right sides face together, and accuracy is the prime requisite in piecing.

Source: ONE HUNDRED AND ONE PATCHWORK PATTERNS, revised edition. by Ruby Short McKim. Dover Publications, New York, 1962. 124 pages. illustrations. paperback edition $2.00.

beautiful things. If you've got it—well, you just naturally make things that are beautiful. If you turn them out any old way, you can see it by just looking at them. Can't you tell the difference between these homemade quilts and the machine-made ones? In the ones done by hand, you can see the love, and the thought, and the care.

Rug Making

HANDMADE RUGS FROM PRACTICALLY ANYTHING. by Jean Ray Laury and Joyce Aikens. Countryside Press, 1972; 125 pages. distributed by Doubleday and Company. illustrations, photographs (some color). $7.95.

When the English settlers of America first arrived in the colonies, they adhered to the English rugmaking designs and procedures with which they were familiar. However, life in the New World was difficult and supplies were long in arriving; the colonists soon had to resort to their own initiative. Before long, colonial women were transforming remnants salvaged from old clothes into warm lap robes and attractive rugs.

Fine yarns and materials are available to rug makers of today, but the authors of this book feel that much of the fun and challenge in this craft comes from the use of old scraps and leftovers—the joy of making something from almost nothing.

Jean Ray Laury and Joyce Aikens inject a new life into felt rugs, offering instructions, ideas, and inspiration for machine-appliquéd rugs, hand-appliquéd rugs, button rugs, and cut-through rugs. A brief chapter on macrame and rope rugs offers some general directions for the making of a macrame rug but presupposes a knowledge of knotting and so would benefit only the macrame aficionado. This same type of deficiency is evident in their chapters on latched, hooked, and rya rugs. They provide instruction for the basic techniques, but it is of such a cursory nature that the inexperienced would have a hard time following. However, the sections on hoop and box frame rugs are more adequate. The real value of this book lies not in its treatment of the how-to aspects of its subject, but in the possibilities it opens up to the enthusiastic and imaginative hobbyist.

THE TECHNIQUES OF RUG WEAVING. by Peter Collingwood. Watson-Guptill Publications, New York, 1969. 480 pages. illustrations, photographs (some color), suppliers list, bibliography, index. $17.50.

This is the prime reference book on the subject of rug weaving. Interspersed throughout the wide technical coverage is a wealth of historical detail and reflection. Three chapters are devoted to the various types of wet-face rugs in plain weave, and additional chapters deal with wet-face weaves of as many as eight shafts. Also treated in detail are block weaves, pickup weaves, corduroy pile rugs, warp-face rugs, and other rug techniques of an astounding variety.

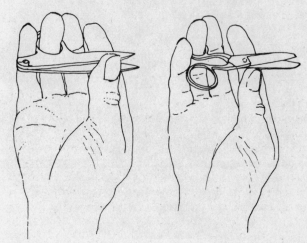

HOLDING WEAVER'S SCISSORS   HOLDING NORMAL SCISSORS

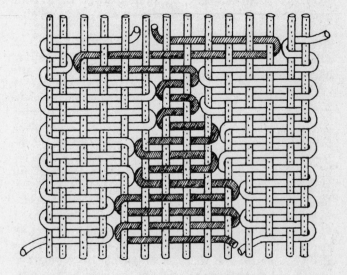

Kilim, weaving a triangle with wefts in contrary motion

RUG WEAVING FOR BEGINNERS. by Margaret Seagroatt. Watson-Guptill Publications, New York, 1972. 104 pages. illustrations, suppliers list, bibliography, index. $7.95.

Techniques and equipment of rug making differ in many specifics from the techniques of fabric weaving. The warp in rug making is usually of unresilient mat, and the tension must be extremely tight in order to beat the weft enough to cover it. The strain that this imposes upon the framework of a loom could cause it to fall to pieces if not properly constructed for rug making. The author offers useful buyer's tips and economical instruction for improvising frames from picture frames, bedsteads, and deck chairs. The instructions and diagrams are acceptable but could be clearer in the beginning sections on loom preparation. In addition to providing instruction on a variety of tapestry techniques, the author also covers other methods of rug making, such as the hooked, braided, and wrapped cord.

On the whole, this is a book that is not exceptional, but a good place for beginners to begin.

STEP-BY-STEP RUGMAKING. by Neil Znamierowski. Golden Press, Western Publishing Co., Racine, Wis., 1972. 96 pages. illustrations. $2.95.

This is an inexpensive, complete and clearly written and illustrated guide to the techniques of embroidery, latch hook crochet, knitting, braiding, hooking, and weaving. Each technique is accompanied by a project that allows beginners to implement what has just been learned. The book also contains information on the making and buying of frames, methods of transferring design, finishing techniques, care of rugs, dyeing, design, and design sources. An additional helpful feature is a list of suppliers, schools, and workshops featuring information and instruction in rug making.

ORIENTAL RUGS AND CARPETS, PLEASURES AND TREASURES. by Stanley Reed. G. P. Putnam's Sons, New York, 1967. 120 pages. photographs (some color). $5.95.

This book describes the development of the Oriental rug both geographically and historically from the thirteenth century to the present day. The area between Spain and China, with particular attention to the qualities of rugs made in the towns and districts of Persia, Asia Minor, the Caucasus and Turkestan, Isfahan, Tabriz, and Herz, of course, receive special emphasis. Photographs of rugs are numerous and colorful and offer a great source of inspiration as well as historical information.

١ ٢ ٣ ٤ (۴۵) ۶ ٧ ٧ ٨ ٩ ٠

1 2 3 4   5 6 7 8 9 0

Typical Arabic numerals used on rugs to indicate date of construction

ORIENTAL RUGS AND CARPETS. by Fabio Formenton. McGraw-Hill, New York, 1972. 252 pages. illustrations, photographs (some color), bibliography, index. $12.95.

At the heart of this book lies a systematic list of the important centers of Oriental carpet making, divided into five zones: Turkey and the Caucasus, Iran and Turkestan, Afghanistan, China and India. The centers are arranged alphabetically, with maps of each region and color plates of the most representative carpets and rugs.

EUROPEAN CARPETS. by Michele Campana. Cameo Series, Textile Book Service, Plainfield, New Jersey, 1969. 158 pages. 70 color plates. $5.00.

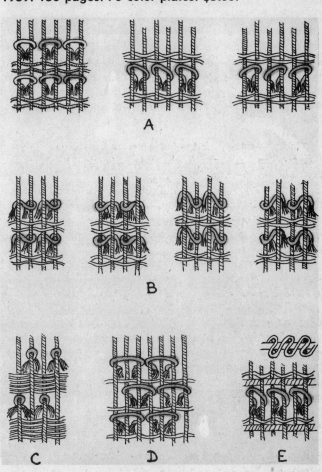

A *Variations on the Turkish knot*

B *Variations on the sehna or Persian knot*

C *Spanish knot*

D *Knotting over three warp threads*

E *Bidyar weave*

This book concerns itself with the Oriental, or knotted, carpet which gradually achieved a prominent place in the textile centers of western Europe.

Spain was the first European country to possess knotted Eastern carpets, to learn the techniques of manufacturing them, and the first to distribute them and acclaim them throughout Western Europe. The technique of knotting employed in Spain differed from that of the East in that

the thread which created the pile was a single warp knot twisted onto a single even or uneven warp thread; the Eastern carpets were executed with a double warp knot. The Spanish technique resulted in the knots forming a zig-zag pile that prevented a linear design from being achieved. The Spanish knot was very popular and used in the best carpets from Cuenca, Letur, Lietor, and Alcaroz. Later, it was alternated with the Persian or Sehna knot and the Ghiordes knot. Eventually, the Ghiordes knot completely replaced first the Spanish and then the Sehna.

The author concentrates primarily on the carpets produced in Spain, France, Portugal, and England, and places a particularly heavy emphasis upon those woven in the mid-seventeenth to -nineteenth centuries, which she feels were the highest expression of taste and harmony of composition of all the art forms of that time.

THE BOOK OF CARPETS. by Reinhard G. Hubel. Praeger Publishers, New York, 1970. 348 pages. illustrations, photographs (some color), bibliography, index. $15.00.

This is an appreciative history of the art and manufacturing of Oriental rugs, and a guide to rug identification. Beginning with the earliest days of carpet weaving, the author traces the distinctive development of the carpet in Persia, India, and China, and relates it to pertinent examples from North Africa and Europe. Most Oriental rug designs are imitated in regions not native to that of their inception. The collector or buyer must be able to determine authenticity, and this can be done by closely examining structure rather than design. The author provides illustrations of various weaves and knots and discusses the materials and dyes used for a number of different carpets. He also provides a method of classification based upon weave and material, pattern, motif, and color.

NAVAJO RUGS, PAST, PRESENT, AND FUTURE. by Gilbert S. Mazwell. Best West Publications, Post Office Box 757, Palm Desert, California, photographs (some color), paperback edition

When Coronado's army set out from Compostela to conquer the New World, his entourage included 5000 sheep, the first progenitors of the beasts that would eventually alter profoundly the lives of the Indians of the Southwest.

The Pueblo Indians raised, among other things, cotton and had a highly developed art of textile weaving. Under the yoke of the Spaniards, wool joined cotton on their loom. The Navajos, like the Apaches, were raider-hunters at this time and it wasn't until 1690, when a Spanish attack forced the Pueblo Indians to flee into the Gobernador area of New Mexico inhabited by the Navajo, that the two tribes intermarried and the Navajo learned the art of weaving. Textile production became increasingly important to the Navajo as the settlement of America snuffed out the old raider's way of life. They were captured and enslaved by the Spaniards and put to work weaving blankets for their masters. The Navajos continued to produce blankets until the 1890's when they found themselves in conflict with the fabricated clothing from the east. They were saved from critical circumstances by the traders who, noting that more people were tossing their blankets on the floor, insisted that the Navajos modify their product to make it more suitable for use on the floor. The weavers developed a heavier type of fabric with borders instead of stripes, and the Navajo rug was born.

No two Navajo rugs are alike, but certain distinctive features of style, pattern, and color, which the author discusses in detail, can help the knowledgeable viewer to pinpoint a rug's place of origin and authenticity. He also discusses weaving equipment and techniques and the evolution of Navajo design.

WORKING WITH THE WOOL, HOW TO WEAVE A NAVAJO RUG. by Noel Bennett and Tiana Bighorse. Northland Press, Flagstaff, Arizona, 1971. illustrations. paperback edition $4.95.

This is *the* book to have on Navajo weaving. It is clear and comprehensive.

HOOKED RUGS AND RYAS: DESIGNING PATTERNS AND APPLYING TECHNIQUES. by Xenia Ley Parker. Henry Regnery Company, Chicago, Illinois, 1973. 152 pages. illustrations, photographs, suppliers list, index. $6.95.

This is an excellent introduction to the major techniques of latchet hooking, punch needle, and rya knotting, which are explained and accompanied by clear photographs. There is a design chapter, but it appears to be fairly gratuitous, although the author does give some good suggestions on using new fibers and yarns to achieve special effects. She also offers some sound practical advice on choosing materials, such as her admonition to all but the very wealthy to buy their yarn by the skein rather than precut yarn when working on a large project.

RUG HOOKING AND BRAIDING, FOR PLEASURE AND PROFIT: A STANDARD GUIDE. by Dorothy Lawless. Thomas Y. Crowell Company, New York, 1962. 286 pages. illustrations, photographs (some color), index. $5.95.

The somewhat experienced rug hooker who is seeking new ways of executing and designing rose petals will probably derive the greatest amount of information and gratification from the author's presentation.

HOOKED AND KNOTTED RUGS. by Ethel Jane Beitler. Shuttle-Craft Series, Sterling Publishing Company, New York, 1973. 48 pages. illustrations (some color), photographs, index. $2.95.

This is an excellent first book for beginning rug makers. It offers good step-by-step instructions for building a frame, winding the yarn, hooking, knotting, latch hooking, and rya knotting. The usual section of design ideas is included with good examples of the effects of loop length variation.

The Rug Hooker, News and Views
Joan Moshimer, editor
Kennebunkport, Me. 04046
Bimonthly. $6.00 a year.
New ideas, patterns, features, exhibit news, and so on.

GETTING STARTED IN HANDMADE RUGS. by Kathryn Andrews Marinoff. Bruce, Beverly Hills, California, 1971. 86 pages. illustrations, photographs (some color), bibliography, index. $2.95.

This is a revision of the author's earlier *Handmade Rugs*, containing basic but clear instructions for a variety of rugs. The author explains the differences between the Susan Bates needle, Susan Burr shuttle hook, and the Columbia Minerva, and gives instructions for the use of each. She dwells only briefly upon weaving, but her recommended Popsicle loom is one which anyone can make and experiment on, the best way to learn any technique. The only really outstanding

section is that on braided rugs, which is both detailed and comprehensive. The instructions for all other techniques are rather superficial and do not adequately dispose of problems most frequently encountered by novices.

RUGMAKING, TECHNIQUES AND DESIGN. by Mary Allard. Chilton Book Company, Radnor, Pennsylvania, 1963. 160 pages. illustrations, photographs (some color). $7.50.

This is a good book for a weaver with a grasp of the fundamentals. The author discusses pile rugs, knotted, looped, floated, and flat rugs, double weave, and soumak. The chapter on hooked rugs is inadequate and the photographs do not clearly show the process of rug making. The design section is less flashy than most, but the author offers some sound, practical advice about using pile and flat rug techniques as variants, and on color, theme, and motif development.

Rug Making Suppliers

Berry's of Maine
20-22 Main Street
Yarmouth, Me. 04096
brochure $.10.
rug frames.

Cambridge Wools Ltd.
Box 2572
Auckland, New Zealand
brochure.
rug making canvas.

Colonial Textiles
82 Plants Dam Road
East Lyme, Conn. 06333
samples $.25.
rug shuttles.

Coulter Studios
118 East 59 Street
New York, N.Y. 10022
catalog; samples $.50.
rug making canvas.

Craft Yarns of Rhode Island
603 Mineral Spring Avenue
Pawtucket, R.I. 02862
catalog.
rug making canvas.

Creative Fibres, Inc.
1028 East Juneau Avenue
Milwaukee, Wis. 53202
catalog $1.00.
rug filler.

Dick Blick Company
P.O. Box 1267
Galesburg, Ill. 61401
catalog.
rug frames.

Earth Guild, Inc.
149 Putnam Avenue
Cambridge, Mass. 02139
brochure.
rug shuttles.

Edgemont Yarn Service
RR 2, Box 14
Maysville, Ky. 41056
brochure.
rug filler.

Gager's Handicraft
3516 Beltline Boulevard
St. Louis, Mo. 55416
catalog $1.00.
rug frames.

George Wells Rugs, Inc.
565 Cedar Swamp Road
Glen Head, N.Y. 11545
brochure.
rug frames, rug making canvas.

Gillian's Specialties
P.O. Box 623
Solona Beach, Cal. 92075
brochure.
rug shuttles.

Harlan's Handweaving
Nanticoke Drive
Box 68A
Endicott, N.Y. 13760
brochure.
rug filler.

Harris Looms
North Grove Road
Hawkhurst, Kent, England
catalog.
rug shuttles.

House of Kleen
P.O. Box 265
Hope Valley, R.I. 02832
catalog, sample charge $.35.
rug making canvas.

J. C. Larson Company
7330 North Clark Street
Chicago, Ill. 60626
catalog $1.00.
rug frames.

Jean Malsada, Inc.
P.O. Box 767
Roswell, Ga. 30075
catalog.
electric rug hookers, rug shuttles.

Kay and EE Corporation of America
200 Fifth Avenue, Room 325
New York, N.Y.
brochure.
rug frames.

Kessenich Looms & Yarn Shop
7963 Harwood Avenue
Wauwatosa, Wis. 53213
catalog.
rug shuttles.

Lamb's End
165 West, 9 Mile
Ferndale, Mich. 48220
brochure; samples $1.00 to $1.50.
rug filler, batting, rug backing.

Lily Mills Company
Handweaving Department
P.O. Box 88
Shelby, N.C. 28150
catalog; samples $.25.
rug filler.

Looms and Lessons
Ruth Nordquist Myers
6014 Osage Avenue
Downers Grove, Ill. 60515
brochure.
rug filler.

Magnolia Weaving
2635-29th Avenue, West
Seattle, Wash. 98199
catalog.
rug filler, rug shuttles.

The Mannings
RD #2
East Berlon, Pa. 17316
catalog; samples $.50.
rug making canvas, rug frames.

Naturalcraft
2199 Bancroft Way
Berkeley, Cal. 94704
catalog $.50.
rug shuttles.

Newcomb Loom Company
P.O. Box 3204
Davenport, Ia. 52808
catalog $.10.
rug shuttles.

Nilus Leclerc, Inc.
P.O. Box 69
L'Islet, Quebec, Canada, GOR 2CO.
Also Leclerc Corporation
Box 491
Plattsburg, N.Y. 12901
catalog.
rug shuttles.

Norden Crafts
P.O. Box 1
Glenview, Ill. 60025
catalog.
rug frames.

Northwest Handcraft House, Ltd.
110 West Esplanade
North Vancouver, British Columbia,
Canada
catalog; samples $.50 to $1.00.
rug making canvas.

Norwood Loom Company and Weaving
  Shop
Baldwin, Mich. 49304
brochure; send self-addressed envelope.
rug shuttles.

Owl and Olive Weavers
4232 Old Leeds Lane
Birmingham, Ala. 35213
samples $1.50; deducted from orders of
  $10.00 or more.
rug shuttles.

The Pendleton Shop
Handweaving Studio
Box 233, Jordan Road
Sedona, Ariz. 86336
catalog.
rug shuttles.

Schacht Spindle Company
1708 Walnut Street
Boulder, Colo. 80302
brochure.
rug shuttles.

The Sheep Village
2005 Bridgeway
Sausalito, Cal. 94965
rug shuttles.

Some Place
2990 Adeline Street
Berkeley, Cal. 94703
catalog.
rug shuttles.

Textile Crafts
856 Genesee Avenue
P.O. Box 3216
Los Angeles, Cal. 90028
catalog.
rug frames.

Valley Handweaving Supply
200 West Olive Avenue
Fresno, Cal. 93728
brochure; samples $.50.
rug making canvas.

Schools

The following is a partial list of institutions and workshops offering courses or degrees in crafts. It makes no claim to being definitive; the number of schools providing such courses grows every day. The type of course offered in the past is noted after the name of the school. Write or call for a current schedule; most schools change their offerings from semester to semester, and what was offered in September may not be available in April. The adult education programs in many communities and local Ys usually feature craft courses and you should consult those nearest you.

Alabama
Auburn University
Auburn 36830
  Offers an undergraduate degree in crafts and an M.S. in textile design.

Livingston University
Livingston 35470
  General courses in crafts, woodworking, and ceramics.

Troy State University
Troy 36081
  Offers a large variety of craft courses.

University of Alabama
Box F
University 35486
  B.A., B.F.A., M.A., and M.F.A. in crafts.

University of South Alabama
307 Gaillard Drive
Mobile 36688
  Offers a B.F.A. in ceramics, and features courses in silversmithing and jewelry.

Alaska
Anchorage Community College
2533 Providence Drive
Anchorage 99504
  General craft courses in metal, silversmithing, spinning, jewelry, macrame, and so on.

Sheldon Jackson College
Sitka 99835
  General crafts and crochet.

Arizona
Clay Pottery Workshop
517 North 6th Avenue
Tucson 85705
  Ceramics.

Mohave Community College
1971 Jagerson Avenue
Kingman 86401
  General crafts course, metalsmithing, jewelry, lapidary, and others.

Northern Arizona University
FAC Box 6020
Flagstaff 86001
  B.F.A. in general crafts, glassblowing, metalsmithing, ceramics, textiles.

Pendleton Fabric Craft School
P.O. Box 233
Jordan Road, Sedona 86336
  Courses in weaving, crochet, and other textile crafts.

Pima Community College
2202 West Anklam
Tucson 85700
  General crafts course and courses in other special areas, such as metalsmithing, textile design, lapidary, and crochet.

Tucson Art Center School
179 North Main Avenue
Tucson 85705
  Spinning, macrame, and other craft offerings.

University of Arizona
Tucson 85721
  B.F.A. in metal; M.F.A. in silversmithing, ceramics, and jewelry. Also features courses in other craft disciplines.

Yavapai College
1100 East Sheldon
Prescott 86301
  A wide offering of craft courses.

Arkansas
Arkansas State University
State University 72467
  B.F.A. in ceramics. Also has classes in glassblowing and jewelry.

Little Firehouse School
Southeast Arkansas Arts and Sciences
  Center
1516 Laurel, Pine Bluff 71601
  General craft courses.

Mountain View Branch of Foothills
  Vo-Tech School
P.O. Box 359
Ozark Folk Center
Mountain View 72560
  A wide offering of craft courses.

California
Arts and Crafts Cooperative
1652 Shattuck
Berkeley 94709
  Quilting.

Augustine Glass Works
711 Colorado Avenue
Santa Monica, 90401
  Glass crafts.

Barnsdall Arts and Crafts Center
Los Angeles Department of Recreation
  and Parks
4800 Hollywood Boulevard
Los Angeles 90027

Big Creek Pottery
Davenport 95017

California College of Arts and Crafts
5212 Broadway
Oakland, 94618
  B.F.A. and M.F.A. in glassblowing, metal, ceramics, and textiles as well as courses in many other craft fields.

California Polytechnic State University
San Luis Obispo 93401

California State College at San Bernardino
5500 State College Parkway
San Bernardino 92407
  B.A. in general crafts, wood, furniture, ceramics.

California State College at Sonoma
1801 East Cotati Boulevard
Rohnert Park 94922

California State University at Chico
Chico 95926
  M.A. in glassblowing, ceramics, wood; M.F.A. in ceramics.

California State University at Fresno
Maple Avenue
Fresno 93710
  An extremely wide offering of craft courses.

California State University at Fullerton
800 North State College Boulevard
Fullerton 02632
  B.A. in general crafts; B.A., M.A. in silversmithing, jewelry, ceramics, textile and textile design, weaving, as well as many other nondegree crafts courses.

California State University at Long
  Beach
6101 East 7 Street
Long Beach 90840
  B.A. in general crafts, silversmithing, jewelry, ceramics, textiles; M.A. in general crafts, metal, jewelry, ceramics, and textile design.

California State University at
  Los Angeles
5151 State University
Los Angeles 90032
  M.A. in general crafts, plastics, wood carving, metal, jewelry, enameling, ceramics, textiles, weaving, stitchery, printing and dyeing, batik, tie dye, macrame, and lapidary.

California State University at San Diego
5402 College Avenue
San Diego 92115
  B.A., M.A. in weaving, jewelry, enameling, ceramics, wood as well as many nondegree craft offerings.

California State University at San Jose
Washington Square
San Jose 95114
  B.A. and M.A. in glassblowing, plastics, metal, ceramics, tie dye, weaving, stitchery, printing and dyeing, batik, textile design, crochet, knitting, and macrame.

College of Marin
College Ave.
Kentfield 94904
  B.F.A., M.F.A. in glass, enameling, ceramics; B.A., M.A. in metal, silversmithing, jewelry, textiles, as well as other nondegree craft courses.

College of the Pacific of the University
of the Pacific
3601 Pacific Avenue
Stockton 95204
Many craft courses.

The de Young Museum Art School
Golden Gate Park
San Francisco 94118
**General craft course and courses in
glassblowing, metal, textile, ceramics,
and more.**

Ginger Dunlap Pottery
514 North Hoover Street
Los Angeles 90004

Fiberworks
1940 Bonita Avenue
Berkeley 94704
Variety of textile crafts.

Ida Graw Weaving Workshop
424 LaVerne
Mill Valley 94941
**Classes in fabric arts for which the
California College of Arts and Crafts will
give credit.**

Hallie's Alley Jewelry School
13045 Ventura Boulevard
Studio City 91607

The Loft Weaving Classes
522 Ramona Street
Palo Alto 94301

McGroarty Cultural Art Center
7570 McGroarty Terrace
Tujunga 91042
**Classes in metal, ceramics, textile,
weaving, stitchery, printing and dyeing,
lapidary, and more.**

Young, Joseph, Art in Architecture/
Mosaic Workshop
1434 South Spaulding Avenue
Los Angeles 90019
Courses in stained glass, mosaics.

Nervo Studios
2027 7th Street
Berkeley 94710
Glassblowing and stained glass.

Otis Art Institute of Los Angeles County
2401 Wilshire Boulevard
Los Angeles 90057
B.F.A. and M.F.A. in ceramics.

Pacific Basin Textile Arts
1659 San Pablo Avenue
Berkeley 94702

Pepperdine University
24255 Pacific Coast Highway
Malibu 90265
**B.A. in glassblowing; M.A. in general
crafts.**

The Pot Shop
324 Sunset Avenue
Venice 90291

The Pottery
5838 Perry Drive
Culver City 90230

The Pottery Workshop
110A Camino Pablo
Orinda 94563

Richmond Art Center
25th and Barrett
Richmond 94804

Rio Hondo College
3600 Workman Mill Road
Whittier 90608

Rudolph Schaeffer School of Design
2255 Mariposa
San Francisco 94110
**General craft course plus weaving,
dyeing, batik, tie dye.**

Santa Barbara Art Institute
2030 Alameda Padre Serra
Santa Barbara 93103
B.F.A. in glassblowing and ceramics.

San Francisco Art Institute
800 Chestnut Street
San Francisco 94133

Scripps College
9th Street
Claremont 91711
B.A. in ceramics and textile design.

Mary Sharp
6219 Alviso Avenue
Oakland 94618
Courses in enameling.

Straw Into Gold
5550 College Avenue
Oakland 94618
**Courses in spinning, natural and chem-
ical dyeing.**

William Tapia, Bindery
7513 Melrose Avenue
Los Angeles 90046
Courses in bookbinding.

Textile Crafts
856 Genesee Avenue
Los Angeles 90046

University of California at Berkeley
234 Worster Hall
Berkeley 94720
**Courses in weaving, ceramics, jewelry,
and metal.**

University of California at Los Angeles
1300 Dickson Art Center
Los Angeles 90024
**B.A., M.A., and M.F.A. in glass, glass-
blowing, ceramics, textile design, weaving, printing, and dyeing.**

University of California at Santa Barbara
Santa Barbara 93106
B.A., M.F.A. in ceramics.

University of Redlands
Peppers Art Center
1200 Colton Avenue
Redlands 92373
**B.A. in metal, ceramics; M.A. in jew-
elry, weaving.**

University of Southern California
Los Angeles 90007
M.F.A. in glassblowing and ceramics.

Woman's Workshop
17042 Devonshire
Northridge 91324

The Yarn Depot, Inc.
545 Sutter Street
San Francisco 94102
Courses in weaving, spinning, stitchery.

Colorado
Colorado State University
Fort Collins 80521
**B.F.A. in metal, textile design, ce-
ramics; M.F.A. in ceramics.**

Halcyon
1121 California Street
Denver 80204
Courses in fabric crafts.

Trimble Court Artisans
114 Trimble Court
Fort Collins 80521
A wide variety of craft offerings.

University of Colorado
Boulder 80302
**B.A., B.F.A., M.F.A. in weaving, jew-
elry, ceramics.**

University of Northern Colorado
Greeley 80639
**B.A., M.A. in general crafts, silver-
smithing, jewelry, ceramics, weaving,
stitchery, batik, macrame.**

The Weaving Shop
1708 Walnut Street
Boulder 80302

Western State College
Gunnison 81230
B.A. in jewelry, ceramics, weaving.

Connecticut
Central Connecticut State College
Stanley Street
New Britain 06050
Courses in general crafts, macrame, jewelry, ceramics, and a few others.

Edgerton's Handcrafts
210 West Town
Norwich 06360
Courses in spinning, weaving, dyeing.

Hartford Art School
200 Bloomfield Avenue
West Hartford 06117
B.F.A. in ceramics.

University of Connecticut
Storrs 06268
B.F.A. in ceramics.

Wesleyan Potters, Inc.
350 South Main Street
Middletown 06457
Many crafts taught other than ceramics.

The Works
175 Post Road West
Westport 06880
Offers a course in pewter working along with ceramics, jewelry, wood, batik.

The Workshop of Nickie Von Dulon
44 Wilridge Road
Georgetown 06829
Spinning, puppetmaking.

Delaware
Alexis I. DuPont Continuing Education Program
50 Hillside Road
Greenville 19807

University of Delaware
Newark 19711
B.A. in general crafts, plastics, jewelry, ceramics, textiles.

District of Columbia
Catholic University of America
4th and Michigan Avenue, N.E. 20017
M.F.A. in ceramics and textiles.

The Silver Shuttle
1301 35th Street, N.E. 20007
Courses in weaving.

Smithsonian Institution
Smithsonian Associates, 20560
Courses in general crafts, stained glass, jewelry, enameling, ceramics, weaving, stitchery, printing and dyeing, metal, spinning, lapidary.

Florida
Barry College
11300 North East 2nd Avenue
Miami 33161
B.F.A. in metal, jewelry, ceramics.

Ceramic League of Miami, Inc.
8873 South West 129 Street
Miami 33156
Courses in ceramics, mosaic.

Craft House
1091 North Military Trail
West Palm Beach 33406
Courses in jewelry.

Daytona Beach Community College
Welch Boulevard
Daytona Beach 32015
M.F.A. in general crafts, metal, jewelry, silversmithing, ceramics, enameling, weaving.

Florida Gulf Coast Art Center
222 Ponce de Leon Boulevard
Belleair 33516

Miami-Dade Community College
North Campus
11380 North West 27th Avenue
Miami 33167

University of Miami
1300 Campo Sano
Coral Gables 33124
B.A., B.F.A., M.F.A. in ceramics, weaving.

University of Tampa
Plant Park
Tampa
B.F.A. in ceramics, metal.

Georgia
Berry College
Mount Berry 30149
B.A., B.S. in jewelry, ceramics, weaving.

Georgia College
Milledgeville 31061
Offers a number of courses in crafts such as ceramics, silversmithing, textile.

Georgia State University
33 Gilmer Street
Atlanta 30303
B.V.A. (Bachelor of Vocational Arts), M.V.A. in general crafts, metal, silversmithing, jewelry, ceramics, weaving.

Mercer University
1400 Coleman Avenue
Macon 31207
B.A. in general crafts, ceramics.

University of Georgia
Athens 30601
B.F.A., M.F.A. in glassblowing, metal, jewelry, ceramics, textile design.

Wesleyan College
Forsyth Road
Macon 31201
B.F.A. in ceramics.

Hawaii
Kapiolani Community College
620 Pensacola Street
Honolulu 96822
General craft course.

Idaho
Idaho State University
Pocatello 83201
B.A., M.F.A. in metal, ceramics.

Illinois
Chicago Academy of Fine Arts
86 East Randolph Street
Chicago 60601
B.F.A. in general crafts.

Contemporary Art Workshop
542 West Grant Place
Chicago 60614
Courses in ceramics, wood carving, jewelry.

Eastern Illinois University
Charleston 61920
General craft course and some specialty courses such as silversmithing, ceramics.

Evanston Art Center
2603 Sheridan Road
Evanston 60201
Wide craft offering including tie dye, batik, weaving, plastics, metal.

Illinois State University
Normal 61761
B.S., M.S. in glassblowing, metal, jewelry, ceramics, textile, weaving, silversmithing.

Looms and Lessons
6014 Osage Avenue
Downers Grove 60515
Courses in weaving.

Northern Illinois University
DeKalb 60115
B.A., B.F.A. in general crafts; B.A., B.F.A., M.A., M.F.A. in jewelry, ceramics, weaving.

Rockford College
5050 East State
Rockford 61101
M.A. in ceramics; M.F.A. in wood, textile design. Additional offerings in batik, spinning, knitting, macrame, weaving, tie dye.

Southern Illinois University
Carbondale 62910
B.A., M.F.A. in glassblowing, metal, ceramics, weaving, and many more nondegree craft courses.

University of Illinois
143 Fine Arts Building
Champaign 61820
B.F.A. in general crafts.

Weaving Workshop
3352 North Halsted
Chicago 60657
Courses in weaving, basketry.

Western Illinois University
Macomb 61455
B.A. in silversmithing, jewelry, ceramics.

Indiana
Ball State University
Muncie 47306
B.A., B.S. in silversmithing, jewelry, ceramics, weaving.

Craft Kaleidoscope
6551 Ferguson Street
Indianapolis 46220

Indiana Central College
4001 Otterbein
Indianapolis 46227
B.A., M.A., M.F.A., B.A.E. (Bachelor of Art Education), M.A.E., M.S. in general crafts; B.S., M.F.A. in metal, jewelry, silversmithing, enameling; B.S., M.A., M.F.A. in ceramics; B.A.E., M.A.E., M.S. in textile, weaving, printing and dyeing, macrame.

Indiana University
Bloomington 47401
A.B., B.S., B.F.A., M.A.T., M.F.A. in silversmithing, jewelry, enameling, ceramics, textile, printing and dyeing.

Purdue University
West Lafayette 47907
B.A. in general crafts, silversmithing, jewelry, ceramics, textile design, weaving.

Saint Mary's College
Notre Dame 46556
B.A., B.F.A. in general crafts, metal, ceramics, textiles, weaving.

University of Evansville
1800 Lincoln Avenue
Evansville 47714
B.A., B.F.A. in metal, jewelry, silversmithing, ceramics.

Iowa
Coe College
1221 1st Avenue
Cedar Rapids 52402
B.A. in plastics; M.F.A. in ceramics; M.A. in batik, tie dye.

Creative Craft Center
Iowa Memorial Union
University of Iowa
Iowa City 52240
A very wide selection of craft offerings including quilting.

Drake University
25th and University
Des Moines 50311
B.F.A., M.F.A. in plastics, wood, silversmithing, jewelry, ceramics.

Graceland College
Lamoni 50140
M.F.A. in ceramics.

Grinnell College
Grinnell 50112
B.A. in silversmithing, jewelry, ceramics, weaving.

Iowa State University
Ames 50010
B.S., M.S. in wood, furniture; B.F.A., M.S. in silversmithing, jewelry, enamel; B.F.A., M.F.A. in ceramics; B.S., B.A., M.S. in textile design, printing and dyeing; B.S., M.S. in weaving, stitchery.

Luthor College
Decorah 52101
B.A. in ceramics, weaving, batik.

Mount Mercy College
1330 Elmhurst Drive
Cedar Rapids 52402
B.A., M.A. in ceramics.

The Octagon Art Center
232½ Main
Ames 50010

University of Iowa
Iowa City 52240
B.A., B.F.A., M.A., M.F.A. in silversmithing.

University of Northern Iowa
Cedar Falls 50613
B.A., M.A. in general crafts, metal, jewelry, ceramics.

The Weaving Studio
812 South Summit Street
Iowa City 52240

Kansas
Fort Hays Kansas State College
Hays 67601
B.A. in general crafts, wood carving, silversmithing, jewelry, ceramics; M.A. in ceramics.

Friends University
2100 University
Wichita 67213
Courses in general crafts, wood, silversmithing, ceramics, weaving, macrame.

Jennie B. Weaving and Yarn Studio
P.O. Box 52
Linwood 66052

Kansas State Teachers College
Emporia 66801
B.A., B.S.E., M.A. in glassblowing, metal, ceramics.

Kansas State University
Justin Hall
Manhattan 66506
B.A. in weaving, B.A., B.F.A. in general crafts, silversmithing, jewelry, ceramics; M.A. in ceramics.

University of Kansas
Lawrence 66044
B.F.A. in silversmithing, jewelry, ceramics, textile design, weaving.

Washburn University
1700 College
Topeka 66621
B.F.A. in jewelry, ceramics.

Wichita State University
Wichita 67208
B.F.A., M.F.A. in ceramics.

Kentucky
Asbury College
Wilmore 40390
M.A. in general crafts, enameling, textiles; M.F.A. in metal, ceramics, glassblowing. Other nondegree craft courses.

Berea College
Berea 40403
B.A. in ceramics, textiles; B.S. in metal, general crafts, wood.

Centre College
Danville 40422
B.A. in metal, ceramics.

Louisville School of Art
100 Park Road
Anchorage 40223
  B.F.A. in metal, ceramics, textiles.

Murray State University
Murray 42071
  Courses in plastic, wood, silversmithing, jewelry, spinning, weaving, printing and dyeing, and others.

Thomas More College
Box 85
Covington 41017
  M.F.A. in ceramics.

University of Kentucky
205 Fine Arts Building
Lexington 40506
  B.A., M.F.A. in ceramics, textiles.

Western Kentucky University
Bowling Green 42101
  B.A., B.F.A. in ceramics, weaving.

Louisiana
Newcomb Art Department
Tulane University
New Orleans 70118
  B.A., B.F.A. in ceramics.

Nicholls State University
Thibodaux 70301
  B.A. in ceramics.

University of Southwestern Louisiana
University Avenue
Lafayette 70501
  M.F.A. in jewelry, ceramics.

Weavers Workshop
1538 Dante Street
New Orleans 70118

Maine
Portland School of Art
93 High Street
Portland 04101
  Courses in silversmithing, jewelry, ceramics.

University of Maine at Portland-Gorham
Gorham 04038
  B.A. in ceramics.

Maryland
Baltimore Museum of Art
Art Museum Drive
Baltimore 21218
  Courses in ceramics.

Bowie State College
Jericho Road
Bowie 20715
  B.S., B.A. in ceramics.

College of Notre Dame of Maryland
4701 North Charles
Baltimore 21210
  Several courses offered including rug hooking and basketry.

Maryland Institute College of Art
1300 Mount Royal Avenue
Baltimore 21217
  B.F.A. in general crafts.

Montgomery College
Manakee Street
Rockville 20850
  Courses in general crafts, weaving, ceramics, jewelry.

St. Mary's College of Maryland
St. Mary's City 20686
  Courses in general crafts, silversmithing, jewelry, ceramics, weaving.

Towson State College
York Road
Baltimore 21204
  Courses in wood, metal, jewelry, ceramics, textiles, weaving.

Massachusetts
The Art Institute of Boston
700 Beacon Street
Boston 02215
  B.F.A. in ceramics, batik.

Boston Center for Adult Education
5 Commonwealth Avenue
Boston 02116
  Wide offering of craft courses.

Boston University
855 Commonwealth Avenue
Boston 02215
  B.F.A. in general crafts, jewelry, ceramics.

Castle Hill-Truro Center for the Arts
Castle Road
Truro 02666

Craft Center
25 Sagamore Road
Worcester 01545

Decordova Museum
Sandy Pond Road
Lincoln 01773
  Large variety of courses including ones in stained glass, spinning, silversmithing.

Endicott Junior College
Hale Street
Beverly 01915
  B.S., M.Ed. in general crafts; B.F.A., M.Ed. in ceramics.

Hudson Institute, Inc.
Hosmer Street
Hudson 01749
  Courses in general crafts, wood, metal, ceramics.

Mudflat
196 Broadway
Cambridge 02139
  Courses in ceramics.

The Old Schwamb Mill
17 Mill Lane at 29 Lowell
Arlington 02174
  Classes in spinning, printing and dyeing, stained glass, weaving, textiles, wood, metal, jewelry, lapidary.

Project, Incorporated
141 Huron Avenue
Cambridge 02138
  Courses in textiles, ceramics, tie dye, batik, macrame, bookbinding, lapidary.

The School of Fashion Design
136 Newbury Street
Boston 02116
  Courses in textiles, jewelry, macrame, knitting, spinning, crochet, and others.

School of the Museum of Fine Arts
230 Fenway
Boston 02115
  B.S. in education; B.F.A., M.F.A. in stained glass, plastic, mosaic, metal, jewelry, silversmithing, ceramics, tie dye.

Southeastern Massachusetts University
North Dartmouth 02747
  B.F.A. in textile design. Other non-degree craft courses available.

Springfield College
263 Alden Street
Springfield 01109
  B.A., B.S. in general crafts, ceramics.

Workshops in Creative Arts-Boston
  YWCA
140 Clarendon Street
Boston 02116

Michigan
Alma College
Superior Street
Alma 48801
  B.A., B.F.A. in general crafts.

Central Michigan University
Mount Pleasant 48858
  B. A., B.F.A. in metal, jewelry, silversmithing, enameling, weaving, macrame.

Cranbrook Academy of Art
500 Lone Pine Road
Bloomfield Hills 48013
B.F.A., M.F.A. in metal, ceramics, textiles, in addition to many other nondegree craft offerings.

Eastern Michigan University
Ypsilanti 48197
B.F.A., B.A. in education, M.F.A., M.A., M.A. in education in mosaics, metal, silversmithing, jewelry, enameling, ceramics, textiles, weaving, stitchery, printing and dyeing, batik, tie dye, macrame, spinning, crochet, knitting.

Henry Ford Community College
5101 Evergreen
Dearborn 48128
Courses in general crafts, weaving, metal, ceramics, batik, tie-dye, macrame, knitting.

Kalamazoo Institute of the Arts
314 South Park Street
Kalamazoo 49006
Courses in jewelry, ceramics, weaving.

Kalamazoo Public Museum
315 South Rose
Kalamazoo 49006
Courses in weaving.

Michigan State University
East Lansing 48823
B.A., B.F.A. in jewelry, ceramics.

Northern Michigan University
Marquette 49855
B.S., B.F.A., M.A. for education, in wood, silversmithing, jewelry, enameling, ceramics, textiles.

Rockford School of Weaving
11 Old Mill Square
Rockford 49341
Courses in colonial crafts, spinning, weaving, tie dye, batik, textiles.

Scherer Handweaving Studio
Trout Lake 49793
Courses in spinning, loom and backstrap weaving, dyeing.

University of Michigan
Ann Arbor 48104
B.F.A. in jewelry, textiles; B.F.A., M.F.A. in ceramics.

Wayne State University
Detroit 48202
B.A., B.F.A., M.A. in metal, jewelry, ceramics, textiles, weaving, printing and dyeing, batik, tie dye.

Western Michigan University
Kalamazoo 49001
B.F.A., M.F.A. in metal, jewelry, ceramics, textiles.

Minnesota
Gail Kristensen Ceramic Studio
1775 Hillcrest
St. Paul 55116

Mankato State College
Mankato 56001
B.F.A., B.A., B.S., M.A., M.S. in general crafts, glass, metal, jewelry, ceramics, weaving.

Minnesota Museum Art School
30 East 10 Street
St. Paul 55101
Courses in metal, ceramics, jewelry, weaving.

Rochester Art Center
320 East Center Street
Rochester 55102
Courses in jewelry, ceramics, weaving, stitchery, batik, tie dye.

St. Cloud State College
1st Avenue South
St. Cloud 56301
B.A., M.A. in glassblowing, metal, silversmithing, jewelry; B.S., B.A., M.A. in ceramics.

School of Associated Arts
344 Summit Avenue
St. Paul 55102
B.F.A., M.F.A. in general crafts, stained glass; B.F.A. in wood, furniture, metal, ceramics, printing and dyeing, tie dye.

University of Minnesota at Duluth
2400 Oakland Street
Duluth 55812
B.S., B.A. in weaving, stitchery, batik, tie dye, macrame; B.S., B.A., M.A. in general crafts, metal, jewelry, silversmithing, enameling, ceramics, lapidary, leather.

University of Minnesota
208 Art Building
Minneapolis 55455
B.F.A., M.F.A. in glassblowing, plastics, ceramics.

University of Minnesota
St. Paul 55101
B.S. in jewelry, textile design.

Mississippi
Mississippi State College for Women
Columbus 39701
M.F.A. in plastic, wood carving, silversmithing, jewelry, enameling, ceramics.

University of Mississippi
Fine Arts Center
University 38677
M.F.A. in ceramics. Other nondegree courses in metal, jewelry, and so on.

William Carey College
Tuscan Avenue
Hattiesburg 39401
B.A., B.S. in general crafts, ceramics.

Missouri
Central Missouri State University
Warrensburg
B.F.A. in wood carving, metal, ceramics.

Kansas City Art Institute
4415 Warwick
Kansas City 64111
B.F.A. in glassblowing, ceramics, textiles.

Lincoln University
Dunklen at LaFayette
Jefferson City 65101
Classes in general crafts, glass, jewelry, enameling, leather, ceramics, lapidary.

Northeast Missouri State University
Kirksville 63501
B.A. in ceramics, weaving.

Northwest Missouri State University
Maryville 64468
B.F.A., B.A., B.S. in education in plastics, wood carving, metal, ceramics, silversmithing, printing and dyeing, batik, tie dye, macrame.

Southeast Missouri State University
Normal Avenue
Cape Girardeau 63701
B.S., B.S. in education; A.B. in general crafts, jewelry, ceramics, weaving.

Southwest Missouri State University
Springfield 65805
B.F.A., B.S., B.A. in silversmithing, jewelry, ceramics, weaving.

University of Missouri at Columbia
Columbia 65201
A.B., M.A. in jewelry, ceramics, weaving; B.S. in general crafts.

Washington University
Skinkes and Forsythe
St. Louis 63130
B.F.A., M.F.A. in metal, ceramics.

William Woods College/Westminster College
Fulton 65251
B.A., B.S., B.F.A. in jewelry, ceramics.

Montana
Archie Bray Foundation
2915 Country Club Avenue
Helena 59601
 Courses in glassblowing, ceramics.

College of Great Falls
1301 20th Street South
Great Falls 59401
 Courses in general crafts, stained glass, mosaics, silversmithing, jewelry, ceramics, weaving, enameling, textiles.

Miles Community College
2715 Dickinson
Miles City 59301
 B.F.A., M.A. in general crafts, jewelry.

Montana State University
Bozeman 59715
 B.A., M.A.A. in metal, jewelry, ceramics.

Northern Montana College
Havre 59501
 B.S. in education in ceramics.

Montana State University
Bozeman 59715
 B.A., M.A.A. in metal, jewelry, ceramics.

University of Montana
Missoula 59801
 M.A., M.F.A. in general crafts, jewelry, ceramics.

Yellowstone Art Center
401 North 27th Street
Billings 59101
 Courses in jewelry, ceramics, batik, tie dye, macrame.

Nebraska
Haymarket Art Gallery
119 South 9th Street
Lincoln 68508
 Courses in jewelry, batik, backstrap weaving.

Kearney State College
Kearney 68847
 B.A., B.A. in education, B.F.A., M.S. in glassblowing, ceramics, textiles, weaving, stitchery, batik, macrame.

Peru State College
Peru 68421
 B.A., B.S. in general crafts, plastic, metal.

University of Nebraska at Omaha
Box 688, Downtown Station
Omaha 68132
 B.F.A. in ceramics.

Wayne State College
Wayne 68787
 M.A. in general crafts, jewelry.

Nevada
University of Nevada at Las Vegas
Maryland Parkway
Las Vegas 89109

University of Nevada at Reno
Reno 89507

New Hampshire
Franconia College
Franconia 03580
 A.A., B.A. in metal, jewelry, ceramics, weaving, spinning.

Franklin Pierce College
Rindge 03461
 B.A. in glass, metal, jewelry, silversmithing, ceramics.

Keene State College
Keene 03431
 B.A. in ceramics.

Manchester Institute of Arts and Sciences
148 Concord Street
Manchester 03104
 Silversmithing, jewelry, ceramics, weaving, stitchery, leather.

New England College
Henniker 03242
 B.A. in jewelry, ceramics.

Notre Dame College
2321 Elm
Manchester 03104
 General crafts, ceramics, textiles, macrame.

Sharon Arts Center
RD 2
Peterborough 03458

University of New Hampshire
College Road
Durham 03824
 Courses in furniture, metal, silversmithing, jewelry, ceramics, weaving.

New Jersey
Artist and Craftsman Guild
17 Eastman Street
Cranford 07016
 Large variety of courses.

Caldwell College
Caldwell 07006
 M.F.A. in general crafts, metal, ceramics.

Craft Concepts, Inc.
41 Hudson Street
Ridgewood 07450
 Large offering of courses including spinning, ceramics, textile design, weaving.

Earth and Fire Ceramic Studio and
 Gallery
20 Morris Street
Morristown 07960

Jersey City State College
2039 Kennedy Boulevard
Jersey City 07305
 B.A., in weaving; B.A., M.A. in jewelry, ceramics.

Middlesex County College
Woodbridge Avenue
Edison 08817
 Courses in ceramics, weaving.

Montclair State College
Upper Montclair 07043
 B.A., M.A. in metal, jewelry, ceramics, textiles, and other craft offerings.

Newark State College
Union 07083
 Courses in glassblowing, jewelry, weaving, others.

The Salem Craftsmens Guild
1042 Salem Road
Union 07083
 Courses in ceramics.

The Salem Craftsman Guild
3 Alvin Place
Upper Montclair 07043
 Courses in stained glass, jewelry, ceramics, weaving, stitchery, more.

Stitch Witchery
Denbrook Village
Route 10
Denville 07834
 Courses in needlepoint.

Trenton State College
Pennington Road
Trenton 08625
 M.F.A. in jewelry, ceramics, textile design.

Weiss Studio and Craft Workshop
161 Culberson Road
Basking Ridge 07920
 Courses in stained glass, enameling, ceramics, weaving, stitchery, rug hooking, macrame.

William Patterson College
300 Pompton Road
Wayne 07470
A very extensive selection of courses including lapidary, macrame, leather, ceramics.

New Mexico
The Craft House
Box 178
Arroyo Seco 78514
Courses in weaving, spinning.

Folk Art Workshop
Route 4, Box 58Z
Santa Fe 87501
Courses in general crafts, enameling.

New Mexico Highlands University
Las Vegas 87701
B.A., M.A. in general crafts; courses in jewelry, weaving, ceramics, silversmithing.

Turley Forge
P.O. Box 2051
Santa Fe 87501
Courses in blacksmithing.

University of New Mexico
Albuquerque 87106
B.F.A., M.A., M.F.A. in jewelry, ceramics.

New York
Adamy's Plastic Workshop
19 Elkan Road
Larchmont 10538

Clay Art Center
40 Beech Street
Port Chester 10573

Corning Community College
Corning 14830
Courses in general crafts.

Craftsmen Unlimited, Inc.
16 Main Street
Bedford Hills 10507
Class selection includes basketry, decoupage, tole, bobbin lace, quilting, canning.

Garrison Art Center
Depot Square, Box 4
Garrison 10524
Courses in metal, spinning, leather, weaving, tapestry, batik, macrame, jewelry.

Great Neck Public Schools, Adult Program
10 Arrandale Avenue
Great Neck 11024
Wide variety of courses includes plastic, furniture, ceramics, weaving, enameling, jewelry.

Hofstra University
Hempstead 11550
Courses in general crafts, jewelry, ceramics.

Kirkland College
Clinton 13323
B.A. in glassblowing, ceramics.

Langston Hughes Center for the Visual and Performing Arts
25 High Street
Buffalo 14203
Varied selection of courses including weaving, metal, ceramics, lapidary, leather, macrame, tie dye, enameling, wood, jewelry, textiles.

Lighthouse School of Art
654 Route 9W
Upper Grandview 10960

Charlotte Malten Ceramic Studio
193 Germonds Road
West Nyack 10994

Manhattanville College
Purchase 10577
Courses in textile design.

Marymount College
Tarrytown 10591
B.A. in wood carving, ceramics, weaving. Also offers a course in Scandinavian crafts.

The Naples Mill School of Arts and Crafts, Inc.
33 Academy Street
Naples 14512

Nassau Community College
Stewart Avenue
Garden City 11530
General crafts courses.

Old Water Mill Museum
Old Mill Road
Water Mill 11976
Courses in wood carving, spinning, quilting, hooking, weaving, macrame, ceramics, batik.

Phebe Allen Blake
68 Frost Pond Road
Glen Cove 11542
Courses in jewelry, silversmithing.

Rochester Institute of Technology
School for American Craftsmen
1 Lomb Memorial Drive
Rochester 14623
A.A.S., B.F.A., M.F.A., M.S.Textiles in furniture, metal, textiles in addition to a multitude of nondegree craft courses.

Rockland Center for the Arts
27 Old Greenbush Road
West Nyack 10994

Rosary Hill College
4380 Main Street
Buffalo 14226
B.F.A. in metal, jewelry, enameling, ceramics, textiles, weaving.

St. Lawrence University
Canton 13617
B.A. in ceramics.

St. Thomas Aquinas College
Sparkill 10976
Courses in jewelry, ceramics, textiles.

Skidmore College
Saratoga Springs 12866
B.S. in jewelry, enameling, ceramics, textile design, weaving, printing and dyeing, batik.

Southampton College of Long Island University
Southampton 11958

State University College at Brockport
Brockport 14420
B.A., B.S. in plastics, furniture, wood carving, silversmithing, jewelry, ceramics.

State University College at Buffalo
1300 Elmwood Avenue
Buffalo 14222
B.S. in wood, metal, jewelry, ceramics, textiles.

State University College at Geneseo
Geneseo 14454
Offers a number of craft courses including spinning, lapidary, textiles.

State University College of New Paltz
New Paltz 12561
B.F.A., M.F.A. in metal, ceramics.

State University College at Potsdam
Potsdam 13676
B.A. in ceramics.

State University of New York, College of Ceramics at Alfred University
Alfred 14802
B.F.A., M.F.A. in ceramics, glassblowing.

Syracuse University
Lowe Art Center
Syracuse 13210
B.F.A. in metal, ceramics, textile design, weaving.

Thousand Islands Museum Craft School
314 John Street
Clayton 13624

Westchester Art Workshop
County Center
White Plains 10606
Courses in general crafts, silversmithing, ceramics, jewelry, weaving, stitchery.

Workshop Five
100 Wells Road
Northport 11768
Courses in weaving, ceramics, jewelry, wood, silversmithing, silk-screening.

New York City
The Art Students League of New York
215 West 57 Street
Manhattan 10019
Courses in tie dye.

Baldwin Pottery
540 LaGuardia Place
Manhattan 10012

Bronx Community College
120 East 184 Street
Bronx 10468
Courses in general crafts.

Brooklyn College
Adult Education
Bedford Avenue and Avenue H
Brooklyn 11210
Classes in wood, stitchery, macrame, crochet, knitting.

Brooklyn Museum Art School
188 Eastern Parkway
Brooklyn 11238
Courses in glass, wood, jewelry, ceramics, enameling, batik, tie dye, welding.

City College of New York
Convent at 138 Street
Manhattan 10031
B.A. in wood, metal, jewelry, ceramics.

Clayart Inc.
121 East 29 Street
Manhattan 10016

Clayworks
332 East 9 Street
Manhattan 10003

Columbia University, Teachers College
525 West 120 Street
Manhattan 10027
M.A. in education in stained glass, silversmithing, jewelry, enameling, ceramics. textile design, woven forms.

Craft Students League
West Side YWCA
840 Eighth Avenue
Manhattan 10019
Wide variety of craft classes including quilting, puppetry, needlepoint.

Creative Art Center
1442 Third Avenue
Manhattan, 10014
Courses in ceramics, wood.

Spencer Depas Studio
227 Cumberland Street
Brooklyn 11205
Courses in weaving, macrame.

Durhan Studios, Inc.
115 East 18 Street
Manhattan 10003
Courses in stained glass.

Earthworks Pottery
251 West 85 Street
Manhattan 10024

Erica Wilson Needleworks
717 Madison Avenue
Manhattan 10021
Courses in stitchery.

Fashion Institute of Technology
227 West 27th Street
Manhattan 10001
Courses in jewelry, textiles, weaving, silk-screen.

Fibre Workshop
458 West Broadway
Manhattan 10012

Good Earth Pottery
357 Bowery
Manhattan 10003

Grand Street Potters
135 Grand Street
Manhattan 10013
Courses in ceramics (including raku, Japanese).

Greenwich House Pottery
16 Jones Street
Manhattan 10014

Henry Street Settlement
265 Henry Street
Manhattan 10002
Courses in general crafts, jewelry, enameling, ceramics, batik, tie dye, macrame, knitting, etc.

Hicks Street Clay Studio
46 Hicks Street
Brooklyn 11201

Hunter College
695 Park Avenue
Manhattan 10021
Courses in metal, ceramics, textiles.

Jewish Museum, Tobe Pascher Workshop
1109 Fifth Avenue
Manhattan 10028
Courses in silversmithing (Jewish ceremonial art).

John Harra Studio
6 West 20 Street
Manhattan 10011
Courses in wood, furniture.

Juliette Hamelcourt
Hotel Chelsea, Studio 710
222 West 23 Street
Manhattan 10011
Courses in stitchery.

Kulicke Studio
2231 Broadway
Manhattan 10024
Courses in silversmithing.

Laura Young
21 Claremont Avenue
Manhattan 10027
Courses in bookbinding.

Michelle Lester Studio
55 West 26 Street
Manhattan 10010
Courses in weaving.

Marymount Manhattan College
221 East 71 Street
Manhattan 10021
Courses in stitchery, ceramics, decoupage.

Nautique Arts
215 Thompson Street
Manhattan 10012
Courses in macrame.

The New School
66 West 12 Street
Manhattan 10011
Very diverse offering of craft courses including plastics, jewelry, spinning, leather, ceramics, silversmithing, textiles, batik, macrame, crochet.

New York Phoenix School of Design
160 Lexington Avenue
Manhattan 10016
Courses in weaving, textile design, furniture.

New York University
80 Washington Square
Manhattan 10003
Courses in jewelry, stitchery, general crafts, plastics.

The Nimble Thimble
49 West 16 Street
Manhattan 10011
  Courses in stitchery.

92nd Street YM-YWHA
1395 Lexington Avenue
Manhattan 10028
  Wide offering of courses including silversmithing, glass, weaving, crochet.

Parsons School of Design
66 Fifth Avenue
Manhattan 10011
  Courses in textile design.

Paula Adler Weaving Course
228 N. Houston Street
Manhattan 10014

The Plastics Factory
119 Avenue D
Manhattan 10009

The Pot Shop
356 Bowery
Manhattan 10012

Potluck Pottery
165 West 74 Street
Manhattan 10023

The Potter's Workshop
186 West 4 Street
Manhattan 10014

Pratt Institute
Brooklyn 11205
  B.F.A., M.F.A. in ceramics.

The Riverside Church
Arts and Crafts Program
490 Riverside Drive
Manhattan 10027
  Large offering of courses including spinning, natural dyeing, quilting, rug making, silk screen, basketry.

Rose H. Sulymoss Studio
32 Union Square
Manhattan 10003
  Courses in mosaic.

School of Visual Arts
209 East 23 Street
Manhattan 10010
  Courses in ceramics, general crafts, textile design, batik, furniture.

Sculpture House
38 East 30 Street
Manhattan 10016
  Courses in ceramics.

78th Street Pottery
169 West 79 Street
Manhattan 10024

Sharon Hedges
176 Clinton Avenue
Brooklyn 11202
  Courses in crochet, spinning, dyeing.

Sheepshead Bay Adult School
Avenue X and Batchelder Street
Brooklyn 11235
  Courses in weaving, knitting, ceramics, jewelry, quilting, macrame.

Stained Glass Workshop
136 Henry Street
Manhattan 10002

Studio Del
19 East 7 Street
Manhattan 10003
  Courses in crochet.

Studio Workshop
10 West 18 Street
Manhattan 10011
  Courses in ceramics, jewelry.

Richard Minsky, Bookbinding and
  Repairing
105-21 Metropolitan Avenue
Forest Hills 11375

Threadbare
20 Cornelia Street
Manhattan 10014
  Courses in weaving, spinning, natural dyeing, knitting, crochet, needlepoint, basketry, macrame, stained glass.

Ultimate Bread
237 East 12 Street
Manhattan 10003
  Courses in macrame.

Weaver's Loft
29 West 19 Street
Manhattan 10011

North Carolina
Arts and Crafts Association, Inc.
610 Coliseum Drive
Winston-Salem 27106
  Courses in jewelry, weaving, ceramics, lapidary, crochet, stitchery, macrame.

Duke University
6605 College Station
Durham 27708
  Courses in general crafts.

East Carolina University
Box 2704
Greenville 27834
  B.F.A., B.S., A.B., M.F.A., M.A. in education, M.A. in general crafts, jewelry, enamel, ceramics, textiles, weaving, printing and dyeing, batik, lapidary, leather.

Fayetteville State University
Murchison Road
Fayetteville 28301
  Courses in general crafts, ceramics.

Gaston College
New Dallas Highway
Dallas 28034
  Courses in stained glass, ceramics, jewelry, macrame.

John C. Campbell Folk School
Brasstown 28902
  Courses in general crafts, wood, wrought iron.

Mint Museum of Art
501 Hempstead Place
Charlotte 28207
  Sometimes offers a course in stitchery.

N.C.A. and T. State University
Greensboro
  M.S. in general crafts, metal, ceramics, textiles, weaving.

Penland School of Crafts
Penland 28765
  Courses in weaving, ceramics, glassblowing, etc.

University of North Carolina
Columbia Street
Chapel Hill 27514
  Courses in ceramics.

University of North Carolina at Asheville
Asheville 28801
  B.A. in general crafts, ceramics.

West Carolina University
Cullowhee 28723
  B.F.A. in glassblowing, jewelry, ceramics, weaving, textiles, lapidary, stitchery.

North Dakota
Jamestown College
Jamestown 58401
  B.F.A., M.F.A. in general crafts.

Minot State College
9th Avenue, North West
Minot 58701
  Courses in general crafts, other craft offerings.

Ohio
Bowling Green State University
Bowling Green 43403
  M.F.A. in general crafts, glassblowing, wood, jewelry, textiles, ceramics.

Cleveland Institute of Art
11141 East Boulevard
Cleveland 44106
   B.F.A. in glassblowing, silversmithing, jewelry, enameling, weaving, textiles.

Edgecliff College
2220 Victory Parkway
Cincinnati 45206
   B.A. in ceramics, weaving, batik.

Kent State University
Kent 24420
   B.F.A., M.F.A. in ceramics, weaving, enameling, glassblowing, jewelry.

Malone College
515 25th Street, North West
Canton 44720
   B.A., B.S. in education in general crafts.

Ohio University
School of Art
Athens 45701
   B.F.A., M.F.A. in ceramics.

Riverbend Art Center
142 Riverbend Drive
Dayton 45405

School of the Dayton Art Institute
Forest and Riverview
Dayton 45405
   B.F.A. in ceramics.

Toledo Museum of Art
Box 1013
Toledo 43697
   Courses in glassblowing, silversmithing, ceramics, jewelry.

University of Akron
Akron 44325
   B.F.A. in silversmithing, ceramics, jewelry, enameling.

University of Cincinnati
Cincinnati 45221
   B.F.A., M.F.A. in ceramics.

The Working Hand Craft Center
515 Conneaut
Bowling Green 43402
   Apprentice program in jewelry.

Oklahoma
Bacone Junior College
Bacone 74420
   Courses in general crafts, weaving, spinning, silversmithing, jewelry.

Central State University
400 East Hurd
Edmond 73034
   Courses in weaving, ceramics, general crafts, jewelry.

Contemporary Handcrafts
2927 Paseo
Oklahoma City 73116
   Courses in weaving, macrame.

Firehouse Art Station
444 South Flood
Norman 73069
   Courses in weaving, ceramics, jewelry, stitchery.

Northeastern State College
Tahlequah 74464
   Courses in general crafts, plastics, macrame, lapidary, ceramics, jewelry.

Oral Roberts University
777 South Lewis
Tulsa 74102
   B.A. in ceramics.

Phillips University
University Place
Enid 73701
   B.F.A. in ceramics.

University of Tulsa
600 South College
Tulsa 74104
   B.F.A., M.A., M.F.A. in ceramics.

Oregon
Coos Art Museum
515 Market Street
Coos Bay 97420
   Courses in spinning, weaving, textiles, stitchery, jewelry, silversmithing, wood, batik, macrame.

Corvallis Arts Center
700 South West Madison
Corvallis 97330
   Courses in general crafts, ceramics, weaving, stained glass, bobbin lace.

Eastern Oregon College
8th and K Avenue
La Grande 97850
   Extensive selection of craft offerings, including spinning and lapidary.

Lewis and Clark College
0615 South West Palatine Hill
Portland 97201
   B.S., B.A. in jewelry, ceramics.

Maude Kerns Art Center
1910 East 15th
Eugene 97403
   Courses in stained glass, wood, spinning, stitchery, weaving, ceramics, macrame, silversmithing, kite building.

Oregon College of Education
Monmouth 97361
   Courses in general crafts, and other offerings.

Oregon State University
Corvallis 97331
   B.S., B.A. in metal, enameling, jewelry, silversmithing, textiles, ceramics, weaving, printing and dyeing.

Portland State University
P.O. Box 751
Portland 97207
   B.A., B.S. in jewelry, silversmithing, weaving; M.F.A., M.A.T., M.S. in Textiles in ceramics. Classes also held in nonloom weaving techniques, glassblowing.

School of the Arts and Crafts Society
616 North West 18th Avenue
Portland 97209
   Many crafts taught, including spinning, natural dyeing, ceramics.

Southern Oregon College
Ashland 97520
   Courses in general crafts, silversmithing, etc.

Umpqua Community College
Adult Education
P.O. Box 967
Roseburg 97470
   Courses in ceramics, stitchery.

University of Oregon
Eugene 97403
   B.A., B.S. in wood, jewelry, ceramics, weaving.

Pennsylvania
Allegheny College
North Main Street
Meadville 16335
   Courses in ceramics.

The Arts and Crafts Center of Pittsburgh
Fifth and Shady Avenues
Pittsburgh 15232
   Extensive offerings including stained glass, plastics.

Bloomsburg State College
Bloomsburg 17815
   B.A. in general crafts, ceramics.

Carnegie Mellon University
Schenley Park
Pittsburgh 15235
   B.F.A. in metal, ceramics, weaving.

Cedar Crest College
Allentown 18104
   B.A. in wood, metal, enamel, ceramics.

Cheltenham Township Art Centre
439 Ashbourne Road
Cheltenham 19012
   Courses in silversmithing, ceramics, weaving, macrame, batik, jewelry, tie dye.

Drexel University
32nd and Chestnut Street
Philadelphia, 19104
   Courses in weaving, furniture, jewelry.

East Stroudsburg State College
East Stroudsburg 18301
   B.S., M.A. in general crafts, stained glass, jewelry, ceramics.

Edinboro State College
Edinboro 16412
   B.F.A., B.S. in education in general crafts, wood, furniture; B.F.A. in jewelry, silversmithing.

The Fringe
5600 Walnut Street
Pittsburgh 15232
   Courses in weaving, knitting, spinning, macrame, tie dye, batik, lace-making.

Indiana University of Pennsylvania
Indiana 15701
   B.A., B.S. in education in general crafts, silversmithing, jewelry, weaving, ceramics, enameling.

Juniata College
Moore Street
Huntingdon 15552
   B.A. in ceramics.

Kutztown State College
Kutztown 19530
   B.S. in jewelry; M.Ed. in weaving.

The Mannings-Creative Crafts
R.D. #2
East Berlin 17316
   Courses in spinning, weaving, tie dye, macrame.

Mansfield State College
Mansfield 16933
   M.F.A. in knitting, lapidary, wood, silversmithing, jewelry, enameling, ceramics, weaving, stitchery, textiles, printing and dyeing.

Marywood College
2300 Adams Avenue
Scranton 18509

Mercyhurst College
501 East 38 Street
Erie 16501

Moore College of Art
20th and Race Street
Philadelphia 19103
   B.F.A. in silversmithing, ceramics, textile design.

Philadelphia College of Art
Broad and Pine Streets
Philadelphia 19103
   B.F.A. in metal, ceramics, wood, glassblowing.

Tyler School of Art
Temple University
Beech and Penrose Avenues
Philadelphia 19126
   B.F.A., M.F.A. in silversmithing, metal, jewelry, ceramics, textiles, weaving. Courses in electroforming, blacksmithing.

Westminster College
New Wilmington 16142
   B.A. in wood carving, jewelry, ceramics.

Wilkes College
South Franklin Street
Wilkes-Barre 18703
   B.F.A. in wood carving, jewelry, enameling, ceramics.

Rhode Island
Rhode Island School of Design
Providence 02906
   B.F.A. in textile design, weaving, metal, furniture, glassblowing, general crafts; M.F.A. in general crafts, furniture, ceramics.

South Carolina
Clemson University
Clemson 29631
   M.F.A. in wood, metal, ceramics.

University of South Carolina
Columbia 29207
   B.A., B.F.A., M.F.A. in ceramics.

South Dakota
Mount Marty College
1100 West Fifth
Yankton 57078
   Courses in general crafts, glass.

Northern State College
Aberdeen 57401
   Courses in general crafts, lapidary, jewelry, ceramics.

Tennessee
Austin Peay State University
Clarksville 37040
   B.S. in plastic, metal, wood, ceramics, leather.

Carson Newman College
Box 1901
Jefferson City 37760
   B.A. in ceramics.

East Tennessee State University
Johnson City 37601
   B.A., B.S., B.F.A., M.A. in jewelry, ceramics, enameling, weaving.

Memphis Academy of Arts
Overton Park
Memphis 38112
   B.F.A. in textiles, metal, general crafts.

Memphis State University
Memphis 38111
   B.F.A. in general crafts, plastics, jewelry, ceramics, weaving.

University of Tennessee
Knoxville 37916
   B.S., M.S. in general crafts, metal, jewelry, enameling, silversmithing, ceramics, textiles, weaving, stitchery, printing and dyeing.

Texas
Baylor University
Waco 76703
   B.F.A., B.A. in ceramics, metal, general crafts.

The Craft Guild of Dallas
Museum of Fine Arts
Fair Park
Dallas 75226
   Metal, silversmithing, jewelry, ceramics, weaving, bookbinding.

East Texas State University
1603 Walnut
Commerce 75428
   B.S., B.A., M.A., M.S. in general crafts, plastics, wood, metal, ceramics, jewelry, silversmithing, printing and dyeing, lapidary, macrame.

Fort Worth Art Center Museum
1309 Montgomery
Fort Worth 76107

The Museum of Fine Arts
School of Art at Houston
909 Berthea
Houston 77005
Courses in wood, jewelry, ceramics, metal.

North Texas State University
Denton 76203
   B.F.A. in jewelry, ceramics, weaving.

Sam Houston State University
Huntsville 77340
   M.F.A. in ceramics; M.A. in textiles.

Southern Methodist University
Dallas 75275
    B.F.A., M.F.A. in ceramics.

Southwest Texas State University
San Marcos 78666
    B.S. in education jewelry, ceramics,
textile design.

Texas Lutheran College
West Court, Seguin 78155
    B.S., B.A. in ceramics.

Texas Woman's University
Box 23548, TWU Station
Denton 76204
    B.S., B.A., M.A. in silversmithing,
ceramics, textile design.

University of Houston
Houston 77004
    B.F.A. in silversmithing, ceramics,
jewelry.

University of Dallas
Irving 75060
    B.A., M.A., M.F.A. in ceramics.

University of Texas at El Paso
El Paso 79968
    B.A. in metal, silversmithing, jewelry,
enameling, lapidary, ceramics.

West Texas State University
Canyon 79015
    B.A., B.S. in general crafts, mosaics,
wood, enameling, ceramics, textiles,
weaving, stitchery, printing and dyeing,
macrame; M.A. in metal, silversmithing,
jewelry.

Utah
Artistic Glass
315 East 2100 South
Salt Lake City 84115
    Courses in stained glass.

Pioneer Craft House, Inc.
3271 South 5th East
Salt Lake City 84106
    Varied and extensive selection of craft
courses including puppetry.

Southern Utah State College
Cedar City 84720
    B.A. in ceramics.

Utah State University
Logan 84321
    B.F.A. in metal, ceramics, textiles.

Weber State College
Ogden 84403
    B.A., B.S. in metal, jewelry, ceramics.

Vermont
Bennington College
Bennington 05201
    B.A. in ceramics.

Goddard College
Plainfield 05667
    B.A., M.A. in glass, glassblowing, weav-
ing, ceramics, metal; B.A. in furniture.

Judy Fox
Waitsfield 06573
    Courses in weaving, spinning, dyeing.

University of Vermont
Burlington 05401

Virginia
The Hand Work Shop
315 North 24th Street
Richmond 23223
    Courses in macrame, weaving, etc.

Madison College
Main at Grace Streets
Harrisonburg 22801
    B.A., B.S. in metal, ceramics, textiles;
M.F.A. in ceramics.

Radford College
Radford 24141
    B.A., B.S., M.S. in general crafts, jew-
elry, ceramics, enameling, textiles.

Virginia Commonwealth University
901 West Franklin Street
Richmond 23220
    B.F.A., M.F.A. in furniture, metal,
jewelry, ceramics, textiles.

Virginia Museum
Boulevard and Grove
Richmond 23221
    Courses in glassblowing, ceramics.

Washington
Crockery Shed
826 102nd North East
Bellevue 98004
    Courses in ceramics.

Eastern Washington State College
Cheney 99004
    B.A. in general crafts, mosaics, wood,
metal, silversmithing, weaving, enameling, ceramics, macrame, spinning, lapidary.

Factory of Visual Art
5041 Roosevelt Way North East
Seattle 98105

Loom and Leather
South 208 Wall Street
Spokane 99204
    Courses in weaving.

Hella Skowronski, Studio and Workshop
9923 South East Bellevue Place
Bellevue 98004
    Courses in weaving, sprang.

The Loomery
3239 Eastlake East
Seattle 98102
    Courses in spinning, dyeing, weaving.

Pacific Lutheran University
Tacoma 98447
    B.F.A. in glassblowing, wood, metal,
ceramics, textiles.

Skagit Valley College
Mount Vernon 98273
    Courses in lapidary, jewelry, ceramics.

University of Washington
Seattle 98195
    B.F.A., M.F.A. in wood, metal, textile
design, ceramics; B.F.A. in furniture.

Washington State University
Pullman 99163
    B.A., M.F.A. in jewelry, ceramics.

Whitworth College
Spokane 99218
    M.F.A., M.A. in education in general
crafts, jewelry, ceramics, batik.

West Virginia
Huntington Galleries
2033 McCoy
Huntington 25701
    Courses in weaving, ceramics, wood
carving, stitchery.

Oglebay Institute
841½ National Road
Wheeling 26003
    Courses in general crafts, stained glass,
ceramics, stitchery, macrame, knitting,
crochet, needlepoint.

West Virginia State College
Institute 25112
    B.A., B.S. in education in ceramics.

Wisconsin
Cardinal Stritch College
6801 North Yates Road
Milwaukee 53217
    B.F.A. in wood, jewelry, ceramics,
textiles.

Carroll College
Waukesha 53186
    B.A. in jewelry, ceramics, textiles.

Lawrence University
Appleton 54911
    B.A. in silversmithing, jewelry, ce-
ramics.

Mount Mary College
2900 Menomonee River Parkway
Milwaukee 53222

St. Norbert College
De Pere 54115
    B.A. in metal, jewelry, ceramics, textile design, printing and dyeing, lapidary.

University of Wisconsin at Eau Claire
Water Street
Eau Claire 54701
    B.F.A. in metal, ceramics.

University of Wisconsin at Green Bay
Green Bay 54302
    B.A., B.S. in jewelry, ceramics.

University of Wisconsin at La Crosse
La Crosse 54601
    B.A., B.S. in silversmithing, jewelry, ceramics.

University of Wisconsin at Madison
455 North Park
Madison 53706
    B.S., M.S., M.F.A. in glassblowing, wood, metal, ceramics.

University of Wisconsin at Milwaukee
Milwaukee 53201
    B.F.A., M.S., M.F.A. in metal, ceramics, weaving.

University of Wisconsin at River Falls
River Falls 54022
    B.F.A., B.S. in general crafts, glass, plastics, furniture, metal, jewelry, silversmithing, enameling, ceramics, textiles, weaving, stitchery, plastics, crochet, knitting, macrame, spinning, lapidary.

University of Wisconsin at Whitewater
Main Street
Whitewater 53190
    B.A., B.S. in general crafts, metal, jewelry, ceramics, textiles, weaving.

Weaving Workshop
817½ East Johnson Street
Madison 53701
    Courses in weaving, spinning.

Wyoming
Northwest Community College
Powell 82435
    Courses in general crafts, jewelry, ceramics, crochet, bookbinding, knitting.

Selling Your Crafts

Recently, the American Crafts Council compiled a survey from the results of a questionnaire mailed to 1,187 craft shops and galleries in September 1972. Five hundred thirty-two retailers responded and, of these, a representative portion—269 questionnaires—were tabulated for computer analysis. The results are telling and can be read in toto in the May-June 1974, Volume 15, Number 3 issue of ACC/Outlook, the bulletin of the American Crafts Council. Some of the more interesting statistics are as follows: Proprietors of craft shops may be even more vulnerable to the difficulties encountered by all small businessmen and 50 percent of all small businesses are sold or liquidated within the first two years, one-third make it through four years, and only 20 percent through ten. The ten most frequently stocked crafts in descending order were pottery (by far the leader), jewelry, wall hangings, ceramic sculpture, woven accessories, wood accessories, candles, stained glass, blown glass, and leather. There was not a great deal of agreement about what were slow moving items. Frequently mentioned in this category were: "anything big," "anything expensive," sculpture, and various forms of fiber (which was also listed as a hot item). Twenty-three percent of the proprietors buy all their stock; 13 percent sell on consignment. The preferred method, however, is a combination of both, and 48 percent indicated that this was the way in which they worked.

Craftspeople cannot expect to be paid back for their time.

    —Susan Toplitz, professional knitter

SELLING YOUR CRAFTS. by Norbert N. Nelson. Van Nostrand Reinhold, New York, 1973. illustrations, index. paperback edition $3.95.

This book is directed toward craftsmen who are more interested in a cottage industry type of production than an operation based upon commission sales or a generally less commercial set up. The author strongly recommends the preparation of a line of products and has a number of reasons why and how this should be done. He discusses pricing and the establishment of a sales plan and a sales force, and the advantages and disadvantages of different markets are set forth. The most useful and interesting chapter is that on legal pointers for the craftsman.

If the potential profits, in an exclusive market, of a design you have make it seem worthwhile to protect that design through legal action, there are steps you can take, not to prevent it from being used as a source of inspiration to other designers, but to prevent it from being reproduced in direct copy providing you are properly protected. If your work can be classified as art, it can be copyrighted. This is the cheapest and most effective way to protect a design. All you need do is send two photographs of the object and a completed copyright blank (supplied free by the Copyright Office) plus a $4.00 fee to the Register of Copyright, Library of Congress, Washington, D.C. The office does not check to ascertain whether or not the design originated with the filer and others may contest your claim on those grounds. Uncontested, a copyright is good for twenty-eight years and renewable for another twenty-eight.

If, on the other hand, your design is a useful object and not subject to copyright protection, it can be guarded by a design patent. This protects its mode of operation. When an application to obtain a patent is made, the patent office searches its records to make sure nothing like it has been patented before. The patent examiner tries to prove by examining literature and museum collections and anything else that the idea is not new. A design patent costs at least $150 to $200 and it is advisable to employ a patent attorney to settle the transaction rather than attempt it single-handedly. Once the patent has been obtained, the appearance of the object is protected. Some people mistakenly believe that they can get around patents by making slight alterations in the appearance of a patented object. This is not true. The final test is whether or not an unsuspecting observer, seeing the two objects separately (not together so that the differences are emphasized), will think them identical.

Despite the higher price of a patent, it does not really offer more protection than a copyright. More patents have been invalidated by courts than copyrights, and a patent trial means that the craftsman must successfully prove his design is totally unlike anything else ever done. This is an especially difficult task for anyone working in an artistic field, since creation is more a matter of nuance of perception and artistic innovation than invention.

HOW TO MAKE MONEY WITH YOUR CRAFTS. by Leta W. Clark. William Morrow and Company, New York, 1974. 240 pages. $7.95.

This is a particularly good book for anyone, though the author directs it toward women. Legal and official recognition are only small parts of what is needed for true metamorphosis of woman's role. Women must throw off the burden of economic dependence, and the well-developed hand skills they probably never thought much of could become the means.

The author supplies good, practical information on loans, leases, trade rags, costing, gallery pieces versus retail, and so on. There are appendixes with addresses of Small Business Administrations nationwide, trade journal addresses, and other important places to know.

SELLING WHAT YOU MAKE. by Jane Wood. Penguin Books, Baltimore, Maryland, 1973. 105 pages. illustrations. paperback edition $2.25.

The handwritten, counterculture type layout of this book makes it hard to get concrete information amidst all the cuteness. Anyway, we find it hard to read this type of thing.

Rural Selling: A Letter From Nancy Colin, Maine craftswoman

RFD ROBBINSTON MAINE 04671

Dear Paul,

We're in the middle of haying, which is a rough business, so this letter will be short as I want to get it out.

I'm not quite sure what you want, a countryside craftperson's experience? Well, I'll assume it's that. First off, we're sort of into a self sufficiency trip. We raise all our milk, butter, cheese, yogurt, and eggs. These items also pay for the animals' feed and we could sell more if we could produce more. We heat and cook with wood we cut and split. We grow our vegetables and forage for seafood as we're 5 min. walk to the ocean.

Craft is just one part of our lives. I've been working with pottery for about three years, but I don't consider myself a professional and destroy much of what I produce I have a wheel and a kiln, but the electricity for the kiln is prohibitive so I don't use it. I go to a workshop twice a week and use their kiln.

The goat t-shirt business is mail order. We advertise in trade magazines and sell them at $5.50 each or $8.50 for two. We buy plain white t-shirts wholesale and silk screen whatever breed of goat they want on front and the herd name on back. Thru friends in N.Y. we are able to sell goat t-shirts with only a goat on front for $3.25. We usually dye these shirts.

We also have a line that pertains to gay women (which in your book would be special interest groups). We do "Killer Dyke" t-shirts and a small magazine/folio silk screened and hand printed called Uva Ursi, which we sell for $1.00. We also do posters, etc. and we sell more than we can make.

Markets for your/our wares. No, we do not have a roadside stand. But there is a leather craftsman whose home/shop is on the highway with big signs north and south of his place. I understand he does very well. Rte 1 is the only way to Canada around these parts and the highway is dotted with craft places. Last year the Indian reservation opened a shop in Calais to sell their baskets and did very well, they kept the store open all year and this summer, the local technical school sponsored a craft shop, which has pottery, weaving, dye (batik, etc.) and is not doing well. The best places to sell your stuff, for a rural craftsperson, are the fairs. Each state (or rather most states) have craft councils and sponsor sections of county and state fairs as well as crafts fairs. There is also a national crafts organization that has a big fair in Vermont (I guess for this part of the country) and this fair is the place to make wholesale contacts.

We brought our t-shirts, ceramic goat tiles, goat paintings, pottery, etc. to goat fairs and did alright. This can be done for horse, cattle, etc. shows and in wealthy areas probably could bring dynamite results.

Love,
Nancy

What I was looking for specifically were not those things which were salable, but those things which were special, the things that were being made for love not to be sold. When I take things because I think they will sell they never do. When I take things because I like them, because I love them, those are the things that inevitably do very well.

Magazines and Pamphlets

Profitable Craft Merchandising
Profitable Hobby Merchandising, Inc.
Pleasantville, N.Y. 10570
Monthly. $3.00 per year. $.50 a single issue.

Has features on how to set up handicraft departments in stores, how to market a number of craft products.

"Mail Order Regulations and Business Practices"
Booklet from the
United States Department of the Treasury
15th Street and Pennsylvania Avenue
Washington, D.C. 20220

The Small Business Administration has many booklets for free and for sale (none sells for more than $1.25). They publish one of particular interest to craftspeople, "Handicrafts and Home Business." Check the white pages of the phone book for the office nearest you.

LEGAL FORMS FOR THE DESIGNER. by Lee Epstein. Contract Books, Suite 1500, 2 Penn Plaza, New York, N.Y., 1969. 134 pages $9.95.

This is an informative survey of the costs for banking services and how to determine the best services for you.

THE VISUAL ARTIST AND THE LAW. by the Associated Councils of the Arts, The Association of the Bar of the City of New York, and Volunteer Lawyers for the Arts. Praeger Publishers, New York, 1974. 87 pages. $5.00.

This is a good reference for information on copyright, gallery agreements, publisher relationships, commissioned works, and taxes.

Urban Selling

Julie's Artisans Gallery is a small boutique on New York's Madison Avenue. It features one-of-a-kind handmade garments, wall hangings, sculpture, and jewelry, ranging in price from $10 to $2,700. Julie takes her artisans on a consignment basis. She claims that final selling price is generally determined by a consensus. Unlike most boutiques, Julie's gallery features four shows per year. These highlight the work of an individual artisan, or articulate a theme common to the work of a number of artisans.

In the year since its opening, Julie's Artisans Gallery has experienced an almost dizzying success, a success that Julie attributes to a combination of prime location and selective merchandise:

Women's Craft Exchanges

Exchanges are nonprofit enterprises and depend upon the willing services of volunteers who wait on customers and receive shipments. Usually, members rotate this task so that each ends up sacrificing only about one day out of every month to shopwork. Depending upon the volume of business, a paid, part-time bookkeeper might be employed.

If you decide to set up a craft exchange, be prepared for a lot of committee work. One committee usually examines the goods submitted for sale, checking on the quality and setting a fair price; another committee is needed to mark prices and display items as they arrive; another one usually takes charge of notifying craftswomen when to deliver more wares.

Most exchanges specialize in homemade needlework and handicrafts, although some also sell antiques, baked goods, hand-decorated furniture, and frozen foods (a few even operate restaurants or catering services); others take orders for custom-made works such as portraits or special-size quilts. The majority of exchanges now in operation turn down submissions similar to merchandise already being sold in the shop and thereby afford protection to their consignors. The exchange commission generally runs about 20 to 25 percent of the sale price with the creator receiving the balance of the money. People who sell their wares through exchanges also usually pay a fee of between $1.00 and $3.00 a year.

It is not necessary to be a member of the community in which an exchange is located to submit wares. Do not, however, send any of your crafts to any exchanges without writing or telephoning first for approval.

Arizona
Family Arts Exchange
5807 North 7 Street
Phoenix 85014

Woman's Exchange
Specialties of Tucson
4215 North Campbell
Tucson 85719

Connecticut
Fairfield Woman's Exchange, Inc.
332 Pequot Road
Southport 06490

Greenwich Exchange for Woman's Work, Inc.
28 Sherwood Place
Greenwich 06830

Litchfield Exchange for Woman's Work, Inc.
Cobble Court
Litchfield 06759

The Stamford Woman's Exchange
45 Prospect Street
Stamford 06901

The Woman's Exchange
993A Farmington Avenue
West Hartford 06107

Heritage Village Woman's Exchange
Southbury 06448

Georgia
Unique Corner, The Woman's Exchange
of Athens
Taylor-Grady House
634 Prince Avenue
Athens 30601

Indiana
The Hen House
4816 Tippecanoe Drive
Evansville 47715

The Little Turtle Woman's Exchange
Time Corner Shopping Center
Fort Wayne 46804

Maine
The Women's Exchange
32 Exchange Street
Portland 04111

Maryland
Woman's Industrial Exchange
333 North Charles Street
Baltimore 21201

Massachusetts
Dedham Woman's Exchange, Inc.
445 Washington Street
Dedham 02026

The Hay Scales Exchange
24 Johnson Street
North Andover Center 01845

The Mulberry Gallery
28 Court Street
Westfield 01850

Old Town Exchange
Lincoln Center 01773

New Jersey
The Depot
217 First Street
Hohokus 07423

The Hunterdon Exchange
155 Main Street
Flemington 08822

Newark Exchange for Woman's Work
32 Halsey Street
Newark 07102

The Village Exchange
De Forest and Woodland Avenues
Summit 07901

Woman's Exchange of Monmouth County
32 Church Street
Little Silver 07739

New York
Craftsmen Unlimited, Inc.
16 Main Street
Bedford Hills 10507

The Elder Craftsmen Showcase
859 Lexington Avenue
New York 10021

New York Exchange for Woman's Work,
Inc.
541 Madison Avenue
New York 10022

Scarsdale Woman's Exchange, Inc.
33 Harwood Court
Scarsdale 10583

Woman's Exchange of Brooklyn, Inc.
76 Montague Street
Brooklyn 11201

North Carolina
The Country Store
113 West Franklin Street
Chapel Hill 27514

The Sandhills Woman's Exchange
Pinehurst 28374

Ohio
The Woman's Exchange
3507 Michigan Avenue
Cincinnati 45208

The Sassy Cat
88 North Main Street
Chagrin Falls 44022

Pennsylvania
Chestnut Hill Community Center
8419 Germantown Avenue
Philadelphia 19087

The Elder Craftsmen
1628 Walnut Street
Philadelphia 19102

Ladies Depository Association of Philadelphia
109 South 18 Street
Philadelphia 19103

The Old York Road Woman's Exchange
429 Johnson Street
Jenkintown 19046

Woman's Exchange of the Neighborhood League
185 East Lancaster Avenue
Wayne 19087

The Woman's Exchange of Reading, Inc.
720 Penn Avenue
West Reading 19602

The Woman's Exchange of West Chester
10 South Church Street
West Chester 19830

The Woman's Exchange of Yardley
47 West Afton Avenue
Yardley 19067

Woman's Industrial Exchange
541 Penn Avenue
Pittsburgh 15222

Tennessee
The Woman's Exchange of Memphis, Inc.
88 Racine Street
Memphis 38111

Texas
St. Michael's Woman's Exchange
5 Highland Park Village
Dallas 75205

Spinning and Dyeing

And all the women that were wise-hearted did spin with their hands.

Exodus 35:25

CREATIVE SPINNING, WEAVING, AND PLANT-DYEING. by Beryl Anderson. Arco Publishing Company, New York, 1973. 31 pages. illustrations, photographs (some color). $3.25.

Beryl Anderson is a successful textile designer whose products are used by world-famous couturiers. The slant of this book reveals her interest in design. She states in her prologue that it is her intention to give a simple explanation for the beginner and new methods and experiments for the more experienced craftsman, but this book will probably perplex the beginning weaver as much as it will inspire one with a grasp of fundamentals.

She begins with an excellent discussion of wool and wool classifications. Insofar as all wool is suitable for spinning, she cautions the spinner to choose fleece with characteristics appropriate to the article being made. A superfine Merino, famous for exquisitely fine-textured wool, would not be a wise choice for a floor rug. She recommends a crossbred with 48/50s count and a staple length of 46 inches for beginners. The fleece should be strong with a reasonable crimp in the individual fibers and without matted or cotted patches. It should be soft to handle, lustrous, and have sufficient natural grease without much yellow yolk. She also pleads a case for the long-neglected wool of the black sheep which in recent times has become prized for natural blends.

There is a nice chapter on plant dyeing, complete with a dyeing table and three recipes for dyeing with coccus cacti (cochineal). She also offers some suggestions for obtaining interesting color variation and unusual effects such as cramming wool into the dye bath so that the dye is prevented from circulating evenly; placing a number of skeins in the same dye bath after first treating each skein with a different mordant; and overdyeing gray fleece to create heather mixtures.

The general discussion on handling the wool is excellent but breaks down on the particulars of working on a spindle. No diagrams accompany the text, and a novice would have a hard time without them. Similarly, the chapters on weaving and knitting presuppose a knowledge of these crafts and no instructions are given on technical aspects other than those of design. Ms. Anderson provides patterns for a woven casual coat, poncho, and sweater, among others.

The knitting chapter contains some helpful advice on accurate fitting and on the making of a stitch gauge. She recommends using the yarn and needles to be used for the garment, but that the stockinette stitch be used no matter what the texture stitch planned for the actual execution. The loops on the needle should never be measured, but rather the extent of the wool itself. A sweater knitted with correct measurement, she maintains, should not have to be blocked.

The appendix features color photographs of Ms. Anderson's fabrics and articles made from them.

YOUR HANDSPINNING. by Elsie Davenport. Selective Books, Clearwater, Florida, 1970. 130 pages. illustrations. $4.25.

This is a number one book on hand spinning. It begins with a discussion of wool and sheep, then continues on to sorting fleece, learning to make a continuous yarn, and carding and spinning wool. There is an excellent section on the construction, use, and maintenance of spinning wheels and hints on what to look for when buying a wheel. There is information on the cultivation and preparation of flax, and the spinning of fibers such as silk, angora, camel, even

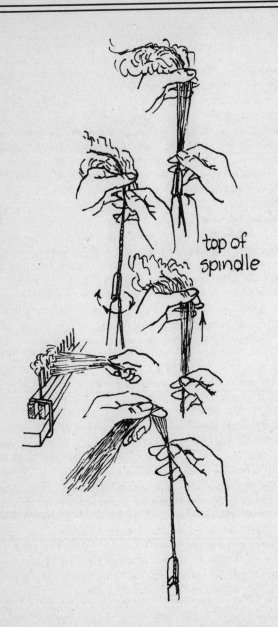

top of
spindle

the author learned to spin, and her wool grading categories which would horrify a professional sorter but which serve her purposes completely.

SPIN, DYE, AND WEAVE YOUR OWN WOOL. by Molly Duncan. Sterling Publishing Company, New York, 1973. 72 pages. illustrations, photographs, suppliers list, index. $3.95.

There is a lot of material to cover in the space of seventy-two pages, and consequently clarity and comprehensiveness lose out to concision.

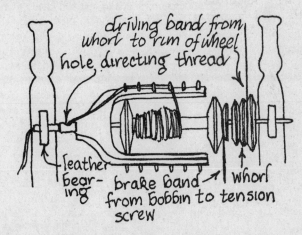

Mother-of-all that moves to adjust tension

HANDSPINNING, ART AND TECHNIQUE. by Allen Fannin. Van Nostrand Reinhold, New York, 1970. 208 pages. illustrations, photographs. $12.50.

Here is another top-notch book on hand spinning. It's technical, up-to-date, and aesthetic in emphasis. The author revitalizes old procedures and turns them to the service of design. Garnetting, for example, is most often used by mills to produce lower-quality goods. It consists of the reuse of previously spun yarns which are broken up or garnetted. Hand spinners don't usually employ this method, but perhaps they should. It offers an additional way to design yarns with texture, and as such, has much potential for the hand spinner.

dog. Many dogs yield combings or clippings which can be spun into useful yarns. Poodle clippings, according to the author, make a very pleasant "woolen" yarn while the luster of Spaniel hair needs a worsted spin. The author recalls no instance of the use of cat hair for spinning, but sees great possibilities for the spinning of fine-haired Persian combings, especially if carded with suitable wool. She does not, however, recommend that anyone duplicate her experiments with a mixture of Siamese and camel.

THE JOY OF SPINNING. by Marilyn Kruger. Simon and Schuster, New York, 1971. 187 pages. illustrations, index. $6.95.

This book offers a wealth of practical information, including where to buy raw wool; how to spin wool, flax, camel's hair, angora, cashmere, and dog's hair; where to order spinning wheels and accessories by mail. All is interwoven with personal and historical anecdotes, such as how

Interview

Eileen Waters teaches spinning and natural dyeing, and she weaves for fun and profit. She lives in New York City, and so must purchase fleece rather than raise it. She recommends that anyone looking for fleece go to a country agricultural agent and ask if he knows anyone with fleece to sell. This is generally the cheapest and best way to make your contacts. She washes her fleece in the washing machine, but doesn't agitate. Eileen attributes the rising interest in spinning to two primary causes: primitive hand-spun yarns are now so popular in weavings and wall hangings; and spinning is a very enjoyable, very relaxing thing to do.

Eileen's loft is crammed full of spinning wheels, looms, assorted flora, and pots for dyeing. These are primarily enamel and stainless steel pots. Copper and aluminum are never used for dyeing because the metals act as mordants. In the past, people dyed in big iron pots. This accounts for the darkness of their yarns.

I'm not opposed to chemical dyes. I enjoy vegetable dyeing. I think it's a lovely process. It's historic and it's fun to get good colors from natural things. It's a good excuse to go to the country and pick things if you live in a city. And with natural dyes, you can mix reds, greens, blues, and so on in the same piece and sometimes if you dye them all on the same day, they'll have a certain feeling about them and all go together. But then, I can do that with chemical dyes, too. I can reproduce anything I do with natural dyes with chemical dyes. In fact, I did a job of dyeing forty pounds of yarn for a company in vegetable dyes because they wanted to reproduce the colors of their fall line in aniline dyes. One thing that is nicer about vegetable dyes, though, is that as they fade as the years go by, they fade softly and don't look washed out. A lot of aniline dyes as they fade just sort of wash themselves out. But chemical dyes are not sinful to me. I'm not into that "back-to-the-earth" trip.

I like to do vegetable dyeing, and spinning, and weaving, but that's because I don't want to do any other kind of work. I can work at home and make enough money to continue. Technological advances are things that we all take advantage of every time we turn on a light bulb, so let's not kid ourselves. I'm doing this because I like it. It's not a big spiritual or moral thing. I find it very exciting to get colors from plants and most of the materials are free; I just pick up garbage from the area.

I usually use two basic mordants when I dye the color. I split the dye pot up and I always dye a whole lot of skeins at a time so I can go through the whole variety: I blossom one with tin, sadden one with iron, and if it's a yellow, I green one over with copper sulfate. I like to dye a whole family of colors at a time.

I don't work from recipes and I don't cook from a cookbook. That's just the way I am. But I do remember most of the time how I dyed something and I keep intending to keep a notebook one of these days. One of my favorite formulas is for a really nice chocolate brown. John built a rosewood cabinet one time and I went out every day and collected all the sawdust and boiled it for about six hours to get the color out. I put in some yarn that was mordanted with alum and cooked it for about an hour. The color was icky brown. I didn't like that at all so I added (for a pound of yarn) a quarter ounce chrome and put the yarn back in. I ended up with a really beautiful brown.

Another successful dye was from Helianthus, a wild sunflower I pick over by the railroad tracks in New Jersey. I took the flower heads and cut them up and soaked them. I heated them very slowly and the water turned purple. I had heard you could get purple from Helianthus. Well, I dyed the yarn—one alum and one chrome—and I got two very nice greens. Then, I boiled the Helianthus for a while and I got a terrible yellow. So, just by heating it very slowly and not boiling it I got a good color. It's hard to get a green like that right off the bat. Usually you have to do a yellow and a blue, but this makes a definite green. I've tested it in the sun and the colors are fast. I would like to experiment some more, though, and find out whatever happened to that purple! I think maybe I have to use only the seeds rather than the whole head.

"FROM RAISING SHEEP TO WEAVING CLOTH," in *Fox-fire 2,* edited by Brooks E. Wigginton, Anchor Books, Doubleday and Company, Garden City, New York, 1973. 83 pages. illustrations, photographs. $4.50.

This is an article about shearing, preparing the wool, spinning, building a loom, and weaving.

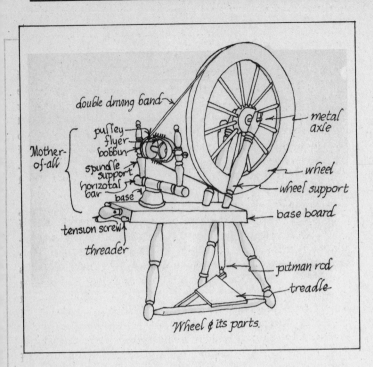

Wheel & its parts.

The hands of the dyer reek like rotting fish and his eyes are overcome by weariness.

—Papyrus Anastasi

NATURAL DYES AND HOME DYEING. by Rita J. Adrosko. Dover Publications, New York, 1971. 154 pages. illustrations, bibliography, index. paperback edition $2.00.

In 1856, W. H. Perkins' accidental discovery of a lavender dye artificially produced from a coal tar substance marked the first step in the decline of the natural dye and the rise of the synthetic dye industry.

Today, craftsmen are returning to the use of natural dyes, probably for the same reasons manufacturers have rejected them: difficulty of standardization. Natural dyes produce one of a kind, off beat colors difficult to reproduce.

This book begins with a discussion of the dyestuffs used in eighteenth- and nineteenth-century America. It supplies historical and technical information on dyes used by manufacturers as well as home craftsmen. Included are excerpts from herbals, natural histories, and manufacturing records. Then, the author moves on to the subject of home dyeing with natural materials. She provides information on the preparation of yarn and tools techniques, and fifty-two recipes for natural dyes.

The more practical side of this book certainly deals adequately with the methodology of home dyeing, but the real value lies in the historical section which contains a wealth of fascinating material.

Coffee Beans

Note: Coffee does not produce fast colors on cotton.

1 lb. wool
1¾ lbs. ground coffee

Chrome mordant: yields a dark yellow-tan wool with good colorfastness.

Boil the coffee in water for 20 minutes. Strain grounds and add cold water to make a dyebath of 4 to 4½ gallons. Thoroughly rinse the wool and squeeze out excess moisture. Immerse wool; heat to boiling; boil 30 minutes, rinse and dry.

Source: NATURAL DYES AND HOME DYEING. by Rita J. Adrosko.

VEGETABLE DYEING. by Alma Lesch. Watson-Guptill Publications, New York, 1971. 146 pages. suppliers list, bibliography, index. $7.95.

A tripartite organization forms the basic structure of this manual. The first section, "General Information," provides a background in methods of preparation and procedures relating to dye substances, fibers, and dyes. The second section contains information for making dyes in primary and secondary color ranges and ranges of low intensity (blacks and browns). There are 151 recipes using a variety of yarns in combination with different dye substances and mordants and illustrating the properties of these mordants and their effects on color and fiber. The third section, "Reference Material," lists sources of supply for chemicals, fibers, and dye substances not easily obtained. There are charts to provide a quick information guide in the areas of color and dye substances and a bibliography listing books on additional areas of vegetable dyeing.

The colors obtained from seaweed can vary according to the geographic location and variety of the plant. The seaweed for this particular dye was gathered along the coast of Deer Isle, Maine. A word of warning, the odor from boiling seaweed is rather pungent.

INGREDIENTS:
1 lb. wool yarn
4 oz. copperas crystals (ferrous sulfate)
4 gallons seaweed
4 tbsp, tartaric acid
½ cup Glauber's salts

Place seaweed in a five gallon container, cover with water and boil for about two hours. As it boils, add extra water to maintain level and keep covered to reduce odor. Cool. Remove refuse. Add 4 oz. of copperas crystals to liquid and stir until completely dissolved.

Add wet, wool yarn and simmer for 30 minutes. The yarn should be kept covered with the dye bath to prevent streaking. Dissolve 4 tablespoons of tartaric acid and half a cup of Glauber's salts in one pint hot water. Add to dye bath. Simmer 30 minutes more. Rinse yarn in warm water until water runs clear. Shake excess water from yarn and hang in the shade to dry.

This recipe makes a dark yellow-green. Do not use the dye bath more than once or the color will turn muddy. Do not use silk fibers as copperas should not be used on that fabric. Linen and cotton dye a muddy shade of greenish gray.

Source: VEGETABLE DYEING. by Alma Lesch.

DYES FROM PLANTS. by Seonaid Robertson. Van Nostrand Reinhold, New York, 1973. 144 pages. illustrations, photographs, suppliers list, bibliography, index. $8.95.

Plants, in addition to supplying food, perfume, and medicine, are also a source of beautiful and varied dyes. The production of these dyes does not pollute the environment with harsh chemicals since they are derived from natural sources. Dyeing fabric with plants has become a very popular craft along with the allied interests of weaving and spinning.

Dyes from Plants is a great source of information, not only on the techniques of natural dyeing, but also on historical, cultural, botanical and aesthetic considerations relating to plant dyeing. Dye plants of every season and locale are presented in a drawing, and full instructions for its preparation and color yield are given. A section on "Dyes of Historical Importance" is a fantastic source of general information, and an additional list of dye recipes is given.

Most of the plant dyes presented are for wool, although the author does provide additional recipes for cotton, linen, and silk dyeing, making this quite a complete text on the subject useful for both beginning and advanced craftsmen.

Cochineal

Cochineal, a famous red dye known throughout history, comes from an insect that produces carminic acid. This, when combined with the appropriate mordants yields pink to carmine on wool and silk. The Mexican Indians would brush the wingless female insects from cactus plants with fine brushes onto trays. They then dried the insects in the sun or over a stove and ground them into a powder. Most ancient American embroideries contain the pinks and carmines of cochineal. It is not as fast as kermes or madder, but it is adequate for textiles not exposed to continual bright light.

NATURAL PLANT DYEING. Brooklyn Botanic Garden, 1000 Washington Avenue, Brooklyn, N.Y., 1974. 64 pages. $1.50.

This is an excellent and inexpensive reference. You can't beat it.

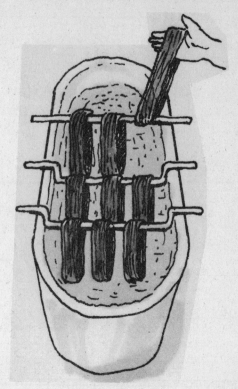

Dyeing in an old fashioned bath tub

RECIPE FOR COCHINEAL

Mordant: Alum gives rose to pink, chrome gives warm pink to purplish red, tin gives strong scarlet, iron in the dyebath yields violet to gray-purple.

Method: Add salt to water and warm to hand-heat. Stir in cochineal. Add clean, wetted wool and heat slowly (it should take about 1 hour to reach simmering point.) Simmer for 1 hour. Add iron for violet and stir, or, for a brighter colored scarlet on alum-mordanted wool, leave wool in the bath to cool and add tin at this point. Rinse the wool twice and dry.

½ oz. cochineal powder
½ tsp. common salt
½ tsp. ferrous sulfate or scant ½ tsp. stannous chloride (for scarlet)

Source: DYES FROM PLANTS. by Seonaid Robinson.

NATURAL DYES: PLANTS AND PROCESSES. by Jack Kramer. Charles Scribner's Sons, New York, 1972. 144 pages. illustrations, photographs (some color), suppliers list, bibliography, index. $9.95.

Jack Kramer has written a host of books on plants and gardening. In this one, he suggests various plants and trees for a "dyer's garden." For each plant he includes gardening instructions and, of course, recipes for dye-making.

Instructions for preparing the fiber and dyeing it are illustrated with large black-and-white photographs of each process. The plants are depicted in beautiful line drawings by Charles Hoeppner. But, best of all, there is a color chart composed of dyed woolstuffs colored by each recipe, and the variations produced by different mordants. This is a fine feature that makes the recipes and principles of natural dyeing much clearer.

Privet Leaves

Boil 2½ lbs. of privet leaves for 1 hour. Strain dye liquid into pot and add cool water to make a 4 to 4½ gallon solution. Let cool. Add premordanted yarn and bring solution to 200° F.; simmer for 1 hour. Let yarn cool in dye bath. Remove and rinse. Alum will yield yellow-green; chrome will yield chartreuse green.

Source: NATURAL DYES: PLANTS AND PROCESSES. by Jack Kramer.

A HISTORY OF DYED TEXTILES. by Stuart Robinson. The M.I.T. Press, Cambridge, Massachusetts, 1970. 112 pages. photographs (some color), bibliography, index. $10.00.

Spanning a period from ancient Egypt to modern times, this book offers a concise history of textile dyeing techniques, including the tie dye and batik methods. From the time of the Middle Ages, dyeing became a prosperous trade and the concern of the government. This resulted in a rapid rise of technical and social innovations, a development described here in considerable detail. Serious students of dyeing will be especially pleased by the outstanding and comprehensive appendixes of information for further research.

Silk dyeing. An illustration from Giovanni Ventura Rosetti's Plictho de l'Arte de Tentori, Venice, 1540. A work of great importance in the development of dyeing. From A History of Dyed Textiles *by Stuart Robinson.*

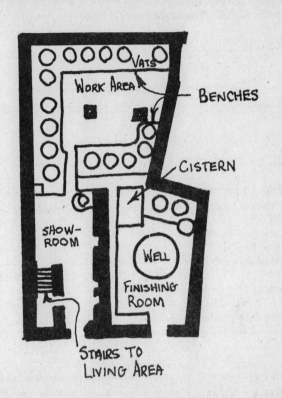

Plan of an Egyptian dyer's workshop belonging to the Roman period. It consists of three rooms. The actual work area contained sixteen vats lined with cement, and it let into a stone bench along three sides of the room. Most of these still showed signs of the blue-black of indigo and some were red when the workshop was discovered among the ruins of Athribis by Sir W. Flinders Petrie at the turn of this century. To the south is a rinsing room with a large, central well, a bench with a tiled wall, a deep cistern, and three vatlike pits. A very thick wall separates this room from what was probably a reception room for the customers, a necessary division due to foulness of the air in the other rooms caused by the large quantities of urine used in the dyeing process. From the showroom led a staircase to the living rooms and from there to a flat roof where the stuffs were probably dried.

Source: A HISTORY OF DYED TEXTILES. by Stuart Robinson.

Spinning and Dyeing: Magazine Articles and Pamphlets

H. Bigham, "Dyeing Yarn for Weaving," *School Arts*, Vol. 70 (February 1971).

K. Boydston, "Successful Experiment: Michigan Group Explores Natural Dyes," *Handweaver and Craftsman*, Vol. 14, No. 1 (Winter 1963).

George Cranch, "Unusual Colors From Experiments with Vegetable Dyes," *Handweaver and Craftsman*, Vol. 13, No. 3 (Fall, 1962).

S. Edelstein, "Historic Works on Dyeing," *Plants and Gardens*, Vol. 20 (Autumn 1964). Bibliography.

The Bureau of Indian Affairs, Publications Service, Haskell Indian Junior College, Lawrence, Kansas, offers a variety of pamphlets. Write to them for their current list and prices.

Spinning and Dyeing Suppliers

Albion Hills Farm School of Spinning, Dyeing, and Weaving
R.R. #3
Caledon East, Ontario, Canada
brochure.
spinning wheels.

Angora Diablo
805 La Gonda Way
Danville, Cal. 94526
catalog; samples $.25.
fleece.

Ankh Guild
7130 South Exchange Avenue
Chicago, Ill. 60649
brochure.
spinning wheels.

Anne G. Bjorklund
1900 North San Marcos Road
Santa Barbara, Cal. 93111
brochure; samples $.50 per card.
fleece, natural dye.

Arachne Webworks
2390 North West Thurman
Portland, Ore. 92710
brochure; yarn samples $.35.
unspun alpaca, flax, fleece, aniline, natural and Procion dye, mordants.

Ars Nova Craft Shop
P.O. Box 1388
Portland, Ore. 92707
brochure.
drop spindles, fleece, natural dye.

Ashford Handicrafts Ltd.
P.O. Box 12
Rakaia, Canterbury, New Zealand
brochure.
spinning wheel kits, spinning wheels, fleece.

Black Sheep Weaving and Craft Supply
318 South West Second Street
Corvallis, Ore. 97330
drop spindles, flax, fleece, natural dye, mordants, spinning wheels and kits.

Cambridge Wools Ltd.
Box 2572
Auckland, New Zealand
brochure.
fleece, spinning wheels.

Clara Creager
75 West College Avenue
Westerville, O. 43081
catalog.
spinning wheels.

Clemes and Clemes
665 San Pablo Avenue
Pinole, Cal.
brochure; samples $.50.
drop spindles, flax, fleece, spinning wheels.

Colonial Textiles
82 Plants Dam Road
East Lyme, Conn. 06333
samples $.25.
unspun cashmere and camel hair, flax, fleece, natural dye, spinning wheels.

Colonial Woolen Mills, Inc.
6501 Barberton Avenue
Cleveland, O. 49102
catalog; sample charge $.50.
spun and unspun angora and camel, drop spindles, mordants, spinning wheels and kits.

Craft Kaleidoscope
6412 Ferguson Avenue
Indianapolis, Ind. 46220
brochure.
natural dye, spinning wheels.

Creative Handweavers
P.O. Box 26480
Los Angeles, Cal. 90026
catalog; samples $2.00.
spun and unspun camel hair and wool, spun human hair.

Dharma Trading Company
1952 University Avenue
Berkeley, Cal. 94704
catalog; samples $.50.
spun and unspun camel hair and wool, fleece, cold water and natural dye, drop spindle, spinning wheels.

Earth Guild, Inc.
149 Putnam Avenue
Cambridge, Mass. 02139
brochure.
natural and Procion dye, mordants, drop spindles, spinning wheels.

Elizabeth Zimmerman Ltd.
Babcock, Wis. 54413
brochure.
unbleached and undyed wool.

Fab Dec
Box 3062
Lubbock, Tex. 79410
brochure.
Procion dye.

Fezandie and Sperrle, Inc.
103 Lafayette Street
New York, N.Y. 10013
brochure.
aniline dye.

Fibrec, Inc.
2815-18th Street
San Francisco, Cal. 94110
catalog.
cold water dye, mordants.

Gallagher Spinning and Weaving Tools
318 Pacheco Avenue
Santa Cruz, Cal. 95060
catalog.
drop spindles.

G. H. Watson
15 Birdwood Road
Lowe Hutt, New Zealand
catalog.
fleece.

Glen Black
1414 Grant Avenue
San Francisco, Cal. 94133
brochure.
aniline, Procion dye, mordants.

Golden Gate Herb Research, Inc.
P.O. Box 77212
San Francisco, Cal. 94116
catalog.
natural dye.

Good Karma Looms
440 West 4th
Chadron, Neb. 69337
catalog.
spinning wheels.

Greentree Ranch Wools-Countryside
   Handweavers
163 North Carter Lake Road
Loveland, Colo. 80537
brochure; samples.
drop spindles, fleece, spinning wheels.

Haldane and Company
Gateside, Strathmiglo
Fife, Scotland, Ky 14 7ST
brochure.
spinning wheels.

Haltec Corporation
32123 Winona Road
Winona, O. 44493
catalog.
spinning wheel kits.

Handcraft Wools
Box 378
Streetsville, Ontario, Canada
catalog; samples $.50 to $3.00.
unspun camel and cashmere, flax, fleece,
   aniline dye, drop spindles.

The Handweaver
111 East Napa Street
Sonoma, Cal. 95476
catalog; samples $.50.
flax, fleece cold water and natural dye,
   mordants, spinning wheels.

Harold Kattau
415 Riley Avenue
Indianapolis, Ind. 46201
catalog.
spinning wheels.

Harrisville Designs, Inc.
P.O. Box 51
Harrisville, N.H. 03450
catalog $.25.
spun and unspun alpaca and camel hair,
   unspun cashmere.

The Heddlecraft
713 Grant Street
Denver, Colo. 80203
brochure.
spinning wheels.

Jean Malsada, Inc.
P.O. Box 767
Roswell, Ga. 30075
catalog.
unspun horsehair, Procion dye, drop spindle, fleece, spinning wheels and kits.

Jones Sheep Farm
R 2, Box 185
Peabody, Kan. 66866
brochure; samples $1.00.
fleece.

Keystone Aniline and Chemical Company
321 North Loomis Street
Chicago, Ill. 60607
catalog.
aniline and Procion dye.

K M Yarn Company
18695 Wyoming Avenue
Detroit, Mich. 48221
catalog.
undyed and unbleached wool.

Lamb's End
165 West, 9 Mile
Ferndale, Mich. 48220
brochure; samples $1.00 to $1.50.
unspun angora, alpaca and cashmere,
   fleece mordants, drop spindle, spinning
   wheels.

Lenos Handcrafts
2037 Walnut Street
Philadelphia, Pa. 19103
brochure.
spinning wheels, drop spindles, natural
   dye, fleece.

Lewis Looms
Pigeon Cove Weave Shop
12 Landmark Lane
Rockport, Mass. 01966
newsletter.
drop spindle.

Looms and Lessons
Ruth Nordquist Myers
6014 Osage Avenue
Downers Grove, Ill. 60515
brochure.
natural dye, drop spindles, spinning
   wheels.

The Makings
2001 University Avenue
Berkeley, Cal. 94704
catalog.
unspun alpaca, cotton, camel, drop spindle, spinning wheels.

Mary Anne Mauro
19 Hewitt Drive
Northport, N.Y. 11768
brochure.
fleece.

Mary Hixon
Box 356
St. Johnsbury, Vt. 05819
brochure.
drop spindle.

Nilus Leclerc, Inc.
P.O. Box 69
L'Islet, Quebec, Canada GOR 2 CO
Also Leclerc Corporation
Box 491
Plattsburg, N.Y. 12901
catalog.
spinning wheels.

The Ohio Wool Growers Association
3400 Groves Road
P.O. Box 27068
Columbus, O. 43227
newsletter.
fleece.

Owl and Olive Weavers
4232 Old Leeds Lane
Birmingham, Ala. 35213
samples $1.50; deducted from orders of
   $10.00 and over.
goat hair, mordants, fleece, drop spindles,
   spinning wheels.

Oy Varpa-Looms Ltd.
Osmonite (St.)
Myllykoski 5, Finland 46800
catalog.
spinning wheels.

Penguin Quill
Sunshine Canyon, 1
Boulder, Colo. 80302
brochure.
spinning wheels.

Rupert, Gibron and Spider
470 Maylin Street
Pasadena, Cal. 91105
catalog; color chart $1.00.
Procion dye.

Schacht Spindle Company
1708 Walnut Street
Boulder, Colo. 80302
brochure.
drop spindles.

School Products Company, Inc.
312 East 23 Street
New York, N.Y. 10010
catalog.
cold water dye, spinning wheels, drop
 spindles, fleece.

The Sheep Village
2005 Bridgeway
Sausalito, Cal. 94965
samples: yarn $.25, spinning $.25.
unspun camel, cotton and cashmere, natural dye, mordants, fleece.

Spincraft
P.O. Box 332
Richardson, Tex. 75080
catalog.
spinning wheels.

The Spinster
34 Hamilton Avenue
Sloatsburg, N.Y. 10974
catalog.
unspun angora, cashmere, camel, cotton,
 mordants, natural dye, spinning wheels.

Straw Into Gold
4440 College Avenue
Oakland, Cal. 94618
catalog, send stamped, self-addressed envelope; fiber samples $1.00.
unspun alpaca, angora, cashmere, cotton,
 camel, mordants, natural dye, Procion
 dye, drop spindles.

Textile Crafts
856 North Genesee Avenue
P.O. Box 3216
Los Angeles, Cal. 90028
catalog.
drop spindles.

Tromp 'n Treadle
41901 Woodbrook Drive
Wayne, Mich. 48184
brochure; sample card $1.00.
spinning wheels.

Valley Handweaving Supply
200 West Olive Avenue
Fresno, Cal. 93728
brochure; samples $.50.
unspun alpaca, fleece, drop spindle,
 spinning wheels.

Warp, Woof and Potpourri
514 North Lake Avenue
Pasadena, Cal. 91101
catalog; samples $.50.
fleece, mohair, cold water dye, spinning
 wheels.

The Weaver's Corner Studios
P.O. Box 560125
Miami, Fla. 33156
catalog; samples $.50.
unspun cotton, mordants, fleece.

The Weaver's Place
12490 Black Forest Road
Colorado Springs, Colo. 80908
samples $.50 to $1.00.
fleece.

William and Victoria Ralph
Village of Orwell
RD #1
Rome, Pa. 18837
catalog.
spinning wheels, fleece.

William Condon & Sons Ltd.
P.O. Box 129
Charlottetown, Prince Edward Island,
Canada
catalog.
fleece, undyed and unbleached wool.

Wool In Works
126 Orange Avenue
Suffern, N.Y. 10901
$1.00 for catalog of yarns and fibers.
fleece, mohair.

Yellow Springs Strings
P.O. Box 107
68 Goes Station
Yellow Springs, O. 45387
catalog.
cold water dye, mordants, spinning
 wheels.

Textile Design and Construction

**THE TEXTILE ARTS: A HANDBOOK OF FABRIC STRUC-
TURE AND DESIGN PROCESSES. by Verla Birrell. Harper and Row, Publishers, 1959. illustrations, photographs (some color), index. $14.00.**

**THE TEXTILE ARTS: A HANDBOOK OF WEAVING,
BRAIDING, PRINTING, AND OTHER TEXTILE TECH-
NIQUES. by Verla Birrell. Schocken Books, New York,
1973. illustrations, photographs (some color), index.
paperback edition $7.95.**

These cover all phases of fabric formation and decoration, with particular emphasis on textile hand arts and
skills. The author traces the history of important textiles
tools and processes from simple forms of the ancient beginnings to the machinery of the industrial era. She provides clear and complete instructions for each of the
various textile processes and lists all tools and materials
needed. There is also information on macrame, tatting, and
knitting.

AMERICAN FABRIC ENCYCLOPEDIA OF TEXTILES: AN ILLUSTRATED AND AUTHORITATIVE SOURCE BOOK ON TEXTILES PRESENTING A COMPREHENSIVE AND PRACTICAL COVERAGE OF THE ENTIRE FIELD. by the editors of American Fabric Magazine. Doric, 1960. distributed by Prentice-Hall. 702 pages. illustrations, photographs (some color). $39.50.

One of the major objectives of the editors of this volume has been to describe and interpret the revolutionary impact of man-made fibers and the modern finishing process on the field of textiles and to "understand them from the perspective of world textile history."

The largest section, "The Textile Fibers," is a tripartite exposition on the origin and history of man-made and natural fibers, their chief characteristics and uses, manufacturing processes, and directions for their care. It features a glossary of man-made fibers, a cotton glossary, a lexicon of wool terms and of silk fabrics, microphotographs of the structure of man-made fibers, and illustrations of wools and worsteds.

The historical information is treated as a chronology of textiles from prehistoric to modern times. It includes events up to 1950, and the developments in fibers and textiles from 1950 to 1960 are cross-referenced to the special sections dealing more specifically with them. Also presented is a section on "Inventors and their Inventions," and the "Origins of Fabric Names."

The second major division, "Textile Design," is also broken down into three parts: "Masterpieces of Textile Design," consisting of forty-eight pages of black-and-white reproductions showing historical textiles; "Textiles Across the Centuries," sixteen pages of color plates; and a list of museums of special interest to textile designers.

A brief history of textiles in the United States and Peru is the concern of the section entitled "Textiles in America."

The final division, "Dictionary of Textile Terms," includes over three thousand textile terms and includes the generic names and the definitions of manufactured fibers as they were established by the Textile Fiber Products Identification Act of 1960.

About half the book is devoted to textile fibers and the manufacturing and finishing processes. These subjects are treated in a popular and nontechnical manner and are illuminated by many black-and-white illustrations and a clear, direct style of writing.

This is a book of such large scope, the aim of which has been to "provide in one comprehensive volume a much-needed source of inspiration and up-to-date fact," that it must necessarily be little more than a condensation of the most vital information on the subject. However, the editors do cover their subject in detail sufficient to enable the reader to understand the great changes textiles have undergone recently, and thus they accomplish what no other publication has been able to do in quite the same way. Unlike *Manmade Textile Encyclopedia* (edited by J. J. Priss, New York Textile Book Publishers, 1955) which is quite technical and concerned only with man-made fibers, the *American Fabrics Encyclopedia* is easily understood,

well, illustrated and comprehensive, and though it is designed for practitioners in the field of textiles, it can be useful to the layman as well.

ART AND DESIGN IN TEXTILES. by Michael Ward. Van Nostrand Reinhold, New York, 1973. 112 pages. illustrations, photographs (some color), bibliography, index. $8.95.

Textile design falls into a limbo somewhere between art and technology, a difficult spot to be in considering the gap usually believed to separate these two.

Design is not just a facile skill for drawing curves and painting pretty colors. It involves an understanding of the never-changing factors important to the subject and of the ever-changing emphasis imposed by the economic considerations of any particular time.

The student designer faces many difficulties in reconciling the seemingly opposing considerations of his profession, due to his training in the disciplines and attitudes of art, while confronted with a world in which technological factors seem to rule the day.

In order to help a newcomer solve the problems of this profession, Michael Ward begins by describing the various stages and processes involved in the production of textiles. He supplies a concise glossary of all terms used to help the uninitiated acclimate themselves. Afterward, he turns to a consideration of the building up and organization of pattern, and demonstrates how closely pattern is linked to textile structures. He offers useful suggestions for pattern order, color, surface, and finish.

All in all, the author sets some hard facts before the beginning textile professional, but he also offers some consolation and reinforcement. Although the textile designer must remember that he does not design for himself, the rewards of the profession are still many. It is easy for many people to be creative on their own terms, but only a few can achieve the satisfaction of successfully creating when the limitations are severe.

BEYOND CRAFT: THE ART FABRIC: by Mildred Constantine and Jack L. Larsen. Van Nostrand Reinhold, New York, 1973. 294 pages. photographs (some color), bibliography. $35.00.

This is a beautiful collection of the works of international artists creating with fibers and thereby producing art fabric, constructions that may be woven on the loom, off the loom, knotted, knitted, crocheted, or made with any other technique.

Today's artist who works with natural fibers or synthetic yarns uses his materials to produce works possessing form and space, with surface and mass interchangeable. His work clearly expresses the pure design qualities inherent in his technique, structure, processes, and materials as well as his experience and inspiration.

The authors trace the germs of the movements which have contributed to the diversity of the fabric field today, noting as the turning point the London Crystal Palace

Great International Exhibition of 1851, which incited the arts and crafts movement in England to call for an overthrow of the machine and a return to hand quality and simplicity. They also place great emphasis on the Bauhaus with its preoccupation with formalized geometry and research into materials and textiles leading toward an industrial aesthetic that overshadowed any concept of fabric design without function until 1960.

CREATIVE TEXTILE DESIGN: THREAD AND FABRIC. by Rolf Hartung. Van Nostrand Reinhold, New York, 1964. 144 pages. photographs (some color). $5.95. paperback edition $3.95.

This book has sparse text, but a playful and interesting attitude. It encourages adults young and old to experiment with knots, ropes, and fabric collage.

Interview

A talk with Sandy Lowe, the owner-director of Threadbare Unlimited, 20 Cornelia Street, New York, N.Y. Threadbare carries supplies for all kinds of fiber crafts and offers lessons in weaving, spinning and dyeing, basketmaking, embroidery, crochet, knitting, macrame, and needlepoint.

I was a weaver. I learned in California, lived in California, and I came back to New York and there was nothing here. I had to send away for yarns and stuff and I said, "You know what this town needs? A good weaving shop"; and it wasn't two months after I said that when someone handed me five thousand dollars and said go ahead.

When I got the money I didn't know where to start—it was just an idea. I sat down and took an old *Handweaver and Craftsman* and an old *Shuttle, Spindle and Dye Pot*, and I just wrote everybody. I started building up contacts and I went to see as many people as I could. I've done very little advertising. My business is tremendous word of mouth. I'm going to start advertising now because I need more volume. Right now I need to expand, but it will never get beyond me because it's part of me, as you can see; it looks lived in, it is lived in.

We're in the process of expanding the school and the school will be, you know, a legitimate school because there is a need for it. But I won't have more than six people in a class because there is a need to really learn. For every one of our courses there will be a children's component course. Maggie Ramsey started taking teachers from the shop into the prisons and is teaching there now. We want to expand that into the hospitals. We want to teach faculty to teach children and we also want to design on a consultant basis.

The prison teaching is paid for by a thing called Hospital Audiences, but it's just the teacher's salary and materials and it's not a grant. We will be going for children so that we'll start out without grants but the fees will be fairly high since the classes are so small and we want to get people who can't afford it, so we'll go for grants.

SANDY ON SEXISM IN CRAFTS

About thirty percent of our clients are men. They're mostly in weaving, but a lot do take knitting, crochet, and a lot of them do needlepoint, but I mean really expressive needlepoint. Some of them do rugs. I have one man now who's making himself a coat. Most of the men who do it

are professionals—doctors, lawyers, publishers, people I guess who've achieved a certain amount of success and don't think of themselves as pansies—do you know what I mean? They're not threatened by it. Even a lot of black men are beginning to get into crochet and I can dig that. It's opening up, it's happening.

SANDY ON LOOMS

We sell looms, we don't stock them because we don't have space. We're the only people who sell the Herald loom. It is a beautifully made loom. The beams on it will never warp because of the construction. It's a pretty object, it's just a fine design, a good tool. Immediately behind it is the Harrisville, designed by John Colony and some other people up at Harrisville. His family owned the town mill, and when the milling business got to be extinct, the town was dying. He's a marvelous person and he wanted to employ all these people so he developed this loom which comes in a kit. It's a hundred and twenty-eight dollars—it'll probably go up but it's 22 inches, it's a wonderful loom. It folds to 10 inches, it's an excellent beginner's loom. You can put it together in about two hours, you can keep it in a closet, and it's a real beginner's tool and you'll never find a loom in its class at that price.

Now Leclerc is what we call a fine old name. They've been in business so long that everybody has heard of them. They are very production oriented. Now look at the difference. You see that Leclerc loom? That is about a two-seventy, two-eighty, maybe even a three-hundred-twenty-dollar loom, I don't remember. Now, look at the treadles on the Herald loom. You see how much wider they are? That means something to a weaver. I mean it really facilitates it. Little subtleties in a good tool. The treadles on the Leclerc are very skinny and they're always popping out of this thing. I mean there's no necessity for this. This loom is not a low-priced loom. Their bigger model, their sturdy model is better.

SANDY ON THE CRAFT EXPLOSION

First of all, I think the economy has something to do with it and it's a cyclical thing. The economy has a lot to do with it in that if you've noticed in every period in which there has been a recession or a depression, fashions have gotten fuller and crafts have gone up. Then there's another situation. This is the offshoot of the hippie movement—alternative life-styles, self-sufficiency—but people stuck with it because even if their life-styles change, there is something very essential about it.

SANDY ON LEARNING TO WEAVE

Very few people can learn to weave from a book. It's very hard and a waste of money to try. You have wasted that much in time and materials. People can learn only certain kinds of weaving from a book.

Weaving is not that complicated. Even at its most complicated it's not that hard because it's mathematically reducible. It's very logical.

Another reason why I opened up this business is there was a tremendous snobbery among weaving stores in California. If you walked in and you didn't know exactly what you wanted and how much you needed for the warp, there was no one to ask; you felt intimidated because they looked at you as if, well, what are you doing weaving? It's the same kind of bias that says weaving is something mystical and the gifted can do it and the ungifted can't. It's just not true.

Emma's writing a book [Emma Levine, Threadbare's weaving teacher] and the first line in that book is "any idiot can weave," which is true. There are other things to weaving besides weaving, but any idiot can weave. Since man's been wearing fiber he's been weaving on a loom, so it can't be that difficult. However, on a four-harness loom the problem is multiplied because how do you get all the threads the same length? How do you get it warped? And warping is the basis of everything. If you have a good warp, you have a good fabric; if you have a lousy warp, the fabric is no good. That's the process, and books do show you, *The Joy of Weaving* shows you, but they're just words, there are too many steps to absorb it from a book.

I've met maybe three or four people who said they taught themselves weaving from a book and four years later came with what they considered their first piece, and why anybody would want to go through that is beyond me, it's just too available, even in New York. The quickest way to frustration is to handle two hundred threads and get them all wound around each other and not know what to do about it. Tapestry weaving is readily accessible to a person who has a good book. There is an excellent book called *Working with the Wool* (by Noel Bennett and Tiana Big Horse. Northland Press, Flagstaff, Arizona, 1971. illustrations. paperback edition $4.95), that is Navajo weaving, but as a book on elementary tapestry weaving it's excellent.

SANDY ON ART VERSUS CRAFT

I know from a historical point of view there is a problem. Since women are very into what Emma calls loving hands at home, and only after two centuries does it become a piece that somebody will pay two hundred dollars for—you know, a quilt, primitive art, whatever you want to call it—there is a tremendous defensiveness about it and so many people ask, "Why am I not recognized? Why when it takes so much longer to do a weaving than it does to do a painting, and the elements of design are inherent in both things, why can I only get fifty dollars for my weaving and you get two thousands dollars for your painting? Why isn't it on the level of art?"

SANDY ON CRAFT AS ART

I think weaving as an art form is valid, but that's with a reservation. I like function in design, and it is not enough to soothe the eye. I believe in art, even paintings, as having a function. I believe things reach their highest point when they function well and they are beautiful, and that to me is the happy blend. I went to the Rhinebeck fair and I went to the Ithaca fair and I saw very little weaving that was any good. It was competent, but the craft was not carried through. The craftsman was incomplete. If you make a piece of fabric and it's going to have a function, not only has the piece of fabric got to be good, but the dress has got to be a dress and the same elements of art and design have to go into making that dress. . . . "The weave is the thing" and anything else means nothing? Well that can't be, that just can't be.

What makes a good pot? It's something that turns you on and functions as a good pot. A teapot has got to function as a teapot. If it burns your hand every time you pick it up, no matter how beautiful it is you're not going to use it, and that's a flaw in its character.

SANDY ON BUSINESS

When I entered business I wanted to see if I could enter business and really be ethical, keep all my principles. Maybe that's why I'm not a millionaire.

I feel that when something is good, it's worth paying for, and if it is good it practically sells itself. I don't mind saying, "Look, I don't think you should get this, I think you should get that," and I don't mind sending somebody up to Coulter Studios to get the Varpa. Now those looms are six hundred and seven hundred dollars, and that commission goes to them not to me, but the fact is I want them to have a good tool and not something that's going to wear out or be used for something it shouldn't. I just handle people the way I would handle myself. It's not that hard. My customers are very loyal, very loyal, really. I have an excellent reputation and you can't buy that.

Magazines: Textiles

Textile Book Service
266 Lake Avenue, P.O. Box 178
Metuchen, N.J. 08840
   Titles pertaining to textile construction, design, and trade.

Textile Crafts
Box 3216
Los Angeles, Cal. 90028
Quarterly. $5.00 per year.

Textile Museum Journal
Published by the Textile Museum
2320 "S" Street North West
Washington, D.C. 20068
Annual. $3.00 subscription.
   Interesting articles on various textile arts, design, symbolism, history, and technique. Illustrations.

Textile Equipment and Supplies Directory
Laura Glazier and Stephen Thurston
Textile Department, School of American Craftsmen
1 Lomb Memorial Drive
Rochester, N.Y. 14623
   Annual publication listing most of the sources of materials available for use by the serious-minded student or professional craftsman of hand weaving and textile design.
   Materials are briefly described, though they are not evaluated. Wherever possible, prices of sample cards are indicated.

DESIGNING WITH THREAD: FROM FIBRE TO FABRIC. by Irene Waller. The Viking Press, New York, 1973. 183 pages. illustrations, photographs (some color), bibliography, index. $14.95.

This book is more inspirational than instructional. It begins with the origin of design concepts and ways of choosing working methods and materials to achieve desired results. After some reflections on the basics of workroom layout and equipment, the author goes on to survey the various methods of fiber constructions, such as winding, wrapping, twisting, knotting, and weaving. Each technique is examined in terms of its own particular qualities, as well as its practical, economical, and aesthetic advantages when compared to other techniques.

A particularly interesting feature is the discussion of machine knitting. Machine knitting has a terminology and notation all its own. A loop pulled toward the knitter is called a face loop, a loop pulled through away from the knitter is called a back loop. A horizontal row of loops is called a course, a vertical row is called a wall. Plain fabric is composed of nothing but face loops, the front being the technical face and the reverse the technical back. Alternation of front and back loops in vertical walls is known as 1x1 rib. A 1x1 purl is a fabric composed of alternate courses of face and back loops. Notation is by symbols, but these may differ according to type of equipment, fabric, or region. In most general notation systems, a stitch is represented in position on graph paper with x standing for the face loop and *o* the back loop. Additional symbols indicate such things as missed or tucked stitches.

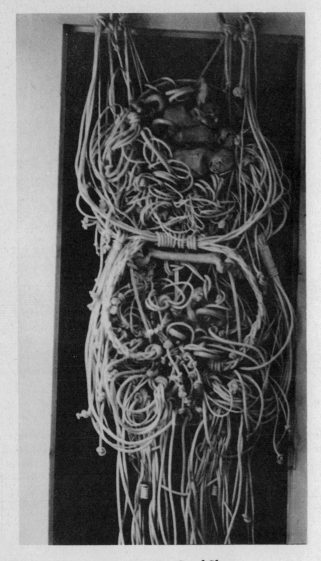

Rope and ceramic construction, Carol Sloane

A tapestry is a thing alive, for it has body and spirit; it breathes and so exudes warmth; it grows with color and responds with verve to every change of light or of human contact. It embraces by its amplitude all things within its reach, drawing them graciously under the spell of its dominance. It is the link between buildings and their contents, the harmonizing back-drop against which man more dramatically inhabits the stage of his environment.

Source: AMERICAN TAPESTRIES. introduction by Mildred Constantine. critical notes by Irma B. Jaffe. Charles E. Slatkin Inc., Galleries, 115 East 92 Street, New York, 1968.

TAPESTRY: CRAFT AND ART. by Maurice Pianzola and Julien Ciffinet. Abner Schram, New York, 1972. 127 pages. photographs (some color), bibliography. $9.95.

The first section of this book consists of a brief discussion of the differences between high- and low-warp tapestry, accompanied by photographs of weavers in Gobelins and Savannerie ateliers performing the various procedures. The second section presents a history of tapestry-making enhanced by black-and-white photographs and beautiful color plates. The historical information is not detailed or specific, but of a rather general and appreciative nature covering the earliest tapestries up through the middle of the twentieth century. The discussion is summed up by a useful chart showing the parallel developments in tapestry arts and historical events from 1580 B.C. in Egypt and ending in 1962 with the First Tapestry Biennial at Lausanne, paralleled by the continuing evolution of Western art toward abstractionism and new realism, and the Cuban Missile Crisis.

TECHNIQUES OF RYA KNOTTING. by Donald J. Willcox. Van Nostrand Reinhold, New York, 1971. 136 pages. photographs (some color), suppliers list, bibliography. $8.95.

Rya is a knotting technique that creates a pile which looks very much like fur. Most people are familiar with rya knotting as a technique used in rug-making, but it has countless other, often overlooked, applications for clothing decoration and interior design. The author is apparently attempting to open the reader up to the other-than-rug potentials of rya by presenting a photo gallery of rya-decorated clothing. Many of these are very beautiful, like the hand-woven rya maxi-coat; others, like the rya knotted jockey shorts, are simply ludicrous.

The author presents a very brief introduction to the techniques of knotting itself, which ordinarily are not difficult, but manage to become very confused in his presentation.

SPRANG: THREAD TWISTING, A CREATIVE TEXTILE TECHNIQUE. by Hella Skowronski and Mary Reddy. Von Nostrand Reinhold, New York, 1974. 100 pages. illustrations, photographs (some color), bibliography, index. $8.95.

Sprang, or Egyptian plaitwork, is a very ancient art. Fragments of what appear to be caps, stockings, and hairnets executed in sprang sometime between 1500–1100 B.C. have been found in Danish and Norwegian peat bogs. The name "sprang" comes from an ancient Swedish word and the name Egyptian plaiting is the term used to identify the lacy woolen pieces of sprang-like material found in Coptic graves of the 4–5 centuries B.C.

Basically, sprang is a network of threads twisted over each other to form a type of net or mesh. The threads are first placed on a loom and then rows of twists are made from the bottom up. The unique property of sprang is that operations performed at the bottom of the frame are automatically performed at the top. As the work progresses the two halves meet in the middle where they must be fastened.

Sprang is experiencing a rebirth of interest, and new techniques are continually being uncovered. Two such new techniques are that of applying a continuous warp on the frame and spranging in sections. A continuous warp does away with the previous limitations of size according to the size of the frame, and spranging in sections enables the craftsman to work on a number of different designs simultaneously. These two methods can be combined to form large hangings, ponchos, table runners, and other such items. The authors explain just how this is done through how-to instructions and clear diagrams. A glossary at the end of the book allows for quick reference to forgotten terms.

Magazine Articles: Sprang

Peter Collingwood, "A Sampler in Sprang," *Threads in Action*, Vol. 2, No. 2 (Winter 1972).

Peter Collingwood, "Sprang, Revival of an Ancient Technique," *Handweaver and Craftsman*, Vol. 15, No. 2 (Spring 1964).

Jeanette Luno, "Sprang," *Threads in Action*, Vol. 2, No. 1 (Fall 1970).

OFF THE LOOM: CREATING WITH FIBRE. by Shirley Marein. The Viking Press, New York, 1972. 96 pages. illustrations, photographs (some color). $8.95.

The author, an experienced teacher and noted craftsman, selects those techniques which quickly build a wide range of skills and supply a diversity of surfaces and structure. The directions and diagrams are explicit and easy to follow, and provide information on braiding, finger weaving, sprang, twining, warp wrapping, crochet, and macrame. The author also delves into rug and tapestry techniques and methods.

There is a special chapter on the dyeing process with alternatives provided for city craftsmen who do not have a great deal of natural vegetation with which they can work. Those who find themselves in such a predicament would do well to follow the author's advice to "try everything." The most unlikely candidates heading for the trash can be turned into a source for natural dyes. Onion skins, for example, will yield a shade of allium cepa (burnt orange).

To dye a pound of wool, you would need a pound of dry outer onion skins. Place them in a copper pot and soak in softened water. Then strain the liquid, return it to the pot, and add to it wetted wool treated with alum mordant. Simmer for thirty minutes and then remove the wool, rinse, and dry. To make the color fast, repeat the process several times, rinsing and drying between each dip. By using different mordants, a variety of tints and tones can be obtained.

NEEDLE LACE AND NEEDLE WEAVING. by Jill Nordfors. Van Nostrand Reinhold, New York, 1974. 159 pages. illustrations, photographs (some color), bibliography, index. $9.95.

Needle lace is a type of lace-like embroidery in which every stitch does not go into the background fabric, but is attached only at the edges or to an outline or border. The stitches are useful for filling in any shaped space and may be worked on a background or suspended airily on an open warp.

Needleweaving is similar in construction to some forms of traditional drawn thread. It involves a warp which is stitched onto a background or wrapped around a supporting frame. A filling is woven into the warp using simple over and under darning and needle lace stitches.

Needle lace and needle weaving work well together and can be easily combined to create all kinds of decorative effects.

Jill Nordfors covers basic materials, preparation of the background for stitching, collecting and attaching found objects, as well as the stitches themselves which are presented categorically as looped-filling stitches, insertion stitches, woven-filling stitches, borders and interlacing stitches, bars, and stitches done on planned, random, and detached warps. The instructions are clear and to the point, supported by many clear line drawings and photographs. This excellent book is further enhanced by the numerous black-and-white and color plates of historical and contemporary needle lace and needle weaving examples.

TIAHUANACO TEXTILE DESIGN. by Alan R. Sawyer. Museum of Primitive Art, Studies Number 3, 1963. distributed by New York Graphic Society. 13 pages. illustrations, photographs. $1.75. Also published in the *Textile Museum Journal*, Volume 1, number 2, December 1963.

Profile, feline (puma?) heads facing each other along a central axis suggests a human frontal face.

This is a scholarly exploration and discussion of the ancient Peruvian textile motifs of the Tiahuanaco empire (700 to 1200 A.D.), which are outstanding for their consistently high standard of craftsmanship, abstract and powerful design, and striking color harmonies.

COPTIC WEAVES. by Margaret Seagroatt. Exhibition catalog on the Coptic textile collection in the City of Liverpool Museums, distributed through Unicorn, Craft and Hobby Book Service, Box 645, Rockville, Maryland, 1965. 160 pages. illustrations, photographs, bibliography. $2.50.

The Copts were the earliest Egyptian converts to Christianity. They were brutally oppressed as a minority under the Greeks, Romans, and even Christian conquerors, and were frequently forced to flee into the desert where they formed exclusive communities which often became textile centers. The isolated nature of these communities caused their culture to become more individuated and textiles of specifically Coptic character began to appear.

Almost all extant Coptic textiles were found in graves in Upper Egypt in the late 19th and early 20th centuries. Dating is difficult and inaccurate owing to the fact that styles overlapped, however, certain major periods and tendencies are identifiable.

The motifs used in Coptic weaving reflect the influence of the Copts' various conquerors and were executed in tapestry techniques still employed today.

THE TEXTILE TOOLS OF COLONIAL HOMES, FROM RAW MATERIALS TO FINISHED GARMENTS, BEFORE MASS PRODUCTION IN THE FACTORIES. by Marion L. Channing. Channing Books, 1971. 64 pages. illustrations, index. paperback edition $2.00.

This book offers descriptions and pictures of tools, machines, and equipment which were used in the colonial home textile industry. Many of these tools are the result of the users' inventiveness, and the specific functions of some of the odder gadgets is still unknown. Most tools differ in design and name according to the section of the country in which they are found. In addition, blueprints were not available in rural areas, and a man generally went home and tried to copy something he had seen in a neighbor's house, sometimes altering it slightly in the process.

Current price and ordering information for this book can be obtained by writing to the author at 35 Main Street, Marion, Massachusetts.

SYMMOGRAPHY: THREE DIMENSIONAL CREATIVE DESIGNS WITH YARN WITHOUT KNOTTING OR KNITTING. by Lois Kreischer. Crown Publishers, New York, 1971. 62 pages. illustrations, photographs (some color), index. $4.95.

The word symmography is derived from "symmetry" and the suffix "graphy." These are combined to describe a linear representation which uses proportion, balance, and harmony to create the proper relationship between rays of yarn.

Symmography requires primarily simple and inexpensive tools and materials. The only indispensibles are nails, a hammer, a piece of wood, and yarn, although the creation of a truly "finished" work would require a few nice to have items, such as sandpaper, woodstain, and so on.

The actual symmographic process is accomplished by placing nails in the piece of wood in an already established pattern, and then connecting them with different weaves. The author instructs new symmographers in all the fine points of this craft, beginning with the creation of simple circles and progressing to butterflies, flowers, free forms, abstracts, and so on. She also provides information on mounting, finishing, and framing completed designs.

TEXTILE CONSERVATION. edited by J. E. Leene. Smithsonian Institution Press, Washington, D.C., 1972. distributed by George Braziller. 275 pages. illustrations, photographs (some color), index. $15.00.

Twenty leading authorities from Europe and America contributed chapters to this book, which, though aimed at restorers of textiles, curators, and scientists working in museum laboratories, is of interest to craftsmen and textile artists for the basic information it provides on the characteristics of textiles and dyes and principles of cleaning and repair.

Tools

THE MAKING OF TOOLS. by Alexander G. Weygers. Van Nostrand Reinhold, New York, 1973. 93 pages. illustrations, photographs. paperback edition $3.95.

This book offers lessons for the artist and craftsman on how to make your own tools, and how to design, sharpen, and temper them. Using mostly scrap steel and simple equipment, one learns how to make the simplest tools, gradually progressing to more difficult ones.

The simple tools presented include: a screwdriver, cold chisels, center punch, chasing tools, and some stone carving tools. More advanced tools include: hammers, tin snips, pliers, wire and nail cutters, and sculptor's wood-carving gouges.

The instructions for making the tools are clear and well illustrated with drawings and diagrams. General techniques are discussed along with the specific construction methods so that many variations on each type of tool can be performed.

COMPLETE BOOK OF POWER TOOLS, BOTH STATIONARY AND PORTABLE. by R. J. DeCristoforo. Popular Science Publishing Company, New York, 1972. 434 pages. illustrations, photographs, index. $9.95.

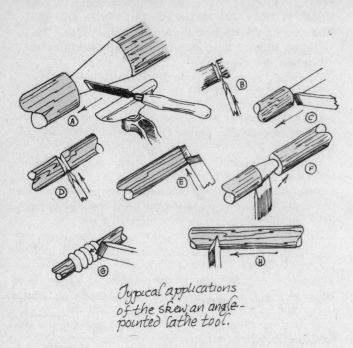

Typical applications of the skew an angle-pointed lathe tool.

This is an excellent book, including extensive chapters on table saws, radial arm saws, jig saws and band saws, drill presses, lathes, jointers, shaper, belt and disk sanders, and bench grinders. There is also information on portable tools such as circular saws, saber saws, drills, routers, polishers, hand grinders, and flexible shafts. A thorough discussion of techniques, jigs, and fixtures, as well as safety precautions and unusual uses for each of the tools, makes this book a very valuable addition to any craftsman's workshop.

HOW TO USE HAND AND POWER TOOLS. by George Daniels. Popular Science Publishing Company, New York, 1968. 160 pages. illustrations, photographs, index. $3.95.

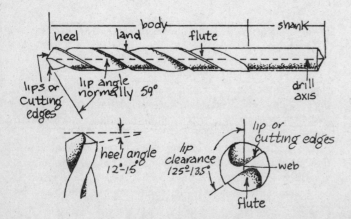

This is a practical book on the selection and use of the most important hand and power tools. The illustrated text describes the purpose of each tool and what it can and cannot accomplish. There are clear instructions for the correct and safe use of the tools, especially in the sections on hand tools. In addition, the advice is quite good regarding the use of glue, clamps, and abrasives, and how to select the correct hinges, brackets, wall fastenings, and so on.

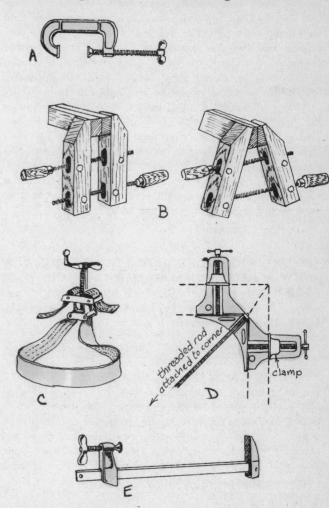

A   *C-clamp. Use scrap of wood under jaws.*

B   *Hand clamps may be adjusted to hold angular surfaces. They will not scratch work.*

C   *Canvas strap is used to hold irregular shapes snugly.*

D   *Corner clamps with threaded rod are used to hold opposite sides of mitred work.*

E   *Bar clamp can accommodate large objects to be glued.*

HOME AND WORKSHOP GUIDE TO SHARPENING. by Harry Walton. Popular Science Publishing Company, New York, 1967. 160 pages. illustrations, photographs, index. $3.95. paperback edition $2.50.

A SHORT HISTORY OF MACHINE TOOLS. by L. T. C. Rolt. The M.I.T. Press, Cambridge, Massachusetts, 1967. 256 pages. illustrations, photographs, bibliography, index. $7.50.

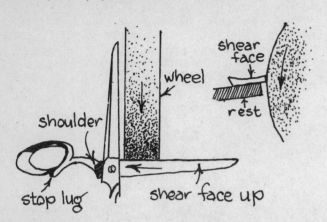

Ornamental turning lathe with template, after Jacques Besson, 1578

The importance of proper edge angles, the uses of honing, hollow grinding, and all the basic sharpening tools employed—from simple hand stones to deluxe grinder hones—are described and explained in this book. There are precise illustrated instructions for putting the best cutting edge on yard and garden tools, common household tools, hand and power saws, and woodworking tools. Sharp tools give good results.

This book is concerned primarily with the history of tools and technology. However, there is a very interesting section on craftsmen's tools. The text is accompanied by lots of old woodcuts of tools, toolmakers, and craftsmen.

The Sjoberg workbench, obtainable from School Products for about $125. A really fine, well-made shop accessory

Straight-backed Egyptian saw, painting from the tomb of Rekhmara, c. 1480 B.C.

Weaving

NEW KEY TO WEAVING. by Mary Black. Macmillan, New York, 1961. illustrations. $12.00.

If you could own just one book on weaving, this should be that book. No other we know of covers such a vast amount of material as well. After providing guidance on choosing a loom, Ms. Black meticulously discusses the various methods of loom dressing and gives encyclopedic descriptions of all weaves possible on a hand loom. Her chapters cover plain weaves, loom controlled; plain weaves, finger controlled, such as knotted and lace techniques; twill and miscellaneous weaves on twill threading; overshot; crackle weave; summer and winter weaves; Bronson; one shuttle weaves, such as huck, Swedish lace, Ms and Os, waffle weave; tartan weaves; tapestry weaves; and others. The book ends with down-to-earth, helpful information on how to overcome the many little problems weavers must face, such as repairing broken warp threads, determining the correct sley for threads of unknown sizes, and so on. An entire chapter is devoted to the theory of weaving, so that the weaver will be able to develop new designs of his own or elaborate on traditional patterns.

ELEMENTS OF WEAVING. by Azalea Thorpe and Jack L. Larsen. Doubleday and Company, Garden City, New York, 1967. 257 pages. illustrations, photographs, index. $9.95.

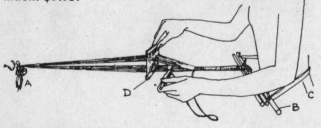

Parts of backstrap loom as set up:

A *Hitching point*

B *Cloth stick*

C *Back strap*

D *The rigid heddle*

This is probably the best book for beginners currently available. The section on setting up the loom is particularly good. No book, however, can take the place of actual experience, and the authors themselves stress this. They believe that weaving is learned by doing rather than reading, and so they suggest work projects as the best means of getting under way. They select simple equipment and equally simple projects in order to enable the individual with no previous weaving experience and with little or no

equipment to master the techniques of the craft with relative ease and with minimum expense. They also offer practical purchasing suggestions.

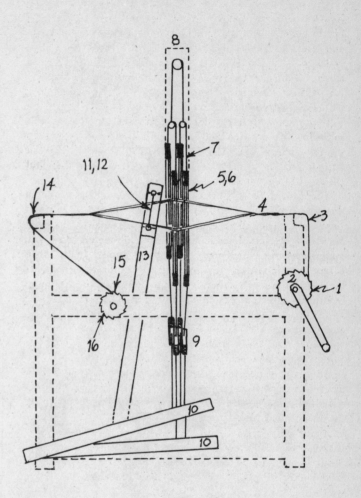

Side view of working parts of counterbalanced foot powered loom:

1	Warp beam	9	Lams
2	Ratchet	10	Treadles
3	Back beam	11, 12	Reed and dents
4	Lease sticks	13	Beater
5, 6	Heddles	14	Breast beam
7	Harnesses	15	Cloth beam
8	Castle	16	Front ratchet

Buying a Loom

The main considerations in buying a loom are: its size, its width and weaving space, number and type of harnesses (including noise); its harness action, type of warp beam and finally, cost.

As far as considerations of size and width go, in most cases, the first, or major, loom should be as wide as possible. Narrow cloth can be woven on a wide loom, but wide cloths can be woven only on a wide loom.

If portability is a consideration, a small floor loom or a table loom is an excellent choice. This small loom may be used for experimentation, in addition to a wider loom for actual weaving projects. Folding looms can be sturdy, but those with an X-form base rarely are.

The height of the breast beam is the major factor in considerations of size. Generally, the higher the breast beam, the easier the weaving. This is especially important for a tall person. Looms with overhead beaters have tall superstructures which may make them appear to be much larger than looms of the same size with underslung beaters.

The width of a loom is designated by the maximum width of cloth that can be set up on it. That is, the width of the loom is put in terms of the weaving width available, not the over-all width of the loom which is approximately 6″ wider than the weaving width, and as much as 10″–12″ wider than the maximum finished cloth.

Standard widths for looms vary from manufacturer to manufacturer. Generally, looms can be bought in sizes ranging from 20″ through 24″, 30″, 40″, 48″, 54″, and up to 60″ wide.

Space requirements are, of course, a very important consideration in choosing a loom. Dedicated weavers have been known to give up their bedrooms, living rooms, or play rooms in order to have sufficient space for a weaving studio.

Source: ELEMENTS OF WEAVING. by Azalea Thorpe and Jack Lenor Larsen.

ON WEAVING. by Anni Albers. Wesleyan University Press, Middletown, Connecticut, 1965. 204 pages. photographs (some color), bibliography. $17.50. paperback edition $6.95.

This is an indispensable book for the thoughtful weaver and textile designer. World-famous artist and designer Anni Albers discusses textile fundamentals and underlying principles in a sharp analysis that reaches back to the pre-ceramic age and forward to the possibilities of the future. Her emphasis is on the interrelation of medium and method in design organization. She calls for a "comprehensible orderliness" which should underlie the designer's organization and whose form is ultimately that of art.

Material form becomes meaningful form through design, that is, through considered relationships. And this meaningful form can become the carrier of a meaning that takes us beyond what we think of as immediate reality. But an orderliness that is too obvious cannot become meaningful in this superior sense that is art. The organization of forms, their relatedness, their proportions, must have that quality of a mystery that we know in nature. Nature, however, shows herself to us only in part. The whole of nature, though we always seek it, remains hidden from us. To reassure us, art tries, I believe, to show us a wholeness that we can comprehend.

WEAVING IS FOR ANYONE. by Jean Wilson. Van Nostrand Reinhold, New York, 1966. 144 pages. illustrations, photographs (some color), bibliography, index. $8.95.

This book explores a wide range of what to weave on and ways to do it. Almost every type of inexpensive, easy-to-make loom is included, as well as a good discussion of Peruvian, Chilean, Salish, Navajo, Ghanaian and Coptic weaving.

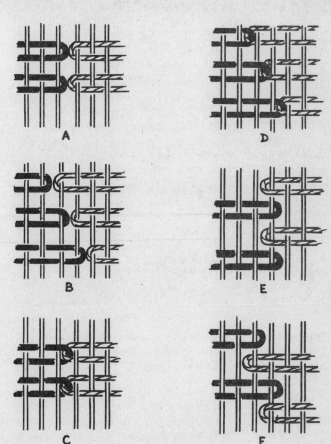

Methods of making color changes and joinings: plain weave tapestry techniques.

A *Straight slit*   D *Diagonal interlock*

B *Diagonal slit*   E *Straight dovetail*

C *Straight interlock*   F *Diagonal dovetail*

Nine simple projects in chapter 8 provide instruction in basic tapestry technique, plain weave, Swedish knotting, Egyptian knotting, Oriental and Greek soumak. The author also has special advice and instruction for those who wish to weave with natural and found materials.

This book will probably be most interesting to beginning weavers, although Ms. Wilson herself maintains that experienced weavers can also benefit from it since they must do a great deal of sampling and experimenting in order to learn exactly what happens when yarns of different colors, weights, textures, and lusters are placed in spacing and juxtapositions. The small cardboard looms and frames she suggests enable the weaver to achieve a close approximation of a weaving without having to use a large loom.

WEAVING IS FUN. by Jean Wilson. Van Nostrand Reinhold, New York, 1971. 140 pages. illustrations, photographs, bibliography, index. $8.95.

This is a guide for teachers, children, and beginning weavers. It includes a chapter of special advice to the teacher featuring hints about some of the more bothersome points of weaving the more experienced teacher might tend to take for granted, but which often bewilder the student. Although this book is especially directed toward teachers of children in the lower grades, it is by no means limited in scope. There is enough technical information, variety in projects, and suggestions for utilizing individual creativity to interest weavers at more advanced levels of experience and students of more advanced age.

WEAVING IS CREATIVE. by Jean Wilson. Van Nostrand Reinhold, New York, 1973. 268 pages. photographs (some color). $14.95.

A unique feature of this excellent book is a notebook section conveying diagrams for easy reference to projects presented in preceding chapters. There are also two very good charts on techniques and name comparison; the first for brocade and its variations, and the second for tapestry.

WEAVING YOU CAN WEAR. by Jean Wilson and Jan Burhen. Van Nostrand Reinhold, New York, 1973. 128 pages. illustrations, photographs. $8.95. paperback edition $4.95.

Working from the premise that everything that comes off a loom is basically a square or rectangle since it is constructed of threads at right angles, the authors present a variety of methods for weaving and assembling units for clothing. It is not a book for the beginning weaver and does not present detailed information on fundamental techniques, but rather tells how to weave specialized fabrics and suggests ways to turn hand-woven textiles into functional garments. Those who don't know how to weave at all can use the book as a guide for making patterns for the variety of interesting ethnic garments that can also be constructed from store-bought cloth. These pattern designs reflect the authors' belief that what primitive craftsmen did long ago is important to the craftsmen of today, and the book reveals

a sound historical and ethnological base for the projects presented, which include a Coptic tunic, a Mexican huipil, African shirts, South American ponchos, and a Japanese parasol.

> A shady friend—for torrid days—
> Is easier to find—
> Than one of higher temperature
> For Frigid—hour of Mind—
>
> The Vane a little to the East—
> Scares Muslin souls—away—
> If Broadcloth Hearts are firmer—
> Than those of Organdy—
>
> Who is to blame? The Weaver?
> Ah, the bewildering thread!
> The Tapestries of Paradise
> So notelessly—are made!
> —Emily Dickinson, cir. 1861

THE JOY OF HAND WEAVING. by Osma Gallinger Tod. Crown Publishers, New York, 1964. 326 pages. illustrations, photographs, bibliography, index.

For more than twenty years the author taught weaving to various groups of students. In this book she has transformed her practical experience into a clear, step-by-step course for home weavers to follow.

The book begins with a simple discussion of the various types of thread, the way in which fiber becomes thread, and a brief historical survey, and then progresses to the first project—the weaving of a bookmark. All the projects found in part I can be carried out on a weaving frame constructed of cardboard or small pieces of wood. The author believes that it is important for the new weaver to make his own frame as the planning and construction of each part leads to a clearer understanding of the workings of the loom.

Part II requires more complete equipment and investigates possibilities of weaving patterns. The various weaves are analyzed and grouped according to families, such as twill, monk's belt, summer and winter, Ms and Os, and so on. In addition to instructions for making traditional patterns, the author offers advice for outlining and weaving original patterns.

THE PLEASURES OF PATTERN. by William Justema. Van Nostrand Reinhold, New York, 1968. 240 pages. illustrations, bibliography. $15.00.

"For many years now, pattern has taken a back seat to design in texture and color." The author has set out to revitalize the weaver's interest in the possibilities and pleasures of pattern. He begins with a general discussion of the characteristics of pattern, the most important of which he considers to be repetition and variation. Repetition makes the pattern, and variation makes it interesting. A successful pattern requires careful planning and attention to its essential properties: structure, scale, and coverage. Above all, pattern making depends upon the dexterity of the weaver.

The first section of the book consists of a comprehensive survey of pattern from the earliest motifs to contemporary designs. The second section is comprised of eight lessons: two each on line, shape, texture, and color. In the third section the author discusses some aspects of pattern with specific reference to the work of William Morris. A pictorial quiz at the end enables the serious reader to discover just how much information he has absorbed.

WEAVING AND NEEDLECRAFT COLOR COURSE. by William and Doris Justema. Van Nostrand Reinhold, New York, 1971. 160 pages. illustrations (some color), bibliography, index. $9.95.

Yarn and cloth, for the most part, have little in common with paint. Materials used by weavers and needlecraftsmen depend for color on their thickness, luster, and the way in which they are woven or manipulated. Unlike pigments, yarns do not undergo physical change when mixed together. Modern weavers who wish to seriously study color must use theoretical color outlines and modify them according to their personal experience. William and Doris Justema provide such a theoretical outline in their first chapter in addition to a synopsis and history of color theory. In the second chapter they present the basics of the physical factors involved in the craft. The authors have designed a useful color wheel and describe ten types of color schemes with the finite palette of the needleworker in mind. Their approach is theoretical and devoted to principles rather than to technical considerations and methods (such as split composition).

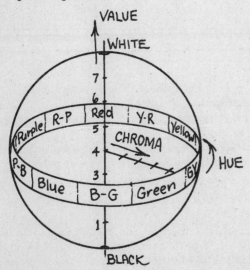

Munsell color solid

HANDWEAVING PATTERNS FROM FINLAND. by Helvi Pyysalo. Charles T. Branford Company, Newton Centre, Massachusetts, 1960. 49 pages. photographs (some color). $1.95.

This is a collection of 122 Finnish hand-weaving patterns. These present some difficulty even to the more knowledge-able weaver since looms, reeds, and threads in Finland are somewhat different from ours. Finnish reed is a metric reed that threads 12½ per inch. The nearest available size for us is 12 and this results in the weaving of a little finer or a little coarser cloth. Similarly, Finnish weaving threads are not exactly like those found in the United States, and to help American weavers over this difficulty, the authors have provided a table of comparisons. Ultimately, the weaver must be willing to do a bit of experimentation in order to determine the threads and yarns that suit him best.

FLEMISH WEAVING: A GUIDE TO TAPESTRY TECHNIQUE. by Gertrud Ingers. English edition prepared by Anne Briston. Van Nostrand Reinhold, New York, 1972. 112 pages. illustrations, photographs (some color). $7.95.

Flamskuavnad, or Flemish weaving, is the name given to the method of weaving tapestries introduced by the Flemish into Sweden in the 16th century and modified by the Swedes to suit their own materials and designs. In this form of tapestry the closely woven weft threads completely cover the warp with plain weave interlacing. Certain characteristics of technique are endemic: the way in which an area of weft color is joined to another color by interlocking or "hatching" so that a vertical join between two colors will be woven with a weft-interlock method. This results in a dovetail line in the tapestry. Another distinct feature is the way in which shapes of one color can be woven separately and then outlined, rather than weaving color changes row by row. The various weaving techniques for changing colors are thoroughly explained and the degree of difficulty of each project is indicated at the beginning. The author also includes information and recipes for home dyeing.

This history of a specialized tapestry technique makes interesting reading and presents some beautiful patterns hard to come by elsewhere.

THE NAVAJO BLANKET. by Mary Hunt Kahlenberg and Anthony Berlani. Praeger Publishers, New York, 1972. 112 pages. photographs (some color), bibliography. $10.00.

This is a beautiful and informative exhibition catalog featuring the work of eighty-one women artists. Unlike the Pueblo from whom the Navajo learned weaving and in whose society men have always been the weavers, the Navajo did not regard weaving as a separate profession; it was part of the cycle of life for the Navajo woman. Weaving remained an important aspect of Navajo society and every woman functioned as an artist. There are those people among us who are unable to consider even the greatest of Navajo blankets as beyond the realm of craft since they are woven rather than painted. "This cultural bias with regard to both the materials of art and the social role of the artist is contradicted by the Navajo weaving tradition."

NAVAJO AND HOPI WEAVING TECHNIQUES. by Mary Pendleton. Collier, New York, 1974. 158 pages. illustrations, photographs (some color), suppliers list, bibliography, index. paperback edition $4.95.

Mary Pendleton, an experienced and well-reputed weaver, has worked with Navajo and Hopi weavers for more than fifteen years. It is difficult, she admits, to learn from the Indians because they do not have a set of rules to impart, nor do they explain why they do something a certain way. Her purpose in this book is to clarify many of the finer points of Navajo and Hopi weaving techniques that have yet to be available in print. Every aspect of weaving is covered: how to make a loom, how to prepare yarn as the Indians do, what to know before you start weaving, and how to analyze finished pieces. The instructions are clear and the photographs remarkably good. The first half of the book covers the whole process of weaving a Navajo rug, and the author has even built in flaws in her sample rug to illustrate problems beginners are most apt to encounter. The second half of the book discusses in equal detail the weaving of Hopi belts.

WEAVING ON CARDBOARD: SIMPLE LOOMS TO MAKE AND USE. by Marthann Alexander. Taplinger Publishing Company, New York, 1972. 88 pages. photographs. $5.95.

A variety of suggestions for cardboard looms of different sizes is offered. Each loom is accompanied by a project. However, the procedural steps are not illustrated by diagrams, and the occasional photograph of the weaving process is not enough to guide beginning weavers.

An appendix presents some ideas for color harmonies.

CREATING WITH CARD WEAVING, A SIMPLE NON-LOOM TECHNIQUE. by Sally Specht and Sandra Rawlings. Crown Publishers, New York, 1973. 96 pages. illustrations, photographs (some color), bibliography, index. $4.95. paperback edition $2.95.

Card, or tablet, weaving is an ancient art believed to date back to the Bronze Age. As frame loom weaving, card weaving creates a fabric by interlacing warp and weft. However, the warp threads in conventional weaving are stretched and fastened to a wooden loom, and in card weaving one warp end is fastened around the weaver's waist and the other around a stationary object. The card weaver himself creates the tension on the warp by pulling back on his end of the threads. A set of four holed cards holds and separates the warp threads in this human loom just as the heddle and harness do in frame loom weaving.

The weaving process involves turning the cards clockwise or counterclockwise and inserting the weft through the shed (opening in the warp) after each turn. The turning of the cards causes the four threads to twist into one four-ply warp strand, and as the weft passes through the shed this strand is locked into place, producing an exceptionally strong fabric unique in that only the warp threads are visible in

the finished material. Card weaving usually produces a narrow band of fabric since it is difficult for a weaver to hold more than a limited number of cards. These strips of fabric are perfectly suited for belts, watchbands, and straps, but contemporary weavers are experimenting with new methods and materials to create everything from wall hangings to luggage racks.

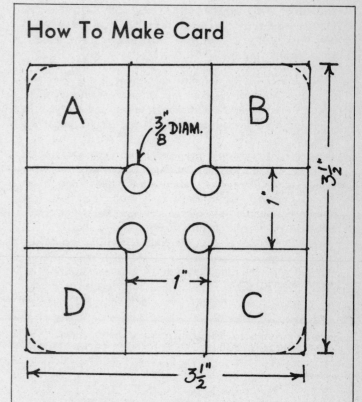

How To Make Card

⅜″ paper punch where sides of square meet.

Letters starting at left hand corner.

Round edges using a penny as a guide so that cards are easier to handle.

Mark edge of each card with a colored ink so that you know at a glance if cards are in proper position.

Source: CREATING WITH CARD WEAVING, A SIMPLE NON-LOOM TECHNIQUE. by Sally Specht and Sandra Rawlings.

OFF-LOOM WEAVING. by Rose Naumann and Raymond Hull. Charles Scribner's Sons, 1973. 190 pages. illustrations, photographs. $8.95.

The authors recommend off-loom weaving as a source of pleasure, relaxation, creative outlet, and also as an inexpensive means of discovering whether or not loom weaving is for you before you make the initial investment of money and time. This last reason is somewhat questionable. Off-loom weaving is not loom weaving. A predilection for one does not necessarily indicate a fondness for the other, and perhaps it would be wiser not to enter upon off-loom weaving if you are going to regard it simply as a trial run.

Directions are given for various types of off-loom weaving, which, incidentally, do require portable frames, all of which can be made at home. One such frame is the Salesh, named after the Salesh Indians of the Pacific coast who wove large blankets on it. The frame allows for the weaving of articles twice as long as the frame is high, since the warp goes around both the back and the front of the frame.

Magazines: Weaving

Shuttle, Spindle and Dyepot
1013 Farmington Avenue
West Hartford, Conn. 06107
Quarterly. $7.00 per year.
The publication of the Handweavers Guild of America and the number one magazine for the craft weaver. Articles on technique, products, design, and craftsmen.

Handweaver and Craftsman
220 Fifth Avenue
New York, N.Y. 10001
Bimonthly.
We've been told that this magazine is temporarily defunct, but the duration of its stasis is uncertain.

Warp and Weft
Robin and Russ
533 North Adams Street
McMinnville, Ore. 97128
Monthly. $4.50 per year.
Bulletin for four-harness weavers. Sample swatches and directions included in each issue.

Drafts and Designs
Robin and Russ
533 North Adams Street
McMinnville, Ore. 97123
Monthly. $5.00 per year.
Bulletin for five- to eight-harness weavers. Sample swatches and patterns.

The Looming Arts
The Pendleton Shop
Box 233
Sedona, Ariz. 86336
Bimonthly. $4.50 per year.
Features hand-woven designs by Mary Pendleton, samples, directions, and four-harness designs. Four harness and multiple designs bulletin $6.00 per year.

Quarterly Journal of the Guilds of Weavers, Spinners, and Dyers
William Evans
China Court
Church Lane
Petham near Canterbury
Kent, England
The only magazine in Great Britain devoted entirely to textile crafts. It is illustrated and contains articles of general, historical, and technical nature.

Swedish Looms

The Swedish looms are all string tie-ups. Everything on the loom can be made. If a peg falls out you don't have to write to the company, you can whittle another out of a piece of wood. You can make the string heddles.

Because everything is tied with knots, things will tend to come apart. If it's a rainy day, for instance, the humidity will loosen the tension and they'll all fall out.

When you get the loom, you have to assemble it. You have to decide for yourself the height of the harness. You should know about weaving before you get a Swedish loom otherwise you're not going to know that the eye of the heddle should hit the middle of the warp and that that should be in the middle of the weave—a whole number of things like that.

A Swedish loom is much stronger than most American (and Canadian) looms. If you want to make a rug, you've got to have a heavy front beam. You've got to have treadles that won't crack.

The Swedish loom is a counter balance. My preference is to an American counter balance with rolling action. It doesn't seem to fall out of adjustment as much. I talk to people who have studied in Sweden and they find no problem with it after learning the Swedish method of doing things, but that method is very inaccessible here.

—Amy Haus
(Amy Haus is a weaver and works
for School Products in New York.)

SHUTTLE CRAFT GUILD MONOGRAPHS. published by Harriet Tidball. Write: William H. Colburn, 4499 Delta River Drive, Rt. 1, Lansing, Michigan.

Weaving Inkle Bands. by Harriet Tidball. 1969. $4.00
Weft Twinning. by Virginia Harvey and Harriet Tidball. 1969. $4.00
Peru: Textiles Unlimited, Ancient Weaves and Modern Applications. by Harriet Tidball. Part I, 1968, $4.00. Part II, 1969, $4.00
Design and the Handweaver. by Mary Atwater. 1961. $3.00
Peter Collingwood: His Weaves and Weaving. by Harriet Tidball. 1963. $4.00
Contemporary Tapestry. by Harriet Tidball, 1964. $4.00
Color and Dyeing. by Harriet Tidball. 1964. $4.00
Contemporary Costume. by Harriet Tidball. 1968. $5.00

THE TECHNIQUE OF WOVEN TAPESTRY. by Tadek Beutlich. Watson-Guptill Publications, New York, 1971. 128 pages. photographs (some color), index. $10.95.

Woven tapestries can be divided into two groups: those woven on a vertical loom (high warp) and those woven on a horizontal loom (low warp). There is no visible difference between these two types and occasionally a red thread is inserted into the border of a high warp tapestry to identify it.

A low-warp loom allows for quicker weaving, but a high-warp loom gives the craftsman more freedom insofar as it is accessible and allows him to see what he is doing. It also permits more than one weaver to work if a large tapestry is being woven. A large low warp tapestry is usually woven in strips and then sewn together afterwards.

Tadek Beutlich discusses both high- and low-warp weaving, and advantages, disadvantages, and method of approach for each variety. His purpose has been to encourage the would-be weaver and to "abolish the fallacy that this craft is a very difficult one and that it takes years of practice to accomplish."

THE SHUTTLE-CRAFT BOOK OF AMERICAN HAND-WEAVING. revised edition by Mary Atwater. Macmillan, New York, 1966. 341 pages. illustrations, index. $8.95.

This book gives patterns for summer and winter weaves, the Bronson weave, double weaving, leno, rug-making, and native weaves from Peru, Mexico, Guatemala, and the American Southwest. Ms. Atwater traces the origins and development of weaving, how and in what forms it arrived in this country, and its eventual decline. She also presents working diagrams for many of the famous traditional coverlet patterns illustrated in Eliza Calvert Hall's book *A Book of Hand-Woven Coverlets.*

SIMPLE WEAVING: DESIGNS, MATERIALS, TECHNIQUES. by Grete Kroncke. Van Nostrand Reinhold, New York, 1973. 95 pages. illustrations, photographs. $5.95. paperback edition $2.95.

The author concentrates on two aspects of simple weaving rather than attempting to present a general introductory text. The first section, "Looms with a Difference," demonstrates some basic ideas for looms, almost all of which can be made cheaply at home. The emphasis is on the development of weaving techniques rather than on the finished products, but the reader is shown how the looms can be used to make various articles.

The second section, "Making String Things," shows how much can be done with cord and twine. Sisal, jute, hemp, cotton, twine, and paper string are all used to decorate and make a variety of objects.

Film

"The Weaving Studio at Peters Valley" 12 minutes, color, 16mm, sound. Sale $150; rental $25.00. Produced and distributed by Hilton Associates, 208 Grayson Place, Teaneck, N.J. 07666.

This film was not intended as a teaching aid per se and no technical information on weaving or spinning is presented. It attempts rather to instill an appreciation of the craft and craftsmanship through an exploration of the reasons why people go into crafts.

This film is suitable for audiences of all ages, including the very young, and will awaken interest in those disposed toward weaving but who do not know very much about it.

SIMPLE WEAVING. by Hilary Chetwynd. Watson-Guptill Publications, New York, 1969. 104 pages. illustrations, photographs, suppliers list, bibliography, index. $2.50.

This is a basic introduction to the techniques of weaving on a variety of looms plus some good advice for solving certain often encountered problems. This is not a step-by-step course complete with projects to reinforce newly acquired skills, but it is comprehensive in its own terms and reasonably priced. The shy novice should look elsewhere, but a confident beginner, who feels comfortable with handcrafts, would probably benefit from Ms. Chetwynd's approach.

A BOOK OF HAND-WOVEN COVERLETS. by Eliza Calvert Hall. Charles E. Tuttle Company, Rutland, Vermont, 1966. 411 pages. illustrations, photographs. $8.75.

When this book was first published in 1912, the author was already looking back wistfully at the fast-fading art of making coverlets. Her book is an attempt not to explain how to make these beautiful and classic coverlets, but to instill an appreciation of their value. The tone is historical and anecdotal, for understanding comes not just from looking but from knowing and listening as well; ". . . Only one who has studied the names of coverlet patterns can know the full depth of magic that a name can hold. Here are the flowery, leafy, and poetic names. Listen how sweetly they run:"

> Flower of the Mountain (North Carolina)
> Sunrise on the Walls of Troy
> Rose in the Wilderness (Kentucky)
> World's Wonder
> Rose of the Valley
> Old Roads (West Virginia)
> Lily of the West
> Spring Flower
> Fading Leaf
> Kentucky Snowballs
> Flowers of Edinboro (Kentucky and Tennessee)
> Rose in the Garden (North Carolina)
> Islands of the Sea (Connecticut)
> Path of the Sunbeam (Maine)
> Primrose and Diamonds
> King's Garden (Maine)
> Folding Leaf
> Pine Bloom (Kentucky).

CREATIVE DESIGN IN WALL HANGINGS: WEAVING PATTERNS BASED ON PRIMITIVE AND MEDIEVAL ART. by Lili Blumenau. Crown Publishers, New York, 1967. 213 pages. illustrations, photographs (some color), index. $7.95.

This is a useful book for the beginning weaver who needs some fundamentals, as well as for the experienced weaver seeking new ideas and for anyone interested in the history of tapestry-making from the Coptic and Inca weaver to today's modern artists. Included is a description of equipment, a discussion of yarns and materials, directions for preparing loom, the basic methods and techniques of weaving, and finally the entire process of designing and making a wall hanging. Pictured alongside the work of the earliest weavers is the work of some of the most well-reputed weavers of today, including Lenore Tawney, Ted Hallman, Spencer Depas, Antonin Kybal, and George Wells.

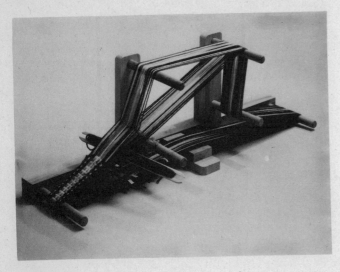

Inkle loom.
Photo courtesy of School Products.

NEEDLEWEAVING, EASY AS EMBROIDERY. by Esther Warner Dendel. Countryside Press, 1972. 128 pages. distributed by Doubleday and Company. illustrations, photographs (some color). $7.95.

A piece of cardboard and a curved needle become a loom upon which a variety of objects ranging from greeting cards to banjo covers can be woven. The needle weaver is free from many of the constraints placed upon loom weavers; the cardboard loom gives great flexibility to the woven products so that the weaver is able to be more spontaneous and imaginative in the process. Moreover, a cardboard loom costs practically nothing and can be carried around to help pass the time.

FINISHING TOUCHES FOR THE HANDWEAVER. by Virginia M. West. Charles T. Branford Company, Newton Centre, Massachusetts, 1967. 102 pages. illustrations, photographs. $5.75.

This much-needed book is devoted solely to methods of finishing. Included is a study of fringes in all their manifold variety and detail—how to secure fringes, how to weave fringe at the sides of the loom, how to keep the weft from raveling. Also, there is information on how to attach handles for handbags, and new ways to apply embroidery techniques.

Weaving Suppliers:

Ankh Guild
7130 South Exchange Avenue
Chicago, Ill. 60649
brochure.
tapestry, i harness, four-harness.

Ayottes Designery
P.O. Box 287
Center Sandwich, N.H. 03227
brochure; membership $2.00.
table looms.

Black Sheep Weaving and Craft Supply
318 South Second Street
Corvallis, Ore. 97339
inkle looms, backstrap.

Dick Blick Company
P.O. Box 1267
Galesburg, Ill. 61401
catalog.
eight-harness, backstrap, tapestry, Leclerc, portable, table, four-harness, inkle, twelve, sixteen, harness.

Colonial Textiles
82 Plants Dam Road
East Lyme, Conn. 06333
four-harness.

Craftsman Guild
Rt. 1, Box 146-D
Cornelius, Ore. 97113
inkle.

Clara Creager
75 West College Avenue
Westerville, O. 43081
Leclerc.

Crystal River Loom Company
Box 261
Carbondale, Colo. 81623
eight-harness.

Dharma Trading Company
1952 University Avenue
Berkeley, Cal. 94704
catalog.
table looms, inkle looms, tapestry looms.

Dorset Looms
Woodin Road
RD 1, Box 1076
Waterford, N.Y. 12188
catalog.
portable looms, four-harness.

Earth Guild, Inc.
149 Putnam Avenue
Cambridge, Mass. 02139
brochure.
four-harness, backstrap, inkle, table
  looms, portable, tapestry.

Edgerton Handcrafts
210 West Town
Norwich, Conn. 06360
brochure.
Leclerc.

Gallagher Tolls
318 Pacheco Avenue
Santa Cruz, Cal. 95060
catalog.
backstrap, tapestry, table.

Gilmore Looms
1032 North Broadway
Stockton, Cal. 95205
brochure.
four-harness, inkle, six-harness.

Good Karma Looms
440 West 4th Street
Chadron, Neb. 69337
catalog.
inkle.

Bernard Gordon
2608 West Farwell Avenue
Chicago, Ill. 60645
brochure.
inkle looms.

Greentree Ranch Wools
163 North Carter Lake Road
Loveland, Colo. 80537
brochure.
table looms, Leclerc looms for the handi-
  capped, rigid heddle.

Gunnar Andersons Vavskedsverkstad
  Oxberg
S-79200 Mora
Sweden
catalog $2.00.
tapestry looms, eight-harness looms, four-
  harness, inkle, tapestry.

Hammet Company
Hammet Place
Braintree, Mass. 02184
catalog.
backstrap.

Handcrafters
1 West Brown Street
Waupun, Wis. 53863
brochure $.50.
tapestry.

The Handweaver
111 East Napa Street
Sonoma, Cal. 95476
catalog.
backstrap, inkle, tapestry.

Harmony Acres Studio
Bag. 1550
St. Norbert, Manitoba ROG 2HO
Canada
brochure.

Harris Looms
North Grove Road
Hawkhurst, Kent, England
catalog.
tapestry, rug, four-harness.

Harrisville Designs
P.O. 51
Harrisville, N.H. 03450
catalog.

Robert F. Heartz
Yankee Looms and Brentwood Press
RD 1
Barrington, N.H. 03825
catalog.
inkle looms.

Kay and EE Corporation of America
200 Fifth Avenue
Room 325
New York, N.Y.
brochure.

Kessenich Looms and Yarn Shop
7463 Harwood Avenue
Wauwatosa, Wis. 53213

Lamb's End
165 West, 9 Mile
Ferndale, Mich. 48220
brochure.

Nilus Leclerc, Inc.
P.O. Box 69
L'Islet, Quebec, Canada Gor 200
tapestry.

Leclerc Corporation
Box 491
Plattsburg, N.Y. 12901
catalog.
backstrap, inkle, rug.

Lenos Handcrafts
2037 Walnut Street
Philadelphia, Pa. 19103
brochure.
inkle.

Anders Lervad and Son A/s
Askov, 6600
Vejen, Denmark
brochure.

Lewis Looms
Pigeon Cove Weave Shop
12 Landmark Lane
Rockport, Mass. 01966
letter, inkle.

Lillistina Looms
P.O. Box 1373
Binghamton, N.Y. 13905
catalog.

Lily Mills
Handweaving Department
P.O. Box 88
Shelby, N.C. 28150
inkle, tapestry.

The Loom Factory
Star Route
Marcola, Ore. 97554
brochure.
inkle.

Looms and Lessons
Ruth Nordquist Myers
6014 Osage Avenue
Downers Grove, Ill. 06515
brochure.
backstrap, inkle, tapestry.

MacMillan Arts and Crafts
9520 Baltimore Avenue
College Park, Md. 20740
catalog.

L. W. Macomber
AD-AO Harness Looms
566-570 Lincoln Avenue
Saugus, Mass. 01906
brochure.

Magnolia Weaving
2635-29th Avenue West
Seattle, Wash. 98199
backstrap, inkle, rug, tapestry.

The Makings
2001 University Avenue
Berkeley, Cal. 94704
four-harness, eight-harness, tapestry.

Jean Malsada, Inc.
P.O. Box 28182
Atlanta, Ga. 30328
Also P.O. Box 767
Roswell, Ga. 30075
catalog.
tapestry.

Nadeau Looms, Inc.
725 Branch Avenue
Providence, R.I. 02904
brochure.

Nasco Arts and Crafts
Nasco West
Fort Atkinson, Wis. 53538
Also P.O. Box 3827
Modesto, Cal. 95352
inkle, rug, tapestry.

Naturalcraft
2199 Bancroft Way
Berkeley, Cal. 94704
catalog $.50.
inkle.

Robert C. Nelson
69 Pleasant Street
Concord, Mass. 01724
brochure.
backstrap.

Newcomb Loom Company
P.O. Box 3204
Davenport, Ia. 52808
catalog $.10.
rug.

Northwest Looms
Rt. 4, Box 4872
Bainbridge Island, Wash. 98110
brochure.

Norwood Loom Company and Weaving
  Shop
Baldwin, Mich. 49304
brochure, send self-addressed envelope.
tapestry.

Owl and Olive Weavers
4232 Old Leeds Land
Birmingham, Ala. 35213
inkle.

Payton Loom Shop
19630 South West Shaw Street
Aloha, Ore. 97005
catalog $.35.

Pendleton Shop
Box 233
Jordan Road
Sedona, Ariz. 86336
catalog.
tapestry.

Putney Mountain Looms
RFD 3
Putney, Vt. 05346
brochure.

Robin and Russ Handweavers
533 North Adams Street
McMinnville, Ore. 97128
catalog.
backstrap, inkle tapestry.

Schacht Spindle
1708 Walnut Street
Boulder, Colo. 80302
brochure.
inkle, tapestry.

Scoles Looms
Box 26029
Denver, Colo. 80226

School Products
312 East 23 Street
New York, N.Y. 10010
inkle, rug, tapestry.

Sears Roebuck and Company
4640 Roosevelt Avenue
Philadelphia, Pa. 19132
inkle.

Sheep Village
2005 Bridgeway
Sausalito, Cal. 94965
ridge heddle, inkle, tapestry.

AL Snickeriversstad
Oxaback, 51100 Kinna
Sweden
brochure.

Some Place
2990 Adeline Street
Berkeley, Cal. 94703
catalog $.50.
backstrap, tapestry.

Straw Into Gold
5550 College Avenue
Oakland, Cal. 94618
catalog.
backstrap.

Karen L. Swanson
1810 Kemery Road
Akron, O. 44313
backstrap.

Threadbare
20 Cornelia Street
New York, N.Y. 10014

Threadbare Shop
Heritage Square
Golden, Colo. 80401
brochure.
inkle.

Toijalan Kaidetehdas
Haittilantie 6 Pl 25
37801 Toijala, Finland
catalog.
Finnish tapestry.

Frederick Traub
D-705 Wliblingen, Lange Str. 32
Germany 3290
brochure.

Turnbull Engineering Company
P.O. Box 4296
Mobile, Ala. 36604
brochure.

Vavstolsfabriken
S-280 64 Glimakra
Sweden
catalog.
tapestry.

Oy Varpa Looms Ltd.
Osmontie (street)
Myllykoski 5
Finland 46800
catalog.
rug.

Warp, Woof, and Potpourri
514 North Lake Avenue
Pasadena, Cal. 91101
inkle, tapestry.

Whitney Looms
514 Myrtle Place
Lafayette, La. 70501
catalog.

Yellow Springs Strings
P.O. Box 107
68 Goes Station, O. 45387
catalog.
tapestry, inkle.

Wood

Gary Williams

Woodworking is very much a generic term. It includes many separate disciplines, such as framing, joinery, marquetry, cabinetmaking, furniture framing, stair building, housewrighting, finishing, carving, turning flooring, box making, picture framing, fitting, even lumberjacking. Clearly, no one is simply a woodworker.

I call myself, and try to be, a cabinetmaker. The trade of cabinetmaking is, I think, the most general of all those listed above. Its operations in toto are the closest to what people seem to think of woodworking as being. So, I've written all this as a cabinetmaker, implying, If you want to learn about this subject, follow my advice. Read certain books, get particular tools. It's easier than learning the hard way.

I consider myself a tradesman. From my impartial view, I consider being a tradesperson more challenging and rewarding than being a craftsperson. In the trades, even if one designs one's own products from the beginning, there are more limitations, more restrictions in design and structural requirements, but the product must still be beautiful. In the trades, a person must be able to work with either hand as circumstances require. And, in the trades, a person must be aware every minute, trying to increase efficiency without compromising (and hopefully, augmenting) quality.

After being occupied in this trade for a while, I've developed a feeling of control over the materials and constructions of the world. Not only is almost any conceivable thing possible to make, it can probably be made from wood. The limitations are those of the imagination, not the material. Curiously, at the same time the imagination is demanded, it is being constricted. In this line of work, a person very quietly grows to approach life with a sense of strict causality. A good mechanic depends completely upon his ability to predict.

With this increased feeling of potency vis à vis the world's materials, there grows an atrophy of language. Working with one's body (and without other people) is direct, without translation or symbolism. A hemisphere of the mind fades. I don't care how romantic you are, the wood does *not* talk back.

I bring up these qualifications because as both trade and craft, woodworking is anachronistic. The environment, in a subtle and monstrous way, is hostile to it. These are days of reproduction and verbalization. Fine design and craftsmanship demand too much of each viewer to be successfully communicative. But, because woodworking is out of place and frustrated by our surroundings, one is the more satisfied and confident by accomplishing what he or she has set out to do, even if it's only the building of a little stool. Obsess yourself with appearance rather than meaning—that's what you must do. It is an eccentric road.

Tools

One way to approach the procurement of tools is to think about their commercial circumstances. The wisdom of the saying "buy the best you can possibly afford" is demonstrated by industry, which always uses high-quality tools. Obviously, it's easier to do good work with good tools. However, both outfits that produce top-notch work and those which produce garbage use good tools. Companies that produce inferior goods are generally more interested in making money than in the integrity of their product. Yet they are willing to invest in good tools because quality tools are actually cheaper in the long run.

Toolmakers cater, in a sense, to industry and to professionals. A century ago, shops weren't electrified, since most woodwork wasn't mass produced, and standards of construction were more circumscribed. The professional market was one of hand tools. High quality was built into many of these tools, and the variety available was enormous.

Nowadays, the preponderance of work is done in factories, so the emphasis, for toolmakers, is on stationary power tools which are very well made, effective, and varied. The other professional work done these days is by small shops and individuals. Their requirement is for small and portable power tools, so good ones of this variety are available, too.

Where does that leave hand tools? Well, there is and has been a market of dilettantes, "handymen," who want tools, don't want to spend much, and aren't too particular about their results. For them, the toolmakers have always made a lot of junk (no, your great-granddaddy's planes aren't necessarily beauts).

When I spoke of standards being more circumscribed in the past, I meant that an awful lot of stuff made these days is garbage. That's common knowledge. Many operations once standard have been dropped from practice because they take more time than others, in less adequate ways. The smaller shops in particular take constructional shortcuts to remain in competition with the big operations. Both large and small industries have drastically depleted the design variables of each job or piece to reduce cost. The idea is to design everything so that it can be produced with power tools alone.

The design simplifications and defaults have narrowed the variety of hand tools on the market. Just like today, much of eighteenth- and nineteenth-century woodwork was made to less than the highest standards, but when things are made one at a time, design exceptions don't seriously alter production. Thus, there was a place for many hand tools for a variety of designs.

Insofar as complexity is undesirable to most professionals, the market for good hand tools has evaporated. The professional can't take the time to cut a joint by hand with a dovetail plane (or he doesn't care to take the time), and the handyman doesn't usually even know what a dovetail plane is.

Of course, there is still the need for good hand tools on the part of the craftsperson. They offer a wider range of operations, more accuracy in some cases, lower capital expenditures, and an intimacy between worker and object unobtainable with power tools. They are also much quieter and use no electricity.

Today, the only quality hand tools available are the ones that a professional can't easily replace with power tools or otherwise do without. These would include: nail hammers, rules and measuring tapes, squares, sharpening stones, and clamps. It's safe to buy an American brand of any one of these tools. Generally, the top of Stanley's line is reliable. The same is true with Craftsman's (Sears) best. And there are companies, like Lufkin, that specialize in a single type of tool. However, with the exception of the above-named tools, try to avoid American hand tools. Which means, write off the corner hardware store.

The change in professional tool requirements has not gone as far in Europe as it has here. It is therefore possible to still get some decent tools from European companies. The major outlet for these is Woodcraft Supply Corporation, 313 Montvale Avenue, Woburn, Massachusetts 01801. Please send them half a buck for their catalog. Really, there's no sense thinking about buying woodworking tools if you're not familiar with Woodcraft. They sell only woodworking tools and know their customers' needs better than most of their customers do. They import the top English and German brands, such as Tyzack, Ulmia, Marples, and Record. If you intend to buy any of the most important tools (plane, saw, or chisel), theirs is the only place to do it.

Sometimes Woodcraft is out of stock on certain items. If you can't wait, write to London's best tool store, Buck and Ryan, Ltd., 101 Tottenham Court Road, London W1, England. They only carry English products, but within that limitation their selection is very complete (even more so than Woodcraft's). Mailing charge for catalog is $1.00.

Carving tools are a special category. The best places I know of to get them are:

Frank Mittermeir
35-77 East Tremont
Bronx, N.Y. 10465

Ashley Iles, Ltd.
Fenside
East Kirkby
Spils, Lincs
England

Carl Heidtmann
563 Remscheid-Hasten
Unterholterfelder Str. 46
West Germany

All the above offer free catalogs. Incidentally, Woodcraft also carries excellent carving tools.

There are a few distributors of Japanese tools in the United States. Don't bother. First, these outlets deal in goods roughly equivalent to the Stanley "Handyman" line. Need I say more? Even if they were of some quality, most operations done by the Japanese woodworker are different from their Western counterparts. The woodworker is more respected in Japan than here. His tools, at their best, are beautiful and efficient, and frequently Japanese woodwork is exquisitely designed and executed. However, it's futile for a Westerner to try sawing or planing on the pull stroke when his conditioning has taught just the opposite. It's not easy to teach yourself to sharpen a Japanese saw through trial and error. Even chisels are used differently in Japan. So, you may respect both styles of work, but use only one.

Now about the notion, "They don't make them like they used to." Of course, as far as power tools are concerned, that's completely false, but it is half true of hand tools. There are three things usually considered when buying the crucial hand tools: durability, feel, and edge quality. For durability, I think the older tools (cir. 1915 to 40) are slightly superior to the new, high-quality ones. The same is definitely the case with feel, balance, and working comfort. Some of the old handles seem made for your hands alone. However, the older tools will not hold an edge as well. The older steel sometimes crumbles and, though you might attain the requisite razor's edge by sharpening, it will dull sooner than the newer alloys normally will. It is true that the older steel doesn't rust as readily, but I've not found that an important asset since I customarily do not store my tools in the sink.

If a type of hand tool was not in common use before 1910, it's probably worthless. You can buy a tool, say, a plane, of higher quality today than you could eighty years ago, but any operations you'd want to perform have been done for centuries, and somewhere along the line there have been qualty tools for its accomplishment. Don't fall for recent gimmicks like "stud finders" and "seven-in-one-holesaws."

By dwelling at length on hand tools, I have not meant to totally discourage the use of power tools. Certain operations can be performed by power tools as well or even better than with hand tools. If you spend hours with a hand drill, you may become too tired to work carefully and precisely on operations that require something besides stamina. It's just that power tools have limited scope, can lead to sloppy work, and sometimes aren't worth their expense. Quality in most power tools depends upon a group of factors: bearings, motor power, accuracy of assembly, durability, tolerance of adjustment. Although in choosing power tools, you get what you pay for, a few tips might be helpful.

In the United States there are a number of companies that market good hand power tools, namely: Rockwell, Black and Decker, Craftsman (Sears), Skil, Bosch-Lesto, Stanley, and Milwaukee. Most of these companies have different grades ranging from standard duty (lowest) to superior duty (highest). It's odd, but no single company makes the best of everything. This is unlike the case with hand tools where, if, for example, you want a wooden plane of any type, Ulmia is the best. I can only offer my preferences in each category. I've also been particular in my choice of categories, that is, I specify ⅜-inch variable speed drill (without reverse) because a ⅜-inch is much more useful than a ¼ inch and variability of speed is a valuable feature, whereas reversibility really isn't.

⅜-inch variable speed drill (nonreversing)—Rockwell 386
½-inch drill (reversing)—Milwaukee 1650
sabre saw (portable jig saw)—Bosch-Lesto 8554
¼-inch router—Craftsman "Commercial" 9HT 17385
½-inch router—Stanley R51
3 • 24 dustless belt sander—Rockwell 360
4½ • 9 finishing sander (10,000 r.p.m.)—Rockwell 505
4½ • 4½ finishing sander (12,000 r.p.m.)—Rockwell 330
7¼" Skil saw (portable circular saw)—Skil 857
electric screwdriver (positive clutch)—Rockwell 7791

The best way to obtain these tools is through a local distributor or hardware or tool wholesaler. A few mail-order outfits offer discounts, but it's hard to know just which model they carry, not to mention the difficulty of getting service. Moreover, their prices can be beaten. If you intend to sell what you make, if you consume a lot of supplies, or, if you're a convincing talker, you can be treated as one "in the trade." This qualifies you to a discount of anywhere from 15 to 40 percent from wholesalers, where you can order exactly what you want. This is the very best way to buy portable power tools.

As far as stationary power tools are concerned, I would recommend buying them used. Their use value often remains high over a long period. I would also recommend not buying too many of them. The average woodworker requires, at most, a table saw and a band saw. Some things, like a radial arm saw, are a complete waste of money. Virtually every operation they perform can be done better by a table saw.

When picking such tools, what you should be looking at is the "chassis," its condition and accuracy. Motors can be overhauled, bearings replaced, blades will be sharpened, but if the tool cannot be adjusted precisely and remain stable, it's not of much use.

Again, you pretty much get what you pay for. Availability of many models is restricted by area, but I can offer a priority list of tools according to their relative usefulness.
1. table saw
2. band saw
3. jointer
4. thicknesser (surface planer)
5. drill press
6. lathe
7. jig saw, shaper, grinder

FINISHING SUPPLIES

Good finishing supplies for automobiles are easy to get. Getting good wood finishing materials is another story. The spray lacquers used by industry have replaced oils and varnishes once available. However, you can still get fine oils and liquid waxes from Watco. Also, Pratt and Lambert

varnish and paste filler are reliable. A rough equivalent to Woodcraft Supply for finishing materials is H. Behlen and Brother which is a subsidiary of Mohawk Finishing Products, Amsterdam, N.Y. 12010. Their catalog is free and it lists scores of varnishes, stains, fillers, and the like. Mohawk, the parent company, has a very complete line of refinishing and repair supplies.

WOOD

You can buy lumber and veneer through the mail. However, it's bad practice since the prices are outrageous and you can't really see what you're getting. Nevertheless, with clenched teeth, I'll offer the names of the top suppliers:

Constantine's
2050 Eastchester Road
Bronx, N.Y. 10461

Craftsman Wood Service
2727 South Mary Street
Chicago, Ill. 60608

Both companies offer free catalogs. The best bet in either is Constantine's box of fifty veneer samples for $6.00. It comes in very handy.

On the whole, making the best of local goods is apt to be much more fruitful than dealing through the mail. Of course, Honduras mahogany and satinwood aren't indigenous to the States, but walnut, gum, oak, maple, beech, and many others do grow here. If you search your area for these woods, you'll have the opportunity to choose the board you want at a reasonable price. If you can't do beautiful work with some of the American woods, a foreign pedigree isn't going to save you. Perhaps you'll have to resort to mail-order houses for veneer, but that's not as risky as lumber. Just make sure you get pieces from a single flitch (consecutive pieces).

Nowadays some very good plywood is made, with anything up to a Phillipine mahogany core and avodire faces. There are dozens of veneers on plywood available. Find out the specifics from your best local yard or a U.S. Plywood or Weyerhauser dealer.

HARDWARE

The variety of hardware available today is unbelievable. Imagine anything you'd like to do with wood and there's probably hardware made to facilitate it. Of course, some of it's good quality and some of it's junk. Among the better companies are: Stanley, Ires, Baldwin, Modric (English), and Jado (German). The best way to introduce yourself to some of the many devices is to go to your nearest hardware store and start thumbing through catalogs. When you near the point of exhaustion, take down some addresses and write for catalogs of your own.

Magazines: Woodworking

There aren't very many magazines on woodworking of any use to the craftsperson. You can pretty much write off *Woodworker* and *Handyman*. There are publications such as *Wood and Wood Products* intended for industry, but these have little relevance to the individual. Two English magazines, however, are informative: *Practical Woodworking* (Fleetway House, Farringdon Street, London EC4A England), an $11.00 a year monthly, and *Woodworker* (which can be obtained from Eastern News Distributors, 155 West 15th Street, New York, N.Y. 10011), a $6.00 a year monthly. The former is slightly preferred. Each month it features sections on using tools, book reviews, projects, tips, and so on. The information is accurate and the descriptions complete. Reading these magazines is a bit like having another person nearby to offer a broad range of advice. I warn you, though, sometimes their designs are from left field (but good for a little amusement). Most students of the art will find these quite helpful.

National Carvers Museum Review
7825 Claremont Ave., Department AC
Chicago, Ill. 60620
Quarterly. $1.00 sample issue.

Official publication of the museum, which is located at 14960 Woodcarver Road, Monument, Colo. 80132, and which displays a variety of fine wood carvings (free brochure available on request).

Books: Woodcarving

The apprentice system has largely disappeared from the United States, making it necessary to partially learn wood crafts through the medium of print. Without going into the benefits and disadvantages of this system, I sincerely offer advice on choosing books from personal experience. All the books listed are in print and fairly accessible. Expense has been considered, although, unless you'd lay out 250 dollars for an architectural wood specimen encyclopedia, the good books aren't usually the costly ones. Other criteria, of course, were clarity, accuracy, comprehensiveness, and the quality of the illustrations. These selections have been made from hundreds of possibilities. Moreover, they are the books I've bought and found of value for my professional use.

Certain publishers, such as Charles A. Bennett Company of Peoria, Illinois, and McKnight Publishing Company of Bloomington, Indiana, deal in textbooks like *Cabinetmaking and Millwork*, by John L. Feirer, and *Woodworking Technology*, by James Hammond, et. al. Such books can be broad and illuminating at times. Their drawback is that they're principally in reference to the woodworking industry, rather than the techniques likely to be used by the individual. You'll also come across many *Complete Book(s) of. . . .* None of these is what it pretends to be, and you'll end up buying the more modestly titled and detailed volumes anyway.

Some years back, Evans Brothers of London began publishing a "Woodworker" series. Many of their titles have been republished in the United States by Drake. I've drawn disproportionately upon this series simply because it's much better than anything else in English.

It is my conviction that an aspiring woodworker should be acquainted with all the books I've reviewed here, and not necessarily any more. To be unfamiliar with the information in one or more of them would be to leave a gap in the knowledge of the subject. Together they offer a solid ground on which to practice cabinetry.

There are nonbasic areas associated with cabinetwork which require ad hoc training. A list of recommended titles in some of these specialties follows:

Introducing Marquetry, edited by Marie Campkin (Drake Publishers, $7.95).

Practical Wood Turner, by F. Pain (Drake Publishers, $5.95).

The Principles and Practice of Ornamental or Complex Turning, by John Jacob Holtzapffel (Dover Publications, $12.50). (Only covers highly ornate designs.)

Practical Upholstery, by C. Howes (Drake Publishers, $6.95).

Woodcarving, by W. Wheeler and C. Hayward (Drake Publishers, $6.25).

Masterpieces of Furniture, by Verna Cook Salomonsky (Dover Publications, $3.00). (Excellent selections with measured drawings. Highly recommended.)

English Period Furniture Designs, by C. H. Hayward (Arco Publishing Company, $4.95). (Fine selections with working diagrams. Highly recommended.)

Encyclopedia of Furniture Making, by Ernest Joyce (Drake Publishers, $14.95). (Excellent treatise for a broad range of furniture making techniques. Broader range, more data than *Cabinetmaking for Beginners*, though without the depth of descriptions of most important operations.)

Furniture Treasury, by Wallace Nutting (Macmillan, $20.00). (*The* picture book of American furniture, featuring five thousand photos.)

Furniture Repair and Refinishing, by Ralph Parson Kinney (Charles Scribner's Sons, $5.95).

Portable Power Tools, by Leo P. McDonnell (Delmar Publishers, $3.95).

How to Do More with Your Power Tools, edited by Sears Roebuck staff (Midwest Technical Publishers, $1.69).

Rockwell Books—On Router, Band Saw, Circular Saw and Jointer, Drill Press, Shaper. (Rockwell Manufacturing Company, $2.10).

Power Tool Maintenance, by Daniel Irvin (McGraw-Hill, $9.50).

Although I've omitted a group of books which are out of print, time is better spent looking for old books than old tools. In particular, The International Correspondence School series prior to W.W.I and the Audel series prior to W.W.II are fabulous. The information is detailed and accurate and the illustrations are often gorgeous. Since their data pertain more to commerce and its vicissitudes, age in no way affects their relevance.

The largest supplier of woodworking books I know of is Stobart and Son, Ltd., 67-73 Worship Street, London EC2, England. Woodcraft Supply Company, 313 Montvale Avenue, Woburn, Massachusetts 01801, also carry a good selection.

ANTIQUE OR FAKE. by Charles H. Hayward. St. Martin's Press, New York, 1972. 56 pages. illustrations, photographs. $8.95.

Today, when we praise (and rightly so) the skill of men who had only the labor of their hands to do everything, we know that we would never go back to that system. Much of it, skillful as it was, was pure drudgery. Who, for instance, would want to go back to ripping out boards in the saw pit? If ever there was a soulless job it must have been that, the creeping forward one eighth inch at a time, the man below in semi-darkness, a mere human machine covered with sawdust which clung to his half-naked, sweating body.

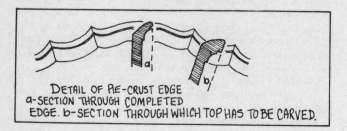

DETAIL OF PIE-CRUST EDGE
a-SECTION THROUGH COMPLETED
EDGE. b-SECTION THROUGH WHICH TOP HAS TO BE CARVED.

People would not want to go back to the labour and tedium that is inescapable when every operation calls for human work, but they cannot but help feel admiration for things that were made in that way. It is one thing to admire something, another to do it.

This book is requisite reading for anyone who wishes to design and/or build traditional furniture, whether it be reclining chairs or piecrust tables. Ostensibly the contents are an outgrowth of the title, but the special value lies in the demonstration that developments of style and technique have been anything but arbitrary or dependent on formal taste. Not only are the theoretical solutions to certain problems shown, but also the reasons behind one choice or another. It provides a concise and intelligible history of Western furniture construction, and, as such, affords to the reader a context in which to consider the making of wood furniture. Also noteworthy are the photographs of handsome representative pieces, and the diagrams and measured drawings which are quite helpful when one begins to translate two dimensions into three.

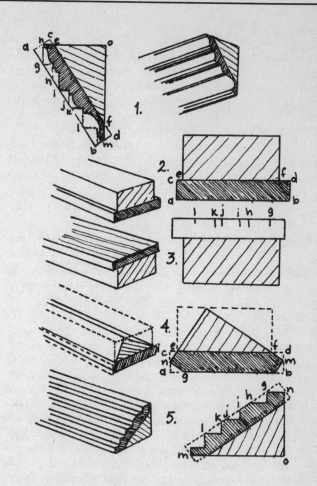

Steps in making a backed cornice molding

TIMBERS FOR WOODWORK. edited by J. C. S. Brough. Drake Publishers, New York, 1970. 232 pages. illustrations. paperback edition $5.75.

If this book is used in conjunction with *Fine Hardwood Selectorama*, the reader will have an ample introduction to the subject of timber. Most woodworking books offer sections on lumber, but they are too brief to describe a wide range of woods in detail, or the complete growth process of a tree, and usually they end up by merely sketching why a certain board from a certain tree looks the way it does. *Fine Hardwood Selectorama*, on the one hand, is most importantly a visual demonstration. *Timbers for Woodwork* relies on verbal material, such as the commercial histories of various timbers, methods of conversion from log to board, and typical working properties. Despite idiosyncracies owing to the fact that it was originally published in England, this is one of the most useful references for the woodworker.

The grain of timber should not be confused with its texture. Grain refers to the direction or scheme, simple or complex, of the fibres and other woody elements. By texture we mean the distribution, arrangement, and fineness or coarseness of these elements. Grain is something in the nature of a pattern we can trace; texture is the background through which the pattern runs.

Source: TIMBERS FOR WOODWORK. edited by J. C. S. Brough.

FINE HARDWOOD SELECTORAMA. Fine Hardwood Association, 666 Lake Shore Drive, Chicago, Ill. 58 pages. illustrations. $1.00.

Published as a means of increasing the demand for hardwood, this is an inexpensive and handy catalog despite its commercial intent. It includes a small chart on comparative physical properties of various hardwoods, and illustrations of different ways to match veneers. The text, which is generally descriptive, is aimed at the buyer and user of lumber, the architect, and the woodworker. An especially helpful feature is the number of plates (forty-two in black and white and thirty-six in color) of full-size boards which fairly represent typical specimens as they would normally be viewed.

A REVERENCE FOR WOOD. by Eric Sloane. Ballantine Books, New York, 1965. 111 pages. illustrations. $2.00.

At first glance this work seems to have no relevance to cabinetmaking. It is concerned with some of the uses of wood in early America, large scale (houses and barns) and small (kitchen utensils and garden tools). The point is that there are more ways of utilizing a tree than leaving it to look at or ripping it into planks. And, regardless of what is done, that wood will never cease being responsive to and dependent upon its environment. This affords a sense of proportion to the reader, a method different from that of ingrown, compulsive, European cabinetry. Each attitude has its place, of course, but it's nice to be able to take the break as it is offered by this book.

CABINET MAKING FOR BEGINNERS. by Charles H. Hayward. Drake Publishers, New York, 1971. 209 pages . illustrations. $5.95.

This is the best introductory book available. Its scope is broad, although therefore its depth is relatively shallow. However, all the information is correct, all bases are touched, and if a person were to follow this treatise strictly, it would probably result in the creation of beautiful cabinets. Indeed, most "professionals" would do well to read it a few times and amend their malpractices accordingly. The book is well illustrated and emphasizes the proper ways of building things.

HAND WOODWORKING TOOLS. by Leo P. McDonnell. Delmar Publishers, Albany, New York, 1962. 294 pages. illustrations. $4.00.

It is a false economy for any mechanic to buy a saw that is not produced by a reliable manufacturer, and upon which the name and grade are not stamped on the blade. A good saw, handled properly, will last the average carpenter at least 15 years. A poor quality saw is a detriment to good work and is never satisfactory. In the selection of hand saws, there are some rule-of-thumb methods to judge the quality of the blade. They apply more to hand saws or the rip and cross cut type, but some may apply to compass and keyhole saws.

1. To test the quality of steel in a saw blade, hold the saw tightly in one hand, by its handle. With the other hand, catch the toe of the blade under the thumbnail and snap the blade. The blade should emit a clear, lasting ring. The clearer the ring, the better the blade. A dull, short ring denotes inferior spring steel, or, in some cases, the steel may be of good quality, but too thick for carpentry use.

2. Bend the blade toward the handle. If it snaps back to its former shape quickly, it is of good spring steel.

3. Notice if the edge where the teeth are located is thicker than the back edge. If it is, this is a sign that the saw blade has been ground and that the saw is of good design.

4. Examine the surface of the blade. Good saws have their surfaces finely ground and polished.

5. Examine the handle to see if it is of hard, close grain wood and finished to protect it from moisture.

6. Observe whether there are brass studs in the handle and that there are enough to hold the handle firmly to the blade.

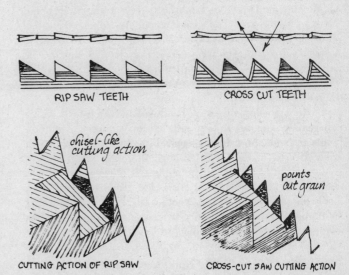

RIP SAW TEETH   CROSS CUT TEETH

chisel-like cutting action

points cut grain

CUTTING ACTION OF RIP SAW   CROSS-CUT SAW CUTTING ACTION

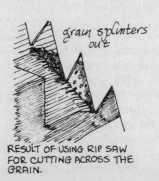

grain splinters out

RESULT OF USING RIP SAW FOR CUTTING ACROSS THE GRAIN.

In addition to Mr. McDonnell's advice, I would add the following suggestions: Try to procure a saw whose teeth have been created by filing rather than stamped out. The steel should be hard enough to hold an edge, but if it's too hard, as that of some popular models, the teeth will break when being reset. See how the handle accommodates your hand. This is important. And don't buy any saw with a plastic or metal handle.

Regardless of cost, the best saws available in the United States these days are the following:
1. Spear and Jackson, "Double Century"
2. Tyzack "Nonpareil 154"
3. Spear and Jackson "88"
4. Disston "D 95"
5. Sears "Craftsman Kromedge"
6. Disston "D 23"

Hand Woodworking Tools is basically the best book on the subject. It is somewhat directed toward carpentry and joinery but is still applicable to cabinetmaking. Lots of clear drawings complement the text which discusses the care and use of marking tools, saws, boring tools, and more, as well as fasteners and abrasives. Sections on sharpening are excellent for a book of this type. Other books may be more exotic, but none covers the material more widely or soundly for a beginner's purposes.

Two alternative selections are: *Tools for Woodwork*, by C. H. Hayward (Drake Publishers, New York, $6.95) and *How to Work with Tools and Wood*, by Robert Campbell (Pocket Books, New York, $1.25). The former is intended primarily for cabinetmakers and is occasionally vague. The latter was written by an employee of Stanley Tools and is pretty decent, though it is misinformative in places, and therefore dangerous.

There is no single book on hand woodworking tools which adequately and accurately satisfies the subject's demands. Tools become the worker's appendages and this makes it a difficult area to deal with through literature. Tool choices and techniques vary with practitioners. Once a person has had some experience, he or she is less likely to return to a book on tools than one on another area, such as finishing or timber. However, a proper start is important, and in this respect, books have their place.

PLANECRAFT. by C. W. Hampton and E. Clifford. C. and J. Hampton, Ltd., Sheffield, England, 255 pages. Available from Woodcraft Supply Company, illustrations. $5.00.

This book is a classic, a gem of erudition and experience, replete with tips and tricks about metal planes and spokeshaves. Its only fault lies in its being published by the manufacturer of the world's best metal planes, Record, which affects its objectivity. (For some operations, such as jointing and final surfacing and cleaning up, high-quality wooden planes are preferable to metal ones.) This bias notwithstanding, *Planecraft* so thoroughly covers the wielding of every metal plane worth laying hands on that the only people who couldn't be helped by it should be writing

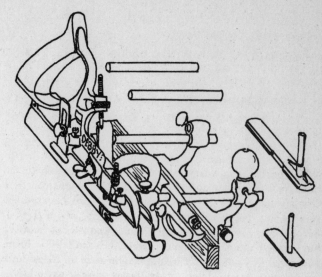

Record multi-plane, showing parts

their own books.

Planes themselves are critically important in cabinetmaking. If you don't know how to use a plane, don't bother to buy the wood. Once planing is mastered, the quality of results achievable is surprisingly high—you will learn to love your plane.

Another nice feature of this book is the inclusion of practical applications. The reader is told not only how to make a plane perform an operation, but why and when the results of that operation are useful to good construction.

WOODWORK JOINTS. by Charles H. Hayward. Drake Publishers, New York, 1970. 176 pages. illustrations. $5.50.

This book is desirable because all the joints one would normally need to use are comprehensively covered. Most often construction fails at a joint, rather than in midmember, and the first details scrutinized in any piece are the joints. In good work, pieces are held together by the joining wood, not the glue or the screw. Through time, many joints have been devised, and the Western cabinetmaker alone should have perhaps seventy-five possibilities at hand. The information supplied by a general woodworking book may suffice for the simplest work, but in more demanding circumstances, *Woodwork Joints* should be consulted.

STAINING AND POLISHING. by Charles H. Hayward. Drake Publishers, New York, 1970. 214 pages. illustrations. $5.75.

Like others of the author's books, *Staining and Polishing* is just specialized enough for people with fewer than seven good years in the field. The section on French polishing is especially complete.

A good finish is not only necessary for handsome appearance but also to protect and preserve. Typically, books on finishing are filled with waste—often half or more of the advice given is of use to no one. This book is the exception to the rule.

I think there is a natural tendency for people to seek finishing instructions when they think the piece is ready to be finished—after it's "made." This is too late; like all other operations, finishing must be considered and planned for at the project's outset. *Staining and Polishing* is narrative rather than encyclopedic, and as such encourages a deliberate and comprehending reading, making the better of a fairly tedious literary subject.

The best quality varnish is made from the finest selected fossil resin and the purest refined Baltic linseed oil, at a carefully regulated and steady heat over sandbath-protected furnaces to prevent its firing, and is used for high-class decorations, carriage, and other work, when cost is not the first consideration. It is a slow dryer, but is of great lustre and durability. It should be applied in a room of uniform temperature, from which all drafts are rigidly excluded.

Source: STAINING AND POLISHING. by Charles H. Hayward.

Required Reading

PRACTICAL VENEERING. by Charles H. Hayward. Drake Publishers, New York, 1949. 170 pages. illustrations. $5.50.

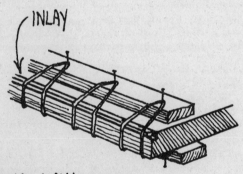

HOLDING INLAY LINE IN POSITION AT EDGE WITH STRING PASSED AROUND NAILS.

A person can make perfectly fine cabinets without knowing anything about carving or wood turning or marquetry, but there is scarcely a piece of furniture or cabinetry extant which has not, or could not have been, veneered. Furthermore, instead of being the cheap solution to problems some think it to be, veneering often represents high-quality work. It is a difficult process requiring the best wood. It can be employed to achieve certain effects impossible with solid stock. It allows forms to be built which would otherwise be structurally unsound. And remember, some woods are in short commercial supply, so if they are to be cut at all, it should be minimally. Therefore, veneering constitutes an integral part of cabinetry, not an ancillary one.

This book, though the best I know of on the subject, is often incomplete. This is because little about veneering is immediately apparent or derived from everyday experience, and of course, its necessary precision is intimidating. However, its worth outweighs possible apprehensions and makes this book required reading.

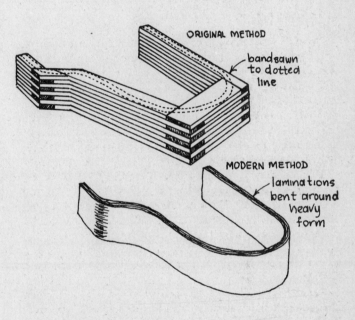

Original and modern methods of forming rim of grand piano

The environment tends to either encourage or discourage people from doing certain things. I'm thinking of wood, for example. Women don't want to go to lumberyards because they'll be intimidated and ostracized. The same is true for hardware stores and tool stores. And therefore, even if they have an opportunity or inclination to participate in some sort of program, once they are forced to deal with the real world they find themselves frustrated. I think the same thing is probably true for men in something like weaving.

—Gary Williams, cabinetmaker

Miscellany

He who works with his hands is a laborer.
He who works with his hands and his head is a craftsman.
He who works with his hands and his head and his heart is an artist.

—Saint Francis of Assisi

National Crafts Foundation
Hospitality House
Silver Dollar City, Mo. 65616

This foundation's objectives is "the preservation of rare and historic skills of American handcraftsmanship." It sends administrators on roving assignments to discover additional practitioners of handcrafts. It also sponsors the National Festival of Craftsmen, in early October at Silver Dollar City, Missouri.

American Crafts Council
44 West 53rd Street
New York, New York 10019

The American Crafts Council is a national non-profit educational and cultural organization founded in 1943 to stimulate interest in the work of contemporary craftsmen. It is supported solely by membership dues and contributions. Membership is open to all having an interest in crafts.

Among its several activities, ACC maintains the Museum of Contemporary Crafts in New York City where the work of established and emerging artists in a variety of craft media can be seen. Craft Horizons, the bi-monthly magazine published by ACC since 1942, presents many aspects of craftsmanship including coverage of national and international events in the arts. ACC Outlook, a members' newsletter printed six times a year, informs readers of Council programs and offers a calendar of crafts activities in each issue. The Research & Educational Department of ACC maintains a unique portfolio system of pictorial and biographical data on contemporary American craftsmen and operates a nationwide slide sales/rental service known as "Your Portable Museum." It publishes annually a Directory of Craft Courses and other references on crafts in all media which can be seen in the ACC Library at 44 West 53rd Street in New York or purchased by mail. Through the Council's Regional Program, fairs, workshops, and other educational projects are carried out under the aegis of regional assemblies of craftsmen from the fifty States.

Comprehensive Catalogs of Craft Books Available from:

Museum Books, Inc.
48 East 43 Street
New York, N.Y. 10017
send $.50 handling charges.

Craft and Hobby Book Service
P.O. Box 626
Pacific Grove, Cal. 93950

Unicorn
Box 645
Rockville, Md. 20851

Freebees (or almost)

Craft and Hobby Helps
National 4-H Supply Service
59 East Van Buren Street
Chicago, Ill. 60605
Variety of 15-cent pamphlets and leaflets. Titles include: "Block Printing," "Soap Sculpture," "Woodcraft."

Foil for Fun
1501 Alcoa Building
Pittsburgh, Pa. 15238
A free 30-page booklet containing instructions for making foil flowers, animals, and other projects.

Industriline Company
Maine, N.Y. 13802
"How to Cast a Trivet Kit" #9001
"How to Cast Panholders and Paperweights" #9002
"Hints for Successful Resin Casting"
Free leaflets containing hints on resin casting, materials, mold charts, flocking, and color charts.

101 Things to Make for Fun or Money
Scholastic Book Services
50 West 44 Street
New York, N.Y. 10036
96-page booklet (#9095) of things to sew, paint, knit, glue. $.60.

Creating with Styrofoam
Dow Chemical Co.
Consumer Information Service
2030 Dow Center
Midland, Mich. 48640
Free leaflet containing designs and instructions for making items with plastic foam.

"A Teachers Guide to Flower Arrangement"
Kenneth Post Foundation
Box 100
Etna, N.Y. 13062
 40-page booklet wtih lesson plans for a unit in flower arrangement. $.50.

American Reedcraft Corporation
417 Lafayette Avenue
Hawthorne, N.J. 07506
 Weaving materials and design uses. Request instruction booklet.

"Artist Projects with Salt"
Morton Salt Company
Public Relations Department
110 North Wacker Drive
Chicago, Ill. 60606

"Let's Have Fun Decorating with Diamond Walnuts"
Diamond Walnut Kitchens
Suite 701
47 Kearny Street
San Francisco, Cal. 94108

Best Foods
Division of Corn Products Company
International Plaza
Englewood Cliffs, N.J. 97632
 Request arts and crafts booklets.

"Modern Simplified Book Repair"
Bro-Dart Ind.
P.O. Box 1120
Newark, N.J. 07101

One Out of Every Five Americans Practices a Craft

According to a national survey conducted by the National Research Center for the Arts, Inc., an affiliate of Louis Harris and Associates, one of every five Americans over the age of fifteen practices a craft, and one out of six paints, draws, or sculpts. The survey, which consisted of more than three thousand 90-minute interviews, also revealed that 89 percent of the people polled feel that the arts are important to the "quality of life in the community," and that 64 percent would be willing to pay five dollars more in annual tax if it were to go to the arts.

The full survey, titled "Americans and the Arts," is available from ACA Publications, Box 4764, Tulsa, Oklahoma 74104 at the cost of two dollars per copy.

Magazine: Crafts

The Craftsman's Gallery
Box 645
Rockville, Md. 20851
Quarterly. $8.00 per year.
 Published by the Guild of American Craftsmen. Subscription includes membership in the guild. Contains photographs of members' work, interviews, and book reviews.

Everyday Art
American Crayon Co.
Sanduske, O.
Published 3 times a year. $1.00 per year.

American Home Crafts Magazine
Rachel Newman, editor
641 Lexington Avenue
New York, N.Y. 10022
Biannual. $1.25 a single issue.

Artweek
1305 Franklin Street, Department AC
Oakland, Cal. 94612
Weekly. $8.00 per year.
 Listings of festivals and sales.

Art Workers Newsletter
National Art Workers Community
32 Union Square East
New York, N.Y. 10003
6 times a year. $5.00 per year; includes membership in community.
 For artists and others interested in issues, sociological and political, pertaining to visual arts. Particularly concerned with the role of government sponsorship.

Creative Crafts Magazine
P.O. Box 700
Newton, N.J. 07860
18 issues a year. $3.00 per year.
 Instructional articles covering all crafts on varying levels of difficulty.

Hobbies and Things Magazine
30915 Lorain Road
North Olmstead, O. 44070
Bimonthly. $4.00 per year. $1.00 sample.
 Hobby and craft articles, patterns, ideas, and letters.

National Calendar of Indoor-Outdoor Art Fairs, and National Calendar of Open Exhibitions
Henry Niles
5423 New Haven Avenue
Fort Wayne, Ind. 46803
Quarterly. $7.00 per year.

Craft/Midwest Magazine
Box 42A
Northbrook, Ill. 60062
$6.00 per year. $1.50 a single issue.
 Articles on how to sell, exhibits, trends, suppliers.

Crafty Ideas
Department H
Evansville, Wis. 53536
Quarterly. $4.00 per year. $1.50 sample.
Articles and patterns for folkarts and needlecrafts.

American Artist
Billboard Publications
165 West 46 Street
New York, N.Y. 10036
Monthly (except July and August). $11.00 per year.
Book reviews, features, new product news for craftsmen and designers, artists, and sculptors.

Art Materials Buyers Guide
Billboard Publications
165 West 46 Street
New York, N.Y. 10036
Annually. $1.25.
Consumer's guide for artists, craftsmen, designers and students. Contains technical tips, product directory, trade name directory, art store directory, index of manufacturers, and art school directory.

Design Magazine (USA)
Review Publishing Company, Inc.
1100 Waterway Boulevard
Indianapolis, Ind. 46202
Bimonthly (September to June). $4.50 per year.
Articles of interest for teachers, artists, and craftsmen.

Creative Crafts
Model Craftsmen Publishing Corporation
31 Arch Street
Ramsey, N.J. 07446
Bimonthly. $3.00 per year. $.50 single issue.
Articles about plastics, leather, paper, needlecraft, flowercraft, fabrics, and so on. Product reviews, how-tos.

Craft Horizons
American Craft Council
44 West 53 Street
New York, N.Y. 10019
Bimonthly. $12.50 per year; includes membership in ACC. $3.00 a single issue.
A beautiful magazine featuring comprehensive and sophisticated coverage of the art-craft world.

Nutmeg House Crafts
Marion Burr Sober
Box 294-3
Plymouth, Mich. 48170
Quarterly. $5.00 per year.
Which describes itself as: "A rich source of craft techniques to use in new and creative ways."

Nutshell News
Catherine B. MacLaren, editor
1035 Newkirk Drive
La Jolla, Cal. 92037
Quarterly. $5.00 per year.
Illustrated and international coverage of miniature collections and collectors.

Ozarks Mountaineer/AC
Clay Anderson, editor
U.S. 160
Forsyth, Mo. 65653
Monthly, except January. $3.00 per year. $.50 a single issue.
Not a craft magazine as such, but it does carry articles on Ozark crafts, craftspeople, and festivals.

Westart
P.O. Box 1396, Department AC
Auburn, Cal. 95603
Quarterly. $4.00 per year.
West coast art-craft scene happenings.

Artisan Crafts
O and E Enterprises
St. Rt. 4
Box 179-F
Reeds Springs, Mo. 65737
Quarterly. $5.00 per year. $1.50 a single issue.
Small, folksy magazine with articles on crafts and craftspeople, and news of general interest to the crafts world. They also publish an annual directory listing subscribing member-craftsmen and suppliers who pay for inclusion.

Decorating Craft Ideas Made Easy
Tandy Corporation
1001 Foch Street
Fort Worth, Texas 76107
Bimonthly. $4.00 per year.

Workbasket
Modern Handcraft
4251 Pennsylvania Avenue
Kansas City, Mo. 64111
Monthly. $1.50.
Patterns and directions for knitting, tatting, crochet, recipes, crafts, hobbies, garden info.

1001 How To Ideas
Science and Mechanics Publishing Company
505 Park Avenue
New York, N.Y. 10022
Annual. $.75.

Design Quarterly
Walker Art Center
1710 Lyndale Avenue South
Minneapolis, Minn. 55403

Carter Assoc. Directory
Box 1477, Department AC4
New Iberia, La. 70560
Annual. $1.25.
Listings of over 550 companies that sell hobby and handcraft supplies, materials, instruction, and periodicals. Brief descriptions of the type of items sold or services offered.

Farmer's Cooperative Service
U.S. Department of Agriculture
Washington, D.C. 20250
Offers technical assistance to craft associations, helps state and regional associations to develop craft marketing services, coordinates state programs that support craft development.

The Society of Arts and Crafts
69 Newbury Street
Boston, Mass. 02116
A non-profit organization for the promotion of fine crafts. Has an information-disseminating service for craftsmen/patrons, provides special custom-design work. Maintains a gallery. Craftsmen interested in being represented, write: Director Cyrus D. Lipsitt.

The Country Store
University Mall
201-45 Estes Drive
Chapel Hill, N.C. 27514
A nonprofit craft outlet sponsored by the Junior Service League. Sells crafts on consignment.

Cumberland Mountain Crafts
Rt. #9
Holiday Hills
Crossville, Tenn. 38555
A nonprofit organization devoted to promoting craft industries, with the objective of providing product markets for native families and improving their standard of living through constructive utilization of talents.

Three Programs from the National Endowment:
Craftsmen's Fellowships
Workshops Program
Craftsmen in Residence
Open to professional craftsmen of exceptional talent, of any age (except students), medium, or aesthetic persuasion. For guidelines and application forms write: National Endowment, Washington, D.C. 20506.

Catalogs

Allcraft Tool and Supply Company
215 Park Avenue
Hicksville, N.Y. 11801
complete line of jewelry making, silversmithing, casting and enameling supplies. catalog price $1.00; deductible.

Bergen Arts and Crafts
P.O. Box 381-H6
Marblehead, Mass. 01945
200-page catalog of ceramics, enameling, jewelry, batik, macrame, candlemaking, etc. $1.00.

Anchor Tool and Supply Company, Inc.
231 Main Street
P.O. Box 265
Chatham, N.J. 07928
150-page catalog of jeweler's findings, tools, supplies, etc. $1.50; deductible.

C. R. Hill Company
2734 West 11 Mile Road
Berkley, Mich. 48072
jewelry-making supplies catalog $1.00; deductible.

Myron Toback, Inc.
23 West 47th St.
New York, N.Y. 10036
jeweler's supplies catalog $1.00.

Aiko's Art Materials Import
714 North Wabash Avenue
Chicago, Ill. 60611
catalog on Oriental art supply, woodcut tools, art books, batik dyes and equipment. $.50 handling charge.

Creative Fibers, Inc.
1028 East Juneau Avenue, Department AC
Milwaukee, Wis. 53202
macrame catalog $1.00.

Mac Leather Company
424 Broome Street
New York, N.Y. 10013
leatherwork catalog.

Pilgrim's Pride
Box 47, Department AC
Roslyn, Pa. 19001
stained glass supplies and tools $1.00; deductible.

Basic Crafts Company
312 East 23 Street, Department AC
New York, N.Y. 10010
illustrated catalog of quality book binding tools, equipment, and supplies.

Macrame and Weaving Supplies
63 East Adams Street
Chicago, Ill. 60003
sample cards $1.00.

Celebration
Box 28
Pentwater, Mich. 49449
candlemaking factory will send free information on where to buy wax and what wax to use.

Leisure Crafts
3061 East Maria Street
Box 5528
Compton, Cal. 90021
general craft supply catalog $1.00.

The Leather Works
628 Emerson
Palo Alto, Cal. 94301
leather kits. catalog full of helpful advice, patterns, dyes, materials, instructions $1.00.

Edmund Scientific Company
Edscorp Building
Barrington, N.J.
complete source for scientific handicraft supplies. catalog free.

Index